ED DELAHANTY

in the Emerald Age of Baseball

For Joe
with best wishes from
your father-in-law Jeannita
Erwin!
with best wishes,

Ed Delahanty, 1867–1903

Chicago Daily News, June 1903.
Negative collection SND-001412. Courtesy of Chicago Historical Society.

ED DELAHANTY

in the Emerald Age of Baseball

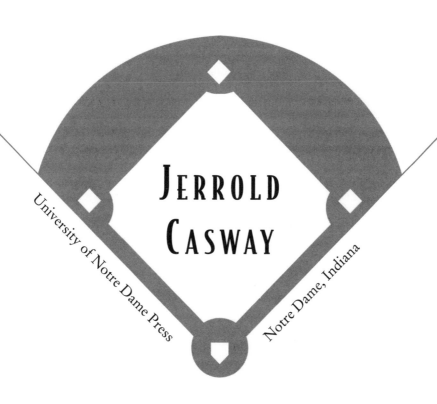

JERROLD
CASWAY

University of Notre Dame Press

Notre Dame, Indiana

Manufactured in the United States of America

.

Library of Congress Cataloging-in-Publication Data
Casway, Jerrold I.
Ed Delahanty in the emerald age of baseball / Jerrold Casway.
p.   cm.
Includes bibliographical references and index.
ISBN 0-268-02285-2 (cloth : alk. paper)
1. Delahanty, Ed, d. 1903.
2. Baseball players—United States—Biography.
I. Title.
GV865.D45C37   2004
796.357'092—dc22

2003024041

Contents

Preface

Baseball is a game learned as a child that is nurtured by the seasons of our lives. Like a lingering melody, the sport and its players are tied to our experiences, linking the progress of years to the succession of baseball campaigns. These recollections do not age in our mind's eye; they are forever etched as we first saw them. For most of us these memories were nurtured by our fathers who were nourished by their own childhood remembrances.

My dad introduced the game to me around the breakfast table, explaining the morning box scores. The names and numbers were brought to life by voices carried over summer-evening radio broadcasts and by the flickering black-and-white images on a small round television screen. The game was taught after dinner by my father in front of our small row house on a narrow city street. The ultimate initiation came when dad took me to old Shibe Park for a Sunday afternoon ballgame. The stadium's vast green fields and the sound of thousands of excited fans nearly took my breath away. The passing decades have not extinguished these keepsakes. I can still call up the many hours spent with my father and younger brother Howard listening, watching, and talking baseball. Perhaps these enduring mementos explain why a wearied historian of seventeenth-century Irish studies became fascinated with the topic of baseball history.

The prospect of putting aside twenty years of research to study an alien topic made no sense, unless it was personally grounded. Having already written one biography, I was not sure I was ready to do another, particularly of a troubled athlete whose career was routed toward a pathetic death. But working on Ed Delahanty had certain advantages. I could draw upon my Irish historical background, and through baseball renew a link to my dad, my youth, and my hometown of Philadelphia.

Ed Delahanty's feats and his bizarre death have always attracted a great deal of attention. But no one has studied him in the context of his community and culture, a son of Irish postfamine refugees, whose career embodied the ethnicity of late-nineteenth-century baseball. Throughout Delahanty's troubled career, the Irish were baseball's dominant ethnic group, sometimes totaling as much as 40 percent of major league rosters. It's what I call the "Emerald Age of Baseball." This prominence was a product of the expansion of urban professional sports and its allure to second-generation Irish-American youths, like Ed and his brothers. Baseball for them, had an acculturating flavor and nonelitist pretensions, a kind of sporting crucible for boys raised in ancestral bat and handball traditions. But to identify Irish athletic ambitions as a conscious medium for social mobility is to ignore the intentions of young men whose expectations were personal and immediate. Baseball for Irish kids was a shortcut to the American dream and to self-indulgent glory and fortune.

By the mid-1880s these young Irish men dominated the sport and popularized a style of play that was termed heady, daring, and spontaneous. This competitiveness was an expression of their survival instincts, a search for advantages and one-upmanship against society and its prevailing norms. Delahanty embodied many of these traits, but unlike the major practitioners of this style of play— Charlie Comiskey, Ted Sullivan, John McGraw, Ned Hanlon, and Connie Mack—Ed struck another popular chord. He personified the flamboyant, exciting spectator-favorite, the Casey-at-the-bat, Irish slugger. The handsome masculine athlete who was expected to live as large as he played.

Ed Delahanty's story is also a baseball chronicle. It's about a player who rarely gave thought to life after baseball or paid attention to the rigors of ordinary living. He drew his identity and expectations from the game he exploited. Delahanty had no other livelihood or training. His life was pillared between baseball seasons and determined by the sport's labor-management disputes. As a young ballplayer these controversies humiliated him and reduced his earning power. A decade later interleague clashes incited Delahanty with a destructive sense of entitlement that led him to squander his options, money, and reputation. These fatal setbacks, unfortunately, were suffered in the public limelight as an active ballplayer and cannot be told without understanding the sport.

The game, when Delahanty played it, was the unrivaled national pastime, a product of the growing popularity of recreational sports and urban living. Baseball was part of a new cultural totem that permeated America in the Gilded Age. These years were marked by unprecedented contrasts. It was an epoch of big business and labor unrest, prosperity and recession, opportunity and racism, and provincialism and national chauvinism. These times and their values determined Delahanty's stage and audience. They even dictated the circumstances of his demise.

Delahanty's story took eleven years to research and write and indebted me to a great many people and institutions. My efforts were made easier by a grant from the Irish American Cultural Institute. Their confidence in the Delahanty project and their generosity got this effort off on the right foot. The Society for American Baseball Research (SABR) was an ideal affiliation for me and my work. This organization provided a forum for my ideas and a venue to understand the character and workings of this neglected era of baseball. Their support, particularly their microfilm lending library, made my work more manageable. I am also appreciative of the assistance I received from the staff at the National Baseball Library in Cooperstown, New York. I benefited greatly from their attention and expertise. The Library of Congress, the National Archives, the Paley Library at Temple University, the Free Library of Philadelphia, the Wagner Free Institute of Philadelphia, the Pennsylvania Historical Society, and the New York Public Library were also generous with their time and resources. Finally, I must thank the staff of the Teaching and Learning Services area of Howard Community College, who were always accommodating and sustaining: Sharon Frey, Sharon Gover, Chris Dodd, Carolyn Wuyts, Ela Ciborowski, and Quentin Kardos. A special appreciation also goes out to David Hinton and his computer design wizardry and to Susan Randt for her genealogical support and guidance in tracking the Delahanty family. Thanks also to Helen Brown, a Delahanty descendant, for her enthusiasm and insights into the family.

Speaking of the Delahantys, my understanding of the family after Ed's death was dependent on the support I received from Earl and Dorothy McDonald of Mobile, Alabama. The McDonalds were friends of Florence Delahanty Randall, Ed's daughter, and the guardians for Norine Randall, his granddaughter. Thanks to the McDonalds I met Norine before her death in November 1993. Their hospitality, trust, and insights were very much appreciated and deserving of my gratitude and recognition.

My thanks are also extended to Bruce Kuklick, Ernie Green, and Robert Lowery, who read drafts of the manuscript and were valuable sounding boards of baseball lore. Bill Wagner, an indefatigable researcher and thoughtful authority on nineteenth-century baseball, also gave me editorial input. His meticulous collecting of Delahanty's game-by-game statistics corrected existing data and was invaluable to this project.

Critical with keeping my work on task was the ability to talk baseball and share experiences with other enthusiasts. Thanks to long-suffering Philadelphia baseball mavens like my brother Howard Casway, my cousins Joel Cassway and Gary Foreman, and long-time mates Craig Horle, Don Insley, and the sage of forebearance, Larry Aaronson. Each was a receptive audience to my thoughts about baseball history.

My understanding of nineteenth-century ballparks was enlarged by conversations and correspondence with Bob Bailey and the late Larry Zuckerman. Talks with Tom Jable helped me understand the history of sports in Pennsylvania, and the late Dennis Clark and Ed "Dutch" Doyle gave me insights into Philadelphia's Irish communities and their passion for baseball. I am also indebted to "Skip" McAfee, of SABR's new bibliography committee, for his discerning indexes, and the supportive editorial staff at Notre Dame Press who guided me through the publication process. And to Donny Insley who was "in" at the right moment.

No expression of gratitude would be complete without giving considerable thanks to my wife, Sandie. She endured my change of fields and tolerated my obsession with this unexpected project. Perhaps this explains why we see more games together than ever before.

Introduction:
Delahanty Is Missing!

It was a typical July Fourth holiday in the nation's capital in 1903. Washington's weather was sunny, hot, and humid with a forecast for late-afternoon thunder showers. Holiday celebrations were to be launched by two baseball games. The home town Washington Senators, well-settled in last place in the three-year-old American Baseball League, had just returned from a twelve-game road trip having lost ten games—seven by shutouts. The prospects for the rest of the season were not good. Over the last two weeks, the team's manager had been suspended for fighting with an opposing player, key ballplayers were out with injuries, and the team's performances were "demoralized." But the Senators were home and about to open a series against the third-place Cleveland Blues, a team which featured former National League stars Napoleon Lajoie and Elmer Flick. The Washington baseball fans dreamed of a fresh start and hoped the team would turn things around.

The first game on Saturday was at 10:30 A.M., the second was scheduled for 3:00 P.M. More than an hour before the gates opened, kids assembled at the entrance to the wooden stands at American League Park on Florida Avenue, Northeast. The crowd that morning was special; 1,300 "little fellows" occupied the bleacher section. These kids, many of whom were orphans, were guests of the Larner Fund, which provided tickets and refreshments for outings of this kind. A "Punch and Judy" puppet show was set up before the bleachers. This performance occupied the kids until the big moment—the arrival of the ballplayers. The youngsters shouted greetings as they leaned over the rail to see, or perhaps, touch one of their heroes.

The rising humidity could not dampen their spirits or the increased noise level. Many of the kids were saving their loudest cheers for the local favorite, last year's batting champ, "Big" Ed Delahanty. But, Ed never appeared. The youngsters' disappointment did not lessen their enthusiasm.

The game was an exciting start to the holiday. The Senators beat Cleveland 10 to 8. Lajoie was ejected for arguing or "kicking" at the umpire and had to be escorted by police from the Cleveland bench. The boys in the bleachers shouted, "Put him out." The crowd loved the game—"A new start, you'll see." Their only regret was not seeing Delahanty. Nobody had overlooked the powerful slugger because he was not at the ballpark. The kids, and for that matter, most of the 4,500 fans, gave no further thought to Delahanty's nonappearance. "Perhaps Del will show up for the afternoon game."[1]

The second contest of the doubleheader never got underway. It was called off because of a large thunderstorm that drenched 3,000 newly assembled spectators. By the time the disappointed crowd returned home, the humidity was broken, and the evening papers hit the street. Only the most avid fan took time on that holiday evening to read a small news item: Washington's famed ballplayer, Ed Delahanty, had not been heard from since Thursday, July 2, when the team ended their western road trip in Detroit.

On this holiday weekend, as newspapers carried stories about the dying Pope Leo XIII, Delahanty's frantic young wife telegraphed inquiries to family members and friends about her husband's whereabouts. Some of his teammates speculated that Delahanty was hanging out with his friend John McGraw in New York or was enjoying himself at some racetrack. Another ballplayer hinted that Delahanty was going through a difficult time and would probably turn up at some health spa. The District of Columbia's police chief saw things differently and started a city search for the missing ballplayer.[2] There were no leads or sightings. On Monday, July 6, the *Evening Star* reported "the big fellow has disappeared as if the earth had opened up and swallowed him."[3]

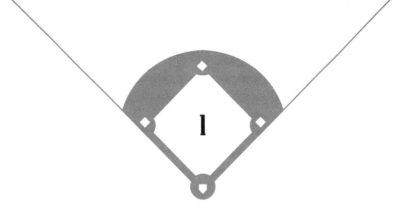

Baseball's Beginnings

Like most Irish-American boys, Ed Delahanty dreamed of playing baseball, the game he loved, in front of thousands of adoring fans. It was and still is one of America's seductive images: achieving fortune and fame through professional sports. Baseball, promoted by journalists and investors as the "national pastime," appealed to every generation of ballgame-playing youngsters. Children, regardless of birthplace or ancestry, were inevitably drawn to the great national sport. Part of the attraction was the degree to which baseball was mythically associated with popular American culture. It was a kid's game that became a kind of cultural totem, identifiable with the country's post-Civil War economic development.

The earliest forms of what became American baseball had shared features and were known by a variety of names. These games spawned a native baseball prototype called townball, which got its name from the practice of playing organized team bat-ball games on town squares. Although the rules differed by region, townball fields were four-sided or based, with the batter standing halfway between home and first base. A pitcher, or "feeder," was positioned thirty feet away. The hitter ran the bases unless the ball was caught or the runner "plugged" (hit) by the thrown ball. In many respects, townball resembled the English game of rounders.

Townball was not exclusive to rural villages. Variations of the game were popular in northeastern cities like Philadelphia and New York. In 1845 one of these variants progressed to a recognizable form of baseball after a New York ball club, the Knickerbockers, refined a new set of playing rules. The New York game, as it was later termed, established a symmetrical diamond-shaped playing field with bases ninety feet apart. Eventually, nine men made up a side, teams had three outs, the pitching distance was forty-five feet, three strikes constituted an out, and outs were made by catching balls or throwing to a base before the runner arrived. The first game played under these new rules was in October 1845 at Elysian Fields in Hoboken, New Jersey.[1]

This prewar decade saw baseball, in the form of the New York or Knickerbocker game, steadily attract participants and followers. By 1858 twenty-five New York–Brooklyn clubs agreed to play in the Knickerbocker fashion in an organization known as the National Association of Base Ball Players. In 1860, sixty clubs, some from as far away as Chicago and St. Louis, joined the association. But the outbreak of the Civil War saw a drop in its membership. This decline was deceiving, because the war promoted and helped spread the popularity of this Northeastern urban game. Two years after Appomattox, the National Association grew to 267 clubs. As Mark Twain said, baseball became the "very symbol, the outward and visible expression of the drive and push and rush and struggle of . . . [our] raging, teaming [and] booming" society.[2] With this expansion a new type of ball player emerged.

Before the Civil War, ball clubs were social sporting fraternities. They attracted young businessmen and artisans with the leisure to play a native-inspired sport that did not require large blocks of time, like cricket. At first, ball clubs met at a member's place of employment and accepted good-natured challenges from other clubs to compete on local playing fields. However, as membership in the National Association grew, the competition between clubs and their respective communities became intense. The demand for talented ballplayers with specialized skills motivated teams to bid for the services of the best baseballers. Toward the end of the war, this competitive one-upmanship evolved into contentious interclub rivalries. Clubs started paying players by the game or supporting them with employment. Less affluent organizations set up cooperative teams that offered players a share of the gate receipts. Other operations, such as the stock company teams, raised money by issuing shares in its local nine. This kind of organization turned baseball from a social-amateur pastime into a professional-commercial venture. Salaries and profits soon underscored each baseball campaign. In 1869, two seasons after Ed Delahanty's birth, the Cincinnati Red Stockings team toured the country with the best baseball players money could buy. After spending close to $30,000, the Red Stockings' profit was less than $1.40. Their season changed the course of American sports. In 1871, with the establishment of the National Association of Professional Base Ball Players, the shift became irreversible.

Cities such as Chicago, New York, Boston, Philadelphia, and Cleveland had stock company teams. Players exerted an extraordinary amount of influence and competed under an agreed set of rules. Salaries averaged about $1,200 a season. But these teams were not run efficiently nor were they effectively shielded from gambling influences. The association lost its credibility and was replaced in 1876 by the National League. Made up solely of stock company teams, the new league was managed like a business enterprise, with the directors, not the ballplayers, making all commercial decisions. One prominent executive declared, "like every other form of business enterprise, base ball depends for results on two interdependent divisions, the one to have absolute control and directing the system, and the other . . . always under the executive branch [performing] . . . the actual work of production."[3]

For team owners, the bottom line was always profit. To ensure success, the owners exerted exclusive rights over territory, rules, and players. Despite the players' limited options, by the mid-1880s, during Delahanty's adolescence, some of the game's biggest stars earned $3,000 to $4,000 for a seven-month season. These wages were ten times greater than what an average factory laborer made in a year. Baseball had become an alluring corporate-run game that expected to make money by showcasing its athletes at unprecedented levels.

The newspapers that noted the growth and popularity of early baseball also detailed the emergence of an unfolding calamity in

Ireland, the devastating potato blight. The collapse of Ireland's agricultural economy and the ensuing famine traumatized its rural countryside. By the outbreak of the American Civil War, more than a million Irish perished, and about two million more emigrated to North America. With survival at stake, America became a haven and land of exaggerated opportunity. Males between the ages of 14 and 24 made up 45 percent of these refugees. Although little thought was given to the games or sporting interests of their adopted homeland, the growth and popularity of urban recreational sports greeted Ireland's dispossessed. It was not by chance that the offspring of these desperate refugees associated themselves so closely with a sport they were destined to transform.

As a son of Irish immigrants, Ed Delahanty and his five brothers viewed baseball as a way to escape the struggles and rigors of many second-generation Irish Americans. They also shared an illusion that there would always be enough money and notoriety to outlast a playing career. Reality said otherwise. Many ballplayers needed off-season jobs to sustain their families. Only a talented few earned enough money for investment or could capitalize on their athletic renown.

Although ballplayers might be great local heroes, to a club director, an athlete remained an employee. If the player did not produce, or if his performance declined, he was expendable. In contrast, many ballplayers understood the realities of the sport and demanded appropriate compensation when their production and bargaining power were great. The result was decades of management-player strife that simmered close to the boiling point during most of Delahanty's fifteen-year career.

Dominant players like Ed Delahanty should have had an advantage at the bargaining table. Unfortunately, collusion among the owners would cost Delahanty tens of thousands of dollars. Player strikes, walkouts, and lawsuits did little to overcome the dictates of management. Delahanty and other great turn-of-the-century ballplayers thrived when there was competition for their services. A rival league or renegade owner was their sole hope of fully capitalizing on their skills or popular reputation.

Aware of the economics of the game, players such as Delahanty needed to live more moderately. Instead, they acted as if their careers were perpetual and baseball would continue to be an inexhaustible source of money and favors. Having a sports persona as the "Great Delahanty," "the king of swat," and the "Only Del" distorted truth and fact. For "Big Ed" Delahanty there was always next season's paycheck or a salary advance. In his mind, great batsmen were to be indulged, and so they lived by different standards. But these ageless adolescents could not dwell forever in the arena, and for some athletes the experience was self-destructive

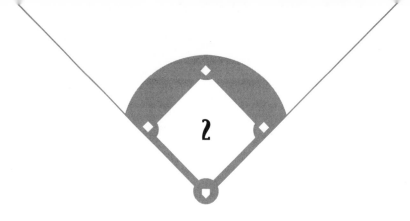

Irish Kid from Cleveland

The "Emerald Age of Baseball" and the career of Ed Delahanty were marked by a strong ethnic-urban flavor. The development of baseball and its speculated origins were steeped in ethnicity. Throughout the last two decades of the nineteenth century, more than 40 percent of the professional ballplayers were of Irish descent.[1]

Although the sport was generally acknowledged as an outgrowth of the English game of rounders, controversy persisted throughout the late nineteenth century over the effort to validate baseball as a nationally conceived pastime. Claiming the game to be American, proponents scoured the countryside for baseball's native antecedents. In a campaign driven by post–Civil War national pride, a variety of bat-ball games were identified that traced the national game through variants of pastoral townball to post-Knickerbocker baseball. Foreign sources, especially claims of English origin, received little credibility. Old World bat-ball games were often attributed to rural Yankee America, but few acknowledged that baseball was shaped and perfected by the descendants of immigrants in the nation's developing cities. This phenomenon was evident in the leading post-Knickerbocker ball clubs of New York and northern New Jersey. By the late 1850s, the influence of new Americans was obvious when players bearing immigrant surnames appeared on the rosters of leading clubs. This popularity among immigrants took on special significance with second-generation Irish-American males. Their association coincided with the game's dramatic transition into a position and skill-specialized sport. The question is why did so many Irish-American boys develop such an affinity for baseball?[2]

In 1902, an article in the *Gael* magazine lauded the number of dominant Irish-American baseball players. The author wrote that "all outdoor games played with a stick and ball have their origin in the ancient [Irish] game of hurling." He went on to say that wherever the "race [Irish] flourished the original game and its various forms of offspring can be found in use."[3] This pride neither discredited English-Yankee influences nor proved Irish evolutionary roots. It only verified the affinity that second-generation Irish-American kids, such as Ed Delahanty, had for a bat-ball game. To a community with a tradition of bat- and hand-ball sports, the attraction to a popular game so closely identified to their new homeland was predictable. To them, the sport represented a vehicle of assimilation and an expression of their new identity.

But if the nature of recreational pastimes was different in America, the social patterns and the community needs of the Irish remained the same. Irish men still congregated and sought social outlets from everyday ordeals. Success and acceptance in these male refuges focused on achievement and community recognition. Here, physical and athletic prowess became compensating factors for immigrant male socioeconomic shortfalls. Baseball, a competitive team sport where individuals excelled, was an ideal expression for this masculinity. Played on fields and on undeveloped and vacant lots in America's swelling cities—Boston, Chicago, New York, Philadelphia, and Cleveland—the baseball craze and the children of Irish immigrants came together.

As athletes in the early 1880s emerged as glorified popular heroes, the British, German, and Scandinavian players on major league rosters were outnumbered by the Irish. For Irish-American boys, particularly those growing up in cities with baseball franchises, the associations were immediate. Pitchers such as Jim Devlin, James "Pud" Galvin, Tony "The Count" Mullane, and "Smiling Mickey" Welch, and hitters such as Jim "the Orator" O'Rourke,

Roger Connor, Dan Brouthers, and Mike "King" Kelly were instant darlings in Irish neighborhoods. Young Ed Delahanty could root for the local National League Cleveland Blues and follow the exploits of his favorite players in the popular growing sporting press.

Cleveland's fascination with baseball was deeply rooted. It took shape in 1866, the year before Delahanty's birth, with the formation of the Forest City ball club. Throughout the next two decades, the people of Cleveland supported a growing number of local teams in a variety of leagues. Therefore, by the time Delahanty was a ball-playing teenager, baseball was very much a part of a young man's warm weather life in the city. When O'Rourke and the Boston Red Caps or King Kelly and the champion Chicago White Stockings came to town, Delahanty and his friends found a way to get inside the Kennard Street ballpark. As an adolescent, Delahanty often went to morning workouts and fielded balls for his local favorites—second baseman Jack Glasscock and shortstop Fred Dunlap, or Louisville's third baseman Jerry Denny.[4] After the games, Ed and his pals could return to their local ball fields and imitate their champions.

Kids were also impressed with an athlete's conspicuous life-styles. To young boys from impoverished families, ballplayers like Mike Kelly, with their bravado, embodied the American dream. In this "Emerald Age" of baseball, when the Irish dominated and affected the character and play of the national game, it was Irish youngsters who emulated their ballplaying idols the way today's urban African American youth mimic their favorite basketball stars. Ed Delahanty, a handsome young Irishman from Cleveland's inner-city, contributed to this tradition.

In 1870 America's large urban centers sheltered more than 44 percent of the million Irish-born and their children.[5] The "first large group of white cultural strangers," they spoke English but were ill-suited for America's urban economic opportunities. Many of these refugees had arrived as unskilled Catholic agricultural laborers, employable only as a casual or seasonal laborer in low-paying jobs. A decade later, manual labor persisted as the largest single occupation for most Irish Americans. This stunted mobility did nothing to help the struggling condition of the Irish, whose general economic plight reinforced unflattering traditional religious and cultural images. Their poverty, rural background, and limited prospects supported society's concept of the childlike and brutish Irish "Paddy." However, the alternatives to pick-and-shovel jobs—working on the canal, laying railroad ties, or laboring in a mine shaft—were scarce. The success of a few enterprising contractors, well-connected politicians, and dutiful municipal workers did little to change the Irish forecast. America's grand promise still eluded the general community.[6]

Baseball for youngsters such as Ed Delahanty and his five brothers was a shortcut to self-indulgent glory and fortune. Their expectations were personal and immediate, quite typical for their class and circumstances. Their parents were immigrants who took leave of rural Ireland for the same reasons other young refugees left the land of their birth. After the potato famine the failing Irish countryside offered no relief as the daily struggle for survival intensified. Like most young Irishmen who emigrated, Ed Delahanty's father, James, was a landless laborer. Del's ancestors resided in the eastern parts of County Kilkenny and worked along the Barrow River canals. His father was simply the oldest son of a small tenant farmer.

O'Dulchainte or Dullahunty was a native Irish surname familiar to the Kilkenny midlands of Ireland. Edward (Ted) Delahanty, Del's grandfather, was thirty-one years old in 1832, when he married a local girl, Mary Phelan of Knockbodaly. He inherited the lease of a seven-acre fee farm in the townland of Cloghasty North, two and a half miles north of the old market town of Graiguenamanagh. Situated along the Barrow River across from County Carlow, Edward and Mary raised seven children, four of whom were boys.[7] In the shadow of the Blackstair Mountains of Carlow, the Delahanty family eked out a living. For the Delahanty brothers the prospects of getting land for sustaining families of their own were remote. Since laws and landed customs made it difficult to bestow or subdivide their limited arable acreage among family members, sons might wait decades for a father or kinsman to resolve the family estate. These constraints forestalled the expectations of distressed young men, who were unable to secure leased lands that made marriage and independent living possible. Rather than expose themselves to these uncertainties, and unwilling to spend their lives as landless rural laborers, young men such as James Delahanty were drawn to the promises of the "golden streets" of America.[8] In the

1850s County Kilkenny, the home of the Delahantys, had the highest rate of emigration.[9] Among the refugees who boarded ships for the New World was Ed Delahanty's father.

Sometime before the outbreak of the American Civil War, James Delahanty and his brother Martin took leave of their family and friends and set out for the port towns of New Ross or Passage East. If they were fortunate enough to travel by steamship, the voyage took two to three weeks before they arrived at their destination, the province of Ontario, Canada, on the northern shores of the eastern Great Lakes. The brothers stayed with relatives who had settled there in the early 1850s. Aside from the joy of reunions, James' experiences were disillusioning. There were no great opportunities awaiting him except the fate of a laborer working in the host of towns and mills that dotted the waterways of the Great Lakes. Toiling ten to fifteen hours a day for low, insupportable wages, the prospects were not any better in America because of the risks and threats of the erupting Civil War. Without suitable alternatives, the brothers accepted their fate and remained in Canada.

It was not until the end of the war that James Delahanty, in search of employment, came south to Buffalo, New York. Here he met the young Bridget Croke, one of four children who came over in 1862 with Edward Croke and his wife, the former Mary Waters. Having lost their farm outside of the Irish port city of Waterford, the Crokes emigrated to Ontario and eventually crossed over to Buffalo. Bridget was thirteen when the family resettled. Although nothing is known about her courtship or marriage, it was not uncommon for a seventeen-year-old girl to marry a man fourteen years her senior.

Headstrong and ambitious, the soon-to-be-pregnant bride persuaded her husband that they should strike out on their own, away from the Croke family hearth. The decision to leave Buffalo was also influenced by the brothers' desire to find work along Lake Erie's southern shore. Sometime early in 1866, James and Bridget moved west to the emerging urban port of Cleveland, where they met up with Martin and his family. The city that would be their home for more than half a century had seen its population double since before the war. Lured by the city's great postwar industrial boom, Irish workers like James and Martin Delahanty constituted 15 percent of the population.

The first few years in Cleveland were difficult for the Dela-hantys. At the beginning of 1867, James' father died in Ireland, and two months before the birth of their first son, Edward James, on October 30, 1867, the family lost a baby daughter to scarlet fever. The loss of their oldest child greatly distressed the eighteen-year-old mother. It made Edward's birth and well-being paramount. He would be Bridget's replacement child. Named after both of his grandfathers, Edward would struggle for his father's approval, but was always his mother's favorite.

Almost two months after Edward's birth, in the wake of the Christmas season, another tragedy struck the family. Martin was killed after he fell from a church roof he was rebuilding.[10] Only twenty-nine years old, Martin Delahanty left a wife and two young children. James bore his sorrow heavily. He buried Martin along-side his baby daughter and assumed the responsibility for his brother's family until the young widow remarried. It was just after the family began recovering from Martin's death that James and Bridget lost another child, her third-born, Marty, who was not yet two. Until the birth of her fourth child, Thomas, in 1872, young Edward James received the full attention of a possessive and griev-ing mother. Fortunately, the next decade was more fulfilling, with the birth and survival of six children—four boys and two girls.

The expansion of the family compelled the Delahantys to move to 42 Phelps Street (later changed to 1431 East 34th Street). Situated in a mixed Irish-German community, between Superior and St. Clair Avenues, the large, wooden, two-story, porched structure with a spacious backyard remained their homestead until 1920. Initially, James Delahanty sustained his new house and growing family by working at a variety of jobs. Beginning as a laborer, he became a stoker at the city gas works before striking out on his own as an independent contractor and teamster. Bridget Delahanty was the matron of Phelps Street, where she ran a boardinghouse and raised her children. By the time Ed Delahanty was a teenager, fourteen people were in residence.[11]

The daily routine and size of the household required organiza-tion and attention. When the boys were old enough, their domestic chores included working with their father or looking after a dis-abled sister. Like all adolescent boys, the brothers usually found ex-cuses to avoid their responsibilities, and with such a large household to run, it was a challenge for mother Delahanty to keep track of her sons when they were not in school. Bridget's priorities for her children were the typical and identifiable "lace curtain," middle-class values of propriety, hard work, and education. But raising six ballplaying boys, especially her headstrong, convivial, and over-indulged oldest son, Eddie, tried the patience and strength of this proud and willful woman.

Ed Delahanty was quiet by nature. In contrast, he was also competitive, frustrated easily, and had a quick temper. Delahanty brooded and dwelled on setbacks and shortcomings but was enlivened by the company of the lads. As a young man, and later as an adult, "Mush" Delahanty, as Ed was known to his Cleveland friends, was dependent on their encouragement and support. This attention also led him to indulgent and intemperate behavior that distressed his mother. Raised in a rigid, matriarchal, Catholic household, Delahanty became a spoiled and weak-willed man, struggling with the constraints instilled by his mother and his own conscience. When focused, Ed Delahanty was a dutiful achiever, and no one was prouder than his mother when he left Central High School to attend St. Joseph's Business College and took courses in book-keeping.[12] Unfortunately, Bridget Delahanty's hopes were upset by her son's preoccupation with baseball and the social camaraderie of Fire Engine House #5.

The neighborhood vacant lot used for baseball and the masculine world of the local fire station played a big role in the lives of Ed Delahanty and his brothers. Located at the north end of Phelps Street, off the St. Clair intersection, it was the kind of gathering place not to Bridget Delahanty's liking. Such assembly spots were popular for male-centered, immigrant, working-class communities. Within a block of the Delahanty house was a billiard and bowling establishment, two saloons, a barbershop, and a firehouse. Each of these masculine leisure centers was a hub for the local bachelor sub-culture. No ethnic group was drawn more to these male social places than the Irish. For immigrant laborers struggling to sustain themselves in an alien and difficult setting, these male enclaves provided men with a much-needed sense of identity, status, and security. Places such as the firehouse drew upon Old World social gathering patterns that fostered gender segregation. It was only natural that these relationships evolved into a kind of surrogate family, one in which the male rites of passage and bonding were consummated. A companion to the saloon, the firehouse often doubled as a local lodge or club. It was a place where men could remain boys, and boys emulated their fathers. Although these havens networked their communities, they also disserved the vulnerabilities of weak and less-mature males.[13] Here masculine deeds were exalted and celebrated with alcohol, gambling, and fraternity. It was not the direction that Mrs. Delahanty intended for her eldest son.

As a strong, athletic youngster, Ed Delahanty excelled in neighborhood sports, which caught the attention of the local firemen. Between drills and alarms, the men of Engine House #5 watched and encouraged "Mush" and his friends. The firemen maintained the field for baseball and oversaw their games. After playing, the youngsters ran errands and made money doing odd chores around the station. Inevitably, the boys were drawn into the social circle of the firehouse. The drinking, betting and boasting that occupied long nonactive hours of those firemen touched the impressionable, good-natured Ed Delahanty. He enjoyed their joviality and good-fellowship.

If someone wanted to find Ed or his brothers, they knew where to look. Frank Delahanty, one of the younger brothers, once told an interviewer how the boys "were practically raised" at the firehouse.[14] An often-told anecdote about Ed and his passion for baseball can be traced to the Phelps Street fire captain. He related that he had been "watching him [Ed] play around here since he was a knee-high kid. He never learned how to play. Every one o' them Delahantys was born with a baseball bat for a rattle. . . . I'll bet any man they know'd a baseball bat before they know'd A,B,C."[15] Delahanty himself joked that he and his brothers had been given "bats, instead of rattles when they were babies."[16] If mother Delahanty's sentiments were not so apparent, a person might be convinced by a newspaper editorial that Irish kids played baseball so well because of a lack of "parental restraint." To that columnist's way of thinking, "American lads," unlike Irish boys, had parents who "won't permit them to devote all their time to the study and practice of the national game."[17] In the case of Ed Delahanty, his mother and father had little choice. His craze for the game inspired local lore about Delahanty being last to leave any ball field. The most frequently told story was how a younger Delahanty was always sent to the corner lot to fetch Ed. "Ma wants you to come home for supper," was the shout. "When I get through battin' this ball," he replied. "But Ma says come on now." "Git away from me," Delahanty retorted, "I'm busy."[18] Laughter and taunts from the fire station usually followed.

His friends at the firehouse reinforced Ed's intensity for baseball in other ways. They sponsored the neighborhood team in community ballgames and tournaments. By the time Delahanty was seventeen, he was a standout player in the rough and bruising semipro leagues of Cleveland. Against older competitors he played on the riverbed grounds, on the west side of the Cuyahoga River. It was said that when a ballplayer was accepted on that part of the river, one of Cleveland's most disreputable areas, he was among the city's baseball elite. Ed Delahanty earned this status with the infamous Shamrocks, "who played anything [one] in northern Ohio, except the big leaguers" and the professional Resolutes. Delahanty and his feats fast became part of local folklore. For years, Cleveland fans or "cranks" retold the story of how Ed Delahanty was the Shamrocks' costliest player because of all the balls he hit into the river.[19] Popular limericks extolled the feats of Ed and his brothers:

> They're products of the vacant lots
> All game as bloodied banties,
> And, holy smoke, ain't there a bunch
> Of baseball Delahantys.[20]

This notoriety did not impress Ed's mother, but it did attract the attention of regional baseball scouts.

It was only a matter of time before letters of inquiry were followed by contract-wielding ball club agents. This attention culminated in early February 1887. Thomas "Sandy" McDermott, the manager and sometimes infielder of the Mansfield ball club in the new eight-team Ohio State League, came to Phelps Street looking for Delahanty. He found his prospect at the firehouse and made an offer. Ed, surrounded by his firemen pals, accepted the proposal and signed a contract for $50 a month. This boldness in front of his friends did not extend to a confrontation with his mother. He put off that meeting and left a farewell note for his parents. At the age of nineteen, he began his career and accompanied McDermott to Mansfield.

The mill town of Mansfield had a reputation as a good baseball hub. It was only seventy-five miles from Cleveland, but to Bridget Delahanty it may as well have been on the other side of the planet. Once she heard about her son's signing, Bridget confronted her husband about the crisis. They considered going after Ed, but James Delahanty did not think the incident was worth losing work over. Troubled by her husband's detachment, Mrs. Delahanty took her reluctant spouse to see their neighbor, J. N. Leach, a bill collector and father of the future major leaguer Tommy Leach. Mrs. Delahanty hoped to persuade her husband or Mr. Leach to go after her son. She complained that her Eddie had no business playing ball. He "should be working" in Cleveland. James Delahanty stood his ground, and Leach laughed and declined her request. He replied, "Listen, you've got a boy who only wants to play baseball. He tells you he's working, and what's he doing? He's always out playing ball somewhere. Give him a break, who knows, maybe he can make the grade."[21]

Delahanty did meet his parents a few days later. He showed up one afternoon in a new suit and told his mother and father he was going to play baseball in Mansfield. "Drat baseball," his mother replied in a heavy Irish brogue, "it's sure ruinin' this family." Ed pleaded, "But Ma, I'm comin home with rocks [money] in my pockets this time." Mrs. Delahanty turned in disgust and remarked, "Yes, just like the times you've come home with rocks on the side of your thick head from playing with the Shamrocks." Delahanty shrugged off her comments by saying that he would make the family proud and one day would earn $3,000 a year as a major league ballplayer.[22]

Despite his stance, Delahanty was disturbed by his mother's reaction. It was the kind of disapproval that struck his conscience deeply. For Ed Delahanty, family and peer acceptance were very critical for his well-being. He always tried to please others and earn their acceptance. This obliging disposition came from his father. Whatever is known about James Delahanty is taken from popular sports lore that promoted the legend of the ball-playing Delahanty family. They applauded James' paternity and suggested he played baseball as a youth, and had mastered "the art of handling a shille-lagh," meaning a hurley stick, a reference to the sport of hurling. The game was Ireland's version of field hockey that was so popular in Delahanty's home county of Kilkenny.[23] But these conclusions were not accurate. Father Delahanty's sport was handball, a very competitive and another popular game in his native county. It was Ed Delahanty himself who commented about his father's athleticism. When asked whether his "old man" would join his three brothers on an Allentown baseball team in the Atlantic League, Delahanty responded, "Well there are worse ball players than dad, and if anyone can beat him playing hand ball I'd like to see him."[24]

The reality is that Ed Delahanty's father saw baseball as recreational pastime and never appreciated the importance of professional sports. He was fifty-one years old when his eldest son signed the Mansfield contract, an ordinary workman with little faith that baseball could sustain domestic responsibilities. A near contemporary writer, who knew the family, said that James Delahanty had "no special interest in [professional] athletics, in fact was inclined to frown upon them."[25] This attitude might explain his reaction to the Mansfield contract. As a parent, James Delahanty did not share his wife's passion or will. He was set in his ways and probably spent much of his time outside of his crowded home seeking work or socializing with his friends. Although a good provider, he always remained a background figure, dwelling in the shadows of his dominating wife and the fame of his sons. In the bustling Delahanty household, James deferred the daily responsibility of raising children and handling family crises to his wife. Every documented family incident testified to either James' passivity or detachment. It is quite conceivable that Ed's disinterest in his father's work, together with James' age and lack of appreciation of professional sports, colored their relationship.

The sole surviving picture of Ed Delahanty's father depicts a tall, somber, good-looking, and well-attired man with a prominent wax-tipped mustache.[26] But a more revealing portrait of the Delahantys is an incomplete daguerreotype of the family taken about 1896. In this picture, the father and three younger sons were conspicuously absent. The paternal presence, instead, was embodied by his eldest son, who imposed a fatherlike figure behind a row of seated Delahanty women. This persona was upstaged by the haughty bearing of Bridget Delahanty.[27] Her posture captured the camera's attention and signaled her role in that matrifocal household.

The self-indulgent immaturity of Bridget's eldest son was obvious after he inked his first professional contract. By the time he was ready to leave for spring training in Mansfield, his advance money was spent. Mother Delahanty would not give him any funds for train fare, so he borrowed five dollars from a friend. Unfortunately, Ed met a few neighborhood buddies on his way to the train station. They "had a little celebration," and when the "hilarity" was over, his cash was squandered. Fearful he would not get to Mansfield on time, Delahanty took his suitcase and jumped a local freight train to the town of Crestline, where he had to change trains. But the Pennsylvania Railroad was not as obliging as the Ohio line, and Ed had to walk the last twelve miles to Mansfield. Along the way, a kind-hearted solicitor for the *Mansfield News* gave him a ride in his horse-buggy. Ed Delahanty, the new professional baseball player, entered Mansfield in style. It was not the first or last time the "good fellow" athlete was waylaid by intemperance. In retrospect, it was also a foreboding of a career that was about to begin.[28]

3

Making the Majors

On a photographic postcard intended for family and friends, Ed Delahanty posed in a Mansfield uniform with teammate George England. The seated England, a one-armed right-handed pitcher, is a mature contrast to Delahanty. Standing with his hands on his friend's shoulder, Delahanty strikes a contrary image with his boyish face and large uncertain melancholy eyes. He appears like a big unsettled kid away from home for the first time.[1] The card announced that both youngsters were in pursuit of a major league career. George England never made it to the top but predicted that Delahanty would soon be playing in the National League.[2]

Delahanty did not disappoint his supporters or the Mansfield organization. In the season opener against Akron, he batted lead-off and went 3 for 5. Ed also caught and made two errors. He never batted in the second game because he was injured by a foul tip in the first inning. This injury persuaded Manager McDermott not to risk the batting prowess of this prospect to the perils of catching. When Ed Delahanty returned to the lineup, his athleticism was put to use, playing every field position, particularly second base.

In his first season, Delahanty performed better than did his club or the league. The eight teams in the Ohio League suffered financially. Two clubs disbanded during the season and another could no longer compete. The Mansfield club lost money and survived the 1887 season by incorporating as a joint stock company. But the prospect of keeping their players under contract for the new season was difficult. Many of their better players left at season's end. Among them was the versatile Ed Delahanty, who played in 73 games, batted .355 with 90 runs scored, and surprised people with his speed and promise as a base runner. Recognized as the team's best hitter, Del was awarded a silver-mounted, rosewood bat.

Delahanty's accomplishments impressed major league scouts and the directors of the Wheeling, West Virginia, ball club. Wheeling, known as "Nails" or "stogie" city, because of its local industries, was considered one of the premier franchises in the Ohio League. Determined to field a team worthy of the city, the new Wheeling manager, Al Buckenberger, convinced Ed that seasoning in the revamped Ohio, now called the Tri-State League, was in his best interest. He signed Delahanty in mid-November at twice his Mansfield salary. Rival owners were disturbed by the unrestrained spending of the Wheeling directors. They wanted to keep salaries at a monthly limit of $1,000 per club and were distressed that the new outlays might put the league in financial jeopardy.[3] But these disputes and the accompanying raids were overshadowed by a more pressing matter, the embroiling racial controversies of the reconfigured Tri-State League.

When Delahanty played in Mansfield, three black players competed in the Ohio League. In 1888 the league changed its policy, banning black players. Only Dick Johnson from Zanesville was allowed to return because of a preexisting contract. Ed Delahanty was not troubled by these events. Like most Irishmen of his time, he was unsympathetic to the economic plight of blacks and the spreading of Jim Crow–type of segregation to professional baseball.[4] These issues were beyond the consciousness of a young, self-absorbed ballplayer intent on getting to the National League.

In February 1888, "without much more of a promise and the price of a cup of coffee," Ed took his spikes and jumped trains on the Baltimore and Ohio Railroad to Wheeling. Delahanty's presence was obviously anticipated because a local paper made note that the young Delahanty was seen walking into town on March 2.[5] Ed was to be the team's second baseman and serve as "change catcher" for future major leaguer Jake Stenzel. Within a few weeks of spring training, the "general verdict" on Delahanty was that "he will be a star player this year." In the language of one of his youthful admirers, "he purty near gets there."[6]

After distinguishing himself in exhibition games against American Association major league teams, Delahanty was ready. In the season's first game, against the Pittsburgh Alleghenies, Delahanty had two singles and hit a home run over the center field wall in four at-bats, but Wheeling lost 13 to 8. Over the next twenty games, Ed terrorized the Tri-State's pitchers. He was batting .408 when major league scouts started descending on Wheeling's Island Park ball field.

The National League Philadelphia Phillies were one of many teams eager to see the young Delahanty play, because he promised to be the kind of player who might replace the late Charlie Ferguson, a dominating pitcher, and part-time second baseman, who batted .337 in 1887. Tragically, he contracted typhoid fever during spring training and died at the age of twenty-five, nine days into the 1888 season.

The Phillies originally hoped that utility infielder Charlie Bastian would hold down second base, but it was soon evident that Bastian was not up to the task. The Phillies' manager, the venerable Harry Wright, told the club president, Al Reach, "We've got to get somebody in there for Bastian. He is losing too many games for us at second base."[7]

At this juncture, Reach and Wright heard about Delahanty through the minor league grapevine. In one story, a traveling shoe salesman from Philadephia tipped off Wright, "There isn't a ballpark in the world big enough to hold his [Delahanty's] wallops." After you see the kid hit, he remarked, "other hitters will make you laugh. He kills em." These comments moved Reach and Wright to dispatch James Randall, an all-purpose scout, detective, and troubleshooter, to evaluate the young prospect. The first time Randall observed Delahanty, Ed hit three home runs. When Wright asked Randall whether the youngster could "place his hits," the scout said, "Place em? The fellow doesn't have to place em. If an infielder got in front of one [hit], that ball simply knock his legs out from under him and goes on."[8] The reports were so flattering that Randall was ordered to start negotiations with the directors of the Wheeling ball club. "You better get him quick," Wright remarked.

"We need somebody who can hit."[9] The Wheeling executives knew they had a marketable player and welcomed Randall's attention.

The Wheeling franchise, as forecasted, was losing money with a winning team and welcomed all offers for Delahanty. Initially, a number of league and association ball clubs were in the hunt. When Randall arrived in Wheeling, managers Bill McGunnigle of Brooklyn and Billy Barnie of Baltimore were already in town. But Wheeling's asking price of $2,500 for Delahanty was very high. Only the Phillies were still interested enough to negotiate. Working through an associate, who owned the local Howell House Hotel, Randall set up a meeting with the club's directors.

Although Randall had been authorized not to pay over $1,000, he knew the talented Delahanty would not come cheaply. He telegraphed President Reach for permission to exceed his limit and was notified that Reach was coming to Wheeling with the purchase money. The Phillies began their bargaining at $1,500, but eventually settled for a near record price of $2,000, including advance money.

Reach, a successful sporting goods manufacturer and great player with the post–Civil War Philadelphia Athletics, arrived in Wheeling while Delahanty was playing in Toledo, Ohio. He transacted the sale and took the train back to Philadelphia. It was James Randall, who went to Kalamazoo to sign Ed Delahanty. Randall found the young ballplayer at the Kalamazoo House, and over dinner, began the negotiations. Manager Buckenberger was disturbed when he learned of the purchase. He had not been consulted and hated to lose his best player in the middle of a successful season. In the bargaining, Del demanded at least $225 per month and said he wanted to finish out the two-game series against Kalamazoo before signing with the Phillies. His final salary, like the purchase price, varied by account. The Phillies were unwilling to pay him what topline players earned, so Delahanty received about $250 per month, making the unproven kid from Cleveland an expensive and well-paid major league ballplayer.

Competing for first place, the Delahanty-led Wheeling ball club knew this was their last chance to play at full strength. Kalamazoo won the first game, 16 to 5. Delahanty had two singles and committed two errors at second base. The final game of the series on Monday, May 21, was a different story. Wheeling won 4 to 2 with Delahanty going 3 for 4 with three stolen bases. Following the game, Delahanty said goodbye to his teammates and accompanied James Randall to Chicago, where he joined the Phillies.

The fans in Wheeling regretted Ed's departure. Without Delahanty in the lineup, the club fell in the standings. It was reported that his sale "took the heart out of the team." The *Wheeling Register,* however, toasted Delahanty's good fortune and splendid play and recognized the "gentlemanly manners" that made him such a local favorite. These sentiments and an accompanying sketch of a clean-cut young Ed Delahanty would have made his mother proud. This same pride also infected Phelps Street and all of Cleveland. Ed was "everybody's hero." Tommy Leach later recalled that Ed Delahanty was all that his dad ever talked about. At the age of twenty-one, the local boy had made it to the big leagues.[10]

The game that Ed Delahanty played in the summer of 1888 would be recognizable to the modern fan. The experiments of the 1880s over the number of balls and strikes per batter, the practice of counting a walk as a hit and the tradition of a batter requesting a high or low strike zone, were over. Catchers, secure with their padless leather gloves, protective masks, and chest padding, began moving closer behind the batter. This positioning gave the pitcher a better target. Some fielders still resisted gloves, but they were a minority by Delahanty's rookie season. Bats, or "wagon tongues," accommodated the contact hitting of that era, with thick tapered handles and wide barrel heads. Hitters also benefited from not having foul balls count as strikes. It was not until the mid-1890s that a foul tip and a failed bunt became a strike, and in 1902, the National League gave two strikes for foul hits. As for the ball that was thrown to Ed Delahanty, it was made of horsehide and stitched with cotton thread. It consisted of a small, hard rubber core that was wrapped in two layers of heavy stocking and worsted yarn. Sealed with rubber cement, these balls had little resilience and were easily disfigured and quickly soiled. This "dead ball," batted in the era's spacious ballparks, defined the offensive character of nineteenth-century baseball.

During Delahanty's rookie year, no substitutions were permitted. These restrictions were lifted in 1891. As for umpires, only one officiated a ballgame, and he positioned himself according to the number of men on base. Often a slow or inattentive umpire had problems controlling a game and frequently was harangued by unhappy spectators and quarreling and scheming players. The most apparent difference with modern baseball was pitching. Throughout Ed Delahanty's career, pitchers threw on a level plane with the batter. It was not until 1903 that pitchers regularly pitched from an elevated mound. Before this modification, the pitcher threw from a 4 by 5½ foot box. In 1888 the box was 55½ feet from homeplate. Pitchers kept their foot on the back line and could only move forward one step. Up to 1886 a pitcher's delivery had a shoulder-height prohibition. The overhand delivery and the short distance to the plate gave pitchers an advantage during Delahanty's early years. The only successful innovation to counter this edge took place in 1893 when the pitching distance was moved back five feet. During these "re-stylings," the dynamics of baseball focused on speed, guile, and daring. Contact hitting of "dead balls" stressed bunting, hit-and-run plays and sacrifice batting. Fielders perfected teamwork defense and tactics that used position and placement to take away offensive advantages.[11] These strategems, often associated with conniving Irish ballplayers, were lost on the untested and free-swinging Delahanty as he struggled through three frustrating seasons.

The Phillies competed in the National League, an organization promoted as an honest and respectable model for the game. In essence, the league ushered in a new era of management control by subordinating ballplayers to the will of the club owners and their stock company investors. With profit, stability, and control in mind, the league's founders cast themselves as vehicles of propriety. Sunday games, liquor sales, and gambling on the grounds were banned. Players were expected to behave properly, and sobriety regulations were fashioned.

On the practical side, the league awarded franchises only to cities with at least 75,000 people. Teams received exclusive territorial and market rights. But these concessions meant nothing if the owners could not control their players. Toward this end, troublesome ballplayers were removed from team and league business. Players had no representation and contracts were not open to negotiations. National League players also were bound to their clubs, and "revolving" or jumping to another league or team was prohibited.

This policy was reinforced by threats of boycotts against any owner who tampered with contracted players. New players such as Delahanty quickly learned that without a freely competing marketplace they could not broker their talents.

As a professional ballplayer, Delahanty's situation was determined by the National League's response to rival organizations that threatened their player-management relations. The league's first challenge, in 1877, came from the International Association, which afforded players expanded control in a cooperative-run league. Their advent forced the National League to pay higher salaries. In the hope of curbing these spiraling expenses, the owners wanted players to assume pedestrian expenses like buying, cleaning, and replacing their uniforms and paying for medical examinations. A player's fitness to play and be paid was tied to his condition and appearance. When Jim "The Orator" O'Rourke of Boston refused to accede to a uniform assessment and jumped to another team, the infuriated Boston owner proposed a measure to curb the problem of "revolving"—the reserve clause. This radical step gave management the right to reserve five players for the next season. With player mobility undermined, salary controls were possible. The reserve clause also coincided with the demise of the International Association. Following its collapse, seasonal wages were again reduced, and the lines between management and labor were redrawn.

A more serious threat to the National League came in 1882 from the American Association. Financed by a number of investors with beer and liquor backgrounds, the association put forward a twenty-five cents admission charge, Sunday baseball, and beer sales on the grounds. The new association endured through 1891, because of an agreement with the National League over the reserving of players. In 1883 both leagues acknowledged each other's existence by signing the National Agreement, which recognized each club's right to reserve eleven players. A year after this accord the Union Association challenged their exclusiveness with nonreserved contracts. Thirty National Agreement players signed with the renegade organization. The National League and the American Association responded by blacklisting jumpers and issuing schedules that conflicted with Union Association games. The upstart league never made it to the second season.

By the time Delahanty was playing with the Shamrocks on the Cleveland sandlots, professional baseball owners were confident that the years of escalating salaries and franchise instability were behind them. This optimism was based on a new National Agreement that expanded reserved lists to twelve, instituted a "roll over" contract clause, and proposed a $2,000 salary cap. By 1889, Delahanty's first full season in Philadelphia, the wages of league ballplayers had risen 30 percent, games expanded from 84 to 132 and club receipts soared by 300 percent.[12]

The ballplayers that Delahanty joined in the National League were disappointed by the failed efforts of the various leagues. Unfortunately, their options and years of productivity were limited. They could continue playing under the National Agreement, join nonaffiliated leagues in smaller urban markets without guaranteed salaries, or retire from baseball. Aware of these constraints, ballplayers turned their attention to the country's growing trade union movement. Professional ballplayers began to see themselves as a special fraternity possessing a "collective pride in [their] . . . unique abilities," something akin to artisans.[13] Their remedy was the creation of an independent union.

In 1885, after the collapse of the Union Association, a group of New York ballplayers organized the Brotherhood of Professional Base Ball Players. Within a few years the brotherhood's membership rose to more than one hundred. The union's aims were for open and guaranteed contracts with protection against pay cuts for reserved players. In return for contract concessions, the brotherhood supported the establishment of a code of conduct for league players.

Five of the nine original founders of the brotherhood were Irish. This ratio exceeded the percentage of Irish players in the two major leagues, but it was an accurate reflection of the role played by the Irish in America's labor movement. Half of all unskilled workers in 1880 were of Irish descent. Laboring in factory, construction, mining, and mill jobs, the Irish contended with the periodic recessions of the Gilded Age. Their responses to working conditions were intensified by the organizing ventures of skilled Irish laborers in America's emerging unions—the Knights of Labor, the American Federation of Labor, and the United Mine Workers.

This ethnic identification with unionism fostered empathy and expectations among the athletes. It was an extension of the American dream of "free labor" to workers on the baseball diamond. The brotherhood's leader and elected president, John Montgomery Ward, played baseball at Penn State before turning professional in 1878. His greatest years were as captain and shortstop of the champion New York teams of the late 1880s. He spoke five languages and earned undergraduate and law degrees from Columbia University. More erudite than most of his followers and teammates, Ward became an articulate spokesman of ballplayers' rights. In an article written for *Lippincott's Magazine,* "Is the Base-Ball Player a Chattel?" Ward equated the traffic in ballplayers to speculation in livestock.[14] Using good trade union logic, Ward and the brotherhood believed a player-worker sacrificed his freedom under the threat of being denied an opportunity to work at his craft. They viewed their "free labor" stance as an inalienable American right. It was inevitable that the debate between the brotherhood and the owners would be carried over into the sporting press and the nation's courts. This impasse and its pending confrontation greeted and tainted young Delahanty in May 1888.

The Phillies wasted little time in getting their prospect into the lineup. On May 22, he started at second base against Chicago. Delahanty batted ninth and went 0 for 4 as the Phillies won 4 to 2. The next day in a 7 to 4 loss, Ed got a single off right-hander George Borchers. Newspapers reported that he played well and hit the ball hard. After closing the Chicago series, the team traveled to Boston without Delahanty. He returned to Wheeling to collect his belongings and say farewell to friends. On Friday, the 26th, Delahanty rejoined the Phillies. With the adrenaline from opposing Mike "King" Kelly and batting against the great John Clarkson and "Old Hoss" Radbourn, his travel fatigue was forgotten. The opening game of the series also inaugurated Boston's new grand pavilion. Nearly 15,000 people, including a host of dignitaries, saw Clarkson, who had led the league with 38 wins in 1887, take on the visiting Phillies. Delahanty responded with his first extra-base hit, a double, as Philadelphia beat the Beaneaters 4 to 1 to spoil Boston's big celebration.[15]

This hit, and the other sixty-four he made in 1888, did not come easy. Delahanty had been progressing well as a hitter, but major league pitchers took advantage of his inexperience and aggressiveness at the plate. They changed speeds and pitched him away, thereby negating the rookie's right-handed strength as a natural pull hitter who tried to slug every ball to left field. Delahanty responded with frustration and self-inflicted anger. He "fumed, scolded, cussed and criticized himself" and threatened to quit the sport. Within a few weeks of his arrival, *Sporting Life* reported that Ed was "too free in his hitting" and was being tempted to go for "balls curved around his neck."[16] The pressure also affected his play at second base. Manager Harry Wright appreciated the intensity of the stressed rookie. Fortunately for Delahanty, no one in the game was more respected and better suited to instruct a talented prospect.

Wright was born in Sheffield, England, in 1835. The son of a cricket champion, Wright grew up in New York, where he made a name for himself as a cricket and baseball star. A thinking, strategy-oriented baseball man, Wright is considered by many to be the real "father of baseball." In 1869 he assembled and managed the professional Red Stockings team of Cincinnati. Dubbed a "baseball Edison," his game strategies and training techniques were viewed as innovative and were the standards for "smart" baseball. Wright was also a sophisticated man, a jeweler by trade, who conveyed a sage-like appearance with his long, well-trimmed beard, his dark suits, and recognizable top hat. In 1884 he was brought to Philadelphia by his old rival, Al Reach, to build the year-old franchise into a championship team. Within a few years Wright made the Phillies a contending ball club. An astute judge of talent and an acknowledged teacher, Wright recognized Delahanty needed patient instruction and paternal encouragement.[17]

Contrary to popular expectations, Delahanty did not "batter down fences." Some fans actually came to think of him as a "shine or flash-in-the pan." There was even ill-founded speculation that he might be released, but the Phillies had invested too much money to give up on him in his rookie year. Instead, Wright, acting the part of a wise father, cautioned Ed about his frustrated outbursts. "Be less impetuous, Edward, less hasty. Calm yourself. Modify your speech. It doesn't do you a bit of good to be too strong in big words. It won't help you be a better ball player." Delahanty accepted the old man's advice—"Damn it, I know it, but what the hell are you going to do if you don't hit the ball to suit you?"[18]

Wright put Delahanty under the tutelage of the team's captain and veteran shortstop, Art Irwin. Born in Toronto, Canada, Irwin was a small, dapper infielder, nine years Delahanty's senior. A student of the game, Irwin was a machinist by trade who developed and merchandised a popular fielder's glove. As a batter, he was a contact hitter, with only five home runs in a thirteen-year career. Nevertheless, Irwin was Ed Delahanty's batting instructor and the person responsible for teaching Ed the patience of waiting on a pitch and hitting the ball to the opposite field. Irwin later recounted how he approached the big brooding rookie about his batting. In a "hopeless tone," Delahanty confessed that he did not know what the trouble was. Instead, he lamented to Irwin, "I can hammer them as far and as often as I did before I came here, but I always hit them right into fielder's hands." The little shortstop responded by telling him he had to learn to stroke the ball to all fields. "Why, I'm a right-handed hitter and I can't hit 'em anywhere, but to left," Delahanty replied. Irwin nodded and told him that every pitcher in the league already knew "you can't hit anywhere but to left field." Del grudgingly replied that he would come to the ballpark early and work on curbing his big swing and practice hitting the ball to the opposite field. Art Irwin also remembered that Delahanty was not always a willing student and frequently threatened him with a $5 fine for pulling the ball.[19] Delahanty complained if he "could only hold myself like that old crab, Cap Anson . . . I would bat better than he ever did. But I can't. When the ball seems to me to be coming to my liking, I am going to belt it. I don't care where it comes. I'll either hit it or miss it, and if I miss it, God knows, I'll miss it by enough."[20]

In spite of Ed's frustrations, the Phillies were pleased with his potential. An early assessment of Delahanty called him a "decided acquisition to the team." Other reports said he fields a ball cleanly, throws very quickly, and covers a good deal of ground, but had a propensity to stop ground balls with his chest and made costly errors with his aggressive play. Harry Wright appreciated Delahanty's potential and tried to ease him into the Phillies' infield. Ed's transition was not helped by an injury to his finger on June 13 that plagued him for the rest of the season. Wright even tried Delahanty in left field. Overall, it was agreed that Del had a great future at both positions.[21]

Delahanty played in seventy-three games, seventeen in the outfield, for the 1888 Phillies, who finished 14½ games behind the league-leading New York Giants. In 286 at-bats, Delahanty hit a disappointing .224. He knocked in 31 runs, scored 40 times on 64 hits with only one home run and 12 walks. Delahanty also committed 44 errors at second base, but surprised the opposition with 38 stolen bases. Harry Wright summarized Ed's season this way: "I thought I would get more hitting out of the big fellow. He meets the ball well, but he can't keep it away from the fielders. But he really can run. Someday, he may be a champion base-runner. And he loves to play ball."[22]

In his 1888 rookie portrait, the one used for his Hall of Fame plaque, Ed Delahanty appeared as a vulnerable young man with large sad eyes and long pomaded hair parted on the right side. Wearing an ill-fitting tie and a wool, double-breasted waist coat, he did not look like a streetwise professional ball player.[23] His pose had the innocence of a graduation portrait, a "gentlemanly" young prospect with a half year of major league baseball behind him.

In the off-season Delahanty, with a salary advance and a new contract for $1,750 in his pocket, returned to Phelps Street with stories and adventurous anecdotes. Having hurt himself sliding in a year-end exhibition game, Delahanty limped off the train and was received like a wounded hero. A welcoming group of admirers serenaded him at the train station. The celebrations continued with Bridget Delahanty's special-occasion dinner of corned beef and cabbage, or "Irish turkey," as Ed called it. The lads at Fire Engine Company #5 were not neglected. They got cigars and exchanged predictions with their protégé. The press also got their first glimpse of Ed Delahanty as a man about town. In a reported incident, Del, a member of the Shattuck Rowing Club, got together with a number of local baseball stars at the annual ball at the Germania Hall. After an evening of drinking and revelry with Blues shortstop Ed McKean and Phillies catcher "Deacon" McGuire, a rumor began that Delahanty was "a drinking man." One source went so far as to suggest that Harry Wright labeled Ed as "incorrigible." *Sporting Life* countered that Delahanty was not that kind of player and said he was owed an apology. In truth, Ed was a young man who enjoyed a night out and a few laughs with his friends. As for Harry Wright, it was said that he only cautioned Ed about excessive smoking.[24]

Harry Wright recognized Delahanty's shortcomings and knew the youngster was not an immediate solution to his team's offensive production. He and Al Reach remedied their needs by signing a dominant player from the bankrupt former champion Detroit Wolverines, the handle bar-mustached "Big" Sam Thompson. At 6'2" and 207 pounds, the twenty-nine-year-old cabinet-maker from Indiana was recovering from a sore throwing arm that threatened to end his career. But Thompson was still an imposing power hitter, who led his team in 1887 to the championship while batting .372 with 166 RBIs. The Phillies were undeterred by his lame arm and gambled by purchasing his release for the princely sum of $5,000. With little bargaining power or redress, Thompson signed a $2,500 contract. Reach and Wright hoped that if their pitching came through and Delahanty continued to progress, a Thompson-led team might successfully compete for the pennant.

When Delahanty reported to spring training in 1889, there was speculation he might do some catching or go to left field. Ed's preference, and position to lose, was second base. Art Irwin said Delahanty was "one of the best handlers of thrown balls in the business and is not intimidated by baserunners."[25] Irwin went so far as to predict that Ed "is going to make one of the greatest players in the country. He is a great batsman and base-runner and can throw the ball like a rifle shot. He isn't 21 years old yet." Agreeing with his field captain, Harry Wright predicted Delahanty would be his regular second baseman.[26] This confidence was part of the team's optimism when they boarded a New York steamer for spring training in Jacksonville, Florida. But team politics and unforseen injuries would dictate a different course.

In a shipboard interview, Harry Wright commented about the team's chances. "I am not in the habit of bragging, and I have never claimed the championship before it was decided, but I have such a splendid set of men this year that I do not believe there is a club . . . that can beat us out." Captain Irwin, standing nearby, concurred.[27] Three weeks later, before the Phillies broke camp, Art Irwin, in a special piece for the *Philadelphia Inquirer,* reported that Delahanty was rapidly improving at second base. "I think he will be the right man in the right place this summer. He is afraid of nothing . . .

baserunners don't scare him a bit. He is always there when the ball arrives and he knows how to touch [tag] them up."[28]

Delahanty reported to camp in excellent shape after spending the winter working out in a Cleveland gymnasium with other major league ballplayers. But the year did not start off well. During a morning practice he pierced his shoe on a rusty nail, and the badly infected foot kept him out of several preseason exhibition games. The Phillies, nevertheless, were pleased with his progress. They moved Delahanty to third in the batting order and were confident that his "over-anxiety" at second base would be cured with experience.[29] Five weeks into the season, Ed's hopes were shattered.

Delahanty's misfortune began in a hotly contested series against the Cleveland Spiders—formerly the American Association Blues—that began on Wednesday, May 23. The opening game, threatened by foul weather, saw both teams caught up in heated plays that sparked on-field incidents and players' fines. Philadelphia won the rain-delayed, protested game, 4 to 3. On the following day, the first-place Phillies lost 5 to 2 in a game marred by Delahanty's hard slide into his old pal, the 5'3", foul-mouthed, Cleveland second baseman, "Cub" Stricker. The Cleveland players were upset about the play, but in appreciation of aggressive base-running they did not draw out their protest. On Friday, Cleveland won another closely contested game, 5 to 4.[30] The pressure was now on the hometown Phillies to win the Saturday, getaway game to even the series. Eight thousand people in attendance saw Cleveland score the winning run in the ninth inning that dropped the Phillies out of first place. The worst setback was the loss of Delahanty to a crippling injury.

Following Thursday's script, Del singled to center field in the sixth inning and, again, tried to steal second base. This time the veteran Stricker stood his ground. The throw from catcher "Chief" Zimmer was breast-high and on the mark, allowing Stricker to greet Delahanty in a crouched defensive position. Stricker's knee hit the left shoulder of the head-first-sliding Delahanty. Called out, Del sprang to his feet, dazed by a "cold chill." The shock was followed by a sharp searing pain. Surrounded by players from both teams, it was obvious that his shoulder was in bad shape. The team physician, Dr. Ziegler, came out of the stands and with the help of the Phillies' trainer, Harry Lyons, and a few teammates, assisted Ed off the field. In the dressing room under the third-base pavilion, Dr. Ziegler confirmed that Del's left collarbone was badly fractured. After the bone was set, Ed, with his arm bound tightly to his side, took the Sunday afternoon train back to Cleveland. It was a month before Delahanty could wear his arm in a sling.[31] When he left the lineup, the Phillies were 15 and 9 and in second place. He was batting .344 and, with 13 errors, was the league's worst fielding second basemen.

The reaction to his loss was immediate. The Phillies lamented their misfortune and accused Stricker of "dirty" ball playing. Delahanty came to Cub's defense by acknowledging the accident was caused by a "stumble which threw him off of the line and against Stricker." As for the injury, the bone needed to be reset after Ed's trip to Cleveland.[32] Delahanty now faced many weeks of restless convalescence and a bleak outlook for the season. As late as August 2, Harry Wright reported that Del might not return that season and asked President Reach to get him an experienced second baseman. Finding a competent replacement during the season was nearly impossible, but the Phillies solved the problem by purchasing Sam Thompson's good friend, Al Myers, from the financially troubled Washington club for $4,000. With Myers holding down second base, the Phillies did not need to rush Delahanty into the lineup.

Back in Cleveland under his mother's care, Ed began to mend and started daily workouts to get himself back into condition. Often Delahanty hung out at the ballpark, and on one occasion, when his Phillies came to Cleveland, he worked at the gate overseeing ticket receipts.[33] But Delahanty was becoming bored and restive and craved the excitement of the emerging pennant race. This desire created an embarrassing moment for Del and the Phillies. According to Cleveland newspapers, Delahanty was accused of stealing signs and tipping off visiting clubs. Since Cleveland was competing with the Phillies for second place, Ed was "chased off" and banned from the playing field. The same papers also reported that Wright and Delahanty were quarrelling over stories of Ed's intemperance. Wright, it was said, refused to pay Delahanty until he reported to the team. Asked about these reports, both Wright and Delahanty denied everything.[34]

When Delahanty was reinstated on August 3, he had missed forty games. During that time, the Phillies played .500 ball and dropped into fourth place. Ed's return, however, did not guarantee his former position. Though Delahanty played an occasional game in the infield, Wright had seen enough of Ed at second base. He felt that Delahanty's speed and strong arm were better suited for left field or first base. Art Irwin later recalled that Ed Delahanty and other young players made their reputations on dirt or "skin diamonds" and did not have the agility to handle balls that skipped off the grass infields.[35] Unfortunately, eight days after his return to the lineup, Ed injured his shoulder sliding into third base.[36] For the rest of the season, Delahanty continued to favor the shoulder, and his play "lacked the dash" he had displayed before the accident.[37]

After much consideration Wright put Del in the outfield. In his first game he made a two-run error, but had only two miscues with five assists in the remaining twenty-nine contests.[38] The Phillies finished fourth, 20½ games behind the Giants and one game under .500. Sam Thompson, in spite of a slow start, lived up to his billing by hitting .296 with an extraordinary 20 "dead ball" home runs and 111 RBIs. Delahanty, playing in only 56 games, batted .293. He had no home runs and drove in 27 runs.

His first full season in the major leagues also laid the groundwork for the next two troubling years. Del and his teammates were very disappointed with their losing season and distracted by its accompanying discord. The festering dissension, fed by the brotherhood's rhetoric, affected the impressionable and self-centered Delahanty. These experiences ensnared him in "revolving" and "jumping" situations that earned him a reputation that he never lived down.

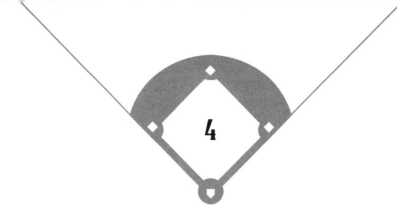

Triple Jumping

A confrontation was brewing between players and management that would trouble major league baseball for more than a decade. To the owners' way of thinking, players were "ingratious," disloyal, and responsible for the sport's misfortunes. Management bemoaned how they invested money in player development only to see ballplayers abandon parent clubs for better opportunities. Albert Spalding, the powerful sporting goods magnate and owner of the Chicago White Stockings, maligned the players' greed. He reminded people that a ballplayer "as a street car driver or conductor, brakeman, a porter, or an assistant at some ordinary trade . . . can only demand ten dollars a week for his services . . . [working] ten to fifteen hours each day; and yet this same individual. . . . given $2000 as salary for six months' services as a ballplayer . . . [work in a] comparatively . . . pleasant recreation, requiring two or three hours work each day."[1]

The editor of *Sporting Life* contested this perception. He said people should not make comparisons of this kind. To him players were entertainers, "as much entitled to proportionate pay . . . as are actors, or other professional men." They were paid "for their aptitude and skill . . . [their salaries] have nothing to do with their intelligence or character outside of [baseball]."[2]

This ongoing debate also took in a ballplayer's worthiness and lifestyle. The owners, who paid the athletes' salaries, felt victimized. They believed ballplayers did not appreciate their advantages, and behaved too often like reckless and pampered employees. Management rarely considered a player's daily rigors to maintain and hone skills that age, wear, and injury eroded. The focus, instead, centered on the fact that these young men were paid well to play for work. The truth was that young prospects often struggled through their early seasons only to fail and return to their former anonymity. A special few, such as Ed Delahanty, endured and found success and fame in the seductive glare of the public limelight.

Adoring fans celebrated the thrills and luster of their heroes, which in turn invigorated self-possessed and virile young athletes to take their prosperity and society's vision of stardom for granted. But much of these titillating images, and its underlying ethnic bias, came out of an emergent popular sporting press. Alert to the large numbers of players of Irish ancestry on major league rosters, the press were drawn to the self-indulgent actions of high-profile Irish players. It was their reportings that reinforced the irresponsible stereotypes of improvident athletes. The great manager-batsman of the Chicago White Stockings, Adrian "Cap" Anson—no man of tolerance, as witnessed by his objection to black ballplayers—held the Irish in low regard. It was said that Anson and others disliked working with willful and immoderate Irish players, and never lost an opportunity to demean players of "Irish blood."[3] And though the actions associated with Irish ballplayers were practiced by other ethnic groups, they did provide distressing models for young receptive players such as Ed Delahanty. But eccentric deeds, or the flawed behavior of ballplayers, also sold more newspapers than on-field exploits. Not having found the balance between public relations and sports coverage, the press frequently concentrated on the drinking habits and adversities of prominent players such as Mike "King" Kelly, Denny Lyons, Curt Welch, Mike Dorgan, James Keenan, Frank Larkin, Charlie Sweeney, John "Peach Pie" O'Connor and Hugh Duffy, all of whom happened to be Irish.

Gambling was also linked to ballplayers. Although betting and pool-selling at ballgames had been curtailed, gambling haunts and racetracks were frequented by such luminaries as King Kelly, John McGraw, and Ned Hanlon. This vice caused a great many players of different nationalities to go through large sums of money. But baseball's gossip columns gave a good deal of their attention to the plight of Irishmen, such as Tom Ramsey, Tony Mullane, Denny Lyons, and Curt Welch.

Most players recognized their good fortune of making a living from baseball. They enjoyed the attention and generally took advantage of what fans willingly offered. However, the life of a ballplayer was expensive and demanding. Often, money was not available to maintain an appropriate off-season lifestyle. This shortfall compelled many players to hold rather pedestrian jobs during the winter, as plumbers, carpenters, store clerks, pipe fitters, and factory workers. Better-paid players opened businesses, and those with an education got white-collar jobs. More career-conscious players, with an eye to the future, learned a trade, returned to school and got college degrees. A few such as John Montgomery Ward, Hal McLure, Jim O'Rourke, and Hugh Jennings became lawyers. Charlie Comiskey, Connie Mack, and John McGraw eventually operated successful major league franchises. Some ballplayers were so gifted, and thus well paid, that they took their expected off-season advances and lived all year at being a baseball idol. An unflattering editorial commented: "The ball player, as a rule, is not a thrifty person and it takes money to see the sights; he generally parts with his money as rapidly as he receives it, so that the end of the season finds him with but a scanty exchequer."[4] Ed Delahanty became one of these year-round heroes. Much later, Del's wife related that her husband never held a regular off-season job.[5] In contrast, the wise athlete thought about retirement, saved his money, and traded on his fame to secure a life after baseball.

In 1889, ballplayers at every level knew that the key to their immediate well-being centered on the Players' Brotherhood. For unproven prospects, such as Ed Delahanty, the leagues' proposed salary scales threatened his marketability and earning potential. At the core of this labor dispute was the National League's ill-advised reneging on their 1887 promise to put aside the $2,000 salary cap in exchange for concessions on the dreaded reserve clause. The brotherhood, represented by John Montgomery Ward, Ned Hanlon, and Dan Brouthers, was troubled by the owners' lack of good faith. At the winter meetings of 1888, the league magnates remained adamant about their position and established a five-step classification salary scale—$250 per increment—with the top wage set at $2,500. The system was tied to the "habits, earnestness and special qualifications" of players' behavior and performance. This proposal followed a concentrated attempt by the owners to split the union by awarding lucrative multiyear contracts to brotherhood leaders and star players. The classification scale, however, reinforced this tactic because it was intended for young and aspiring players of Delahanty's status.

These actions were cleverly timed to coincide with the 1888–89 off-season, when many of the brotherhood's leaders were out of the country promoting baseball on an all-star world tour with Albert Spalding's Chicago White Stockings. Among the twenty men taken by Spalding, eleven were active brotherhood members, of whom eight were Irish. The players were in Egypt when they learned of the classification scheme. Ward abandoned the tour in Germany, stirring rumors of an impending strike. He also stoked the pending showdown with his statement that the reserve clause was akin to a fugitive slave law and a violation of the Thirteenth Amendment. Such sentiments, and the union's agitation, impaired Delahanty's injury-ridden 1889 season.[6]

Delahanty's Phillies were a veteran ballclub with a long affiliation to the brotherhood. Many of the union's leading spokesmen played for Philadelphia, including team captain Art Irwin, leading pitcher Charlie Buffinton, outfielder George "Dandy" Wood, and flamboyant centerfielder Jimmy Fogarty. Throughout the early summer of 1889, Wood and Irwin had bitter fallings-out with management over playing time and their union associations. By midseason both men were playing for other teams. These moves disrupted the ball club, and left Delahanty without his mentor. The swelling discontent that infected Delahanty and his teammates was also sustained by a meddling front office.

It was reported that the club's directors, Al Reach and John I. Rogers, were tampering with Harry Wright's managing. Reach rejected this suggestion, saying that "as far as I know there is complete harmony in every department of the club." Rogers agreed with this statement and related that Wright had "absolute control of the players," and that no decision was made without his input.[7] Closer examination proved otherwise.

Al Reach was highly regarded by the baseball public. The *Sporting News* likened him and his brother, Robert, to the noble-hearted

Cheeryble brothers in Charles Dicken's *Nicholas Nickleby*. The Reach name, the article said, was synonymous with all that was "upright, liberal and good. . . . Were all club presidents like Reach . . . there would be no strike talked of, nor even a brotherhood."[8] The same could not be said for the team's treasurer, John Rogers. A litigious, self-promoting city attorney, he had once been an investor in the early National Association. Rogers also served on the governor's staff as judge advocate general with the rank of colonel. His political contacts made him a logical partner to help Al Reach bring a National League franchise back to the Quaker City. At first, he deferred club decisions to Reach, but his role changed as labor-management strife grew. By 1889 the colonel was the spokesman and legal consultant for the league. Steadfast in support of the reserve clause, he wanted no part of agitated union men like Irwin and Wood.

Delahanty was only a bystander among the dominant personalities in the Phillies' politicized clubhouse. But Ed had plenty of time during his convalescent 1889 summer to digest the grievances recited by his teammates. This exposure, together with the active Players' League dealings in his hometown of Cleveland, contaminated the vulnerable young man. In a revealing moment, an impudent Delahanty told Harry Wright that he did not intend to re-sign for his 1889 salary. Wright, disquieted by his arrogance, sarcastically replied, "Certainly not . . . you have been playing such excellent ball lately that you are deserving of a substantial raise."[9] Harry's sarcasm was lost on Delahanty, who was confident that his maturing talent would be his bargaining lever.

For Delahanty and the rest of his teammates, there was little time to plan an appropriate response to the league's classification scheme. The brotherhood players instead contented themselves with a vision of erecting a players-run league. With this objective in mind, key brotherhood representatives, such as John Ward, Tim Keefe, Jimmy Fogarty, Ned Hanlon, and Mike Kelly, secretly pursued potential backers for their new baseball league during the summer of 1889. It was not until November 4 that the players announced their actual intentions. They asserted that ballplayers were being "bought, sold and exchanged as though they were sheep instead of American citizens! . . . We believe that it is possible to conduct our national game upon lines which will not infringe upon individual and natural rights."[10]

The union's plan was to establish jointly run franchises of "capitalist" backers and ballplaying employees. The purity of this cooperative experiment depended on one's perspective. Many backers viewed the league as an investment opportunity for their existing businesses, such as real estate, streetcar, and hotel ventures. These interests were so alluring they obscured the National League's concessions: the abolishment of the classification plan and the modification of the sale option under the reserve clause.

The new league, which began play in 1890, had eight teams, seven in National League cities such as Philadelphia and Delahanty's home town of Cleveland. Each franchise was regulated by an eight-man board composed equally of players and backers. The league was governed by a senate of sixteen men—two representatives (one player and one backer) from each club. Although reserve and classification contracts were forbidden, each player signed a one-year contract with a two-year option to renew, after which he became a free agent. Trading players without their consent was prohibited. They demanded the rights of American citizens and refused to be treated like livestock. They proclaimed their natural rights and asked to be judged on the quality of their work. Al Reach countered,

> There is not a man with any common sense, outside of the Brotherhood, who will say that the players are underpaid or not being well treated by club owners. They have absolutely no grievances, and are being led by a number of old players who have seen their best days, and, knowing that they will very soon have to retire and make room for younger men, are endeavoring to get up a scheme like this for self protection and to keep them in the service.[11]

Reach's comments paled in response to the opinions of others. One editorial said, "Would to heaven we could all be such slaves and draw salaries from $3000 to $5000 for seven months work—no play." The same writer, after discussing how the touring world players were feted, said, "A. Lincoln to free them, eh? Free them from what?"[12] The *Cleveland Voice,* in support of the owners, declared, "The slavery of to-day, compared with the freedom of those good old days [pre-reserve clause], is as a gilded palace to a hut of straw." The newspaper cautioned players to be careful before they "ruin the one organization to which they owe every dollar they received from the game. Too late they may find that the goose which laid the golden egg is dead."[13] They predicted that the struggle would be decided by finances and vowed to protect the purity and dignity of the national sport.[14]

Players were characterized as revolutionaries, and one commentator, an English-born journalist, Henry Chadwick, warned his readers about the players' sinister "secret council." He was alarmed by the brotherhood's timing of their November Manifesto with Guy Fawkes' Day. Chadwick must have envisioned another seditious Roman Catholic uprising, this time led by Irish ballplayers. He even accused the brotherhood of using "special pleadings, false statements, and a system of terrorism peculiar to revolutionary movements" to coerce players to abandon their true home teams.[15] Albert Spalding said this action was a "dangerous experiment by a few hot-headed anarchists."[16] Spalding was more adamant when the season started. "I am for war, uncompromising and without quarter . . . I want to fight until one of us [leagues] drops dead. . . . The [National] League . . . will hold on until it is dashed to pieces against the rocks of rebellion and demoralization. I stand ready to go out of business and wash my hands clean of it all when the hour comes."[17] It surprised no one that the three leagues went after each other's players in a "fight to the death." Al Reach commented that if the new owners think they are going to make a fortune in baseball, "The light they are chasing is an imaginary one."[18]

For Delahanty's Phillies, finances would be a critical factor in the upcoming baseball war. In 1889 Philadelphia was the only National League team that shared their city with an American Association ball club. The league compensated the Phillies by permitting them to charge twenty-five cents for general admission. Thanks to these lower prices, the Phillies' attendance during the disappointing 1889 season rose from 130,000 to 287,000.[19] This success was important to the ball club because the Phillies reportedly spent about $22,000 for players over the last couple of seasons and had salaries said to be "not far above $32,000."[20] In addition, there was the cost of building and maintaining one of the finest ballparks in America.

It was estimated that Reach and his investors had expended about $200,000.[21] In spite of these costs, the Phillies were said to have had profits between $30,000 and $50,000.[22]

Al Reach and Colonel Rogers anticipated the conflict by instructing Harry Wright to sound out his players about their intentions for the 1890 season. Most ballplayers expressed loyalty to the brotherhood, though some doubted the experiment would succeed. Others, uncertain of their chances, would not disclose their plans even to the honorable Harry Wright. Eventually, twelve Phillies signed Players' League contracts and Buffinton, Fogarty, Myers, and former teammate George Wood each subscribed for $2,000 worth of stock in Philadelphia's Players' League team.[23] Colonel Rogers denounced these "jumpers." He called them pampered "ingrates" and predicted they would soon be "crawling home." As for Buffinton, Rogers said, "I wouldn't go across the street to secure" him.[24] Spending money freely, Reach and Rogers "hustled" their way through the Phillies roster. Those who re-signed included catchers John Clements and William "Pop" Schriver, young pitcher William "Kid" Gleason, Al Myers, and Sam Thompson. Myers resold his Players' League stock and Thompson jumped at a three-year guaranteed pact for $3,200 a season and a $1,000 advance. Henry Love, president of the Players' League team, angrily declared, "Deserters always strengthen any army. The loss of these men will not worry us or cause us to lose any sleep."[25] The *New York World* stated that "a man who signs with a club in the morning and with another in the afternoon is likely to forget he is alive before 9 o'clock in the evening."[26]

It was estimated that Reach and Rogers spent close to $100,000 on multiyear salaries, fees, and expenses. They even signed Harry Wright, who was rumored to be a candidate for president of the Players' League, to a three-year contract at $3,500 a season. In the end, eight players still defected, including the team's leading Irishmen—Joe Mulvey, Jimmy Fogarty, and Ed Delahanty.

Mulvey, the high-strung third baseman, signed with the Phillies but, under the pressure of his brotherhood cronies Jimmy Fogarty and George Wood, kept his advance money and went over to the Philadelphia Players' League team. This move pleased the manipulative and outspoken Fogarty. Assured by his political and business connections in the city, the center fielder proclaimed, "We've got to get more money out of the game. . . . We attract the fans, but the owners pocket the money."[27] In the off-season Fogarty returned to his native California and worked with Mike Kelly to unionize minor league ballplayers. Before the start of the 1890 strike season Jimmy was named captain of the brotherhood's Philadelphia Quakers. Ed Delahanty was a more complicated matter. He was targeted by two union clubs—the Quakers and Albert Johnson's Cleveland franchise.

Johnson, the younger brother of a reform-minded Cleveland politician, was a fascinating individual. A good-natured, large, and imposing man, Johnson worked his way up from a trolley driver in Louisville, Kentucky, to a wealthy investor in electric steetcars. The Johnson brothers owned lines in Cleveland, Indianapolis, Brooklyn, and Louisville and a steel rail mill in Johnstown, Pennsylvania.

Al Johnson's involvement in sports was sparked by his enthusiasm for baseball. A close friend and after-hours companion of many players, such as Mike Kelly and Fred "Dandelion" Pfeffer, Johnson was introduced to the brotherhood's plans by Ned Hanlon, an outfielder and late-season manager for the Pittsburgh National League club. Hanlon also was an active officer in the brotherhood, and like other leading union players, recruited backers for the Players' League during their 1889 road trips. In Cleveland, Hanlon convinced the thirty-year-old Al Johnson that big money could be made from a professional ball team, particularly if an accompanying ballpark was situated along his trolley lines. Johnson was so excited by these prospects that he accepted the chairmanship of the Players' League organization committee and actively recruited investors for many of the new franchises, including the one in Philadelphia. "I'm going into this thing with my eyes open. . . . I can't see failure, and I tell you we will succeed."[28]

The success of these negotiations inspired Johnson to move aggressively to find local gate attractions for his new club. His primary choice was the popular Ed McKean, a fine shortstop who played in Cleveland for the American Association and the new National League Spiders. Three years older than Ed Delahanty and born in nearby Grafton, Ohio, McKean already had three solid years in professional baseball. As a player, he had advantages over the unproven and often-injured Delahanty, who had no experience at the shortstop position he coveted.

Johnson spoke with both players after the 1889 season. Of the two, Delahanty was an especially eager listener. He had gone through two disappointing seasons, been weaned on clubhouse union talk, and was attracted by the prospect of playing before a hometown crowd. According to the Cleveland owner, every club in the Players' League sought Delahanty. "I want him," Al Johnson said. "He lives in my town. I want him. I want to show the Cleveland public what a great ballplayer grew up in their midst." When someone questioned his logic that players do not play well in their own towns, Johnson replied, "That doesn't go here. I want Delahanty and I'm going to have him, because Patsy Tebeau [a skilled infielder and later Cleveland Players' League manager] will make him a greater player than he has been or [sic] anybody else."[29] Johnson's optimism was blunted by two factors. Delahanty's services for 1890 were reserved by contract to the Phillies, and his territorial rights were owned by Jimmy Fogarty's Players' League Quakers.

Influenced by older, streetwise players, Delahanty followed their brotherhood stance. Local sports pages speculated that it was only a matter of time before the major stockholders on the Philadelphia Quakers, Henry Love, a manufacturer of knit clothes, and Ben Hilt, a former financial manager of the Phillies and owner of the Hotel Hilton, signed Delahanty. On November 15, Hilt, on a western trip to sign players, got Delahanty to ink his contract. The pact was for three years at $2,800 per year with an alleged signing advance of $1,000.[30]

Delahanty's decision and his large salary were big steps for a young man only a few years off the Cleveland sandlots. Without a full productive year behind him, he was being paid like a first-class star player. But Delahanty's most pressing concerns were the wisdom and security of his new contract. These apprehensions made him susceptible to the renewed advances of Reach and Rogers, who were not anxious to lose the money they had invested in the young player. Colonel Rogers warned Ed Delahanty that the laws of Pennsylvania could "prevent a player from joining an outside club."[31] Unable to dispute Rogers' claims, Ed's confidence faltered. He was particularly anxious about the new league's finances and the rumor that Ed McKean was about to sign and take the position Del coveted with the brotherhood team of Cleveland. In

Delahanty's mind, his old ball club, the Phillies, loomed as his only secure option.

The provocative issue for Delahanty and his teammates was the nature of these preorganization, nonguaranteed Players' League contracts. These agreements were tied to the "cooperative" team policy of tying salaries to the uncertainties of gate receipts. Though attracted by the brotherhood's promise of big-monied, three-year contracts, unproven players, such as Ed Delahanty, grew nervous about giving up their guaranteed National League wages. Ballplayers of Delahanty's status feared that if the Players' League experiment failed, only the major stars, such as Kelly, Brouthers, and Ward, had sureties of payment.

Contributing to their anxiety was Rogers' pending injunction against Players' League contracts. If he succeeded, then players in the new league could not play or draw salaries from their union teams. Rogers followed this action with an all-out pursuit to re-sign his dissatisfied athletes. It was under these conditions that Thompson, Myers, Clements, and Delahanty took steps to return to the Phillies.

On December 2, 1889, with the ink hardly dry on his Players' League contract, Delahanty pocketed a $500 advance and agreed to a new pact with the Philadelphia Phillies. Nobody was more shocked and surprised than Al Reach when he received Ed's contract in a large official-looking envelope sent by George Howe, the treasurer of the Cleveland Spiders. According to an accompanying letter, Delahanty acknowledged Rogers' warning that the brotherhood could not absolve him from his contractual agreement with the Phillies. These threats had moved Delahanty to seek out friends and a Cleveland attorney to examine his Players' League contract. They all advised that it was a "snare and too one-sided to be considered at all." Delahanty confessed that what appealed to him about his Players' League contract was Ben Hilt's personal assurance that his salary with the Quakers would be regularly paid. This verbal guarantee did not withstand the legal and financial arguments given to Del, or Ben Hilt's alleged nonpayment of advance money to Delahanty. Therefore, after weighing these factors, an intimidated Delahanty accepted the Phillies' new-found generosity. His decision to return to the Phillies was affected by the fear of being stuck with an unguaranteed contract in a depleted Players' League. This alarm moved him to comment that "as long as the people who are to be benefitted by the brotherhood are deserting . . . he doesn't see why he shall stick."[32] Playing on Ed's anxieties and conscience, the Phillies said, "We have a prior claim on Delahanty, and unless he reports to us . . . in the spring we will show what it means to sign two contracts."[33]

Reach and Rogers initiated this process by asking the National League Cleveland Spiders to give Delahanty, on their behalf, a new contract and a cash advance. The *Cleveland Plain Dealer* reported his salary was less than what the Players' League had offered.[34] In a Christmas eve cartoon on the front page of the *Philadelphia Inquirer,* Reach and Rogers admired a Christmas stocking stuffed with Mulvey, Clements, Gleason, Schriver, and Delahanty.[35]

The new league countered with a proclamation that blacklisted and chastised all re-jumpers: "Whereas. The following named under circumstances and for reasons that bring the blush of shame to the cheek of every honorable player, have since made known their intention of violating their contracts and oaths." By name, they "marked" and expelled Delahanty from the Brotherhood of Ball Players. Fogarty responded from California by questioning the certainty of Ed's signing. "I hope for his sake that it is not [true]."[36] But it would take more than Fogarty's threat to alter Delahanty's vacillating resolve.

Within a matter of weeks, Delahanty's questions and doubts were addressed by a brotherhood leadership meeting in New York and by the lobbying of union players who circulated around major league cities. Their arguments moved Delahanty in two ways. He believed that Rogers had legally bullied him into signing, and he still wanted to play in Cleveland before family and friends. According to Al Johnson, Delahanty made "repeated applications" to return to the Players' League. One report said Del was running around Cleveland "almost praying to be taken back." He let it be known that he would play for less than his original Players' League contract. One brotherhood official maintained that "under no circumstances" would jumpers, such as Delahanty, be reembraced.[37] Al Johnson did not concur and kept a watchful eye on Delahanty.

In the meantime, Ed came to Philadelphia on February 21 and met with Reach, Rogers, and Wright. Delahanty knew they were concerned about his commitment and was careful about what he said at the meeting. In a prepared statement, most likely written by Colonel Rogers, Delahanty declared, "It is untrue, I took the step I did only after mature deliberation and I have never for one instant repented my action. I consider that the Brotherhood have broken faith with me and that I am not bound morally or otherwise by the agreement I signed with them. And . . . am fully convinced . . . [the Phillies] have a right to my services for this season. On this point I was fully advised by my counsel, I am glad that I am once more in the ranks of the National League."[38] This denial was rebutted by the *Cleveland Plain Dealer,* who reported that Delahanty sent a friend to make overtures to the brotherhood's new secretary, sports columnist Frank Brunell.[39]

Delahanty was confused and tried to play each side against the other until he was sure about his contractual responsibilities. But Al Johnson viewed Del's actions differently. When Ed McKean finally signed with the National League Cleveland Spiders, Johnson rekindled Delahanty's interest in playing in his hometown.[40]

A critical factor in Delahanty's reconsideration of Johnson's overtures was a disclaimer from the Philadelphia Quakers. According to J. Earle Wagner, a local meat distributor and one of the directors of the Players' League club, the franchise was no longer interested in signing jumpers such as Delahanty, Thompson, or Myers. In disgust, Wagner remarked, "Nothing could induce us to take these men back again, and if any such actions should be taken I would withdraw from the club."[41] In support of this decision, directors Ben Hilt and Henry Love accommodated their friend and benefactor, Al Johnson, by giving up their territorial rights to Ed Delahanty.

During these machinations, a bewildered and overweight Delahanty accompanied the strife-ridden Phillies to spring training in Jacksonville, Florida. Harry Wright was philosophical about the upcoming struggle. He said the rival league would "split up the business a good deal" and the outcome would be a matter of the "survival of the fittest."[42] When talk got around to the actual season, the Phillies' manager said he was glad Delahanty was back and expected a great season from him. Unfortunately, Delahanty's state of mind and physical condition were not ready for Harry Wright's regimen. Ed showed up "too stout" and out of shape for the infield, yet he insisted he could play shortstop or second base. Wright knew Delahanty had become a liability as a middle fielder but believed that Ed would be "a fixture" on the club "no matter who goes off." "Put a pin here," the manager said, "Delahanty is the best hitter on the team."[43]

This faith was premature, for Ed's condition and distracted disposition were aggravated by Johnson's solicitous telegrams. Actually, Delahanty and his friend, the left-handed catcher, John Clements, undermined their failing credibility because they "had no hesitation talking freely of their actions while in Jacksonville." In one instance, intemperate remarks spoken over a few beers caused Delahanty to spend a great deal of time denying his anticipated desertion. The routine became a familiar one; Ed would proclaim his loyalty to the Phillies and then become "indignant" when his word was doubted.[44] On one occasion, Delahanty and Clements signed a telegram from Wright to Colonel Rogers saying, "We have made no overtures in any way to the brotherhood asking to be reinstated."[45] These denials fooled no one. One night after practice, Wright found Delahanty with his trunk packed. After a fatherly lecture, Ed unloaded his clothes and remained with the team.[46]

The ball club's unsettled disposition was also affected by John Rogers' attitude. Considered "one of the best posted lawyers in the country on base ball law," Rogers coerced players by telling the press that neither Delahanty or other disaffected Phillies wanted to play in the rival league. He even threatened equity suits to restrain his contracted players from being signed by other franchises.[47] But as the Phillies traveled north, playing exhibition games with the New York Giants, events drew Delahanty back to the brotherhood. Colonel Rogers brought an equity suit against Phillies' infielder Bill Hallman, using Delahanty's 1889 injury as an example of the risk a team took when signing a high-priced athlete. Rogers argued that because of Delahanty's absence the club's play and attendance declined significantly. Yet the team was expected to keep Del on the payroll.[48] On March 15 the state court of Pennsylvania ruled that the National League contract was nonenforceable. The judge said the eighteenth section of the contract—the infamous reserve clause—was not clear as to whether there was any mutuality in a contract that gave teams a claim on a player's services for an unlimited space of time when the club had the "privilege" of releasing the same player with ten days' notice. A distraught Rogers admitted the cases against his rebellious players were over. The court's decision also cleared the way for Delahanty once he received a final commitment from Al Johnson.

It was in Charleston, South Carolina, on March 21, that a Players' League contract for $2,800 and an advance check for $600 were delivered to Delahanty. Al Johnson also guaranteed him a three-year contract and calmed his fears about his indebtedness to the Phillies. He assured Ed that the Phillies would be reimbursed for their outlay. Moved by these pledges, Delahanty tried to sneak out of his roominghouse. Unfortunately, he walked into Harry Wright and Jim Mutrie, the Giants' manager. They tried in vain to get Del to reconsider his actions. Wright spoke to Delahanty about the "unmanliness" of not honoring a contract. These words had little effect on the high-strung young man. He said the National League had deceived him and unnecessarily pressured him into signing. And so, with McKean out of the way and a Cleveland contract in hand, Delahanty, with "some sandwich money," train fare, and his uncashed advance check, took a late afternoon train on a "flying visit" to Philadelphia where he retrieved a stored trunk from John Clements's house. Rather than return to the south and join his new club, Delahanty went to Cleveland to see Al Johnson. After an all-day meeting, Delahanty visited his family and accompanied Johnson to St. Louis where Ed joined his third team in five months.[49]

Colonel Rogers was "exceedingly irritated" but bullied his way through this episode. He remarked that "the law punishes conspiracy severely," and asserted that he would recover damages by suing the "capitalist" owners, not the ballplayers, "who are not property owners." He telegraphed Al Johnson and warned him not to "entice League players to break their contracts." Johnson responded that Rogers "must think I'm a farmer." Delahanty, he said, was given no cash inducements and his original brotherhood contract was "prior to all others." To this statement, Rogers correctly asserted that Delahanty "never signed a contract with the Cleveland Ball Club," and reminded Johnson that he had "sufficient evidence to prosecute . . . civilly and criminally for conspiracy."[50] The *Sporting News* predicted that Delahanty would never be allowed to play with the brotherhood,[51] but the Players' League Board of Directors unanimously reinstated Delahanty, Mulvey, and others.[52] Al Johnson reaffirmed his position by digging in his heels and saying that if the

Phillies succeeded in "enjoining" Delahanty, he would just pay Ed his salary and keep him on the bench for the season.[53] As for tampering with Delahanty, Johnson said, the ballplayer returned to Cleveland "of his own free will," and that he had never sent him a dollar. Delahanty, he commented, also paid his own train fares and offered to play for the same salary he was to receive from the Phillies.[54]

Al Reach's response was more temperate. He said he had no use for "unwilling players" such as Delahanty or Mulvey because their "presence on the team would be injurious." The Phillies' president believed each man had finally expressed their "preference for playing elsewhere."[55] Harry Wright just shook his head and lamented that "Delahanty has acted very foolishly, and I think he will regret the step he has taken before the season begins." Teammate Ed Andrews, reporting to the *Evening Item,* said Delahanty "is a very sore boy for making a fool of himself."[56] Another columnist wrote that an organization who takes back a contract breaker will find him a heavy burden to bear. The article went on to say that "a man who has not enough principle to keep a contract is not the proper man to play on a team from which honest ball playing is expected."[57] One sportswriter went so far as to predict, "Hearts in one place and hands in another brings about bad results."[58] Ed Delahanty later admitted in a letter to a Philadelphia acquaintance, "I never made a bigger mistake in my life than I did when I left the Philadelphia club. I will never hear the last of it from my friends in Cleveland."[59] John Rogers got in the final word when he called the "triple jumper" Delahanty a "scalawag . . . I thought he was a man of honor."[60] Ed Andrews, writing from Jacksonville, related that the Phillies drank a toast to the brotherhood and the Players' League before leaving their training camp.[61]

Satisfied or not, Delahanty's career was caught in the middle of what the *New York Tribune* called a "war of extermination."[62] Baseball columnist Henry Chadwick frequently referred to the struggle as a "Kilkenny cat war."[63] Labor and union organizations all over the country endorsed these craftsmen of baseball. A spokesman for the Knights of Labor described the players as a "legitimate organization of skilled workmen." P. J. McQuire, the son of Irish immigrants and the vice president of the American Federation of Labor, said, "Baseball would have died out long ago but for the liberal support given it by the laboring man." It was to these workers, he declared, that "baseball clubs must cater if they expect to be in existence for any length of time." The representatives of the Philadelphia Players' League club even conducted unity meetings with Samuel Gompers of the A.F.L. Gompers said his workers wanted "to see the players succeed in freeing themselves from League slavery."[64] Al Johnson went so far as to appoint a union representative to be Cleveland's official scorer and gave another trade union official the right to print scorecards.[65] But this dialogue and the brotherhood's use of union labor accomplished little of real value. The major stumbling blocks were baseball salaries and the players refusal to affiliate with organized trade unionism. As one commentator put it, "Does Mr. Johnson imagine that the horny-handed son of toiling is willing to sacrifice half a day's work to say nothing of his half dollar admission fee for the purpose of backing up the Players' League? . . . The laboring man has little time and less money to spare for such luxuries as base ball."[66] O. P. Caylor, a long-time baseball columnist, proclaimed that labor to a baseball player was like "holy water to the czar of hades."[67]

National League management responded to the actions of the brotherhood with injunctions against the player-employees who broke contracts and jumped leagues. The Philadelphia Players' League club contributed early to the fray with counter-equity suits against Sam Thompson, Al Myers, and John Clements.[68] But the courts, following the Hallman verdict, rejected all pleas on the grounds that the reserve contract was unfair and lacked mutuality. Not to be denied, Colonel Rogers denounced the court's interpretation.[69] Both sides knew the struggle would be won by gate receipts. One editorial warned, "Should the turnstiles not produce, are your [brotherhood] capitalists going into their pockets for the deficiency?"[70]

All franchises spent huge sums of money. Spalding said the Players' League was no longer a brotherhood. He described it as "an organization of speculators from Wall Street" who were backing a hundred revolutionary ballplayers. If the game died, Spalding argued, the Players' League killed it.[71] But union leaders such as Mike Kelly, filled with early optimism, claimed, "We [baseball players] are the people and before the August sun dries up the grass the old league people won't be in it."[72]

This confidence was short-lived. The American Association lost four teams to bankruptcy, and the National League saw a team go into receivership. The backers of the Players' League, as predicted by Rogers and Spalding, were shaken by the never-ending expenses of running a new baseball league. One investor in a brotherhood team put it very simply, "All I seem to be doing all the time is to put my hand in my pocket, and contribute to the support of a lot of baseball players."[73] This sentiment, evident from the very start of the struggle, indicated that the owners would be the ones to decide the fate of the baseball revolt.

By the season's end, the Players League had spent about $340,000, and the National League costs were somewhere between a quarter- to a half-million dollars. Inflated attendance figures accumulated by the 1891 *Reach's Official Base Ball Guide* said the Players' League outdrew the National League by 167,000, but the combined totals tallied less than what the old league drew in 1889. The Phillies attendance dropped by about 150,000. This data also indicated that Delahanty's Cleveland club ran a deficit of $15,000, the Players' League Quakers lost approximately $20,000, and the Phillies were in the red for $16,000.[74]

All of this was too much for the weary first-time magnates of the Players' League. Bluffed and intimidated by their desperate National League rivals, they were enticed by buyouts and less risky opportunities in the preexisting leagues. As a result, the Players' League folded, and weak teams from the two other organizations were dropped, consolidated, or shifted. These decisions were agreeable and mutually beneficial to the major backers from each of the three leagues. After much backroom wrangling, a new eight-team National League rebuilt itself on a revised reserve contract, blacklisting, and lower salaries.

The brotherhood was victimized by both the owners and its membership. Obviously players such as Delahanty, Fogarty, and Mulvey were not the anarchists or revolutionaries the owners made them out to be. They were just athletes seeking to maximize their earnings and leverage while their careers were still productive. United for the purpose of bargaining, the players used the precedent of cooperative sports, the terminology of trade unionism, and the constraints of the Constitution to pursue their stake in the American dream. In their ballpark workplace eighty-one players, or almost 80 percent, of the Players' League rosters were former National League ballplayers. Twenty-eight came from the American Association. The fact that about 40 percent of the brotherhood players, five of its twelve managers, and six out of its ten leading officers were Irish may not tell us very much more. These proportions do not translate into any specific dogma or agenda. They only reflect how the Irish, like other ethnic groups, shared a working-class union value system that for the moment benefited only skilled workers. Polemics aside, the brotherhood movement was clearly situational and self-serving. As John Montgomery Ward remarked, the collapse of the Players' League can be summed up in three words—"stupidity, avarice and treachery."[75] For Delahanty and his fellow players the fallout left them with few options. They could go out on their own and barnstorm, find another occupation, or make amends with their former employers.

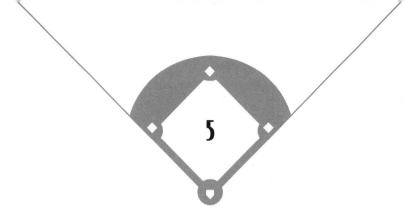

5

From Cleveland to Philly

The 1890 baseball season deeply disappointed the membership of the Players' Brotherhood. They began the season with exaggerated expectations and finished with despair and disillusionment. Ed Delahanty was able to play in front of his friends and family in Cleveland, but with the exception of few productive streaks, he again failed his press notices.

With the league's failure, Delahanty and his fellow players now focused their attention on where they would play in 1891. Many expected retribution, but to their relief, baseball returned to its normal business of pursuing players who could win games and attract customers. John B. Day, the president of the New York National League club, said the league's "whole ambition has been to settle this unnatural war as quickly . . . as possible. The League does not want to knife anybody and it certainly has not issued any boycott against any of the old players."[1]

Brooklyn's Charlie Byrne was more to the point. "The National League proposes to treat everybody fairly. . . . In making up the teams for next season merit alone will be considered."[2] Ballplayers from the defunct league also received a general amnesty and were put on reserved lists drawn from 1889 rosters. In the end, the best players and prospects, regardless of their role in the brother-hood war, were re-signed. Marginal players on the downside of their careers took what was offered or were ignored. The grand experiment did not lead Ed Delahanty or his former Phillies team-mates to their "promised" ball field. Their reward was a scramble to position themselves for employment in the surviving leagues. Over the next decade, lower salaries and management controls pre-vailed in baseball's most monopolistic era.

The tone for the 1890s was set by Delahanty's former employer, Colonel John Rogers, who had been on a three-man "war commit-tee" against the brotherhood. He boasted, "I knew they couldn't last . . . all we had to do was stand firm and see the Players' League collapse from its own inherent weakness."[3] Rogers was equally ada-mant about players he would consider taking back. Union men like Joe Mulvey, Charlie Buffinton, and George Wood were put out and never fully recovered their major league careers. Rogers' resolve, however, was tested with Jimmy Fogarty and Ed Delahanty. Fo-garty weathered the strike season with great difficulty. He endured a public fallout with the Quakers' front office and suffered from lungs weakened by tuberculosis. "Master Jeems," as he was called by the city's adoring press, pushed his body beyond its capacity. Before the 1891 season, it was evident Fogarty was fighting for his life. Prodded by Al Reach, Colonel Rogers kept the stricken and repentant ballplayer on the payroll even though his place in the outfield had been taken over by future Hall-of-Famer Billy Hamil-ton. On May 20, Jimmy died at the age of twenty-seven. The city and all of baseball mourned his passing.

With the exception of the ailing Fogarty, Reach and Rogers val-ued only one player enough to forgive his disloyalty, Ed Delahanty. Ed was twenty-two years old in 1890 when he wore the blue uni-form of the Players' League Cleveland Infants. But the thrill of that experience quickly faded. Al Johnson's team was stocked with vet-erans whose best years lay behind them, including the American Association's great batting champion, the troubled, hard-drinking Pete "The Gladiator" Browning. Another Infants' trademark was horrid pitching, which contributed to their next-to-last finish, 20 games under .500. Their failure was surpassed only by the cross-town National League Spiders, who were 44 games under .500 and 43½ games out of first place. This poor showing by both teams soured the people of Cleveland on baseball. One report estimated that both franchises together lost about $60,000 and drew the least number of people in their respective leagues.[4]

Most of the city's attention during the strike year was given to the two local Irish boys, the shortstops, Ed McKean and Ed Delahanty. Both hit just below .300, but Delahanty was not McKean's equal in the field.[5] One report said that Delahanty was very slow handling the ball, handicapping Cleveland's ability to turn a double play.[6] It was said that Del's problem was the lively Players' League Keefe-Becannon baseball, which was difficult to handle with the leather mitten-style gloves of the era.[7] Playing most of his games at shortstop, Delahanty committed 87 errors.[8] During a damp, July 4 doubleheader in Cleveland, against many of his old Philadelphia teammates, he committed nine miscues. Delahanty remembered the day differently. "I made fourteen wild throws and drove all the people out of the right field seats. To tell you the truth I think I am almost too strong to play an infield position."[9] Actually, he had a sore arm, and as the season wore on his play became so erratic that first baseman Captain Henry Larkin and Manager Patsy Tebeau decided to move him to his original position, second base. But Cub Stricker, who replaced him, was never comfortable at shortstop, and after a few weeks, the grand experiment was over. Del was moved to center field. Overall, Delahanty played 115 games in a variety of positions, the majority at shortstop. Offensively, he lifted his batting mark to .296, scored 107 runs, and in one game against the league's winningest pitcher, Mark "Fido" Baldwin of Chicago, went 6 for 6 with two doubles, a triple, and three singles.

Some of Ed's development as a hitter was attributable to Pete Browning. "The Gladiator" and Del were both powerful contact hitters whose careers were marked by high batting averages. Browning, seeing his young self in the aspiring Delahanty, was generous with hitting suggestions and bat-care techniques. He allegedly owned 700 bats, and many say he introduced John Hillerich of Louisville to bat making. Browning's influence was apparent in Delahanty's obsessive care of his precious "wagon tongues." Later in Del's career, he proudly boasted to having one of Browning's favorite Louisville bats. For Delahanty, his "lumber" was special: "My bat must be like my hat. It must fit or it don't go."[10]

Off the field, Browning may have had a less positive influence on Delahanty. Browning had a grand reputation as a "redlight district" man. And though the 1890 season for Browning was a time of sobriety, this did not mean that his locker room reminiscences did not titillate this young out-on-the-town bachelor.

Less stimulating than Browning's tales were Del's concerns over his failure as a high-profile gate attraction and the repercussions of his "triple jumping." Al Johnson thought people would "flock to see Del . . . he's from Cleveland." Unfortunately, "the fans who pay the freight didn't know Del very well."[11] The biggest problem was that Delahanty's disappointing play was identified with bad Cleveland baseball. He had been billed as the great hometown prospect who in the end never performed well enough to satisfy expectant fans. The *Cleveland Plain Dealer,* commenting on his competitive drive, said he was one of the "hardest losers" on the team. In his first five games of the season, he had three hits in twenty-four at-bats. As Ed began to hit, he was nagged by a variety of injuries.[12] These setbacks bothered Ed greatly. Manager Tebeau appreciated Delahanty's struggles and remarked that this great natural hitter wanted to cry "if he did not get two hits a game."[13]

Del also was frustrated with his inability to play a position for which he was ill-suited. Harry Wright knew that Ed had matured physically and was no longer agile enough to cover the middle infield. Delahanty saw things differently and insisted on playing positions he had outgrown. His determination to be a shortstop was fed by his friendship and hometown rivalry with Ed McKean. Unable to play shortstop at McKean's level, Del bore the weight of unrealistic expectations on his already slumping shoulders. All of this stress was magnified by playing in his hometown, where supporters expected him to produce like an established star. Things got so bad that wherever Delahanty went in Cleveland he was given advice. It eventually reached the point that he dreaded going out with his friends. "Never," Delahanty said, "play ball in your own town. They's too many that gotta talk it over with you."[14] These cumulative pressures took their toll on young Delahanty's performance.

From the very beginning of the season, Delahanty was harassed by an unforgiving John Rogers. It was not until the end of May that the stubborn Rogers was willing to correspond with Al Johnson about the repayment of Ed's $500 advance. But Colonel Rogers was not satisfied, and pestered the young Delahanty for the $94 he said the ballplayer owed for spring training and traveling expenses. Johnson refused to accept this debt, and Rogers whined that the Phillies intended to be compensated for getting Delahanty into shape to play for Al Johnson's team.[15]

On top of these distractions, Delahanty was distressed by the personal animosities stirred up by the Players' League struggle. He never appreciated the divisions and bitterness that the Players' League had summoned. Delahanty wanted to play in Cleveland, and followed his heart and voided whatever principles were at stake. His behavior estranged friends and teammates and showed he was only concerned about his own well-being, not the tenets of the Players' Brotherhood. This attitude and his naïveté were apparent at the end of June when the National League Phillies came to Cleveland. Happy to see his former mates, Delahanty invited them to a Sunday-evening dinner party at Phelps Street. Unfortunately, when some of Delahanty's Players' League teammates dropped by, trouble started. The Cleveland players would not enter the house while the Phillies were there. Before long, harsh words and shoving dampened the evening's festivities.[16] Delahanty's hospitality and attempted mediation could not soften the bad feelings. Ed, always the affable and self-indulgent athlete, acted as if problems would resolve themselves like a game of baseball. His behavior during the "Brotherhood War" confirmed how little this irresponsible young man thought about the consequences of his actions. Wood, Buffinton, and Fogarty were not without their faults, but they understood the issues at stake. Even the narcissistic Mike Kelly remained true to his commitment. When Albert Spalding offered him $14,000 to abandon the brotherhood, Kelly politely refused and told Spalding that if he accepted the money he would be a "traitor" and could never again face his fellow players.[17] More to the point was Kelly's concern for his well-being. "Do you suppose I want to die? Do you think I want to be caught in Boston some dark night by some of the Knights of Labor fellows and disappear suddenly? Oh, no, . . . I have signed my brotherhood contract and will stand [by it]."[18]

The forgiveness and acceptance of gate-attraction ballplayers did not extend to Al Johnson. The "Moses" of the Players' League soon found himself out of major league baseball.[19] He tried to sustain himself by purchasing stock in the bankrupt Cincinnati franchise and keeping ballplayers like Ed Delahanty under contract. But the American Association countered his moves with legal actions and the takeover of the Cincinnati ball club. An editorial in the pro-brotherhood *Sporting Life* bemoaned Johnson's baseball epitaph: "He will . . . sleep sounder and walk the streets more erect than two-thirds of the other capitalists. . . . He made mistakes . . . but nobody can accuse him of treason to his league or base treachery to his friends."[20]

The disturbing prospects brought on by these proceedings moved Jimmy Ryan, an outfielder for the Chicago Players' League team, to bemoan another season of discord. "I've had enough of it. There's more wind than money in it. Let the men who put up the capital manage the game and let the men who do the playing get paid for it and keep still."[21]

The innovations of the Players' League—the two-umpire system, the livelier baseball, and a smaller pitcher's box, with a back line 18 inches further from home plate—were similarly rejected. Though these changes made the Players' League games more exciting and better supervised, the traditionalists in the restored major leagues would not tamper with the "National Game." They ignored these modifications and demanded recalcitrant players be returned to their former teams.

For the 1891 season Delahanty had few options. If he was to remain in major league baseball, he was obligated to play in Philadelphia where his old team drooled at the prospect of adding him to a ball club that had the best record among last year's local teams. The Phillies, playing without Buffinton, Delahanty, Fogarty, and Mulvey, finished third, 9½ games behind Bill McGunnigle's Brooklyn club. Harry Wright's Phillies won a franchise record 78 games, 24 victories over .500. Bill Gleason won 38 games, completed 54 starts, and pitched 506 innings. Sam Thompson batted .313, knocking in 102 runs, and Delahanty's friend John Clements hit .315 and established himself as one of the league's best catchers. The biggest story was the impact of Fogarty's replacement, "sliding" Billy Hamilton, who ignited the team with his hitting and baserunning. The Phillies even put together a remarkable sixteen-game winning streak in late July and contested for the pennant. Adding young Delahanty to this nucleus was tantalizing.

It was not until the close of the 1890 season that Delahanty thought about his next move. In late September he and teammates Henry Larkin and Jim Brennan ran into Colonel Rogers at the United States Hotel in Boston. Rogers insisted they spoke only about the pennant race and no negotiations took place.[22] Regardless of what the colonel said, Ed could do nothing during the season because of his Cleveland contract. Once the ball year was over and the Players' League folded, Delahanty just waited upon events. He visited his mother's family in Buffalo, New York, and returned to Cleveland for the holidays. With the new year, Ed realized his status for 1891 was fast becoming uncertain.

Delahanty's baseball future would be decided in major league board rooms. The National Agreement specified that Delahanty was reserved to the Phillies, but legally Ed was bound by a three-year personal contract to Al Johnson. Unless Johnson released him, Del's obligations were apparent. This situation turned on Johnson's negotiations with the American Association and the National League. His contracts with Delahanty and player-manager Patsy Tebeau provided him with a bargaining tool. He asserted that both players were obligated for two more years and were receiving a regular semimonthly payment on their $2,800 salaries. This condition changed as Johnson's footing in baseball slipped. In a burst of bravado, Johnson projected that he could establish a strong American Association ball club in Cincinnati with Tebeau at third base, Mike Kelly as manager-captain, and Ed Delahanty in left field. Since Delahanty wanted to play in Cleveland, not Cincinnati, there were rumors that Philadelphia might give up his rights to the Spiders if they could get Cleveland's claim to Tebeau.[23]

These speculations had some foundation. Reach and Rogers were trying to sign the veteran Irish slugging legend Dan Brouthers as their first baseman. When Brouthers decided to sign with Boston of the American Association, the Phillies went after Delahanty and gave up on Tebeau. For Ed's part, his decision to return to the Quaker City was tempered by many factors. Johnson was rapidly losing influence, and it was never likely that Philadelphia would surrender Delahanty's rights to Cleveland. With the National League threatening to blacklist any former player who jumped leagues, Cincinnati and the association were no longer options for

Delahanty. After acknowledging contact with the association, he announced, "Do you think I would join a minor league. . . . I would not go to the Association now under any consideration." This remark was ill-conceived and opened him up to accusations of giving a "black eye" to the association.[24] But his diminishing options, with spring training only a few weeks away, meant he had to commit himself. On February 20, he re-signed with the Phillies.

Cleveland Spiders manager Bob Leadley signed Delahanty for the Phillies and reclaimed Patsy Tebeau. Al Johnson put up a brave front. He said the courts would decide where both men would play in 1891. Johnson reminded everyone that his contracts required Del and Tebeau to play ball for "me, not for the Cleveland club." Delahanty, Johnson warned, "can't get away," because all his Players' League contracts were specific and alike.[25] This final hurdle was overcome when Johnson's settlement with the National League nullified his personal contracts. A Cleveland columnist later wrote that Del came very close to staying in his hometown. "He was all but signed, but at the last moment there was a hitch."[26]

Ed Delahanty arrived in Philadelphia and stayed with John Clements while he looked for a seasonal residence. One morning, the two players walked from Center City up Broad Street to the ballpark. There they learned that the Phillies, in another post–Players' League, cost-saving move, had decided against training in the deep South. The new preseason site was to be the beach resort town of Cape May, New Jersey. Accompanied by trainers, groundskeepers, reporters, and the wives of Harry Wright and Sam Thompson, the reconstituted Phillies took up residence at the Aldine Hotel.

Delahanty was pleased to be back with his old ball club and was anxious to show Harry Wright that he was worth the previous year's attention. Although Del had proven last season that he could play the outfield, the Phillies already had those positions set with Billy Hamilton in left, Sam Thompson in right, and young Ed Mayer in center, pending Jimmy Fogarty's return. Keeping Del's infield experience in mind, the Phillies hoped Ed could make it at first base. Delahanty was excited by a move to be where the action was. "It's fun to be right in the middle of the game. In the outfield, you've got to wait too long for a flyball and when you get a bad pitcher in there, you run until your tongue hangs out."[27]

Anxious to get off on the right foot, Delahanty reported in good shape at 175 pounds. But exuberance got the better of him when he ignored Harry Wright's warnings and threw too hard on the first day of practice. He hurt his arm, and for most of training camp, Ed nursed a lame limb. In spite of this setback, he fielded his new position well and made good contact at the plate. To everyone's relief, it was a contented camp, a hopeful sign that former tensions were mending and things were returning to normal.

When the 1891 season began it took just two weeks to determine Delahanty was playing the wrong position. The Phillies had begun the year 6 and 8, but a number of games were lost by Ed's "always over-anxious" fielding. In one game against New York's great fastball pitcher, Amos Rusie, Ed had two singles and a double, but he made two errors that let in two runs. The Phillies lost 6 to 5. With ten errors in eleven games, Harry Wright decided on a switch. He recognized how "indispensable" Delahanty was at the plate and felt Ed would be more comfortable returning to the outfield. With center fielder Ed Mayer not hitting, and the recently acquired "Big Bill" Brown available at first base, Harry Wright moved Del to Fogarty's former turf in center field. Wright hoped to utilize Delahanty's speed and athleticism and believed these moves strengthened the ball club's batting and defense.[28]

Hitting third in front of Sam Thompson and playing center field, Delahanty readied himself for an upcoming four-game series in Cleveland. They swept the series from Ed McKean's Spiders with Delahanty getting four hits, scoring four runs, and commiting no errors. His anxiety about the reception in the hometown he had abandoned was put to rest at his first at-bat. As Delahanty approached the plate, a group of friends and admirers came up behind him with a "gay horseshoe" of roses and flowers. Umpire Tom Lynch gave the "remembrancer" to the startled Delahanty. Ed was greatly embarrassed by the gesture. It was said that the Cleveland pitcher contributed to the ceremony with a base-on-balls so as not to dampen the occasion.[29]

Following the Cleveland series the team moved on to Pittsburgh, where they had to confront an unfortunate Delahanty outburst and the news of a tragic loss. On the way to the first game the quick-tempered Delahanty got into a heated argument with Wright. This trouble took place when the uniformed players were getting into their carriage for the ride to Pittsburgh's Exposition Park. Ed insisted that a young friend accompany the team to the grounds. Wright objected to his companion, and Delahanty argued with his manager. He returned to the hotel and put on his street clothes. Captain John Clements scolded Ed for his childish outburst, but the stubborn Delahanty refused to attend the game. The Phillies lost 11 to 6 and Wright fined his center fielder $100 and suspended him indefinitely. That evening President Reach telegraphed his support for Harry Wright. Disturbed by the reaction of Wright and his teammates, Delahanty wrote a letter of apology and said there would be no repeat of this incident if he was reinstated. Wright, forever the instructive father-figure, accepted Ed's apology and reduced the fine to $25.[30]

The day of Delahanty's repentence, news also reached the Phillies that Jimmy Fogarty had died in Philadelphia. Ed and his teammates knew when they left on their road trip that Fogarty had taken a turn for the worse, but were stunned to learn of his passing. The Phillies and teams in both leagues wore black armbands for thirty days. As the Phillies rode the train to Chicago, Fogarty's black-draped coffin was on its way to his parents' home in San Francisco. Like the passing of Charlie Ferguson, Fogarty's death tore at the soul of the franchise. In both instances, popular talented athletes and team leaders were taken in their prime from the Phillies.

If Delahanty was no Charlie Ferguson at second base, he did measure up to Fogarty's standards in center field. Ed played with vigor and never shied away from a challenge. His first game back after his suspension he tripled and made a great game-winning catch. His outfield play did need some refinement; he had to work on charging hard-hit ground balls and on the accuracy of his strong throwing arm, but he was improving. Unfortunately, injuries to teammates forced Delahanty to play fifteen games at first base. In these contests, Ed made seven errors, often on wild throws. One commentator said Ed Delahanty would be a top first baseman if he was not shifted so much from "post to pillar."[31] On a few occasions injuries even forced Delahanty to take up his old position at second base. But it was apparent that Delahanty was destined for the outfield. He would soon be part of the greatest outfield ever assembled.

The 1891 season was very frustrating for Ed Delahanty. He had hoped to have a productive year and fulfill the expectations of his many admirers. Instead, he pushed himself to do too many things. His immaturity and stubbornness made his task more difficult. Often, he tried to compensate for defensive shortfalls with his powerful batting. This reaction led him to overswing at times as he tried to shoulder the run production needed by a pitching-deficient team. In an era when foul balls did not count for strikes, power-hitting Delahanty averaged about twenty-seven strikeouts per season. In 1891 an over-anxious Delahanty struck out fifty times. But the young batsman was more successful in sacrificing himself in order to move runners along. Responding to Harry Wright's disciplined offense, Ed tempered his hitting to set up Thompson and Clements, who followed him in the batting order. Delahanty was so accommodating that he became the club's most proficient "sacrifice" hitter. It also kept his batting average low. A *Philadelphia Inquirer* editorial questioned this approach and proposed that batters such as Ed Delahanty be allowed to hit away.[32]

All the pressures of the 1891 season took its toll on Delahanty's statistics. He played in 128 games and hit a disappointing .237. Despite this low average, he did score 92 runs, had 86 RBIs, and stole 25 bases. It was a year that would satisfy many ballplayers, but Ed Delahanty, without a major offensive season behind him, was still an unfulfilled prospect. He played the game hard, and his intense competitive style was fast becoming popular with the league's baseball fans. This high profile led to an advertisement endorsing Clafin's Standard Baseball Shoes.[33]

The 1891 season also was a relatively healthy one for Delahanty. His only real injury came in Philadelphia on August 15, when he went after a fly ball hit by Pittsburgh's Fred Carroll. Del collided with the brick, right field wall, hurting his hip and bruising his shoulder. He was hospitalized for a few days and was unable to run for about a week.[34] Sometime after his return, he had another run-in with Wright. Not fully healed from his injuries, Delahanty had trouble bending down for ground balls. In a September 2 game at Pittsburgh, two balls went through his legs, leading to five runs. Ed was so disgusted with himself he failed to run hard after the second error. When he returned to the bench, Wright "called him to task," and Delahanty again "talked back" to his manager. The fans jeered Del, and he was disciplined for his actions.[35] This confrontation was unfortunate. Delahanty revered the old man, often calling him

"Pops," and never intended to be disrespectful. Ed had a flash temper and was more upset with his own performance. Wright knew that, but if Delahanty was to become the kind of player the Phillies anticipated, the sulking young slugger had to bring discipline and self-control to his game. The problem for the franchise, however, was that Delahanty was not the sole factor for their disappointing season.

The 1891 Phillies finished in fourth place, 18½ games behind Frank Selee's Boston Beaneaters. Philadelphia was 68 and 69 for the season, finishing last in home runs and next to last in slugging average with a subpar team average of .252. Their record was perplexing considering the club's productive nucleus. Billy Hamilton, in his second year, won the batting title (.340) and led the league in stolen bases (115). John Clements anchored the club, caught 107 games, and hit .310. Sam Thompson, struggling with an assortment of hand injuries, hit .294 with 10 home runs, 90 RBIs, and scored 108 runs. This offense, including Ed Delahanty, could not compensate for a pitching staff that allowed 5.6 runs a game.

Some responsibility for the Phillies' performance must come from the actions of the front office. Unwilling to burden their already bloated payroll, the Phillies made a number of bad, financially motivated choices.[36] They passed on a number of affordable veteran pitchers and refused to re-sign union man Charlie Buffinton. Instead, the tight-fisted Colonel Rogers swallowed his pride and signed the thirty-four-year-old brotherhood leader, Tim Keefe, after his release from New York. "Sir Timothy," the winner of 310 games, brought a lame and overworked arm to Philadelphia. His performance contrasted with Buffinton, who won 29 games for Art Irwin's American Association Boston club. Many local fans believed that keeping Buffinton might have made Delahanty's Phillies more competitive.

At season's end, Del and his teammates found opportunities for making extra money by playing postyear exhibition games. Ed remained in Philadelphia until the end of October. He signed his 1892 contract, received an advance to see him through the winter and departed for Cleveland. The upcoming year would be a critical one for Delahanty, as he embarked on one of the most productive decades ever enjoyed by a ballplayer.

6

The Emerging Slugger

The recessive national economy of 1892 that coincided with Ed Delahanty's rise as a major baseball celebrity deeply affected the national pastime, moving club owners to reorder the two league alignment and curtail strike-era salaries. In Philadelphia, these policies undermined team morale and contributed to Delahanty's dissatisfaction about his value as a professional athlete. It left him also with a festering sense of bitter entitlement.

A few weeks after Ed Delahanty returned to Cleveland for the off-season, organizational changes in major league baseball were taking shape. Centered on the desperate straits of the American Association, many owners reconsidered the much-talked-about merger of the two organizations into a super league. Matters came to a head when King Kelly's Cincinnati franchise folded, and Mike signed with the National League Boston Beaneaters rather than fulfill his promise to play with their crosstown association rivals. His reneging disrupted National Agreement talks. Without a revitalized pact, a new bidding war was anticipated, particularly when the players from the association's St. Louis Browns announced their intention of signing with the National League. Led by outspoken Irishmen "Tip" O'Neill, Tommy McCarthy, and Denny Lyons, this move convinced St. Louis' owner Chris von der Ahe, an opponent of the merger, that the time was right for an accord. In Indianapolis on December 18, St. Louis, Washington, Baltimore, and Louisville were accepted into the National League. American Association clubs in Columbus, Milwaukee, Boston, Chicago, and the Athletics of Philadelphia were bought out for $130,000.

The new twelve-team "League Association" signed a ten-year pact whereby each team put aside 10 percent of their gate receipts to pay off the defunct association ball clubs. Fifty cents became the standard admission charge, and Sunday baseball and the sale of liquor were permitted where it did not conflict with local ordinances. The new league also restored the fourteen-man reserve list, and rosters were expanded to fifteen players. As a safeguard that the new signings did not disrupt the settlement, a panel of owners oversaw the redistribution of players. To make the game more appealing, and compensate for so many losing teams, a split season was established.[1]

Delahanty's team was affected by the Athletics' buyout. For the first time in the franchise's history, the Phillies did not have to share the city with any other major league club. As for Sunday baseball, Reach and Rogers opposed it, and the laws of Pennsylvania prohibited the practice. The owners also turned their back on the sale of alcohol at the ballpark and grudgingly accepted the fifty cents admission standard. The Phillies only concession was a twenty-five cents section in the left field bleachers.[2]

The demise of the Athletics also affected the makeup of the 1892 Phillies, who signed Gus Weyhing, the winner of thirty games for three consecutive years, and Delahanty's hometown friend, catcher-infielder Lave Cross. They also acquired young pitching prospect Wilfred "Kid" Carsey from Washington and the aging, legendary slugger Roger Connor from New York. These acquisitions strengthened the ball club and offset the jump of pitching ace Kid Gleason to St. Louis.

In the midst of these transactions many people were relieved that the old triple-jumping Delahanty was not incited to change teams. Instead, he asserted, "Let the other players jump contracts; I want no more of that business in mine."[3] This attitude revealed Delahanty's new vulnerability, the result of his tarnished reputation and failed on-field expectations. Therefore, without competitive interleague bidding, Del, like other young developing players, had no choice but to accept a one-third cutback in his contract to $2,100.[4]

Delahanty did not agonize over his setback. He was determined to make the new year a productive and satisfying one. Ed kept in peak condition in the off-season and "did not drink a drop." He worked out nearly every day and reported "as strong as an ox and as spry as an antelope."[5] When he arrived in Philadelphia in February 1892, his disposition was upbeat and positive. This change satisfied many of his doubters who had felt that Delahanty "may need a strict disciplinarian." Now they were encouraged by how well he had taken to playing the outfield. Others said the fans "adored his hitting" because he "smashes at a ball in the style that delights all lovers of savage batting."[6]

Harry Wright was optimistic about the coming season and Delahanty's prospects. "The makeup of the team suits me first-rate," he said, "We will be a strong competitor for the pennant this year."[7] From training camp in Gainesville, Florida, Wright announced that Ed Delahanty was playing with a new zeal, not evident since his "unfortunate collision with Cub Stricker."[8] The only uncertainty was the usual questions about the team's durability, which were answered soon after the season began.

The offensive-minded Phillies opened the year at home against New York. Tim Keefe pitched and lost the game, 5 to 4. But the loss was coupled with Delahanty badly hurting his ankle after he overran second base. He was helped off the field and was on crutches for over two weeks. He missed twenty-five games. This setback was a difficult blow for the team and Delahanty. Again, it appeared as if his injury jinx would ruin another season. In the past, Ed sulked and brooded through his layoffs. This time Del accepted his misfortune and did what he could to get himself back into playing form.

Delahanty convalesced in Cleveland and met up with the Phillies on the team's first road series against the Spiders. While the ankle mended, Delahanty got around with a cane and spent most days at Cleveland's League Park in his favorite grandstand seat. In an interview given at the grounds, Ed downplayed his role on the ball club and modestly replied, "The team would be well enough without me, but men like [second baseman Bill] Hallman when they are missing make big holes."[9] The reporter lauded Delahanty's sentiments and predicted his return would make the Phillies a serious pennant contender. In a subsequent conversation, a local sports-writer related that Delahanty was caught up with the Phillies' progress and constantly kept his eye on their line score. When asked whether he was interested in the game he was attending, Del remarked, "What do I care about the game? I am interested in the Phillies and don't care a rap about the other team." This prompted the reporter to write that unlike some players who think only of money, "This is a player whose heart is in the game."[10]

Delahanty's team was 11 and 14 during his absence. On May 17, he rejoined the club, batted sixth and was hitless in a 7 to 6 loss to Washington. This setback and many of the team's early season games revealed an inconsistent pitching staff, weak baserunning, and the indecisive leadership of team captain John Clements. But Harry Wright was not discouraged. He proclaimed, "The stuff is there and it is bound to make itself manifest. Just let the croakers suspend judgement until we get through this long stand at home."[11] Despite this confidence, on May 30 the Phillies were in tenth place with a 14 and 19 record when they took the field for a morning and afternoon doubleheader against Louisville.

Tim Keefe won the first contest, and Charlie Esper and Gus Weyhing combined to take the next game in fourteen innings. Delahanty played well in both games. In the second contest, he made a game-saving, over-the-shoulder catch and scored the winning run after leading off the fourteenth inning with a triple. More important than Ed's feats, the Phillies rebounded with nine- and sixteen-game winning streaks. The *Sporting Life,* recognizing these successes, reported that Delahanty's "fielding is brilliant and his batting hard and timely."[12] The *New York Herald* gave most of the credit to the managing of Harry Wright. "He didn't shift his nine around, continually threaten men with release . . . [and] paid no attention to the feeble patrons who stayed at home while the club was losing games."[13] By the end of the first-half season, the surging Phillies had too much ground to make up against league-leading Boston for the midseason championship.

During the half campaign, Delahanty elevated his performance. He played in 53 games and batted .303. Ed had 22 doubles, 5 triples, and 3 home runs. More remarkably, he struck out only 8 times and committed just 3 errors in the outfield. The sole complaint was that Delahanty was still timid about going after fly balls near the right-center field wall.[14] This charge was not evident in a home game against Chicago. With the Phillies winning by two runs, Cap Anson hit a hard drive that became entangled in the large American flag flying from a pole based next to a small sloped-roof shed in right field, where the scoreboard boy kept his numbers. Delahanty raced to the top of the terrace at the foot of the brick wall only to see the ball drop behind the structure. Without thinking, Ed "threw himself on his stomach over the roof . . . trying to reach the ball." Unable to get the ball, Del got on his knees and tried to crawl into the shed's small oval doorway. With Delahanty stuck in the opening, Anson and two runners circled the bases, as Ed, "waving his big can and feet," tried to free himself. The fans roared with laughter and applauded him for his gallant effort.[15]

The confidence and good feeling with which the Phillies and Delahanty ended the first half season did not carry over into the second half. In the weeks to come, the team was upset by new management-inspired salary cutbacks, ineffective field leadership, and injuries.

Until the winning streaks, the Phillies drew about 2,000 fans per game. The resulting decline in revenue awakened management's thoughts about cost-saving personnel moves. Sports columnist Henry Chadwick reminded his readers that these conditions were the "true costs" of two years of "needless baseball wars, and the selfish greed of a minority of high-salaried stars."[16] For the Phillies, the new round of cuts began with the release of ballplayers and salary reductions to better paid players such as Tim Keefe and Billy Hamilton.[17] Ed Delahanty was unaffected by these actions. He was playing well and already had his contract reduced.

The effect of the contractions on the club was immediate. Wright became "righteously indignant" about charges in the local papers concerning player dissatisfaction and deflected such reports. "The men," he declared, "have but one idea and that is to win the pennant."[18] No player or reporter questioned Harry Wright's sincerity, but the team regressed to .500 baseball. Again, mediocre pitching exposed the Phillies' weaknesses in on-field leadership and club chemistry.

John Clements, an excellent catcher, lacked the quick-witted, on-field take charge instincts of a John McGraw, John Montgomery Ward, or Mike Kelly. The Phillies needed a player that brought a hard-nosed, in-your-face style of play to the ball field. The magnificent Phillies hitters were not conniving, outspoken motivators. Thompson, Hamilton, Delahanty, and even the veteran Roger Connor relied on their batting to produce victories. Without assertive leadership, Harry Wright's mannerly direction stalled under a barrage of injuries.

For the first time in his career, Delahanty was carrying the burden of the Phillies' offense. He was hitting for power and by September was second in batting with a .347 average. In one game against Cincinnati, he went 5 for 5 with two doubles and a triple against an old nemesis, Billy Rhines. Delahanty's play was so noteworthy that his picture and a career summary appeared on the front page of the *Sporting News*. The piece described him as the brilliant center fielder of the Phillies. "Delahanty is very muscular, is unusually active for a man of his build and always plays to win. He is a great favorite with the Philadelphia enthusiasts."[19]

Everything seemed to be going Delahanty's way until a chilly, drizzling Thursday afternoon home game on September 8, the day of the famous John L. Sullivan–James J. Corbett heavyweight championship fight. In his second at-bat against "Big Mike" Sullivan of Cincinnati, Delahanty was hit in a "delicate," "ugly place" (his groin) by an errant fast ball and was assisted off the field. During the same game, Clements was hit on his bad arm and Thompson took a pitch on the back of his head. But it was Delahanty's injury that proved to be the worst. He remained in bed for a few painful days and was replaced by a deaf-mute outfielder from Camden, New Jersey, "Dummy" Stephenson.[20] Delahanty missed eight games.

At the time of Delahanty's injury, he was hitting .342. His return for the last seventeen games of the season found his batting off and saw his average drop twenty-one points. The Phillies, out of contention for the second-half championship, did put on a spurt but finished in fifth place, 12½ games behind Cleveland. Overall, the Phillies had a composite record of 87 and 66 for a fourth-place finish, 16½ games in back of Boston.

Delahanty and the Phillies closed out the year in their usual fashion with a series of exhibition games against college and minor league clubs. Ed spent more time than usual in Philadelphia after the season in expectation of a contract and advance money that never came. This lack of payment was not the result of Delahanty's 1892 performance; the Phillies did not intend to offer any new contracts until the winter league meetings decided on a new salary cap. While waiting, Delahanty occupied himself by attending shows and accompanying friends to the horse races at the gambling resort in Gloucester, New Jersey. Both he and Philadelphia-born Cub Stricker spent costly afternoons at the Jersey track. He even gambled on the upcoming presidential election and won two suits, three hats, and $95 on the results. By mid-December, Ed returned to Cleveland for some "halcyon enjoyment."[21]

Delahanty earned his winter rest after having his best year in major league baseball. He appeared in 123 games and was one of six full-time players who batted over .300 for the combined season— he hit .306. He led the league in slugging, was second in triples (19), and was third in doubles (32). Del also stroked 6 home runs, knocked in 91 runs, and scored 79 times. His emergence was portrayed in an end of the season team picture. Delahanty, seated second from the left on the front row, was no longer the awkward and insecure prospect of former years. He was a strikingly handsome, muscular, and mature-looking athlete.[22] For Delahanty the 1892 season was a harbinger of his future baseball greatness. Financially, however, he continued to suffer from the new salary standards imposed by the League-Association.

National League baseball, suffering from the monetary strains of the last three seasons, had to contend with fan disillusionment, failing revenues, and latent union sentiment. On some September afternoons, the talent-ladened Phillies played before only a few hundred people. The majority of the 188,000 spectators drawn in 1892 attended the first-half season.[23] Rogers told the *Philadelphia Inquirer* that since Labor Day the club had been losing $200 a day and expected to close the year with a $15,000 deficit. In early October, Rogers suggested that next season's salaries had to be dramatically reduced.[24] Even the pro-players *Sporting Life* editorialized that "baseball depends upon reduction of salaries and retrenchment of expenses, as the clubs would have to go out of business were the present heavy expenses carried over in another season."[25]

Baseball's financial problems were also a product of the country's economic malaise. The most troubling problem was the depressive state of silver, the backing for the country's paper currency.

The nation's failing economy could not overcome the inability of the Harrison and second Cleveland administrations to stabilize the gold and silver standard. By June 1893, 128 banks had failed, the stock market had plummeted, businesses and factories had closed, unemployment and inflation raged, and labor agitation was growing. Within a year, one out of every five workers was without a job, and public confidence was shaken by the violence of the Pullman Railroad strike and the suppression of Jacob Coxey's march on Washington by unemployed workers demanding federal relief work.

These conditions shook the world of baseball. Owners tried to stabilize their investments by curtailing large salaries and multi-year contracts. At the end of 1892, the owners, using the ten-day termination clause in players' contracts, released everyone rather than pay their last checks. The move literally made every ballplayer a free agent. But the owners protected their personnel by not going after each other's players. Some teams like the Phillies allowed Delahanty and his teammates to recoup some money by playing exhibition games. This gesture meant little in the face of new salary standards. The owners decided on a $2,400 maximum salary and a club payroll target of $30,000. And though some teams paid special players under the table, the Phillies' best athletes were awarded contracts in the neighborhood of $1,800. With the average industrial worker making $486 a year, Rogers and Phillies secretary Billy Shettsline believed a six-month contract at $300 a month was a satisfactory wage for their veteran players.[26]

Recognizing their leverage, Philadelphia's front office did not mail out the 1893 contracts until mid-February. Enclosed with the contracts was a statement justifying the reduction of wages. The players reacted predictably. Ed Delahanty was especially upset. After having his best year, he was asked to take a $300 pay cut. Some of his teammates publicly voiced their distress. Bill Hallman threatened to remain on stage as a song-and-dance performer or play baseball and sue for his contracted wages. Roger Connor warned he would play elsewhere. Shettsline was not overly concerned. He expected most contracts back in a few weeks, and boasted, "if they do not sign we will immediately fill their places with reliable men . . . who will sign at a moment's notice."[27]

The Phillies did concede a few points. They invited local players to a meeting about the club's finances and promised each player a share in half of the revenue if 1893 was profitable.[28] The issue was so controversial that Colonel Rogers tried to ingratiate himself to his Irish ballplayers and the "liberal patronage from Irish American" fans. Instead, he aggravated the situation by offending nationalist sentiment with his pro-Irish Home Rule correspondence with English Prime Minister William Gladstone.[29]

Though other teams had better luck signing their players, a few malcontents stood out. Mike Kelly refused to re-sign with Boston and threatened to play with the "colored" Cuban Giants. But Kelly had more leverage than the average ballplayer. He was still a great drawing card and had a theatrical career singing popular songs and reciting poems such as "Casey at the Bat."[30] Eventually he played with New York in a limited capacity and was out of major league baseball by the end of the season. More drastic actions were taken by Ad Gumbert of Chicago. He refused to accept $1,800, was traded to Pittsburgh, and unsuccessfully sued his former club. Bill Joyce of Brooklyn went a step further than Gumbert. He held out, was traded, and sat out the 1893 season. Denny Richardson of Washington lamented the player's dilemma when he said, "Baseball is a big monopoly. Players can't kick with one major league. They must accept their restrictions or retire."[31]

This reality struck Delahanty and his teammates very hard. The Philadelphia organization refused to give any additional ground and reminded the players about their revenue-sharing proposal. Rogers and Shettsline warned ballplayers that they "have certainty and no risk, with the chance for profit if good luck comes to us."[32] Only Roger Connor resisted the Phillies' ultimatum. He refused his pay cut and was sent back to New York for two low-salaried youngsters. The other players waited and took their lead from former brotherhood officer Tim Keefe, who rejected a proposal suggesting the Philadelphia pitchers hold out as a group. Keefe replied, "I was in one [strike] once and it cost me everything I was worth."[33]

Soon after Keefe's signing, Sam Thompson reported to Philadelphia, leaving only the recalcitrant younger players, such as Clements, Hallman, Hamilton, Cross, Delahanty, and Bob Allen unsigned. Hallman eventually worked out an agreement with the Phillies that allowed him to perform on stage during the season, and Hamilton begrudgingly came in after his pleas were rejected. With each signing the resolve of the remaining holdouts was weakened.

Delahanty and Clements resentfully inked their contracts by April 1, and were followed by a disgruntled Lave Cross and Bob Allen. The extent of these reductions was evident and alarming (see table 1).[34]

Delahanty was distressed by these cutbacks. He had shown good faith by accepting his initial 1892 reduction and kept himself in good condition. He had sworn off hard liquor and was working out with other local players like Candy Sommers, Charley Zimmer, and Ed McKean of Cleveland by playing indoor baseball.[35] When a reporter approached Del on a Cleveland street, Ed said he was anxious to play and would be ready when the 1893 season started.[36] As for the rumor about trading a disaffected Delahanty to Cleveland, Harry Wright thought too much of Delahanty "to contemplate even a moment the idea of letting him go."[37]

It was ironic that as Delahanty began to fulfill his potential as a hitter, salaries were dropping and the owners were looking for ways to enliven the game. The magnates believed the low-scoring, pitcher-oriented, dead-ball baseball of 1892 was as unappealing to the fans as the failed split-season experiment. Motivated to change, the National League planners thought about enlarging the infield, liven-

Table 1.   Annual salaries of Phillies Players

	1889	1892	1893
Clements	$2,450	$3,000	$1800
Delahanty	1,750	2,100	1,800
Hallman	1,400	3,500	1,800
Thompson	2,500	3,000	1,800
Allen	—	3,000	1,800
Hamilton	—	3,400	1,800
Cross	—	3,250	1,800
Keefe	—	3,500	1,800
Weyhing	—	3,250	1,800
Total		$28,000	$16,200

ing the baseball, instituting a four-strike rule, or curbing sacrifice hitting. In an effort to negate the advantage of pitchers, the pitching distance was increased from 55'6" [the pivot distance from where the pitcher planted his back foot] to 60'6". They also removed the pitcher's box and replaced it with a 12-by-4-inch pitching slab. These changes, the most drastic since 1887, transformed the batter-pitcher relationship. Until the rule changes of the next decade that elevated mound and counted foul balls as strikes, pitchers were on the defensive.[38]

An assessment of this anticipated new pitching distance remarked that the increase in hitting would not be apparent in batters such as Delahanty and Thompson, "who as it is nearly pound the cover off the ball." The difference, it was said, would be seen in younger and more timid hitters.[39] For the potent Phillies batters, this edge softened the disappointment of reporting to training camp at reduced salaries.

The ball club's cost-saving measures were further evident in Rogers' decision to hold spring training in Philadelphia, with exhibition games against college and amateur teams. His other resolution was to return to the premerger standard of twenty-five cents admission, a move well-received in Philadelphia. It did not play well with the other league owners, who cherished their half share of the gate receipts.[40]

Hoping to get patrons back in the ballpark, Rogers put his faith in the attraction of his emerging slugger, Ed Delahanty. In the exhibition games, Ed hit impressively for power and played "brilliant" center field. A preseason preview reported that the "Buckeye youth" was fulfilling everyone's expectations. "If he ever was a Philadelphia favorite," the paper asserted, "he will surely make the cranks [fans] have great delight this season."[41] Delahanty was penned in to bat third after Hamilton and Thompson. The prognosis was that if the Phillies were as fast on the bases and strong in pitching as their batting "there would be scarcely a doubt as to where the flag [championship] would land."[42]

The excitement for the new season was soon becalmed. The Phillies immediately played .500 baseball and fell from the pennant chase. By the end of May, Harry Wright and his players began to feel the pressure of another failing season. Wright reacted by shifting Delahanty to left field, believing he could cover more ground and could get the ball back to the infield quicker than the left-handed Hamilton.[43] Within a week, Delahanty's standout playing made him a great favorite of the vocal, left field bleacher cranks. Delahanty also contributed with powerful hitting, including an unusual two home–run game in a 16 to 7 win against Chicago. Trying to get the Phillies out of third place, Harry Wright moved to bolster his pitching staff. He signed Tom Vickery and "Brewery Jack" Taylor. With six pitchers, Wright hoped to gain an advantage on the teams ahead of him in the standings.

Before the Phillies could make a serious run on first place, the club had to resolve a distracting grievance. Many of the players, led by Hamilton, Delahanty, and Hallman, believed they left their best playing on the practice field. These ballplayers complained that, when they were playing at home, Harry Wright held two- or three-hour simulated game practices every morning. The players contended that these sessions were draining and sapped their strength for the regular late-afternoon games. Delahanty was particularly concerned about all the wind sprints in the outfield.[44] Del may have had a good point, but it did not prevent him from being roasted by a cynical columnist. "Poor petite Delahanty," wrote O. P. Caylor for the *Sporting News*. Such cruelty, he glibly declared, from a "hard-hearted overseer [Wright]" who worked "these slaves . . . five hours a day instead of the customary two hours." Can you imagine, Caylor asked, Delahanty standing out in left field on his 2-by-9-foot piece of turf from 4:00 P.M. till supper time with only twenty-two hours to rest up. "But the cruelty of it. . . . Talk of serfdom in Russia. Why, Mr. Delahanty's case would form the basis for another historical romance like *Uncle Tom's Cabin*." The columnist concluded that if Delahanty and his friends wanted to compare themselves to actors how would they account for hours of stage rehearsal?[45]

Of course, Caylor made Delahanty appear like a spoiled and pampered athlete, but Ed had a point about over-practicing. Harry Wright was under a great deal of pressure to win a pennant and believed that repetitious hard work was a remedy. But no Phillies player was giving more than Delahanty. He was leading the league in home runs, was batting .390, and struck out for the first time on June 21. Ed was so coveted that the Giants of New York tried to work out a trade with the Phillies. Rumor had it that Delahanty actually met with New York manager John Montgomery Ward to discuss his role with the Giants.[46] E. T. O'Laughlin of the *Philadelphia Evening Item* countered, "When the officials on the New York club get ready to buy out the entire Philadelphia team will they stand a chance of getting Delahanty and not before."[47]

This attention put Delahanty at center stage. On Thursday, July 20, 9,200 people showed up to see a sore-armed Jack Taylor beat lowly Washington 8 to 1. The fans were especially excited when Delahanty came up to bat for the first time. He was met at homeplate by a group of dignitaries, who presented him with a package. The crowd quieted as Del unwrapped his present. Then a mighty roar went out as Delahanty held aloft a regulation-size, silver-inscribed bat. Gleaming in the sun, this bat became his most prized baseball possession.[48]

There was never a let-up in Delahanty's superb play. He was called the "bête noir" of third basemen. Billy Shindle, Brooklyn's exceptional keeper of third base, remarked that when Del starts to "shell the corner of the diamond we [third basemen] all get the tired feeling."[49] Overplaying Delahanty on the left side did not help, because according to *Sporting Life* no one in baseball was better at lining the ball to right field.[50]

Ed's dependable play, however, was again offset by the lack of strong pitching and by injuries to Hallman, Clements, and Thompson. In early August, Billy Hamilton was lost to the team when his heavy cold turned out to be a life-threatening bout of typhoid fever. Beset by these losses, the Phillies were dependent on the versatility of Lave Cross and Ed Delahanty, both of whom filled in at a variety of positions.

Of the two, Cross was more comfortable than Delahanty in the middle infield. Del played the infield without complaint, but his coverage of second base was erratic at best. Some writers went so far as to call it "decidedly poor." His biggest shortcoming was his anxiety about making mistakes. This led him to hold the ball too long when making the double play.[51]

Despite these setbacks, it was not until Labor Day that the Phillies suffered the decisive blow. In the first inning of the opening game, Bob Allen had his right cheek bone shattered by an "ugly bounding ball." Without Captain Allen at shortstop, the team's woes multiplied. Delahanty did the best he could and played wherever Harry Wright required. In early September he remained in the lineup despite a sore back and a bad cold. The desperate Phillies even resorted to a well-worn racist superstition. They recruited a new mascot, a "large head African," whose scalp they rubbed for luck.[52] In the end, despite the hitting of Delahanty, the team again finished fourth, 14 games behind Frank Selee's Boston Bean-eaters. Led by the heads-up playing of Hugh Duffy and Tommy McCarthy, and the 34-win pitching of "Kid" Nichols, Boston always seemed to outplay the faltering Phillies.

What was remarkable about the final standings was that Boston did not lead the league in any category except in wins. The Phillies were on top in seven departments, including runs, doubles, home runs, slugging average, and a remarkable team batting mark of .301. The club also committed the fewest errors and had the best fielding average. Critics could not even fault Philadelphia's pitchers. In the first year of the new pitching distance, the Phillies' staff had a 4.68 ERA, just .25 points behind Boston.

The most frequently heard complaint about Delahanty's Phillies was that they rarely played smart baseball. Supporters read about slow baserunning, thoughtless play, and the lack of bunting and sacrifice hitting. *Sporting Life* reported that Harry Wright and Captain Allen were not at fault because they could not put "alert brains into thick heads or speed into leaden heels."[53] Tim Keefe believed that the players "did not know how to play the game to win." He explained "that it took two weeks before catcher Clements gave him signs to throw to second base to catch a napping runner."[54] A consensus asserted that the Phillies depended too much on "freer batting," where hitters tried "to knock the cover off the ball." Headwork, the *Sunday Item* admonished, won ballgames. Teams such as Boston, the columnist said, when they could not hit a pitcher changed their tactics and used "brains as well as brawn" to gain an advantage.[55]

This approach was not associated with Delahanty and his talented teammates. Their batting averages were high; in 1893 Thompson (.370), Hamilton (.380) and Delahanty (.379) led the league in most offensive categories. But the Philadelphia game was not alert to how successful franchises in St. Louis and Boston and later in Cleveland and Baltimore used scheming and daring baseball to get a competitive edge. Wily field tacticians—the most successful and visible of whom were Irish—often associated with these clubs and approached a ballgame differently than Harry Wright. The gentlemanly strategist of the Quaker City believed a game should be crafted and plotted according to its rules. He did not condone deceit, and like Colonel Rogers, could not abide willful ballplayers that flaunted authority and on-field propriety. A respected teacher of the sport, Wright often was closed out by his masterful Phillies hitters, including Delahanty, who like gifted students expected to succeed with little study or preparation. This attitude, unfortunately, became an enduring Delahanty trademark.

Although the team's shortfalls affected their morale and outlook, it was the season's ledger book that captured the attention of Delahanty's employers. In 1893 the high-scoring Phillies drew almost 290,000 people. There was speculation that the franchise made $40,000.[56] How much of this amount was available for the player's end-of-the-year dividend was not known. No salary complaints or disclosures appeared in the press. Nevertheless, Ed Delahanty and his teammates could not but be disturbed by the club's fiscal policies and failed efforts to assemble a contending team.

The Phillies' unacceptable finish upset John Rogers almost as much as the league's resistance to his twenty-five cents admission price. On a number of occasions, his fellow magnates shortchanged his ticket receipts in retaliation for their share of the gate in Philadelphia. Rogers would challenge the league's authority on this matter and continued to look for ways to make his franchise more profitable. Some players actually accused Rogers of keeping costs down by skimping on expenses, compelling "the players to travel on the cheapest railroads and live at the poorest hotels."[57] Rogers' distress at these disclosures increased his growing impatience with the team and its manager.

Meeting with Al Reach to discuss the state of the franchise, Rogers lamented that, after ten years, Wright had not finished better than second, and was stuck in a fourth-place rut. He complained as to how much money he had spent for a club that was finishing behind less-talented clubs. Reach sympathized with Wright and said he would hate to see a loyal and long-time employee released. "That's the problem," Rogers retorted, "Harry has been too long in the game. He goes back to those Cincinnati Reds of the sixties. We're now playing a different kind of baseball in the nineties."[58]

Wright knew that for the last few years John Rogers wanted to get rid of him. Harry told his players at their last team meeting that he expected to be released.[59] He wrote Sam Thompson that Rogers was holding him "personally responsible" for the club's recent finish. Thompson told the press that the "fall-down" was "due entirely to the disabling of strong players and the filling of their places by amateurs."[60] Whatever the fault, on November 24, Wright was relieved of his duties.

The two leading candidates to succeed "Uncle Harry" were Rogers' dutiful front man, club secretary Billy Shettsline, and the one-time Phillies shortstop and captain, the former brotherhood man, Art Irwin. After much debate, Rogers and Reach selected Irwin, who had managed Washington and guided the American Association Boston Reds to a championship. For John Rogers to take back Art Irwin, after the experiences of 1889, testified to his desperation for a winner. But Irwin embodied the kind of leader he coveted, an active and participatory manager, the equivalent of having a field captain on the bench.

The managerial change greatly affected Ed Delahanty. Despite his problems with Wright, Del respected and was fond of the old man. In many ways, Harry Wright filled the void vacated by Delahanty's standoffish father. It would be Ed's loss that he did not heed everything Wright taught him about life and responsibility. In ethnic terms, Del remarked that despite his English ancestry "God breathed pure Hibernian oxygen into the heart of Harry Wright."[61] But Delahanty also had strong feelings for little Art Irwin, who had coached and mentored him during his first years with the Phillies. He would miss Harry Wright, but he was excited about renewing his ties with the former Philadelphia captain.

For the moment, Del was excited by his own achievements and was looking forward to postseason touring. At one point, Delahanty anticipated playing exhibition baseball in Cuba. Both Cap Anson's Chicago team and Wright's Phillies were invited by Carlos Ayala, the father of Cuban baseball, to the Caribbean.[62] The ballplayers loved the idea of exotic travel and additional earnings. Regrettably, the trip proved to be too expensive for the depression-ridden economy and was canceled. Delahanty, instead, joined a team of former major league Irish stars, including Mike Kelly and Jim O'Rourke. This club played against the touring champion Boston Beaneaters. But after a long season, cities like Milwaukee, Wisconsin, in October did not have the same appeal as semitropical Cuba.

After a couple of games, Ed lost his interest in barnstorming and returned to Philadelphia.[63] A few weeks before Harry Wright was dismissed, Del walked into the Phillies office, signed his contract, and returned to Cleveland.

At home, he spent a great deal of time with Jack O'Connor, the outfielder and part-time catcher for the Cleveland Spiders. Jack and his wife were boarding with Bridget Delahanty on Phelps Street. The two players were close friends and shared a passion for baked fruit pies. O'Connor's nickname was "Peach Pie" and Delahanty, it was reported, was a "regular first class pie fiend." From the point of view of indulgence, the Phillies were willing to accept desserts rather than the liquor that Ed had allegedly foresaken.[64]

His temperance was paramount because the Phillies had great expectations for their young slugger. Ed had just turned twenty-six, and his value to the ball club was immeasurable. There was even talk of Del becoming team captain under the new manager.[65] The interest of other clubs in Delahanty also testified to his potential. However, every Delahanty trade rumor sparked rebuttals in the local press and by the Phillies' front office. John Rogers remarked that if he let Delahanty go "he would have to get out of Philadelphia." The *Sporting News* asked if anyone blamed Delahanty for wanting a salary commensurate to his worth.[66]

Delahanty's value far exceeded what he would earn in 1893, when the mantle of baseball stardom shifted to a new generation of ballplayers. An era of baseball was coming to a close. It was marked by Harry Wright's release, the new pitching distance, and the passing from the ball field of many great personalities and talents. Many of the early heroes of the Emerald Age of baseball, Mike Kelly, Jim O'Rourke, Tim Keefe, and Henry Larkin, soon retired. "Hoss" Radbourn, Pud Galvin, Mickey Welch, and Tip O'Neill were out of baseball and John Clarkson, Dan Brouthers, Roger Connor, and Tony Mullane were at the tail end of their great careers. A cast of younger players with names such as McGraw, Keeler, Hoy, Rusie, Jennings, Duffy, McCarthy, Collins, McGinnity, Kelley, Gleason, and Delahanty were now joined by Hamilton, Burkett, Lajoie, Nichols, Young, and Wagner. It would be an exciting age.

7

King of Leftfielders

Although the Phillies' prospects for the 1894 season looked promising, there were issues and problems that threatened the pennant dreams of Delahanty, the new "King of leftfielders."[1] With the franchise's revenues threatened by the recession, the players wondered whether the ball club would pay the kind of salaries needed to build a championship team. Or, instead, would personnel decisions be determined by gate receipt issues and the maintenance costs of a new baseball park?

The league owners had never been happy about the pricing of Phillies' tickets, or their percentage of gate revenues. The justification that cheaper seats led to more tickets sold was not a convincing argument to greedy magnates. Throughout 1893 Rogers' colleagues attacked his pricing policies. At a November meeting of the owners, it was agreed, by an 11-to-1 vote, that Philadelphia had to abandon their popular, twenty-five-cent admission price. Rogers, who was described by a fellow owner as having "a woman's weakness for talking," argued for lower rates. He was so upset by the verdict that Al Reach and then-manager Harry Wright had to drag the agitated Rogers out of the Fifth Avenue Hotel. During his forced exit, Rogers vowed to fight on into the season.[2] When the owners reconvened in February 1894, they averted a crisis and convinced Rogers and Reach to settle for sharing half of the total gross receipts.[3]

Another concern was the unanticipated expenses created by the infamous Broad Street "hump." This obstruction appeared in October 1893, when the city built a tunnel and new intersection over the Reading Railroad crossing at Broad and Lehigh. This alteration ignored the ballpark's grading and drainage, deformed the right and center field structure and eliminated carriage and spectator space. It also made the Broad Street sidewalks practically level with the top of the brick outfield wall. These conditions forced Reach and Rogers, in the middle of a faltering economy, to erect a twelve-foot wooden fence on top of the original enclosure.[4] These costly outlays and the threat of lost ticket revenues weighed heavily on the managing partners as they considered their preseason roster.

With Delahanty already under contract for the imposed maximum salary of $1,800, the Phillies turned their attention to getting his teammates, particularly Hamilton, Thompson, and Cross to accept their static contracts. The Phillies also gave their attention to getting another starting pitcher, and set their sights on Baltimore's ace John "Sadie" McMahon. Oriole manager Ned Hanlon said Art Irwin offered him Sam Thompson, but that he countered with the names of Delahanty and Hamilton. Irwin replied, he would never hear of such a deal. "I would rather have Hamilton and Delahanty," Irwin declared, "than Hanlon's entire pitching outfit." The Phillies' manager said he was not interested in getting a good pitcher at the expense of trading his best players.[5]

Foiled in his attempt to get McMahon, Irwin argued for his team's talent and potential. He attributed last year's failures to "disjointed play" and dependence on "heavy hitting alone to pull them through." The "boys," he observed, lacked generalship and had "no understanding whatever between the base runner and the batsman." Irwin called them "happy-go-lucky" hitters. He preached that everyone had to have their heads totally into the game with every player "part of a machine to work in unison with others."[6]

Focusing on Irwin's solutions, the Phillies and Delahanty got off to a good start. The team won six of its first eight games led by Delahanty's .375 average. Two of these contests saw attendance exceed 17,000. With expectations on the rise, Boston came in for a three-game series. Manager Irwin and the team gloated that the Beaneaters would be hurt by the new bunt rule that counted failed sacrifice bunts as strikes. But Delahanty had turned his ankle sliding into second base against Brooklyn and missed the first two games against Boston. With Delahanty on the bench, the Phillies took the first game, 14 to 3, and Ed crowed, "We would rather play Boston and New York than the weaker clubs and we will win the series from both."[7]

The teams split the next two games, with Delahanty returning for the getaway-game loss. For the next few weeks, the Phillies prospered on the field and at the gate. They were only a few games out of first place, and Del, in the midst of a 14-game hit streak, had batted .507. This success at the plate was matched by his feats in left field. Therefore, it surprised everyone when Art Irwin moved Del from the outfield to first base to get the hot-hitting youngster "Tuck" Turner into the everyday lineup. But this stratagem and the Phillies' successes were derailed by a rash of injuries and a rebellious player.

The Phillies lost Sam Thompson for six weeks after a line drive shattered the tip of his left pinkie finger, which was later amputated. Two starting pitchers went down with a variety of ailments, John Clements broke his ankle, and Bob Allen had his left cheek splintered by an Elton Chamberlain fastball. Allen needed two surgeries to remove bone fragments embedded in his brain and retired from baseball for two years. Even the team surgeon, Dr. Bolger, was felled by a bout of typhoid fever. By the end of June, the local papers referred to the Phillies as "our cripples."[8]

Replacing everyday players was difficult, but ailing pitchers were next to impossible to replace. Art Irwin had to rely on the tempestuous, hard-throwing Jack Taylor. Unfortunately, "Brewery Jack" had a drinking problem that he conveniently confused with malaria. One local paper remarked that Taylor's disease could be cured with the stiffest kind of fine that "would prevent him from contracting it in the future."[9] When Taylor's pay was docked for missing games, he rebelled and returned to his Staten Island home. His alleged inebriation and sulking could not have come at a worst time for Delahanty's ball club.[10]

The Phillies had little choice but to rely heavily on the versatility of Cross and Delahanty to fill in wherever they were needed.

Del, especially, rose to the occasion. He shifted from left field and played every infield position. Not since the days of Charlie Ferguson, the *Inquirer* wrote, had there been a ballplayer who earned so much praise and admiration. He filled in for injured teammates and even spelled Tuck Turner when he could not handle the difficult sun in right field. "Would we had a whole team of Dels," the paper declared, "the Phillies could challenge anyone."[11]

By the first of July, Delahanty was batting a remarkable .447. In a 19 to 6 victory over Cincinnati on June 16, he duplicated his 1890 feat by going 6 for 6 with five singles and a double. In the field, Del continued making plays as spectacular as his hitting. From the outfield, he routinely threw out runners at third base and home plate. In the ninth inning of a game that the Phillies were winning 9 to 1, he went after a hard-hit ball by Cleveland's "Chief" Zimmer. Delahanty ran up the left field terrace, pushing people aside, and reached out for the "finest" catch "ever seen on the home grounds."[12] *Sporting Life* was so impressed with his all-around play it proclaimed, "Delahanty is an awfully even, well balanced player all around. You look at his batting and say well, that chap is valuable if he couldn't catch the measles, and then you look at his fielding and conclude that it wouldn't pay to let him go if he couldn't hit a bat bag."[13]

Wherever Delahanty played he attracted attention. He was always a favorite of the New York crowds, a point not lost on Eddie Talcott, the owner of the Giants. At the beginning of the year, Talcott had let it be known that he wanted Delahanty for his team. Reach and Rogers dismissed this attention and said they could not let their best all-around player go. "The Phillies want to buy Delahantys not sell them."[14] But now with Bob Allen down with his career-threatening injury, Rogers needed help and inquired about New York shortstop "Shorty" Fuller. The asking price, replied Talcott and manager John Montgomery Ward, was, of course, Ed Delahanty. Their offer astonished the Phillies. "Might," Reach and Rogers said, "let the pavillion go, but if they dared to consent to a trade . . . with Del . . . the entire rank and file of the royal Quaker rooters would be at their ears quicker than a wink." An editorial proclaimed, the Giants did not have enough money to buy the best left fielder since the days of Andy Leonard. "Let Delahanty go? Nit. Not. Nit!"[15]

Still in contention, the Phillies began a twenty-two game western road trip that saw them succumb to more injuries, troubled pitching, and the rigors of their travel schedule. The Phillies won only eight games and were never again a serious contender for the pennant. What was left of the season became a series of offensive highlights interrupted by on-field shenanigans and a destructive fire.

The Phillies' misfortunes did nothing to soothe their intense rivalry with Boston. The defending champions were only a few games behind league-leading Baltimore when they came to the City of Brotherly Love for a three-game series. These games took place immediately after the Phillies' disastrous western road trip. During the seventh inning of the second game, with Boston up 2 to 1, the Phillies battled back with seven runs and took the lead. Throughout the rally, thunder and lightning awakened the skies over the ballpark. Captain Billy Nash of Boston, anticipating a downpour, stalled for time. He hoped the rain would interrupt the completion of the inning and give the victory to Boston. The most active player in this charade was the loud, foul-mouthed Tom Tucker, who had had a run-in with the Philadelphia fans earlier in the season.[16] On this day, he was particularly offensive to the sole and inexperienced umpire, Dan Campbell. The Phillies combated Boston's stall by trying to end the inning, but Tucker and company refused to make any of the outs. After scoring four more runs, Delahanty deliberately struck out, and Thompson was called out when he cut across the diamond on his way to third base.

With their half of the inning over, the Phillies took their places on the field as Boston argued and badgered the umpire. The Beaneaters' Hugh Duffy and Tommy McCarthy led the delay and ignored the umpire's warning to resume batting. After a ten-minute deadline passed, Tucker and his teammates were mobbed by several thousand angry fans who invaded the playing field. Nash, McCarthy, Duffy, and the rest of the Beaneaters fled to the grandstand, leaving Tom Tucker to the bleacher mob. Tucker was saved from harm by the intervention of Ed Delahanty, Jack Taylor, and a few policemen. They pushed and fought their way into the crowd. Del put his arms around Tucker and helped hustle the frightened player to safety under the grandstand. A double line of policemen eventually escorted the Boston players from the pavilion to their waiting carriages. On the way through the streets the players were pelted with stones, bottles, and debris.[17] The Phillies won the game.

The Philadelphia papers condemned Tucker and the "Boston culture," which indulged in unruly and provocative behavior. The *Baltimore Sun* said the league had to prevent these antics against umpires because they incited the fans and detracted from the game.[18] Manager Frank Selee countered that the umpire could not control the local team, and Tucker confessed he did not know why the people of Philadelphia pick on him. Deflecting the blame, he declared, "That's the whole trouble with the Philadelphia club. It has the best players in the business and ought to win the pennant right along, but they haven't the sand to stick up for themselves."[19] Tucker said they needed to play with "more life and spirit." Baltimore, he explained, "isn't to be compared with your [Philadelphia] team, but yet look where it stands [first place]."[20] Injuries aside, his analysis had an accustomed ring of truth to it.

Incidents of this kind exposed both the character and faults of baseball in the mid-1890s. The rough and tumultuous style of play promoted by Boston, Baltimore, and Cleveland brought success at the expense of order. Winning games by any means available became the mark of champion teams. These tactics, set in motion by manipulating managers such as Frank Selee, Ned Hanlon, and Patsy Tebeau, were applied by the McGraws, Jennings, McCarthys, Tuckers, Duffys, Kelleys, and Lathams of the era. It was a style of play frequently associated with "heady" Irish ballplayers, whose "scheming" and "quick-thinking" actions transformed baseball playing before the turn of the century.[21] Delahanty and his Philadelphia teammates might "kick" about a play and go after the lone umpire, but they were usually a step behind their quick-witted opponents. Boston's theatrics were part of the give-no-quarter baseball that provided fans with drama and entertainment. The problem for the league was how to bring fans to the ballpark while restraining play without dulling the game or inciting crowds to violence. Although a two-umpire system and better stadium security might prevent another Tucker riot, each remedy would cost the owners money.

More threatening for spectators and management, however, was a ballpark fire. On Monday morning, August 6, the Phillies were conducting their morning workouts at the ball field when they noticed smoke billowing up from the floor boards along the 15th Street, third base grandstand. Twice during the previous season cigarette fires had been successfully extinguished in the bleacher sections. This time a serious blaze erupted. Early morning spectators fled the scene as park personnel and ballplayers went after the fire. Delahanty, Gus Weyhing, Charlie Reilly, and others "rendered meritorious service," working the buckets and locating stray teammates. But the all-wooden structure, disserved by inadequate water pressure, could not withstand the fire, which had worked its way up the walls and turrets of the grand pavilion. Fanned by a brisk breeze, the fire became a roaring inferno and was well out of control when the fire companies arrived. With their lives in danger, Delahanty and his teammates gathered their belongings and escaped to the streets. Ed lost a new suit of clothes, but was relieved that he saved "all of his base hit bats." Other players lost everything, including their uniforms. Within two hours, what was one of the finest ball fields in the country was "simply a wreck of crumbling walls, charred timbers and twisted iron."[22] The only fatalities were the horses in the nearby trolley stables.

The fire was sparked by a plumber's stove near the ladies bathroom under the 15th Street stands. Initially, there was suspicion of arson because this was the third ballpark to go up in flames that season. On May 15, Boston had lost its grandstand and bleachers in a fire that erupted in the sixth inning of a game. On the day before the Philadelphia conflagration, Chicago's grandstand was partially destroyed by fire. The source of these blazes was the abundance of dry wood and a lack of fire prevention materials in these structures.

The Phillies were stunned by the devastation and believed the "hoodoo" from Charlie Ferguson's death still hovered over the organization.[23] For Reach and Rogers, the problem was threefold. The ballpark had been the nation's most expensive to build, with estimates in the $80,000 range. Insurance only covered about a fourth of the value, and construction projections for a fireproof stadium were approximately $150,000. These costs weakened the franchise's tempered finances. For the next seven years, Delahanty's salary would be a casualty of the new stadium's expenditures.

After a four-game road trip, Delahanty and the Phillies played six games at the University of Pennsylvania's Athletic Grounds at 37th Street between Spruce and Pine Streets, a field designed for football and track. Delahanty did not like the facility. He felt the grounds were not in good shape and the layout of the diamond was unsuitable for his style of hitting. Nevertheless, he batted 14 for 29, with 3 doubles and 3 triples. The Phillies were 5 and 1 at Pennsylvania, averaging 15 runs and 19 hits per contest. In their last game at the university, they stroked 36 hits and beat Louisville 29 to 4. Delahanty had four singles and scored five runs.

On August 18 the Phillies took their heavy hitting back to their hastily rebuilt ballpark. They swept the Cleveland Spiders with an awesome offensive barrage. Counting the last three games at the university, the Phillies, in a six-game sweep, pounded out 99 runs and 120 hits. Delahanty went 8 for 11 in the Cleveland series. In a 16 to 1 shellacking of Cy Young, Delahanty was at his best, going 5 for 6 with two doubles and a home run. But in Del's second at-bat against George Cuppy, in the getaway game, Ed took a fast ball below the heart. He was assisted off the field and missed the next nine games.

In spite of the Phillies' postfire streak, they could not make up ground against Boston and Baltimore. For Delahanty, the remainder of the season was disappointing. He returned to the lineup for a doubleheader against Washington. In the second game, Billy Hamilton stole seven bases, and Del was hit by Bill Wynne in the chest with another errant fast ball, forcing him to miss another five games. He came back, replacing an injured Tuck Turner, but the demands of the season and his sore chest took their toll. He could not swing the bat with authority, or keep pace with Boston's Hugh Duffy for the batting title. In September, Ed was 20 for 76 for an uncharacteristic .263 batting mark. Remarkably, he still finished the year with his first .400 batting average.

Ed Delahanty's on-field successes and his personal charm made him a great attraction wherever baseball was played. In a September 17 exhibition game in Mansfield, Ohio, local fans showed that they had not forgotten their departed hero. Before his first at-bat, a delegation came out and presented a visibly moved Ed Delahanty with a diamond ring.[24]

This same affection was shared by the people of Philadelphia. In a season-long popularity poll taken by the *Philadelphia Press,* Ed received over 31,000 votes and was selected as the fans' choice. "Hurrah for Delahanty, the best player in the world!"[25] A special banquet was planned at the end of the season by his admirers. But this recognition could not erase the campaign's bitter disappointments or an embarrassing season-ending incident.

The Phillies concluded the year with a three-game series in Cleveland and finished their first season under Art Irwin as they had with Harry Wright; they clinched another fourth-place slot, 18 games behind Ned Hanlon's Orioles. The last game of the year would be played for the record. On Friday night, before the closing contest, a number of Phillies went out on the town and got drunk. Apparently remarks were made about their unfulfilled showing and a fight broke out. In the course of the early morning fracas, someone stabbed Bill Hallman through his hand with a sharpened stick cane. In Saturday's game, his place at second base was taken by Ed's brother Tom.[26]

Thomas James Delahanty was the smallest of the Delahanty brothers. Five years younger than Ed and his first surviving sibling, Tom, too, was a product of neighborhood games and local leagues. At the age of eighteen, he had competed with the local semipro Stars at Cleveland's League Park. By 1894 he was playing with Peoria in the Western Association and performing so well that Ed tried to get him a tryout with Philadelphia. The Phillies declined the offer, saying Tom was too young and inexperienced. They did humor their star player with a promise to bring his brother in at the end of the season. After a productive year playing second base, Philadelphia called on him when Bill Hallman was injured. The Phillies lost Tom's first major league game 11 to 3. Ed played third base and made 3 errors, while Tom went 1 for 4 with no miscues. The whole Delahanty family and several neighborhood friends came to the ballpark to root for the brothers.[27]

The twenty-two-year-old Tom Delahanty was not retained by the Phillies and went to play with Atlanta in the Southern League and finished the year with Detroit in the Western League. His overall performance was so good he was signed as a utility player in 1895 by Cleveland manager Patsy Tebeau. Tommy played hard, but was not ready for the National League. He made 12 errors in 16 games and struggled at the plate, batting .204. Before too long, he was sold for $200 to Pittsburgh, who sent him directly to Toronto in the Eastern League.[28] The following season, he returned to the major leagues and played one game for Louisville before being shuttled back to the Western League, where he regained his old confidence and form. In 1896, Tommy went east and signed with Newark in the Atlantic League. Tommy Delahanty would play a total of 19 games in the major leagues.

For Tommy's older brother the off season was a grand celebration coupled with new responsibilities. It began on Wednesday evening, October 3, when a group of friends and admirers gathered to honor their hero with a banquet at the Hotel Hanover in Philadelphia. Their formal invitation to Ed Delahanty read: "The undersigned lovers of the national game, of which you are such a distinguished exponent, desiring to evidence their appreciation and admiration of your ability as a ball player and worth as a man, would be honored to meet with you." Del responded, "I am deeply sensible to your expressions of good will and hope to be always 'next' in your esteem."[29]

The evening's festivities were described as a "spontaneous tribute" with an "absence of all restraint and oppressive formality." After a sumptuous dinner, a representative of the *Philadelphia Press* gave Ed his popularity award, a large, inscribed, gold watch charm. Another presenter half-jokingly forgave "our friend Delahanty" and his teammates for last season's shortfall and boasted he would put up $10,000 that a year from now the championship banner would belong to the Quaker City. Ed thanked everyone in a short speech, and cigars were passed out. Among the thirty attendees, only two were from the Phillies—Art Irwin and John Clements.[30]

This celebration of Delahanty's great year was a taste of things to come. He was now among the game's elite, and with each productive year, the adulation increased. His record for 1894 would have been more impressive had it not been for his sore chest and a dreadful September. And though he did not lead the league in any category, he batted .404 with a .561 slugging average. Playing in 114 games, Del had 200 hits, including 36 doubles and 16 triples, scored 149 times, and drove in 131 runs. His real value to the team was that he played every infield position and was brilliant in the outfield.

Delahanty's offensive feats were matched by his outfield mates, Billy Hamilton and Sam Thompson. Hamilton led the league with unheard-of statistics. He scored 196 runs, stole 99 bases, and earned 126 base-on-balls in 128 games. He also batted .404. Sam Thompson only appeared in 102 games, because of his amputated pinkie. He still hit .407 with a .670 slugging average. Thompson had 29 doubles, 27 triples, and 13 home runs, scored 115 times, and knocked in 141 runs. Not to be overlooked in the Phillies' remarkable outfield was Tuck Turner, who batted .416 in 80 games. Statistically, no outfield in the history of baseball approached the offensive standards set by Delahanty and his teammates.

The 1894 season was a unique experience for the National League. The fourth-place Phillies set a team batting mark of .349. Ten Phillies hit over .300, and seven batted higher than .370. The team averaged almost nine runs per game. But Delahanty and his club were not alone in their hitting successes. Seventy-four league hitters had averages over .300, and eight of the twelve teams batted higher than .300. The National League average rose 29 points in one season. Hugh Duffy of Boston had an unmatched career season. He won the triple crown with a .438 average, 18 home runs and 145 RBIs. He also led the league with 236 hits and 50 doubles. The overall league ERA was a horrid 5.32.[31]

The nightmare season for pitchers marked the highwater mark of a hitter-dominated era. Many of the great pitchers of the day held their own with the new distance, but young hitters such as Delahanty, Duffy, Hamilton, Keeler, Doyle, McGraw, Jennings, and Joe Kelley made reputations for themselves at the plate. Regrettably, as baseball completed this extraordinary year for hitters, the "Irish King" of the national pastime died.

No player enjoyed the popularity of Mike Kelly until Babe Ruth rocketed on the scene. Kelly was baseball's greatest drawing card and its highest paid player. But the "great one" had serious character flaws. He "made friends too fast" and was very much the "big-hearted" and "whole-souled" sporting idol whose lifestyle centered on the theatre, race tracks, and late-hour clubs of major league cities. As a result, Kelly could not hold onto or save his earnings. "Money had no charm for the King, unless he could make it talk and make his friends merry."[32]

By the end of the 1894 season, Mike Kelly was out of baseball and had to borrow money for a steamship ticket to Boston. Even in his despair, he remained the good-hearted fellow and gave a complete stranger his topcoat as security for his ticket. Without an overgarment, a run-down Mike Kelly caught a cold and arrived home with a fever. He had contracted active pneumonia and in a matter of days was dead at the age of thirty-six. He left behind an infant child and an impoverished wife. "His money went like the mist before a noon day sun, for it came easy and he thought it would last."[33]

The death of the "Only Mike" had little effect on the man who was being touted as the "Only Del." Delahanty, too, had a penchant for glitter and fame. Early in his career, Delahanty curbed his liquor drinking without diminishing his love for the good life. He wore tailored clothes, adored the theater, attended the races, and enjoyed being a popular host at the best clubs and hotels. At the Junction Hotel across from the ballpark, the proprietor's son recalled that Ed was always the congenial celebrity, entertaining in the hotel bar.[34] Lave Cross confirmed Delahanty's profligate ways. In his early career, Cross said, Ed was "as good a spender as he was a batter." The Phillies' third baseman often told stories of Delahanty kidding Billy Hamilton about his "closeness in money matters." Hamilton usually ignored the taunts and "kept banking the best part of his salary. I have everything I want," Billy said, "I don't see why I should throw away my earnings to prove I am a good fellow." But Del always had a quick retort and laughs for Hamilton's responses.[35]

Much of Delahanty's off-season time and money were spent on his fraternal lodge activities. He helped found the Ancient Order of Jabawauks, a nonsense social organization of ballplayers and theatrical and professional men. Every Thursday evening, they assembled to smoke cigars, raise toasts, and entertain themselves. Years later, he affiliated with another fun and social group, the Fraternal Order of Eagles, a lodge made up of theater people. Contrasted with these social clubs was the more somber Knights of Equity Lodge. This organization was founded in Delahanty's hometown of Cleveland and was made up of practicing Catholics of Irish ancestry. The intention of this order was to advance the study of Irish history and culture and promote the cause of Irish freedom. Their immediate attention went to supporting orphans, the elderly, and young men interested in the priesthood. These community and cultural ties were part of Del's strong Irish Catholic upbringing. Ed was proud of his heritage and often he corrected people who misused his surname. "I do not think it fair that a man who has won fame as a swatter of shoots and benders should have his last name misspelled just because some fellow thinks it easier to make an "e" than an "a.'"[36]

These opinions and values often contrasted with his off-field interests, like the theater. Described as "a persistent theatre fiend," Delahanty could be found almost every evening at a local playhouse.[37] His fascination with the stage and his ascendant fame were so great he received offers to perform in Cleveland. This opportunity was quite common in the late nineteenth century. The sporting public could not get enough of their idols, and the theater was the ideal medium for exposure. Plays and musical revues could always write in parts for famous local athletes. Usually they played rescuing heroes, had minimal lines, and sang short musical verses off-key. The most famous player to perform on stage was Mike Kelly, who frequently recited "Casey at the Bat." Other would-be thespians were Arlie Latham, Tony Mullane, Jim O'Rourke, Bill Hallman, Cap Anson, and later "Rube" Waddell.[38] It is doubtful Delahanty had much interest in these offers since he was about to assume the new role of a husband.

Delahanty had met his future bride sometime during the 1894 season, but plans to wed were delayed until Del finished playing baseball. After Ed's end-of-the-year award banquet, he went to the Phillies' office and signed his 1895 contract. He took a $500 advance and made plans to marry young Norine Thompson of North Philadelphia. Marriage was a significant step for Delahanty because it modified his lifestyle and introduced another strong-willed woman into his life. One of the effects of the pending marriage was opening a new bank account. Lave Cross disclosed that Delahanty realized the mistakes of his improvident days, to which Ed replied, "a married man ought to lay up part of his salary for a rainy day." Ed also took back the jokes he made at Billy Hamilton's expense. "I take off my hat to him now. Hamilton was right and I was wrong, but I am in line with him for the rest of my days."[39]

8

Marriage and Maturity?

Ed Delahanty's marriage was an auspicious step in his life and athletic career. For the first time, he needed to think about a person other than himself. His expressions of a new frugality were testaments to his freshly discovered responsibilities. But baseball marriages were not ideal relationships, and the glittering expectations of newlyweds quickly lost their luster. Players' wives faced a variety of rivals who competed for their husband's attention. They had to put up with lengthy road trips, the adulation of admiring fans, coveting women, and the adolescent gratifications of their ballplaying spouses. It would take a sound relationship with a devoted and understanding wife to make it through a baseball career. Wives occasionally did travel with their husbands when money and domestic responsibility permitted. Otherwise, they were expected to stay at home with the children, be dutiful housekeepers or serve as an adornment on the arms of their celebrated spouses. Other marital factors were the unrealistic dreams and the expensive tastes of young wives. The glamor was alluring, the pitfalls many.

From all indications, Delahanty's courtship was quick and heated. It may be better understood by Norine Thompson's background. She was the youngest of nine surviving children. Her father,

Thomas J. Thompson, was a carpenter whose family came to Philadelphia from Dundee, Scotland, in the early nineteenth century. He was a hard-working provider who doted on and spoiled his little girl. She, in turn, reveled in pretensions drawn from her mother's family, the Hutchinsons. Decades later, Ed and Norine's daughter, Florence, wrote how her mother told her that all the Hutchinsons "loved fine clothing and refinements," which confirmed the "good old English and Scotch . . . and the refined Southern blood . . . of [one of] the first families of Virginia."[1] Unfortunately, a North Philadelphia carpenter could not provide the fineries or lifestyle to satisfy a manipulative and wide-eyed romantic teenage daughter.

Used to getting her way, Norine's puerile and foolish side almost got the better of her in 1893. According to family tattle, the fifteen-year-old eloped with a young plumber's apprentice named Phillips. Her misadventure was corrected by her father, who had the marriage annulled. Shortly after this episode, Norine Thompson met Ed Delahanty.

Both Ed and Norine lived only a few blocks from the ballpark. Unlike modern ballplayers, Delahanty was an accessible sports figure, a popular neighbor approachable in the newly developed North Philadelphia, row-house community. The twenty-six-year-old baseball hero probably met the young Norine on his walks to the ball field or at the park itself. It was not uncommon for young girls to gather in all their finery and frills before a ballgame and flirt with the players. Delahanty was quickly smitten by this slender-waisted, round-faced, blue-eyed beauty. For Norine Thompson, Ed Delahanty was the ultimate catch—a handsome, well-paid, and idolized ballplayer.

The relationship did not immediately have her father's blessing; the ballplayer was much older than his underage daughter and was an Irish Roman Catholic. But Thompson knew his future son-in-law had better prospects than a plumber's apprentice. Delahanty was a nationally known sports figure who commanded more money for a seven-month season than Thompson could earn in a couple of years. He also appreciated the ballplayer's honorable intentions, and knew that a man with Delahanty's income could maintain the headstrong Norine in the lifestyle to which she aspired.

Having accepted this union, Thompson dealt with the problem of Norine's youth and Ed's religion. His daughter's age was initially falsified, then later verified by the father when he signed a special child consent marriage form. Norine's birthdate on the marriage licence was given as May 23, 1876. Her real birthday, August 23, was found on her death certificate and tombstone. Although the former gave her birth year as 1877, her tombstone and the 1880 census indicated she was born in 1878.[2] In any case, Norine Thompson was a minor when she married Ed Delahanty.

The religious issue was a bit more troublesome. Ed was raised in a strict Catholic home, and he knew that marrying someone outside the faith would upset his mother. This misgiving provoked a similiar reaction from his Protestant future in-laws. As a result, the wedding was a private and quiet ceremony without the families on October 10 in a small out-of-the-way Catholic Church, St. Charles Borromeo, in South Philadelphia. In their wedding portrait, Delahanty, posing behind his new wife, appeared proud and content with his decision.

Soon after the wedding, Del took Norine to Cleveland to introduce his bride to the Delahantys. If Bridget Delahanty had a problem with the marriage, it did not last long. She was relieved that her bachelor-son was settling down and that their children would be raised in the Catholic faith. In a partial family picture, taken a few years after the marriage, Bridget beamed proudly at her daughter-in-law as they sat together with their arms affectionately interlocked.[3]

The strain and pleasures of marriage coincided with another issue close to Ed's heart—the return of union baseball. By the end of September 1894, an attempt was made to construct a new players' league. Termed the National (later the American) Association, it was rumored that a number of big-name ballplayers were sympathetic to the experiment. In Philadelphia, Delahanty's name was linked with Lave Cross and Jack Taylor as local players pledged to the new association.[4] This claim was unfounded. Delahanty had already signed his 1895 contract, and with marriage pending, he was not in a position to start gambling his career on an unproven league. Neither could he overlook the National League's threat of permanent blacklisting for any jumper. In the end, the still-born association inspired a lifetime banishment decree from the league for anyone supporting a rival baseball circuit.[5]

Relieved of this threat, Reach and Rogers looked forward to attracting large numbers of fans to watch the Delahanty-led Phillies in their new ballpark. This facility had a double-deck grandstand built principally of steel, with platforms hanging from cantilever piers. This process, first developed on bridges, eliminated forward obstructive posts. The new stadium was constructed with safety in mind. Wherever there was wood, it was covered by galvanized iron or soaked with asbestos paint. Stairways were made of steel and slate treads. A new water and pipe system was also installed, making the new stadium the forerunner of twentieth-century ballparks.[6]

With the new stadium in mind, Reach and Rogers used the menace of a new association to support their argument for amending the league's admission charges. At a November meeting of owners a new four-year receipt-sharing plan gave visiting clubs twelve and a half cents for every admission to Philadelphia grounds.[7]

During the off-season Delahanty remained in Cleveland with his bride. When Del returned to the Quaker City in mid-February, his immediate task was setting up house before he left for spring training. But the Delahantys were not stay-at-home types. They were socially active, attending the theatre and eating at fine restaurants. The willful Norine, often in the company of her older unmarried sister, "Nettie," savored going about town as Mrs. Edward Delahanty.

Ed suffered for his new domesticity. Del was about twenty pounds overweight when he returned to Philadelphia. To get himself in shape, he spent a lot of time at the University of Pennsylvania working out with Gus Weyhing, who was coaching the collegiate pitchers. An exceptional handball player, Delahanty played with Weyhing and Bill Hallman at the Quaker City Athletic Club.[8] Del also followed the lead of many professional ballplayers and earned extra money coaching college baseball; he worked with the divinity students at Ursinus College.[9] By the time the Phillies left for Hampton, Virginia, on March 20, Ed had lost most of his newlywed bulk. The most difficult thing about the new preseason was taking leave of his young, teary-eyed bride at the railway station. But Delahanty's sorrow was quickly lifted by the excitement of seeing his teammates. For Norine, it was the beginning of her first season as a baseball wife.

These separations were forgotten by the time the lads got settled at a private hotel, belonging to a soldiers home that overlooked Hampton Roads. Between practices the players walked the strand

and spent hours playing pinochle, the players' favorite card game. Delahanty was acknowledged as the undisputed champ. On occasion, ballgames were celebrated with picnics hosted by community groups. The affable Delahanty was always the center of local attention. On the surface, all seemed well, but looking over Irwin's shoulder, assessing the team's progress was club secretary Billy Shettsline. A loyal organization man, he reinforced Irwin's stance that every player must "subordinate his individual preference to the general good." The Phillies, he declared, "must play for runs and not individual records."[10] Colonel Rogers reaffirmed that "You can take it from me. . . . We are after that pennant, and will have it if there is any possible way of getting it."[11] This confidence incited the team's supporters, and raised their expectations.

Philadelphia fans were always considered among the league's most rabid and knowledgeable "cranks." In 1895 they could hardly wait to see their team compete in the new ballpark. Leading the cheers for Delahanty and his teammates was a core of local enthusiasts with a strong ethnic flavor. In the lead was Ed J. Kelly and his "Kelly Rooters." They were seconded by Billy Morris's "Guards" and Harry Donaghy's "Grey House Rooters." Both Kelly and Morris gave themselves the rank of colonel and organized their fan clubs in a military fashion. They marched in unison into ballparks and directed cheers for their local favorites.[12] When Philadelphia opened the season in Baltimore, these groups led more than 1,000 supporters by train to the game. To their delight, the Phillies scored five times in the ninth as Jack Taylor beat the Orioles 7 to 6. The game was marred by the rowdy and bullying tactics of Hanlon's Orioles. In one instance, Taylor punched Orioles shortstop Hugh Jennings in the mouth when he tried to shoulder Taylor out of the base path. The Orioles later tried to pacify the Phillies by hosting a dinner at a fashionable restaurant.[13]

In the games that followed, the Phillies deflated much of the preseason optimism by going 2 and 5. Delahanty had a sprained leg and did not play in one of the games. Otherwise, he hit safely in each contest and was batting .400. This disappointing start did not, however, deter a huge and enthusiastic crowd of more than 22,000 for the delayed inaugural game at the new ballpark. Many thousands were turned away, and spectators without seats stood along the outfield perimeter and in the aisles to see Jack Taylor take on

New York's Jouett Meekin. To their disappointment, Taylor's arm was ailing, and he did not have good control or velocity. In the seventh inning there was a moment of hope. New York was leading 7 to 2 when the crowd's darling, Ed Delahanty, came to bat with two outs and the bases loaded. The huge gathering rose on their feet to exhort their hero. One reporter said it was like a scene out of "Casey at the Bat," as the great Irish slugger took his position at the plate. Meekin threw Del nothing but off-speed, breaking pitches. Three times, Ed "lunged viciously" at the ball, and each time he missed. A great hush fell over the ballpark, as the great Delahanty threw his bat down in disgust. The Phillies lost the game, 9 to 4. This setback was only part of the day's problems; the fresh paint on the pavilion's seats ruined many a pair of trousers.[14]

Delahanty had a chance to redeem himself two games later when he faced New York's ace, the overpowering Amos Rusie. Both men, it was reported, had "fear and terror" in their eyes when Rusie got two strikes on Del. Ed fouled off two pitches and called time to get a drink of ice water from the bench. When the "king of Philadelphia" returned, he slugged a game-tying double to right field. Delahanty scored the winning run on a single by Lave Cross. With the Phillies' 10 to 9 victory, a shower of seat cushions "made bedlam a slow pace."[15]

This enthusiasm was not shared by local sportswriters, who called the team to task for stupid playing. Both Irwin and new team captain, first baseman "Honest Jack" Boyle, were criticized for slow thinking and for losing their heads in tight situations. Boyle was not the popular choice for captain. Many wanted Delahanty, but Ed, uncomfortable with responsibility, and situated in the outfield, declined the offer.[16] With an inconsistent and ailing pitching staff, Boyle emphasized sacrifice hitting, putting the burden to score runs on the broad shoulders of Delahanty and Thompson.

Playing with a badly sprained leg, Del pressed hard to ignite his team's offense. For many weeks, the newspapers commented that his hitting had fallen off and that he was striking out and stranding runners. But Ed's batting record told a different story. In the team's first thirty-five games, Del hit safely in thirty-three contests. His longest streak was twenty games. Overall, he was batting .416, with 14 doubles, 2 triples, and 3 home runs in 144 at-bats. Ed even extended himself defensively. From left field, Delahanty participated in a triple and double play in a 4 to 3 win in St. Louis. On the same road trip, Ed, playing in front of his old Cleveland neighbors, knocked a home run off Bobby Wallace that cleared the distant left field fence. Fans and opposing players responded with enthusiasm to this unheard-of feat.

Delahanty's exploits could not deflect the pressures on second-year manager Art Irwin. His troubles came in many forms. Colonel Rogers, carried away with his own rhetoric, expected his team to be a contender. He had no appreciation for the wake stirred by his meddling impatience, or the litany of ailments that disrupted his teams. Irwin responded to these presures by shuffling his lineup. Only Delahanty responded well to his manager's crisis. He played second base, shortstop, and different outfield positions. By the middle of July, Irwin's maneuverings came to a merciful end, and Del, a little worse for wear, went back to left field.[17]

The move came none too soon. The Phillies were barely ahead of Brooklyn and New York in seventh place, five games above .500. A writer from the *Philadelphia Record* was so unhappy he wrote, "youse kin bury dem Phillies deep under a hill! But we'd smell 'em a-far wherever dey are. For dey're rotten, simply rotten." Another commentator asked whether Irwin "could manage the front end of the ice wagon."[18] The only good news was Art Irwin's announced intention to take the Phillies and their wives on a postseason exhibition tour of England. The players were delighted with the idea of touring. Delahanty and Kid Carsey were supposed to go abroad the previous season to give instruction to English players, so the prospects of another trip were appealing to Delahanty, and especially to his young bride. For Del it would be an opportunity to visit his Irish roots and receive the attention that Jimmy Fogarty and Mike Kelly spoke about in their 1889 world tour. Norine Delahanty shared these sentiments. She wanted to return to her ancestor's homeland on the arm of her famous and important husband. Unfortunately, bad weather and costs caused the trip to be canceled.[19]

Delahanty looked forward to the trip as a way to get through what was becoming another frustrating and difficult season. He felt sorry for Norine, who saw this proposed tour as her coming-out event. She enjoyed being Mrs. Delahanty and spoke of her plans to anyone within earshot. Although her husband enjoyed her exuberance, he sarcastically confessed that "a man may boast that he

knows his wife like a book, but can't always shut her up like one."[20]
This comment was not intended to embarrass his wife. It was meant
for laughs among his friends and teammates. Del actually was an
attentive husband, and when he learned that Norine was seriously
ill (probably a miscarriage), he hurried home from Chicago. Delahanty missed seven games and the Phillies won three of the contests.[21]

Neither Norine Delahanty's ailment nor the proposed trip to
England could distract Delahanty from the team's poor performance. Ed did his best, but a badly strained throwing arm forced
him to miss another four games. Art Irwin had confidence in Delahanty and believed that the signing of a few pitching prospects,
Cornelius "Con" Lucid and Al Orth, might turn the season around.

Lucid, born in Dublin, Ireland, was purchased from Brooklyn
and Orth, nicknamed the "Curveless Wonder," was bought for
$1,000 from the Lynchburg ball club in the Virginia League. Orth
began with eight straight wins and would finish his major league
career with 202 victories.

The Phillies' revitalized pitching benefited from a twenty-eight
game homestand and Delahanty's recovery. Del regained his batting stroke by trying to hit the ball to right field. Once his timing
and bat control were back, he took aim on the entire playing field.
In a six-game spurt versus New York and Boston, the Phillies took
five games. Against Amos Rusie, Jouett Meekin, Kid Nichols, and
Jack Stivitts, Ed went 18 for 31 for a .580 average. In this mini-streak,
he had four home runs and five doubles. The *Evening Item* began
referring to the left field bleachers as "Delahantytown."[22] From
August 1 to September 24, the Phillies were 35 and 14 and, at one
point, won 23 out of 28 games. The Phillies were now in third place,
only five games behind second-place Cleveland. Attendance was
again on the rise, and Clements, Thompson, Hamilton, and Delahanty were among the league's top six hitters. With eight games left
in the season, it was hoped that the Phillies could overtake Cleveland and be in a position to play first-place Baltimore in the Temple
Cup playoff—an exhibition forerunner to the World Series games
of the next century.

The first four of these remaining games were played against the
league-leading Orioles. The chance of Philadelphia catching Cleveland and gaining a Temple Cup spot was about as rare as the earth-

quake that shook the Quaker City earlier in the month. The Phillies lost three out of the four games, with a tied contest called because of darkness. With no chance to make the playoffs and third-place clinched, the team's play fell off dramatically. Against Brooklyn they ended the season winning one out of four games.

The disappointment in Philadelphia was deeply felt and bitterly expressed. In reality, the Phillies had secured their best finish since 1887, but baseball breeds hope, and the fans were expecting more from their team and Delahanty. During the Phillies dismal stretch run, Del had not batted well. Excluding the last-day victory over Brooklyn, when he went 5 for 5 against Bill "Brickyard" Kennedy, Ed was only 5 for 24. His disappointing performance, and the club's failure, were made worse by the shock of Harry Wright's untimely death.

At the time of his passing, Wright was considered the preeminent baseball manager, the field general with whom everyone was compared. After leaving the Phillies, he oversaw the National League umpires, but his role was undercut by a lack of executive power. In the summer of 1895, Harry fell ill and contracted catharrhal pneumonia. He died on October 3, 1895, in a sanitarium in Atlantic City, New Jersey, at the age of sixty. Accolades and testimonies to his character and career were immediate and eloquent.[23] Irwin and Shettsline served as pallbearers and Reach and Rogers were honorary attendants at the funeral. Philadelphia ballplayers, however, were not among the 1,500 people who attended the service. Delahanty and John Boyle earlier paid their respects and presented a beautiful casket cushion to the family, but the team played a meaningless exhibition game that Sunday in Paterson, New Jersey.[24]

Soon after Harry Wright was interred, speculation began again about Art Irwin's status as Phillies manager. In two years, Irwin had a 149 and 110 record for a respectable .575 percentage. It was a fine accomplishment, but it was not good enough for Rogers and the city's avid "cranks." For nearly a month, the issue was debated, and candidates were evaluated in the press. The debate was resolved at the end of October, when Irwin took matters into his own hands and signed on to manage New York. His successor in Philadelphia, the only real candidate, was Billy Shettsline. "Shetts," as he was affectionally called, had no major league playing experience. He was the organization's all-purpose, hands-on fellow. Popular with the players and the press alike, Shettsline had been with the Phillies from the very beginning. He came over to the ball club as a twenty-year-old law clerk in Rogers' firm. In recent years, the large, rotund, nattily mustached Shettsline served as the "travel nurse," business manager, and secretary to the team. Although he had Rogers' ear, no one had any illusions that Shettsline was another Harry Wright or Ned Hanlon. His job as manager was to make sure that everything functioned smoothly. The real problem was finding a competent on-field captain to make game decisions.

The Phillies required someone with experience, who could coach from the infield, and bring the winning spirit of Baltimore, Cleveland, and Boston to Philadelphia. The Phillies saw such a candidate in Billy Nash, Boston's veteran third baseman, an excellent tactician with a career .275 average. He had become expendable after Manager Selee concluded that young Jimmy Collins was ready to step in at third base. Nash, however, would not come cheaply. With Delahanty an untouchable, talks centered around Billy Hamilton. For more than a year, Hamilton had asked to be traded. He was still upset over his last two contracts, and despite his .389 average and league-leading 166 runs and 97 stolen bases, Billy was seen as a disruptive malcontent. The newspapers spoke of Hamilton as an obstinate "individualizer" and "disorganizer." Team officials believed his disruptive disposition affected team unity, and if they could get a captain such as Nash for him, it was a deal worth making.[25] In 1895 Nash batted a hundred points lower than Hamilton, but most experts thought it was a good trade for both franchises. Nash would displace Lave Cross at third base and was expected to act as Shettsline's assistant. On paper he seemed to be the Phillies' missing part.

The Hamilton trade broke up the greatest outfield in the history of baseball. No trio amassed the numbers and production of a Delahanty, Hamilton, and Thompson outfield. On offense or defense, this outfield stood out. Excluding 1891, when Delahanty was breaking into the Phillies' outfield, the trio's overall batting mark was .372. They individually averaged 191 hits, 106 RBIs, 133 runs, 32 doubles, 15 triples, 9 home runs, and 44 stolen bases per season. On defense, Hamilton was the weakest of the three, and still he averaged 16 assists a year. Modern skeptics might argue that the new pitching distance induced these high numbers, but consistent league-leading figures, defensive percentages, and comparisons with the era's batting averages favor their accomplishments.[26]

The Phillies hoped to recover Hamilton's lost offense by moving Tuck Turner into left field and replacing Jack Boyle at first base with the "Mighty Irish King," Dan Brouthers, who at the age of thirty-seven was at the end of his playing days. The Phillies obtained him in exchange for a reserve catcher and $500, and hoped Brouthers had one good year left in his aching and overweight body.

After the Brouthers' trade, the Phillies made no significant changes. However, during the postseason, they were actively courted by New York and St. Louis. In each instance, these dealings centered around Delahanty. New York's colorful and controversial new owner, Andrew Freedman, who made his money in real estate and Tammany Hall politics, believed he could buy or trade for established stars. With Art Irwin as his new manager, the desire for Delahanty became intense. Freedman even came to Philadelphia and spent a good deal of time dickering with the Phillies' owners. Not for "any sum" was the persistent Freedman going to pry Delahanty away from the Phillies.[27] This interest did not mean that Del wanted to leave a city where he was idolized. But New York, with its big money and glamorous lifestyle, had its appeal to the Irish sporting hero from Cleveland.

A more aggressive pitch for Delahanty was made by St. Louis' Chris von der Ahe. He offered $30,000 for Delahanty, Thompson, Clements, Taylor, and Carsey. Shettsline was dumbfounded by the offer, and asked, "Why don't you buy the whole ball club?"[28] One newspaper lamented the thought of not having Ed Delahanty in the Philadelphia outfield. "Think of no Del in left to plow up the sod with his spikes and cut off those long hits which look as if they were good for anywhere from four to forty bases!"[29] Von der Ahe was not easily dissuaded. Talking with a reporter, he complimented Del by saying that he was the only outfielder in the league worth $2,000 a season.[30] And though Delahanty would have suggested doubling that value, Ed continued his usual routine of signing his contract early and getting his accustomed advance. Al Reach was uncomfortable with the practice of preseason payments, but he could not deny the wishes of his star player. A frugal man, President Reach believed these advances encouraged nonwork and a frivolous lifestyle. In his experience, players without a strict accounting of their earnings incurred debts that led to discontent and a "let down" in their ballplaying.[31]

These sentiments were not specifically directed at Ed Delahanty, who had enjoyed another dominant year, batting .398, second to Cleveland's Jessie Burkett. Ed also led the league in doubles (49), was third in what would later be calculated as slugging percentage (.611) and total bases (294), and fourth in walks (86) and home runs (11). His feats were part of the offensive-minded Philadelphia style. The Phillies again led all teams in hitting (.330), runs, and extra-base hits. Thompson and Clements followed Delahanty in the batting race. "Big Sam" led the circuit in slugging (.654), home runs (18), RBIs (165), and total bases (352). Hamilton took the honors in stolen bases (95) and base-on-balls (96). These statistics, however, clashed with the team's 5.47 ERA.

The Phillies' shortcomings in the standings did not reflect the ball club's prosperity. The team's attendance figures were significant for the nineteenth century, drawing 475,000 people, an attendance record that stood until 1903. The profits for the franchise were estimated to be about $115,000.[32]

Most of the year's revenue went into the coffers of Reach and Rogers or was spent on renovations to the stadium, in particular a new center-field clubhouse locker room. Ballplayers such as Delahanty, despite their on-field deeds, did not share in this prosperity. They had to be satisfied with their advance money and were expected to return in shape for the next season. Nevertheless, at the age of twenty-eight, Ed Delahanty's alternatives were limited. After the 1895 campaign, he remained in Philadelphia for about a month before returning with his wife to Cleveland. In the weeks before the holiday season, "long-legged" Delahanty was described as a "resident of Easy Street—or, rather doing nothing but taking life quietly and looking forward to the time when he will retread the Phillies' left garden."[33]

9

The Great and Only

As Delahanty pursued his usual off-season activities, he put the 1895 season behind him. Del was excited to have Billy Nash and Dan Brouthers in the lineup, and hoped the new season could bring a championship pennant to the Quaker City. Pondering this prospect, the *Sporting News* sarcastically stated that the Philadelphia owners thought the team should have won the "rag" about six times in the past thirteen seasons. In their opinion, Reach and Rogers were not in the business of baseball for their health, and no National League franchise made as much money without winning a championship. The paper suggested if the ball club hoped to win a pennant, management had to learn not to interfere in the daily running of the team.[1]

The team's success hinged on the ability of Billy Nash to run the ball club. An advocate of teamwork, Nash wanted the Phillies to play for runs not just hits. Billy Hamilton, who was exchanged for Nash, said his old team lacked direction and put the blame on "reckless and incompetent" management.[2] Rogers disagreed and assured everyone that Nash would be the "boss of the entire shooting-match."[3] In other words, Captain Nash, not front-office Billy Shettsline, would manage the 1896 Phillies.

This authority was clumsily introduced by a new set of rules that reinforced an existing temperance clause in the players' contracts. Nondrinkers like Thompson and Cross resented the implications. Others were offended by a more detailed code that was described as "fatherly instructions on how to be good little boys."[4] The real intent of these regulations was to reestablish control and accountability on the Phillies. According to his predecessor, Art Irwin, Nash's biggest test would come from ballplayers who defied authority by going over the manager's head to the front office.[5]

When Delahanty and his teammates reassembled for spring training at the Old Soldiers Home in Hampton Roads, Virginia, everyone followed Nash's lead and waited to test the new regimen. Del and his teammates responded well to Nash's first camp with light-hearted camaraderie. On the first day of practice, St. Patrick's Day, the large contingent of Irish players had the waiters decorate the tables in green. But the pace of the training camp was set by Nash and his schedule of controlled and repetitive workouts. Delahanty led the sprints and organized his "midnight jogs." On inclement days, the athletes went for long walks, toured the nearby naval yards, and played cards. A number of Phillies, Delahanty included, took books out of the local library and wrote letters to their wives. Delahanty, Thompson, and Mike Grady sat on a panel that disciplined the old soldiers who took extra rations of ale. Some days, Del even accompanied trainer Mike Scanlon to church services.

The real issue at training camp was how the talent-laden Phillies would benefit from Billy Nash's directions. He concentrated on teamwork fundamentals and asked his players "to play the points of the game for all that's in it." By this he meant sacrificing oneself for the team, competing aggressively and keeping the umpire alert to the club's needs.[6] Delahanty suggested that former Phillies teams played passively. He said that at road games, opponents spiked them and cut across bases while spectators invaded the outfield and targeted his teammates with beer glasses. Del admonished local fans and players for not giving visiting teams a dose of their own medicine.[7] This new resolve was tested in the season's opening three-game series against Nash's former Boston team.

More than 23,000 people attended the first game, and every "crank" rose to his feet when the Phillies marched toward the flag pole behind Professor Beck's Military Band and "Irish" Lucid's red-painted goats. The Phillies' players raised a new American flag to a mighty roar, but the game itself was a great disappointment. "Kid" Nichols beat Jack Taylor 7 to 3. Hamilton went 2 for 4 and scored three runs. Nash was 0 for 3 and made an error. Delahanty had two singles and batted second ahead of Thompson, Brouthers, and Clements. The Phillies recovered by winning the next two games. Some 45,000 fans attended this inaugural 1896 series.

The Phillies went to New York and Brooklyn and won four straight games. A cartoon in the *Philadelphia Inquirer* had a Phillies player seated on the top rung of a ladder reading a book titled "Team Work."[8] These victories thrilled the Quaker City, but New York and Brooklyn were not the best of teams, and the Giants' star pitcher, Amos Rusie was beginning his year-long holdout against club president Andrew Freedman over a contested fine. Nevertheless, the Phillies were in first place when the club set off on their first western road trip. They swept three games from St. Louis, and Delahanty, in the midst of a fifteen-game hitting streak, was batting .433. This success encouraged Delahanty for a three-game set in Cleveland.

Before Del's first at-bat, W. C. Kelley, a newspaperman and member of the Order of Equity Fraternity, approached the plate with a large basket of flowers. Addressing his lodge brother, Kelley proclaimed, "Mr. Delahanty has been in Cleveland a great many times and he has never made one even half-hearted enemy here. On the other hand, he has friends by the score, and those of them, who like myself, are members of the Order of Equity, want to give him a little to remember. They recognize the fact that not only is he the best fellow on earth, but is one of the most clever baseball players in the country." Delahanty was not good at speech-making and greeted the rousing cheers with many bows and tips of his cap. The Phillies won 10 to 2 behind Kid Carsey. Ed had a double in five at-bats.[9]

After Delahanty's presentation game, the Phillies' pitching soured and the team lost eight straight contests. In the fourth setback, the club received a terrible blow when Billy Nash was badly injured. The Phillies had broken Louisville's pitching signals and Nash, anticipating an off-speed pitch, was thrown a fast ball. He was struck on the right temple with the pitch and retired to the bench with an ugly gash on his forehead. From this time forward, he suffered bouts of vertigo that limited his on-field presence.[10]

Nash's injury contributed to the decline of the team's fortunes. From the start of the Cleveland series on May 11 until the end of June, the ball club went 16 and 23. The team's performance was not a sudden freefall. It was a faltering and troubling descent. One columnist described their play as "somnific, dopey and headless," as if they were dosed by morphine.[11] Frank Richter of *Sporting Life* attributed these kinds of remarks to the exaggerated expectations of the local sporting press. He felt the real culprits were injuries, excessive shifting of players, and hard luck. In his eyes the Phillies were not stupid or a bunch of bushers, but a slumping, overrated ball club.[12]

After the Nash beaning, a rash of injuries, including Delahanty aggravating his bad shoulder, decimated the starting roster. The play of the club was also affected by the disappointing contributions of the team's two publicized acquisitions. Nash had become an unproductive and inconsistent starter, and Dan Brouthers fielded poorly and stranded too many base runners. Having lost his starting position to the weak-hitting Jack Boyle, Brouthers was released after a salary dispute. The Phillies also unloaded some disgruntled players. Pitcher Willie McGill, an alleged "lusher," was dropped, and Billy Sullivan, another rumored drinker, was traded with malcontented Tuck Turner to St. Louis for a young outfielder, Dick Cooley.

Ed Delahanty, recovering from the ailing shoulder that hospitalized him and kept him out of the lineup for eight days, verbalized his frustration about playing in Philadelphia. Del said he had outlived his usefulness, and it was time for a change. There was even talk of trading him for younger players. The most prominent trade rumor had Delahanty and Jack Taylor going to New York for the unsigned Amos Rusie. This speculation was tantamount to "heresy." Frank Hough acknowledged the critics by saying that the injured Delahanty had not been playing up to his "natural gait," but, he reminded his readers, "Every local crank knows the ball that Del has played, and there is a heap more of the same kind stored away within his stalwart frame. He's a trifle stall-fed just now,— that's all."[13] Shettsline also spoke up for Delahanty. He said people took Del's great playing for granted. Shettsline professed that Del was doing all he could to win, and had rightfully earned the titles of the "Great and Only."[14] Another complaint leveled at Delahanty was that the harder he tried to win ball games with his bat the more his strikeouts contributed to the team's failing circumstances. His batting record, however, did not justify these midseason charges. By July 4, Ed was in the midst of a nineteen-game hitting streak that would see him bat safely in 27 out of 28 games. Del also was moved to first base to make room for Dick Cooley in the outfield.

Despite these changes, when the team arrived in Chicago on July 12, the Phillies were 0 and 6 on their current road trip, including three losses to last-place Louisville. Chicago paid little attention to the upcoming series. The city had just hosted the Democratic Party convention, and people were excited about the nomination of William Jennings Bryant for president. Few people gave much thought to a Monday afternoon, midsummer game. On a stifling hot and humid July 13, the people of Chicago were more concerned about the warnings of sunstroke and overexertion. And though 133 heat-related deaths were recorded that day, the weather did not deter about 1,000 hearty fans from turning out at Chicago's West End Park for the opening game with Philadelphia.

The Phillies' batters faced the veteran pitcher William "Adonis" Terry, winner of more than 180 career games. Against the handsome, right-handed, curve-ball specialist, Delahanty was 16 for 48 with no home runs. The ball park that hosted this memorable game was oddly fashioned. Each foul line was 340 feet to the perimeter fence, and on-field clubhouses in center field were nearly 500 feet from home plate. The right field wall was forty feet high with a scoreboard and a canvas screen fastened to telephone poles to block the view of roof-top spectators. It was an unlikely setting for the greatest hitting performance of the nineteenth century.

Dick Cooley began the game by getting a walk and being sacrificed to second base. With two outs, Delahanty, batting fourth in Dan Brouthers' former spot, swung at an outside pitch and hit it over the inner, lower bleacher fence in front of the right field wall. Jimmy Ryan chased the ball into the narrow bleachers between the two fences as Cooley and Delahanty scored. In the third inning, Ed hit a vicious line drive toward shortstop that knocked over the leaping Bill Dahlen and went into left field for a single. Del's third at-bat came with two runners on base. This time he struck a towering blow that soared over the scoreboard and canvas-topped right field wall. It landed across the road in a flock of chickens. A young boy picked up the ball and was chased by a panting policeman. This home run was said to be the longest ever hit at West End Park.

Despite this offensive display, the Phillies were losing 9 to 6, when Delahanty came to the plate in the seventh inning with no one on base. He again swatted a fast ball that went over the head of the fleet-footed Chicago center fielder Billy Lange. The ball rolled to the distant clubhouses, giving Delahanty another home run. When Delahanty came to bat in the ninth inning, the fans had forgotten the score and were cheering for another home run. Chicago manager Cap Anson threatened to fine his whole team "the price of three meals at World Fair rates" if any Philadelphia player was put on base before Delahanty got his last at-bat.[15] To make sure everything was in order, center fielder Lange called time and retreated to the farthest part of the grounds, the uncut grass before the center field clubhouses. Ed Delahanty, in his soaking-wet woolen uniform, laughed at the spectacle of the retreating center fielder. With Chicago fans behind him, many standing on their seats, Delahanty fooled everyone and bunted the first pitch foul. His action brought shouts from the grandstand, "Line it out Del!" Delahanty enjoyed this stunt and waited on Terry's next pitch, a slow, outside curve. The bat, it was reported, impacted with the sound of a "rifle shot." The hit carried more than 450 feet, beyond Billy Lange, and bounded onto the roofs of the center field clubhouses. Delahanty easily scored his fourth home run without a throw. As Ed crossed the plate, Adonis Terry was waiting to shake his hand. Outfielder Lange hid the ball under the clubhouse for a souvenir, and the fans remained standing on their seats cheering wildly for about ten minutes. After the game, spectators followed Del to the omnibus and offered him congratulatory claps on his back. A local gum factory recognized Ed's achievement by giving him a box of gum for each home run. One Chicago paper wrote that if it was not for Delahanty's hitting the overheated fans would have "cursed the day baseball was invented."[16]

Nonetheless, the Phillies lost the game 9 to 8, their seventh setback in a row. Ed had five of the team's nine hits. He knocked in seven runs and had seventeen total bases. That evening, back at the hotel, many commiserated with an exhausted Delahanty. They told him it was a tough loss after the way he batted. Delahanty replied, "I did the best I could. I couldn't hit any more."[17] Queried about Adonis Terry, Delahanty confessed that he never hit hard against him, but "Today they came just right. Tomorrow I probably would not get a hit. Those things can't be explained."[18] Only Bobby Lowe, in 1894, had ever hit four homers in a game. Three of his hits at the small Congress Street Grounds, however, were regular 250-foot fly balls over a short outfield fence. Nothing rivaled Ed Delahanty's power display until Lou Gehrig hit four cork-centered baseballs out of Shibe Park in 1932.

The next day, the Phillies broke their losing streak as Delahanty continued his torrid hitting. Ed went 3 for 5 against Clark Griffith with two doubles and a triple. In the closeout game of the series, rookie southpaw Danny Friend held Delahanty to a single in four at-bats as Chicago beat the Quakers 10 to 6. Chicago's team treasurer bemoaned that thousands of disappointed fans failed to see Del hit another home run.[19]

From Chicago, the Phillies proceeded to Pittsburgh, where the hapless team met up with the club's president, Al Reach. He congratulated Delahanty on his great day and spoke with Nash before addressing his ball club about his general concerns. But Reach's words and threats could do nothing for his ball club. The Phillies finished the road trip with a 4 and 16 record. One of the few notable highlights was Del's two-out single in the ninth inning that broke up a no-hitter by Cy Young. Things became so bad, the Phillies (with Delahanty taking a day off) committed six errors and gave up sixteen hits in an exhibition game loss to an Atlantic City team. Their embarrassing play was matched by the havoc on the bench.

With Billy Nash on the sidelines, the on-field leadership went from former Phillies captain Jack Boyle to Billy Hallman and eventually to Sam Thompson. With the team in disarray, the sporting press again belabored the lack of teamwork and chided the Phillies' sulking and undisciplined play. Nash, it was reported, was not respected by the players, who disregarded his orders "when they feel like it." The truth was that the ailing Nash was reporting daily to John Rogers for directions. This relationship, together with Billy Shettsline's interventions, eroded the team's intended lines of authority. The press decried this condition and wrote that if Nash was to be the Phillies' manager the front office had to give him power to do his job.[20] Lacking proper support, Nash's frustrations affected his patience and judgment, as witnessed in an incident involving Ed Delahanty.

Del could be as obstinate as any player on the Phillies' roster, particularly when he believed his bat alone could change the ball club's fortunes. A Cincinnati player recounted how Nash upstaged the dependable Delahanty when he began fouling off pitches to get a pitch to hit. The stressed-out Nash grew impatient and "called him down" in front of everyone and told him to stop delaying the game. Delahanty looked at his manager in disbelief, as the players from both teams tried to understand Nash's intent.[21] The Philadelphia-based *Sporting Life,* appreciating Del's situation, reported that he had been in Philadelphia too long and would welcome a trade.[22]

The strained relationships reached new heights in tough losses to Brooklyn and Baltimore in early August. The *Sporting News* said the Phillies' performances were so bad the games should be investigated. They called the team "a combination of dung hills."[23] But these disparaging remarks did not apply to Delahanty. He hit well in the Baltimore series, going 8 for 15 with three home runs, a triple, and three doubles. It was agreed that he was the "solitary exception" among the team's disappointing and oft-injured veterans. Delahanty's sole weakness, when playing first base, was his erratic infield throws. The remedy was to return Del to left field, and give first base over to a hard-hitting youngster named Napoleon Lajoie.

The powerfully built and graceful player of French-Canadian descent was born in Woonsocket, Rhode Island. Lajoie dreamed of playing in the major leagues and was an admirer of Dan Brouthers and the "great Delahanty." Although he accepted a baseball scholarship to Holy Cross College, Lajoie was drawn into the local semi-pro weekend leagues. He worked as a teamster and, in 1896, signed a contract to play for Fall River in the New England League. His playing was spectacular, and by mid-July, Billy Nash, who had come up to see another player, was convinced that Lajoie, then hitting .429, was a prospect. The asking price for Lajoie and his teammate was only $1,500. Earlier, Andrew Freedman of New York had rejected the offer, saying "I want no Frenchman or Dutchman on my team. Get me a couple of Irishmen." Freedman's blunder was Nash's windfall.[24]

Lajoie was an immediate success. One sportswriter said he was the "most gracefully awkward man on the diamond today and probably the most deceptive."[25] After his first eight games, the twenty-two-year-old Lajoie had fifteen hits. But the team's lethargy was contagious, and even the celebrated rookie was criticized for sluggish and disappointing play.[26] Befriended by his idol Ed Delahanty, Lajoie settled down and finished the season batting .326.

From the time Lajoie took over first base and Delahanty moved back to the outfield, the Phillies were 22 and 18. Not all the success can be accredited to Lajoie. Delahanty batted .413 during this stage of the season. Dick Cooley, in the leadoff spot, provided some of the offense lost after the Hamilton trade and Mike Grady's solid catching restabilized the team's pitching. On the mound, Al Orth and Jack Taylor returned to the rotation, and Kid Carsey recovered some of his former effectiveness.

But the season that began with grand designs disappointed everyone. The Phillies finished in eighth place, the pitching staff had the second highest ERA in the league and the team's batting average fell thirty-five points. Sam Thompson played flawless outfield, but the thirty-six-year-old slugger was faltering at the plate. He lost nearly 100 points off his average, and 65 runs from his RBIs. John Clements, plagued with injuries and illness, caught only 57 games. Billy Nash appeared in only 65 contests and hit an anemic .247, while Billy Hamilton, leading off every game for Boston, hit .365, scored 152 runs and led the league in walks (110) and stolen bases (83). The Phillies knew they were exchanging Hamilton's offense for Nash's leadership. They never imagined Hamilton would leave such a void and Nash would fail to lead.

In fairness to Nash, he was not brought to Philadelphia to be the team's manager. He still saw himself as a regular ballplayer and was too "considerate" to be a proper disciplinarian. Put off by his injuries and subverted by Rogers' loyalist, Billy Shettsline, Nash saw the spirited harmony of training camp dissipated by the strains of the regular season.[27] Sam Thompson confessed that Nash never had full control of the team. "As soon as the players realized that the manager was helpless and that he was not the boss, they commenced to make life a burden for him. There are some men on the team who would drive a saint to drink. Nash took orders every-day from Colonel Rogers. He was a nonentity."[28]

If the Phillies would not retain Nash or reinstate Shettsline as manager, a new search was in order. This time, Rogers was infatu-ated with the twenty-nine-year-old manager of Detroit in the Western League, George Tecumseh Stallings. A month younger than Ed Delahanty, Stallings came from a much different back-ground than Del and his teammates. The son of a Confederate offi-cer, Stallings graduated from Virginia Military Institute and had a failed tryout as a catcher with the Phillies in 1886. He played briefly for Brooklyn in the Players' League and had a distinguished record in the minors as a field captain and player. In Detroit, Manager Stallings played first base and gained a reputation as a disciplinar-ian, a "calculating fellow" who promoted "up-to-date" baseball.[29]

None of these postseason decisions involved Ed Delahanty. He kept his opinions to himself and went about his way being the ever-popular, grand slugger of the National League. Del signed his con-tract and was in Cleveland when Stallings was appointed manager. It made no difference to Delahanty who ran the Phillies as long as the team played competitive baseball. He was on top of his game and was universally regarded as the league's premier batter. In 1896 he had had his injuries and suffered through the team's doldrums, but continued recording remarkable individual statistics. Delahanty was second in batting with a .397 average and led the league in slug-ging (.631), doubles (44), and RBIs (126). Del also scored 131 runs, stole 37 bases, and batted 17 triples and 13 home runs. He struck out only 22 times. In a *Sporting Life* feature, Del was praised: "Amid the wreck of the year the performance of Delahanty shines out luminously and marks him as indeed the star of the team." The article also mentioned that Ed had made no errors in his last thirty games.[30]

Whatever the makeup of Stallings' Phillies, Delahanty would be its central figure. However, there were some questions before the 1897 season as to whether he or his teammates might still be playing in Philadelphia. In all trade talks, the player every ball club wanted was Ed Delahanty. Andrew Freedman of New York re-newed his efforts to get Del, and often the talk revolved around his malcontented ace, Amos Rusie.[31] Chicago, too, coveted the Philadelphia slugger and, at one point, offered three frontline players for him.[32] The only serious chance of moving Delahanty involved Ed's interest in playing again in Cleveland. The Spiders' owner Frank Robison and Manager Patsy Tebeau wanted the power-hitting Cleveland native. The Spiders even considered giving up the unhappy batting champion, Jesse Burkett, for Delahanty. Although Ed never said he favored the move, Cleveland sources related that he was busy setting up a new house on Studley Street in the hope of spending his summers there.[33] Reports from Cleveland indicated that Ed had several meetings with Robison, where he allegedly promised the Cleveland president that he would hit 27 home runs in 1897. With everyone in Cleveland pushing for a deal, Robison initially proposed a one-sided trade, offering Del's friend "Peach Pie" O'Connor, third baseman "Chippy" McGarr, and outfielder Harry Blake for Delahanty and Cross. Rogers would have nothing to do with this absurd proposition.[34] One report declared that there was as much chance of letting Delahanty go "as there is of the corpulent . . . Shettsline ever drawing a salary as the only skeleton in a dime museum." A cartoon in the *Philadelphia Press* depicted a Cleveland ballplayer chasing after a Quaker carrying Delahanty under his arm.[35] What the Phillies wanted was the perceived quick-thinking Irish infielder, such as Ed McKean. With this type of player in mind, Philadelphia unsuccessfully tried to trade Dick Cooley to Baltimore for up-and-coming John McGraw.[36]

While Delahanty awaited news of a Cleveland trade, he busied himself with postseason pastimes. Del and Norine gave attention to their new home, and Ed joined his hometown friends on a hunting trip. Delahanty even organized a group of local players, including his brother Tom and teammate Lave Cross, to form a traveling club that played throughout Ohio.[37] Life was good to Ed Delahanty. If his team had suffered through its worst season since 1884, Del was emerging as the king of his domain.

Despite their poor showing and failing attendance, Delahanty's Phillies again made money. As always, these profits did not benefit underpaid ballplayers like Ed Delahanty, but they soothed the letdown felt by the Phillies' organization. Ever alert to the business side of the national pastime, Reach and Rogers understood what another bad season might do to the franchise's finances, given the political and economic climate of the country.

The depression of the early 1890s perpetuated the debate about the government's monetary policies. In the presidential year of 1896, the raging issue was whether America should follow a free silver course or continue on the gold standard. Baseball magnates favored the Republicans and their gold standard nominee, William McKinley. Worried about inflation, they did not want to see the debasement or cheapening of currency. Players who were earning substantial salaries, such as Delahanty, found themselves allied with their employers against the free-silver Democrats and the rural-based Populists. For Ed Delahanty, the decision was also a personal one. He knew William McKinley, an avid baseball fan, when McKinley served as the governor of Ohio from 1891 to 1896. Del became acquainted with the governor through his main political backer, the wealthy political boss of Cleveland, Mark Hanna. Delahanty moved easily within Ohio's political community by trading on his sporting fame and his membership in various Cleveland organizations.[38] As a result, no one was more pleased than Del when McKinley took the White House, and the free silver program failed. It was a satisfying cap to a difficult year.

10

Princely Jollyers

The failure of Delahanty's Phillies in 1896 contrasted with the winning records of Baltimore, Cleveland, and Boston. Less talented than Philadelphia, the successful style of play of these teams was envied by many and duplicated by few. It was baseball played with a heady, daring, and defiant manner, associated with the all-out style of many Irish ballplayers. No team better epitomized these characteristics than the Baltimore Orioles. Without a dominant pitching staff, they finished first in each of three previous seasons. The Orioles and their main National League rivals had certain things in common: innovative Irish managers, a core of heady Irish ballplayers, and an active on-field leadership from players "of the Shamrock persuasion."[1]

The manager who guided the Irish Orioles to their pennants was "Foxy Ned" Hanlon. An outfielder whose best years were spent with the great Detroit clubs of the mid-1880s, Hanlon inherited in 1892 a reconstituted American Association Baltimore team in its first National League year. Among Hanlon's models for building a winning ball club was Frank Selee of Boston. Selee, who was not Irish and had no major league experience, put together a dominating and winning combination of players. From 1891 to 1893 he won three straight pennants with a style of play that Hanlon admired. With smart, take-charge Irish players such as Tommy Tucker, Tommy McCarthy, and Hugh Duffy, the Beaneaters played alert, aggressive, and intimidating baseball. Another prototype for Hanlon was Cleveland's Oliver "Patsy" Tebeau, whose approach to winning baseball was cruder and more abusive than Selee's. Connie Mack characterized Tebeau's rough persona by saying that he "came over in a potato sack from County Armagh, Ireland."[2] In 1891 Hanlon also played a half-season in Pittsburgh for Bill McGunnigle. A very successful minor league manager, "Cap" McGunnigle's teams won American Association and Players' League titles in 1889 and 1890 with crafty and aggressive ballplaying.

The origin of this kind of baseball is not easily traced. While Harry Wright and Cap Anson emphasized smart and team-oriented baseball, and Mike Kelly popularized conniving tactics, a hybrid style of scheming baseball evolved in the early 1880s under a Chicago-born son of an Irish alderman, Charlie Comiskey. He was brought to St. Louis by his mentor Ted Sullivan, a native of Ireland, who had a reputation as an enterprising schemer and promotional wizard. Known as the "Old Roman" (or more accurately Celt), Comiskey played first base and managed the American Association St. Louis Browns to four consecutive championships. He loved to win and resorted to any trick or device that brought him a victory. Comiskey enjoyed riling and upsetting opponents, believing if players were disturbed and distracted they were less effective. He declared that all was fair "in war and baseball," and nothing should stand in the way of winning a game.[3] Charlie also baited umpires and relished the challenge of molding difficult players into a group of disruptive and wily winners. Epitomizing this rugged style of play was Comiskey's third baseman, Arlie Latham, labeled "The Freshest Mouth in Baseball."[4] His on-field shenanigans and verbal abuses tormented umpires and players and delighted the fans. One of Comiskey's players also gave credit to the Browns' quick-witted catcher and utility infielder, the part-Irish William "Yank" Robinson, for his "cute Irish way" of flattering and scheming to get the upper hand in a game.[5] By winning and playing colorful hardnosed baseball, Comiskey, Selee, McGunnigle, and Tebeau became Hanlon's models for a successful and profitable franchise.

Comiskey influenced these managers through a variety of relationships. Patsy Tebeau, born and raised in St. Louis, was a devoted follower of the Browns and their winning tactics. Comiskey and Selee were linked by players such as Tommy McCarthy, who learned the game from Comiskey in St. Louis. American Association players said that, next to "Long John" Reilly of Cincinnati, McCarthy was "the dirtiest player in the country."[6] Others said he was "brainy, clever and audacious."[7] As for McGunnigle, he benefited from having some of Comiskey's contentious players on his winning teams. Ned Hanlon also knew the Browns' old leader, Yank Robinson. They were teammates in 1882 with Detroit, and in 1890 Robinson played for Hanlon on the Pittsburgh Players' League team. It appears that Hanlon just took from others what had been adapted from Comiskey in St. Louis. The two men shared the title of the "Napoleon" of the sport.

Another factor associated with these teams was the Irish character of those ball clubs. All National League teams, including Delahanty's Phillies, had their share of Irish players. More plentiful than German or English players, the Irish averaged 25 percent to sometimes more than 50 percent of a team's roster.[8] Being Irish was not by itself an immediate prescription for winning. It took a certain disposition, a recklessness and drive to make this kind of baseball successful. In the eyes of many nineteenth-century observers these traits were most often identified with certain winning Irish players.

Actually, Irish dominance followed two baseball traditions. Delahanty embodied one style, and Hanlon's players represented the other. Delahanty was without question the premier batter of the 1890s, the last of his kind—the great Irish slugger, the "Casey at the bat" Irishman. Starting with James O'Rourke, Roger Connor, and Dan Brouthers, baseball always had its powerful and high-average Irish batters. These hitters dominated all batting categories. But winning baseball, as testified to by the Phillies' shortfalls, was more than just having great batsmen. In the 1890s, it embodied a type of play that evolved into Hanlon's Orioles style of baseball.

From the Baltimore coaching lines the cry went out, "Get at 'em."[9] This second tradition was associated with the Irish, particularly Orioles third baseman John McGraw. When the Giants'

Andrew Freedman turned his back on Lajoie for want of a couple of "Irishmen," he was alluding to smart, take-charge, and aggressive on-field leaders such as McGraw. In 1896, *Sporting Life,* picking up on the ethnic flavor of the national pastime, gave the nod to the descendants of the Emerald Isle, by quoting the biased assessments of New York manager Bill Joyce. This Irishman declared, "Give me a good Irish infield and I will show you a good team. I don't mean that it is necessary to have them all Irish, but you want two or three quick-thinking sons of Celt to keep the Germans and others moving." Joyce apologized for any ethnic slight and remarked, "Now you take a German, you can tell him what to do and he will do it. Take an Irishman and tell him what to do, and he is liable to give you an argument. He has his own ideas. So I have figured it out this way. Get an Irishman to do the scheming. Let him tell the Germans what to do and then you will have a great combination." The example he gave was the Orioles' infield of "Dirty Jack" Doyle, Hugh Jennings, John "Muggsy" McGraw, and Jimmy Donnelly.[10]

This idealized style of play was the "smart" and "inside" baseball Reach and Rogers were trying to emulate with Art Irwin and Billy Nash. It was an alert and unrelenting temper that combined both intelligent and coercive playing. Baltimore competed with clever and aggressive base running, bunting, and sacrifice hitting. It was characterized by Comiskey's getting men on base by any means, unnerving opponents and umpires, and capitalizing on game situations. This kind of baseball brought with it a full array of innovative tactics that transformed the sport. The "Baltimore chop," hit-and-run plays, double steals, bunting for a hit, pitchers covering first base, playing off the corner bases, foul ball hitting, cutting off throws, the trap play, hidden ball tricks, and slap and "hit-them-where-they-ain't" batting were part of their daily repertoire. Many of these stunts were encouraged because of the handicapped on-field authority of a single umpire trying to cover the entire playing field. His limited view moved players to cut corners when they ran the bases, trip base runners, obstruct the base paths, and in the case of John McGraw, slow up runners by grabbing their belts and pants. Even the gentlemanly Cornelius McGillicuddy, Connie Mack, perfected the art of using his glove hand to interfere with a batter's swing, when he played for Hanlon's Pittsburgh club in 1891. This caper was not as extreme as "Irish Jack" Corcoran's spitting bird-shot at batter's necks. Other popular ploys saw players leave equipment on the base paths and hide baseballs in unkempt parts of the outfield grass.

What bothered most critics about this style of play was its unsavory side that bordered on rowdyism. Players and umpires were spiked and collisions at first base were commonplace. These antics were directed at upsetting players and intimidating overworked umpires. It was a kind of psychological warfare, what the "pugnacious" Hanlon called "disorganizing baseball."[11] For the Orioles' manager, his "artful kicking" (disputing calls) sent a message to umpires that players "would not slink away like whipped schoolboys."[12] McGraw declared these confrontations were part of the "never say die spirit" of the Orioles and were done to "impress upon the umpire that the players are not going to let anything slip by them." In this tact, he was following a Charlie Comiskey tenet that "kicking" would not reverse a call, but could affect an umpire's judgment about the next close decision. To "Muggsy" McGraw's way of thinking, this stratagem could gain fifty runs a year.[13] It also aroused spectators to the point where debris was hurled on the field and fights and sometimes riots erupted.

Fans enjoyed these antics and found them entertaining. This was especially true of the bleacher "cranks," who sat in the cheap, open-planked seats. Their tastes, and the kind of ballplaying they adored, conformed to the ethnic prejudices and expectations of the period. The owners frequently spoke about curtailing this behavior. Sometimes fines were issued, but if these outbursts brought fans to the ballpark the rowdyism was subtly tolerated. In many ways, this form of baseball provided entertainment that bordered on stage acting. Players dramatically reacted to umpire's calls, preened themselves in the batter's box, and bowed to admiring fans after a good play. Played in this manner, baseball was like an open-air vaudeville show performed before thousands of spectators.

The popular press contributed its perceptions of the new mode of play. Baseball, associated with "brain, pluck and skill," was an Irish trait. One columnist wrote, "Teams need an infusion of Irish blood to make it win," adding that crafty Irishmen provided the sport with its generals and diplomats.[14] The catalog of Irish names at the top of every hitting category at the end of the season testified to this dominance. Only pitching saw a decline in Irish stars. With the mid-decade retirement of Tim Keefe and half-Irish John Clarkson and with "Sadie" McMahon's sore arm, only "Brickyard" Kennedy and Frank Killen were still around at the turn of the century when Rube Waddell and "Iron Man" Joe McGinnity met the challenges of great non-Irish hurlers. The exception was the hard-throwing Amos Rusie whose mother was Irish. By the end of the decade, Hanlon and Tebeau were joined by other Irish managers— Connie Mack, "Scrappy" Bill Joyce, John McGraw, Tommy Dowd, John McCloskey, and Irish-born Patsy Donovan. For most of the 1890s about 35 percent of all National League managers were of Irish descent. Greater percentages persisted for on-field Irish captains.[15] The Hibernian character of the national pastime spilled over into the umpires, groundskeepers, and trainers. The same Irish dominance did not carry over into the front office. Only Ned Hanlon in Baltimore, Charlie Byrne in Brooklyn, and J. Palmer O'Neill in Pittsburgh held management positions during the decade.

Baseball remained an attractive occupation for sons of immigrant families. With hand- and bat-ball games part of an Irish kid's heritage, the athletically gifted few found baseball to be a rapid entry into the "American Dream." Young Irish men such as Ed Delahanty read about the exploits and lifestyles of their childhood heroes and wanted the fame and fortune that baseball's luminaries enjoyed. They were enraptured with baseball as an individual stage for their identities and skills. Explaining the success of this ethnic group is another matter.

If Irish ballplayers were skilled, fleet-footed, and crafty, they could also be "strong-headed" and slow like a "weary elephant." The issue for nineteenth-century sportswriters was determining whether there was a "peculiar trait" that distinguished successful winning Irish athletes.[16] In comparing German and Irish players, the *Sporting News* exposed a popular-held ethnic bias that the Irish were more "active and possess better heads for quick action—think more quickly and devise plans and schemes better."[17] *Sporting Life* noted that Germans were known for their "solidity and persistence," the Irish for their "alertness and aggressiveness."[18] Henry Chadwick, who had been following sports for almost forty years, spoke of young Irishmen's "pluck, courage, endurance and physical activity" in vigorous outdoor athletics.[19] The American Press Association said the Irish player's domination on the ball field was due to "love of a scrap or his proficiency in the use of a club."[20] Another prevailing tact was tried by Ted Sullivan, the manager who brought Comiskey and Latham to St. Louis. He remarked that the sons of Hibernia were natural leaders and responded well to crises. He believed the Irish pass the test when you consider the character and success of the Irish soldier; fighting men known world-wide "for their dash, valor and impetuosity." Returning to sports, Sullivan said the tradition of "shinny" or hurling and the love of the outdoors were inherent in the Irish race.[21] But these popularizing pundits never fully determined if there was something in the Irish character that made the Celts of this period better ballplayers. Talent and physical dexterity were only part of the recipe.

For some writers, the hard-nose, clever, and passionate play that distinguished Irish on the ball field also reflected Ireland's struggle for survival. Free from the constraints of their ancestral homeland, it was believed that the Irish immigrant strove and worked hard at finding ways or angles to beat the system and succeed in their new country. Without the fetters of landlordism and centuries of alien domination, the Irish, it was said, recognized America as a true land of opportunity, a country where success or failure was theirs to be earned or lost. Baseball, like the competition of life, was akin to the Social Darwinism of the era. The fittest won, and one thrived by playing the game to the fullest. Comiskey called his system "beating the rule." Rules were meant to be bent, and authority was there to be challenged. Prominent sports columnist O. P. Caylor asserted, "No one, but a true Irishman . . . can understand what a pleasure it is to badger an umpire."[22] Baseball was also a microcosm of Irish endurance, an alluring prize for skilled young men who shaped the game to their overbearing drive to succeed.

The Phillies had talented Irish players, competent coaching, and the best facilities in the country, yet they continued to fall short of Baltimore, Cleveland, and Boston. Being Irish was obviously not the only prescription for success. As Hugh Jennings cautioned, winning teams scored runs in a higher proportion to base hits. Baltimore, he said, did not have the best pitchers and could not afford to strand many baserunners. The Orioles needed to stay ahead of the league by having something "new up our sleeves" to maximize favorable playing conditions.[23] Hanlon called it the "unexpected game." They never lost track of where they were in a contest, and competed with their heads rather than their hands. Hanlon wanted fast-paced and unpredictable playing. Ned detested loafing, quitting, and stupidity in ballplayers. He sought athletes who were quick-witted and not apt to lose their head in a close game. One writer said, "It was like going through college to watch them [Orioles] work."[24]

Hanlon, Selee, McGunnigle, and Comiskey also stressed playing as a team. And though a batter such as Delahanty might beat the Orioles with exceptional hitting, Baltimore victimized the Phillies with heads-up, team-oriented baseball. For the Baltimore players, the club was like an extended family unit. They were close-knit, cooperative, and singular in their purpose. No Orioles player ever rebuked a teammate in public. Unlike the Phillies, who sulked or went to the front office with their grievances, the Orioles dealt directly with Hanlon and their teammates. The players also lived and socialized together. They attended each other's weddings and encouraged prudent living. With few exceptions, they were well-dressed and good-mannered off the field. The team had no abusive drinkers or high-livers, though McGraw and his buddies frequented the race track. One writer said the Orioles were "regular Jekyl and Hyde beings." They even developed a dual approach to umpires that amazed the irascible Arlie Latham. Catcher Wilbert "Uncle Robbie" Robinson, who played for Frank Selee in the New England League, would sweet-talk and chat politely with the umpires, while McGraw was "barking and snapping" at their heels as if he had eaten "gunpowder . . . for breakfast and washed it down with warm blood."[25] Comiskey said the charges of acting like a hoodlum did not bother him as long as a player behaved like a gentleman off the field.[26] Nothing was left to chance. If the Phillies were not playing well, they fretted and pouted. The Orioles dug in and competed harder. Hanlon often let his three Irish leaders—McGraw, Jennings, and Joe Kelley—handle game situations. Within a decade all three, and Wilbert Robinson, went on to be influential managers.[27]

To the host of Irish fans that followed Delahanty and the Phillies, it was hoped that their team could attain the heights of Hanlon's "rascals." These expectations and models were not lost on new manager George Stallings. He believed his ball club could be properly motivated and disciplined for success. Since Delahanty played in 1896 with thirty different players, Stallings had a lot of pruning to do before his team left for spring training in Augusta, Georgia.[28] Stallings was also concerned about alcohol use, and he was pleased to learn that ten of his men favored the temperance clause in their contracts.[29] Encouraged by these developments, Delahanty said he believed the Phillies would be stronger and more competitive in the upcoming season.[30]

Delahanty and the Phillies began this campaign of recovery by going to the warmer deep south for their training. The owners winced at the projected costs, and the players complained about traveling so far when they were not under contract. But Stallings persuaded the owners to pick up all expenses and soothed the players' fears about a sea journey to southern Georgia.[31]

Once settled in camp, Del came forward and led the players in getting into shape. He set up handball tournaments and organized long nightly runs around the country roads of Augusta. The most popular exercise at training camp was bicycle riding. Introduced to it by Stallings, the Phillies became avid novice riders. Unfortunately, bicycling had its drawbacks. Delahanty had trouble stopping his bike and, in one instance, after taking a tumble, was run over by an equally inept Napoleon Lajoie. Del's remarks were "not a matter of record."

With little to distract them, the Phillies became a part of the Augusta community. Local clubs and lodges extended hospitality to Delahanty and his mates. Besides shows and opera performances at the local theater, Delahanty and his teammates concentrated on the upcoming Corbett-Fitzsimmons heavyweight championship fight in Carson City, Nevada. The Phillies made their wagers, and most players, including Delahanty, a close friend of James Corbett and his ball-playing brother Joe, backed the champion, a 3-to-1 favorite. The evening of the fight the players assembled at a local theatre for a telegraphic reenactment of the bout. When news of Fitzsimmons' fourteenth-round knockout came over the wire, a crestfallen Delahanty paid off his jubilant teammates who had backed the challenger.[32]

On the more serious side, Stallings spent time during afternoon intersquad games devising and perfecting a system of signals. He also selected a new field captain, second baseman Billy Hallman, to lead the team against New York in the season home opener at the refurbished Broad and Huntingdon Street grounds. The park was newly adorned with two matching upper-deck bleacher sections, a fifteen-foot-wide bike track circling the playing field, and a great gallery and promenade situated above the right field wall. On top of this new structure was a thirty-foot-high, heavy wire-mesh screen that kept baseballs in play.

In these new confines, "Brewery Jack" Taylor started the season by limiting the Giants to five hits, beating them 5 to 1. Del was 1 for 2 and made a couple of grand catches in left field. Behind the hitting of Delahanty and Lajoie, Philadelphia got off to an 8 and 1 start. In each of the nine games Ed hit safely and extended his 1896 season-ending hitting streak to twenty-two games. During this early surge Del was 17 for 34 with four doubles, a triple, and a home run. But Delahanty's play could not sustain the team's prosperity. Sam Thompson's sore back and an unspecified kidney ailment forced him out of the lineup and ended his season. Lajoie was banged up after a collision at first base, and Nash suffered a split finger. With Cross at third, and the recovering Lajoie shuttling between right field and first base, the Phillies lost five games in a row, including a hotly contested three-game series with Baltimore, giving the Orioles nineteen straight victories over Philadelphia.

Delahanty, try as he may, was pitched around and walked. On the first western road trip Del showed teammates what needed to be done. After hurting his ankle, he had it wrapped and proceeded to get four singles and a walk. But Stallings could not keep a stable lineup together, and in an act of desperation installed himself in right field. He also gave into the pressure and publicly criticized his players. Indifferent to Delahanty's lame foot, he belittled Ed's efforts, saying his star player covered as much ground "as a sewer manhole lid."[33] Even the presentation of roses to Delahanty in a getaway game in Pittsburgh could not ease the sting of losing, or of Stallings' disheartening comments. One sportswriter mourned that the city "was in sack cloth and ashes," and accused Stallings of being rigid with his system and too openly critical of his players.[34]

As the team arrived in Cleveland, Delahanty's joy at returning to his hometown was absent. Cleveland also was teeming with controversy. The financially suffering Spiders had tried to play an illegal Sunday afternoon game. Police stopped the contest in the first inning and the umpire and the players of both teams were arrested for violating the Sabbath. Team president Robison put up $100 bail for each person and issued refunds and rainchecks.[35] Hoping to remedy their shortfalls, the Spiders also publicized the novelty of their young rookie outfielder, Louis "Chief" Sockalexis, a Penobscot Indian from Maine, who came to Cleveland from Holy Cross College.

Delahanty and his teammates were impressed with the athleticism of Sockalexis, but it was the Phillies' dismal pitching, not the young Indian's play, that contributed to the club's losing ways. Ed's injury and Stallings' impatience aside, Ed still batted over .400 during the disastrous road trip. Undoubtedly, Del was comforted during the western tour by the presence of his wife, who occasionally traveled with him. But the players frowned at the presence of a spouse on road trips, believing gossip and the meddling of wives undermined a ball club's harmony. Norine was unmoved by the players' attitudes. She wanted to travel and thought the trip was a good opportunity to check on their Cleveland house and visit family. Ed actually appeared to welcome her company. On a return train trip, he and Norine socialized with Giants' president Andrew Freedman, who accepted Del's wager that Philadelphia would finish higher than New York.[36] This was an optimistic bet, since the team was in eighth place and was showing signs of internal discord.

No one was more exasperated by the team's failures then Stallings, who vowed personnel moves would shake up his underachieving ball club. Many transactions were pondered, none bigger than the trading of Delahanty and John Clements to Chicago for the clever shortstop-infielder "Bad Bill" Dahlen and speedy, hard-hitting outfielder Billy Lange. Ed Delahanty was the key to this trade, but again neither Reach or Rogers could bare to part with their popular superstar. One newspaper countered, "Why not trade Stallings?"[37] When the Phillies did act, it was a six-player deal with St. Louis. Team captain Bill Hallman, pitcher Kid Carsey, catcher Mike Grady, and a young prospect were traded for "Buttermilk" Tommy Dowd and up-and-coming catcher Ed McFarland. To no one's surprise, the Hallman trade did not silence inquiries about Delahanty. Buck Ewing of Cincinnati wanted Del, and was willing to give lots of money and some young players for him. New York's Andrew Freedman, as expected, had his standing offer for Del's services. Ed Delahanty, however, had his preferences. If he was going to move, the only western team he would favor was Cleveland.[38] This choice did not deter the frenzy that Stallings had set in motion. The first-year manager continued to listen to offers and waited to see how his new players meshed. His decision had disappointing and disquieting results. The Phillies began a two-month slide that alienated the fans, agitated the press, and derailed Delahanty and his teammates.

From spring training on, Stallings had overestimated the quality and compatibility of his players. Beginning with the loss of Sam Thompson, injuries to Nash, Clements, McFarland, and Orth, and Jack Taylor's inconsistency, unsettled and dispirited the team. In a letter to the editor of *Sporting Life*, a fan wrote that the Phillies "play together more like strangers then anything else—just as though one was not acquainted with the other's play."[39] By mid-August, the team was still in eighth place, 10 games under .500 and falling fast. No Phillies player was immune to criticism, including Delahanty. Playing with a bad ankle, and for a time battling a fever, he shouldered the weight of the struggling ball club. It was hoped that young Lajoie would fill the void left by Sam Thompson, but he was "bullheaded" about his power-hitting figures and did not bat supportively.[40] Only Billy Shettsline came to Delahanty's support. He said the criticism of Del's fielding was unfair and remarked that such comments brought tears to his eyes when he considered all that Delahanty was doing for the team. The Phillies' secretary drew special attention to his revitalized fielding and hitting heroics.[41] What Shettsline was alluding to was a batting performance of Joe DiMaggio proportions. In a 73-game stretch, from May 8 to August 5, Delahanty hit safely in 67 games. He had batting streaks of 9, 12, 10, 21, and 11 games. During these weeks he hit .432, putting together some remarkable numbers. In a pair of games against Washington, he went 9 for 10, and, for good measure, he won a hat and tie by hitting a distant advertising sign on the left field wall. On July 7, against Louisville, Delahanty had ten hits in a row, a National League record, and was 13 for 14 in that three-game series. The "cranks" in Louisville were amazed by his performance. Wherever Del played, "it is Delahanty above everyone else."[42]

Nobody appreciated Ed's prowess more than his fellow ball-players. George Wheeler, the Phillies' young pitcher, said Delahanty was the best batter in the world. He proclaimed that when Del came to the plate with men on base, "he is the picture of perfect happiness. His eyes light up and his tongue runs out and pokes up over his lip and he is so happy that he can't stand still and wouldn't if he could." Wheeler believed there was not a living man "who loves to bat as Delahanty does. He seems to fairly live for it and gloat over it."[43] Patsy Tebeau of Cleveland called Delahanty a grand "mysterious hitter," a batsman so versatile that no one knew where he would hit the ball. No batter, according to Tebeau, could knock out his hits like Delahanty.[44]

During this batting streak, pitchers tried to gain the upper hand on Ed by getting ahead in the count. This tactic did not work. Delahanty professed that no batter should ever overlook the first ball if it was hittable. "What difference does it make whether it is the first ball pitched or the last one?" Delahanty believed if a pitcher had good control, he would "do his business" with the first pitch. Ed reminded his interviewer that in the game on July 13, 1896, he hit four home runs, and three of his homers came on first pitches.[45] Cincinnati hurler Red Ehret confirmed that Delahanty was the "hardest man in the league for pitchers to puzzle."[46]

In Philadelphia, with the ball club failing, Delahanty's play was generally taken for granted. Horace Fogel, a not infrequent critic of Delahanty, said that when Del made a phenomenal play at home, it might get light applause. On the road, he said, where Del was seen about a half-dozen times a season, Ed was better appreciated and encouraged.[47] In the eyes of the Philadelphia "crank," his greatness and the team's dramatic failures were hard to reconcile. They asked how could a team with the "great" Delahanty always come up so short?

Reporters put a good deal of the blame for the season's shortfalls on Stallings. They wrote that the young manager was lulled with "jollyism" and insincere comradeship. Stallings was so full of himself that he was blinded to the fact that his players were conniving against him more than their on-field opponents. When he went to the other extreme, imposing discipline and threatening more trades, Stallings alienated many of his contrary players. And so, during Delahanty's great batting streak his team was described as "undisciplined . . . [like a] disorganized mob," "playing like dead men," "laying down," and being "mentally drunk."[48]

Some of the veteran players—Taylor, Clements, and Tommy Dowd—gave up on the season and conspired against Stallings. Their resistance was marked by excessive drinking, late off-field hours, and malcontented backstabbing. Younger teammates such as Cooley and Lajoie took their lead from the older players. They sulked and fell in with the grumblers. The crisis was a suitable time for Ed Delahanty to assert his leadership. Instead, he turned his back on the controversy and remained aloof in the locker room, where his influence was needed. Rogers reacted differently. He required the Philadelphia players to sign a statement saying that there was no discord, only support for their maligned manager.[49]

After a time, Rogers threatened fines and season suspensions for inappropriate behavior. Frank Hough of the *Inquirer* said the Phillies had "the biggest set of ingrates and leg pullers that ever came down the baseball pike." He warned Stallings about the "jolliers, who, like gift-bearing Greeks will throw hobosh into him whenever it suits their purpose."[50] Stallings confessed that his "princely jollyers" had patted him on the back so often his coat was threadbare.[51] These assessments came too late for Stallings and the Phillies. The infection was festering, and only extreme measures could quell the damage.

Many of the malcontents disrespected Stallings and showed their disdain with disruptive bench behavior. They laughed and made snide remarks about his managing. The situation became so bad that on August 11, after dropping two games to lowly Washington, Cooley, Lajoie, and Taylor came drunk to the ball park. Taylor was so intoxicated he could not "navigate at all" and was immediately suspended. Lajoie and Cooley spent the afternoon napping on the bench. At the end of the game, Lajoie tried to steal the baseball and assaulted an abusive spectator as the player was boarding the team coach. Lajoie was arrested, and fined $50 by Stallings.[52] Rogers fumed and fretted about this behavior. Detectives shadowed the ballplayers, and Stallings warned, "from now out I will cease to be a good fellow and there will be the strictist kind of discipline."[53]

In a few days the "staggering Stallingites" imploded. It began with a Saturday night spree that saw the arrest of two unidentified, intoxicated Phillies. A few evenings later, three local ballplayers spent the night in a station house for drinking and disorderly conduct. No names were disclosed, but on August 27, Napoleon Lajoie, again, came to a game drunk. Rather than bench him, Stallings let him play and embarrass himself on the field. Lajoie misplayed balls, dozed at first base, and shouted profanities at jeering "cranks." He was taken out of the game after a disgraceful half inning. He was fined and suspended from the ball club. The press was aghast at Lajoie's "wolfish thirst for liquor." They compared his intemperance to Cleveland's Louis Sockalexis, who had been put off the Spiders for drinking. Some sportswriters said Larry, as he was often called, wanted to be one of the fellows and was led astray by older and more self-indulgent teammates. After lectures from Rogers and Stallings, a contrite and subdued Lajoie was reinstated after a five-day suspension.[54]

Ironically, despite his later problems with alcohol, Delahanty was not implicated in these episodes. Not even in his prodigal pre-marriage years, did he behave inappropriately. Del enjoyed his nights out with Clements and the lads and often spent his money freely, but no one ever likened his behavior to that of Lajoie and his friends. Ed's dissipation when it erupted would be an expression of his inner demons and self-inflicted failures.

In 1897 Delahanty's greatness as a ballplayer was approaching its peak. He was not a veteran whose best years were behind him, nor was he a young player eager to make his mark. What the public and his peers saw was a commanding athlete whose caring and good-natured ways were still untouched by life's cruel certainties. Horace Fogel made it a point to inform his readers that Delahanty was not one of the trouble-making Phillies.[55] In a later column, the caustic sportswriter described Delahanty as having a heart "as tender as a child's." No ballplayer, Fogel said, had more friends and was as greatly admired for his "sterling qualities." When former teammate Joe Sullivan contracted consumption (tuberculosis) and died slowly, Delahanty responded without hestitation. It was Del who collected and raised money in every baseball town to pay for "Sully's" expenses.[56] His solicitations made up for the lack of any form of disability compensation or support for ailing ballplayers. It was always up to friends and supporters to pass around the proverbial hat. This nurturing side of Delahanty complemented his current conditioning routine. George Wheeler proclaimed that Ed "is the most careful man you ever saw about his health and habits and you will never hear of him breaking down before his time if care and prudence can preserve him."[57]

This dedication carried Ed Delahanty through the disappointing season, but the agonizing decline of his beloved Sully and the passing of his sister unnerved the mighty Phillies slugger. The death of Florence Delahanty was particularly difficult. She was eleven years his junior and was afflicted with autism. The Delahantys, particularly her adoring big brother, were protective of Florence. They saw to it that she was a vital member of the large household. Toward the middle of August, Florence became ill. On the day Lajoie came drunk to the ballpark, Ed was notified that his sister was dying. He immediately left Pittsburgh for Cleveland. Soon after he arrived, the eighteen-year-old Florence passed away. Not since the death of Bridget's infant son, Marty, twenty-six years before, had the Delahantys suffered such a grievous loss.[58]

Still mourning his sister, Ed rejoined the team in Philadelphia for a September 4 game against Cleveland. He went 2 for 3, with a double. But Delahanty's heart was not in baseball. He had been o for 9 before his return to Cleveland, and now his grief for Florence and the team's sorry play sapped his enthusiasm for the season's last month. When Sullivan died in November at the age of twenty-seven, Delahanty was despondent.[59]

The 1897 season for Delahanty was a futile year. Even the joy of competing for the batting title lost its meaning. After his return, he hit .250, and the batting crown went to Baltimore's Willie Keeler. Ed finished fifth with a .377 batting average. Delahanty also placed fourth in slugging (.538), fourth in total bases (285), and second in doubles (40). He had 200 hits, 15 triples, 109 runs scored, 26 stolen bases, and 96 RBIs. In the field, Del committed only 9 errors and had 23 assists. Of the Phillies, only Lajoie finished the season with league-leading statistics. He also batted .361 with 127 RBIs, 40 double, 23 triples, and 9 home runs. Larry also led the league in slugging (.569). In spite of their feats, the Phillies finished in tenth place, 38 games behind Frank Selee's resurgent Boston team. This collapse sparked rumors that George Stallings would not be back, and wishful speculators hoped Ned Hanlon was coming over from Baltimore.[60] But Stallings' job was not yet in jeopardy. On the contrary, Reach and Rogers encouraged him to clean house and bring in fresh, coachable talent. In his quest for young prospects, Stallings missed an opportunity that might have affected the future course of Ed Delahanty's career.

From Dayton, in the Interstate League, Stallings signed a hard-throwing left-handed pitcher, an off-season teacher, named Wiley Piatt. He also acquired Elmer Flick, a speedy, power-hitting outfielder who would supplant Sam Thompson in right field, and ultimately, in 1963, precede Sam into the Hall of Fame. Stallings' problems, however, could have been resolved by the one player that got away. Looking for a shortstop, Stallings turned down the chance to sign the top batter in the Atlantic League, Paterson's Honus Wagner. The Phillies scouting report said that Wagner could hit, but was "too clumsy for the National League."[61] Envisioning a lineup with Delahanty, Lajoie, Wagner, and Flick is left to our imaginations. Stallings did not lament Wagner's signing with Louisville. He focused on ridding the club of its malcontents.

Al Reach said "a championship team must have good players. Not necessarily stars." He decried the bad habits and lackadaisical play of the Phillies[62] and supported the decision of Rogers and Stallings to unload Taylor, Clements, Dowd, and with reluctance, Lave Cross to last-place St. Louis for shortstop Monte Cross, utility player Bill Douglass, and pitcher Red Donahue. The sporting press saw the trade as a bad one for Philadelphia but believed it was a necessary move for the well-being of the team. One unidentified player lamented that the ball club needed a clever and determined manager who was allowed to run his team. To his way of thinking, "The Philadelphia people [Rogers and company] will not stand for a thorough good manager. What they want is a figurehead, so if you desire trouble, look in the office, and not on the field."[63]

Delahanty would miss his friends Lave Cross and Jack Clements, but he recognized the team needed to move on. What really ate away at Delahanty was the fact that his emergence as a dominant slugger did not translate into a larger salary or a winning ball club. Instead, Del's fate was linked to a fractious franchise with falling attendance and suffering revenues. Run by the overbearing

John Rogers, the Phillies seemed to be stumbling through the century's last decade. Delahanty could only hope that 1898 would bring better tidings. Norine Delahanty was pregnant and fatherhood enlivened his spirits. Change seemed to be in the air as war clouds loomed on the nation's clouded horizon.

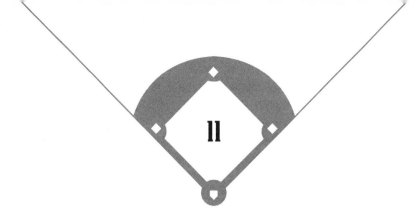

A Season in Wartime

The new year for Ed Delahanty began positively. Once the 1897 season had ended, Ed tied up his affairs in Philadelphia and took his pregnant wife home to Cleveland. Before their departure, he signed his new contract and, together with his advance salary, received a stipend for not talking to any other ball club.[1] By Thanksgiving he and Norine were comfortably settled in Cleveland, awaiting the birth of what would be their only child. It was also the time, free from baseball schedules, to come to terms with his sister's death and soothe mother Delahanty's grief by focusing her attention on the birth of her first grandchild. On January 19, 1898, Norine gave birth to a girl, Florence, named for her husband's deceased sister. The proud father distributed cigars and accepted congratulations at the fire station and all his familar hometown haunts.[2]

However, Delahanty's celebrations, did not dispel his growing dissatisfaction with the Phillies. The team no longer was a contender, and the "cranks" of the Quaker City spent most of 1897 disparaging their favorite ballplayers. Some vocal "hoodlums" raised choruses of "vile epithets" at any player wearing a Phillies uniform, including Delahanty. Things were so bad that Ed and center fielder Dick Cooley often crossed the diamond on their way to the bench rather than pass near the bleacher section of the ballpark. For awhile, Delahanty's "patience was most sorely tried," when spectators addressed him personally and made comments about the women members of his family.[3]

It came as no surprise that Del violated his off-season contract by encouraging the interests of other teams. Ned Hanlon in Baltimore still wanted Delahanty in his outfield, and in Cleveland, rumors abounded that Ed wanted out of Philadelphia.[4] President Robison of Cleveland reported that his mail was full of appeals for a Delahanty trade. He reminded his listeners that Del favored the move and argued against a statement that Delahanty was not popular in his hometown. Robison concurred with local writers, who boasted that two-thirds of Cleveland's patrons "go into ecstasies" over Ed's playing.[5]

Delahanty did not participate in this dialogue. Instead, he philosophized about how "cranks" should react to ballgames. Fans must remember that only one team can win, and on any given day, a team could play "wretchedly" and win a game, and the very next day perform impressively with the same result. He said there were just too many games in a season for people to fixate on a loss. Boosters, he said, should appreciate how well a baseball game was played. "I wish people would learn to love base ball for the skill and science and the 'fight' there is in every contest rather than from the victory and defeat standpoint."[6] These comments were pretentious. Delahanty loved his sport and wanted fans to recognize the game's nuances, but winning ballgames was all that mattered to the clubs and competitive athletes such as Ed Delahanty. The Phillies were no exception and hoped for a winning record after George Stallings' latest rounds of personnel changes.

By spring training, more than thirty players were under contract. Remarkably, only Delahanty, Thompson, and Boyle were left from Harry Wright's fourth-place 1893 club. The team's malcontents were gone and Stallings brought youth, speed, and versatility to the Phillies. With young prospects and new players on board, the fans and management were again optimistic. One newspaper, alluding to the war fever that followed the sinking of the American battleship *Maine* in Havana Harbor, said the Phillies had enough ballplayers to liberate Cuba.[7]

With so many prospects, Stallings had major decisions to make. Only Delahanty, Dick Cooley, and catcher Ed McFarland were assured of their positions. Most of the roster decisions would be determined by the status of Sam Thompson and Billy Nash. "Big Sam" wanted to play again for the Phillies and wired Shettsline that he had his own regimen for getting himself into shape.[8] If the thirty-eight-year-old Thompson recaptured his playing form, young Elmer Flick's career would be stalled. The other uncertainty was Nash, because his return left the young infielders, Lajoie and "Kid" Elberfeld, without settled positions. But while Stallings contemplated his personnel, Reach and Rogers were immersed in league decisions.

On the issue of Sunday baseball, New York and Pittsburgh agreed to play on the Sabbath. Only Boston and Philadelphia held out. With large crowds bringing in revenues of $2,000 per game, it was difficult to turn away twenty lucrative dates. These opportunities did not move Reach and Rogers. They refused to pose as "moralists or interpreters of Holy Writ" and asserted that they did not think "baseball is a work of necessity for our employees or ourselves and therefore we ought not to earn money on the Lord's day by such unnecessary work."[9]

The Philadelphia owners were more supportive when it came to curbing the expenses of team travel. By 1898 annual travel expenses per club were more than $13,000, and a road trip could cost a ball club almost $2,000. With teams traveling more than 10,000 miles a season, railroad costs were critical.[10] To combat these rising expenses, John Rogers, Cincinnati's John Brush, and Cleveland's Frank Robison urged the National Railroad Ticket Agents Association to give them better rates.[11] The railway companies did what they could for the owners, but operating costs still revolved around the game's appeal. Toward this end, John Brush, the author of the 1888 players classification scheme that sparked the baseball revolt, led a crusade to clean up obscene and rowdy behavior. His "purification plan" was to be enforced by umpires and administered by the league's Board of Discipline. During these negotiations, Rogers backed Bush's discipline plan in exchange for recognition of his twenty-five cents admission charge.[12]

Each franchise reinforced the behavior regulations in their own way. Reach and Rogers installed large red signs at their ballpark prohibiting intolerable language and behavior. One sign warned against gambling and pickpocketing. Another forbade profanity and insults to ballplayers, patrons, and umpires. These posted notices pleased Delahanty and Cooley, who had suffered through last season's verbal harangues, but many patrons and sportswriters were insulted by these mandated codes.[13]

With these decisions behind them, the Phillies welcomed Delahanty and his teammates back for spring training camp at nearby Cape May, New Jersey. Delahanty left Norine and the baby in Philadelphia in the care of his sister-in-law and made no comment about his alleged disaffection with the team. He came to camp overweight and hoped his running and time spent in Bill Shettsline's new sweat box would rid him of excessive weight. Del also found a new hunting partner, the hotel proprietor, who said Ed handled a shotgun with "the best wild-woolly-West grace of Buffalo Bill."[14] This proficiency carried over onto the ball field. Delahanty moved well in the outfield, and his batting showed no effect of the winter layoff.

Everyone was excited about the fresh attitudes of the young and hungry ballplayers. Even a rejuvenated Sam Thompson arrived confident of regaining his imposing form. He played so well that Elmer Flick was reconciled to a backup role. On the matter of Billy Nash's salary cut holdout, Rogers said he did not care whether his former manager-captain signed his contract.[15] Rogers was more concerned about Napoleon Lajoie, who was smarting over last year's disciplinary actions and the new sobriety clause in his contract. All players, drinkers and teetotalers, had the same nondrinking clause in their agreements. Lajoie was adamantly against the clause and did not report to camp. It took a face-to-face meeting with Rogers to convince the headstrong youngster that there would be no exceptions on the sobriety issue.[16] Once in camp, Larry impressed everyone with his skills at second base, but it was only after Kid Elberfeld injured his knee that the return of Billy Nash was settled.

With the starting positions set, Stallings had to make a commitment on a new field captain. Delahanty remained the popular choice, though he still resisted the responsibility. It was suggested that he already earned the maximum salary and did not believe the captaincy was worth the money. Lajoie was not acceptable to management, so the decision came down to Boyle, Cooley, or shortstop

Monte Cross. Boyle was not scheduled to be a starter, and out-fielder Cooley was not on the best of terms with Stallings. In the end, a reluctant Cross became the new Phillies captain, much to the relief of Ed Delahanty.[17]

To further motivate the team the front office offered a monied incentive plan. Reach and Rogers publicly declared that $10,000 would be divided among the Phillies if they won the pennant and "faithfully" obeyed the club's discipline covenants. Five thousand dollars was offered for a second-place finish. Third-place would earn $2,500, and finishing fourth brought a $1,250 bonus.[18] The *Evening Item* challenged the players by saying that management had "anteed up" and "sweetened the pot," now it was up to the ball-players.[19] Delahanty and the remaining veteran players were pleased by the offer and began discussing plans for spending the money.

These inducements got the season off on the right foot, even though the players and their supporters were distracted by the talk of the impending war with Spain. Philadelphia's harbor and the entrance to the Delaware Bay were fitted with a dozen eight-inch mortar guns. This led to training camp speculation that Cape May, New Jersey, might be attacked by the Spanish fleet.[20] The fever of war, and its aroused patriotism, was linked with the beginning of the baseball season. *Sporting Life* began the year with a set of cartoons depicting an exasperated Spanish admiral bombarding American soil. On the parapets, ballplayers caught cannonballs and hurled them back at the Spanish ships.[21] The *Inquirer,* under the headline "Spain Must Quit Cuba," had Uncle Sam reading about baseball's opening day in front of posted war bulletins.[22]

War excitement was so high that displayed military notices drew larger crowds than baseball scoreboards. By the beginning of May, Admiral Dewey took the American fleet into Manila Bay, and ballplayers followed the progress of Dewey's ships as if it were a baseball pennant race. Delahanty shared this enthusiasm for the war and anxiously read every newspaper account. Described as a "war fiend," he would debate the subject with anyone.[23] Unfortunately, Delahanty's hitting did not merit the same kind of attention. Distracted by the war, a new baby at home, and pitchers not giving him much to hit, his average by mid-May was uncharacteristically low at .259. In many respects, Delahanty's failures mirrored the struggles of the Philadelphia Phillies.

With the exception of Napoleon Lajoie, who was drawing raves at second, George Stallings' best laid plans were faltering. The team was quicker, and stolen bases were up, with Delahanty second in the league behind former Phillies outfielder Billy Hamilton, but the vaunted Philadelphia offense was disappointing. Delahanty and Lajoie were hitting well below their usual pace, and Cross, McFarland, and Cooley were in miserable slumps. With an unhappy Elmer Flick on the bench, the Phillies depended too much on Sam Thompson. Regrettably, wet, cold weather and Sam's chronic bad back were not a good mix at his age. Without much fanfare, Thompson packed his bags and returned to Detroit, recognizing that his body could no longer endure another baseball season. A thrifty man, Big Sam was prepared for life without baseball.[24] He retired from the game with a .331 batting average, the best home run percentage (home runs per at-bat) for the 1876–92 era, and the highest RBI-per-game ratio in the history of baseball. His exit also allowed Elmer Flick to move into the Philadelphia outfield.

By June 1, the Phillies were 14 and 17 and were playing listlessly. Meanwhile, Delahanty raised his average to .300 and Flick, batting close to .360, exhibited surprising power. This offense should have pleased George Stallings, but the Phillies manager was buckling under front office pressure. He released slumping Billy Nash, moved players around and shouted and cursed at every misplay. He tried team meetings and even resorted to on-field tricks.

With the owners and "cranks" clamoring for wins, it was only a matter of time before the Philadelphia sporting press began to inflame the situation. They accused the team of being a group of "quitters;" "unless they can line 'em out they lay down. . . . they don't keep at 'em. . . . [and] lack the never-say-die spirit of the Bostons, the Baltimores, the Clevelands."[25] Frank Hough, in his Sunday commentary, said the ball club needed a leader, like an orchestra conductor, who knew how to bring everything together.[26] The critical fissures came from players during a ten-game collapse.

It began when eleventh-place St. Louis came to Philadelphia for a four-game series. The locals dropped three closely contested games to former Phillies pitchers, Taylor, Carsey, and Esper. Stallings fumed over these setbacks, as the Phillies moved on to play second-place Boston. After dropping the first two games, Al Orth shut out the Beaneaters, 8 to 0. That evening Cooley and Lajoie celebrated by staying out all night and were fined $25. Cooley, who was now team captain, had had his problems with Stallings in 1897, and it came as no surprise that the fines and the exchange of harsh words alienated Cooley and set off the resentful Lajoie. Both men agitated against the manager, and through Billy Shettsline, they let Reach and Rogers know that they would not play for Stallings. Nevertheless, both men accompanied the team to New York, where the Phillies dropped two one-sided games, 11 to 3 and 16 to 4. In the second contest, the Phillies committed six errors. The *Evening Item* said the Phillies were "unmercifully licked, like Admiral Montijo's Spaniards at Manila [Bay]."[27] On Saturday, June 18, Reach and Rogers removed Stallings as the manager.

Contrary to press speculations, there was no specific player conspiracy. It was the team's on-field performance that convinced the front office that the Phillies were no longer peforming for Stallings. Delahanty played no role in the controversy. He was the first player to learn of his manager's release when he tried to kid around with Stallings before the Saturday game.[28] Frank Richter of *Sporting Life* said Stallings was caught between two millstones. He was not strict enough for the owners and too severe from the players' "selfish and short-sighted standpoint."[29] During his tenure the Phillies were 55 and 104.

As the United States mounted its attack on Spanish Cuba, Reach and Rogers decided on a new Philadelphia manager. One columnist pleaded with John Rogers to "do something big . . . to tingle the blood of thousands of cranks. Do it, Colonel, and in years to come old Philadelphians will recall the past by the season [when] Colonel Rogers made the big deal."[30] Unfortunately, Rogers avoided the "big deal" and selected a reluctant Billy Shettsline, who was traveling with the team. He would be the interim manager, and Dick Cooley remained as field captain. Popular with the players and secure with the front office, Shettsline, as in 1896, hestitantly stepped into the breach.

Shettsline completed the western road trip with a winning record, thanks in part to the quality of their opponents and the renewed batting of Ed Delahanty. Although the Philadelphia slugger had not had a home run since opening day, Ed finished the trip with 24 hits in 48 at-bats. When Philadelphia arrived in Baltimore on July 4, however the team's fortunes did not keep pace with the successes of the American military in Cuba. San Juan Hill was taken, the Spanish Caribbean squadron was trapped and destroyed, and the Phillies dropped five games to Hanlon's Orioles. Delahanty's torrid hitting pace also fell off. Determined to overpower Baltimore's pitchers, Del pressed too hard and went 3 for 17 with no extra-base hits. One observer wrote that Delahanty was trying too much to hit to right field, and it affected his swing and power.[31]

Manager Shettsline was confident that Delahanty would rebound and gave his attention to refining his ball club. The hobbled Kid Elberfeld and substitute catcher Newton Fisher were released, and former captain Jack Boyle was sold to New York. The Phillies countered by purchasing veteran catcher Morgan Murphy from Pittsburgh and signing two Brown University infielders, Billy Lauder and Dave Fultz. Stirred by these moves, the Phillies and Delahanty began to pick up their play. After twenty-six games, Shettsline was 14 and 12, and Delahanty and Lajoie were again making pitchers "quake in their shoes."[32] But Del split two fingers on his glove-hand trying to catch a foul ball. He missed five games and spent time in the upper pavilion with his local admirers. On one occasion, Del found himself surrounded by five clergymen, who were embarrassed by his enthusiastic rooting.[33]

Delahanty brought this intensity back to the field. And though he was not hitting as in former years, he was leading the league in steals and was in the midst of a 35-game stretch without an error. With Del batting .336, the Phillies were struggling to reach .500 and move out of the bottom half of the standings. In contrast, America was triumphant, Spain accepted defeat on August 12, and signed an armistice. The front page of the *Sunday Inquirer* had a full-page cartoon lauding the nation's great victory. America was represented by a proud Uncle Sam attired in a "stars and stripes" baseball uniform. Smoking a large cigar and holding a baseball bat, he said, "Well, gentlemen, having shown ya what modern civilization can do in the way of fighting, I will instruct you in the National Game of this glorious country."[34]

☽ This jingoism and the Phillies' recovery contrasted with the malaise felt by Delahanty's brothers who were mired at the bottom of the new Atlantic League. As the war ended, three of Del's younger brothers played for Allentown, a steel-producing community northwest of Philadelphia. Tom, the eldest, had finished the 1897 season with Newark. Working in the off-season as a boilermaker in Cleveland, Tommy shared his ballplaying ambitions with his two adolescent siblings, Joseph Nicholas, commonly called "Nickles," and James Christopher, known as Jimmy.

Joe Delahanty was four years younger than Tommy. Born in 1876, Joe was trained as a lithographer and pressman but wanted to follow Tom and Ed into baseball. Joe had already made a name for himself on the sandlots of Cleveland before signing in 1896 with Quincy in the Western Association.[35] After unimpressive stints with Quincy and independent Ohio-based teams, he signed on with Fall River in the New England League. In 25 games at third and second base, he batted .344.[36] In 1898 Joe joined up with brother Tommy in the Atlantic League and played third base and right field for the Paterson nine. Though his fielding did not keep pace with his hitting, he caught the eye of Billy Sharsig, the manager of Allentown. Sharsig, from Gloucester, New Jersey, was a prominent Philadelphia baseball figure, who founded and led the old American Association Athletics. An astute judge of baseball talent, he secured Joe Delahanty in mid-June to play third base for his floundering Allentown club.

Tommy Delahanty had been purchased by Sharsig in mid-May from Newark. A few weeks later, the not-yet-twenty-year-old Jimmy Delahanty was brought over to play shortstop. Jimmy, like Tommy and Joe before him, competed at the same Phelps Street corner sandlot where big brother Ed got his start. Over the objections of his mother, in 1897 Jimmy tried out for Fort Wayne in the Interstate League. Unfortunately, his age and inexperience worked against him, and he returned to Cleveland and played semipro ball. Undeterred by this setback, Jimmy wrote to Lima, an independent team in the Northwest Ohio League. The team needed a third baseman and was anxious to give the brother of Ed Delahanty a look. Lima management, impressed with the youngster's strong arm and fielding range, agreed to take him on if he played without a contract. In a matter of a few games, the fans and the players embraced the respectful, good-natured teenager. He was called the "Yellow Kid" because of his fair and boyish looks. Encouraged by his play in Lima, his brothers pushed Jimmy to try for a higher baseball league. In 1898 Jimmy signed to play for Montgomery in the Southern League. After the league folded, brother Tom got him a tryout with the Allentown club.[37]

Billy Sharsig had not seen Jimmy play, and had only heard about the youngster from Tommy Delahanty. But Sharsig liked what he saw. He was impressed by the "Yellow Kid's" range, scrappiness, and potential. On May 27, when first-place Hartford took the field at Allentown, Tommy and Jimmy Delahanty were at the keystone positions. Three weeks later, after Joe's purchase, all three Delahanty brothers played together in the Allentown infield.[38]

After their historic performance, good-sized crowds came to Manhattan Ball Park outside of Allentown for the curiosity of watching three brothers of the great Delahanty play together. Despite a fifth-place finish, Billy Sharsig was pleased with his gate receipts and the prospects of his young club. Tommy Delahanty had a good year at second base, but did not get his National League call. He batted .288 and played in 118 games for Newark and Allentown. Jimmy struggled; playing in 96 games at shortstop, he batted only .200. Joe Delahanty showed the most offensive promise. Before a season-ending injury, he hit .311 with 12 triples in 85 games at Paterson and Allentown.[39] Billy Sharsig spoke highly of the brothers. He said the younger ones were well-behaved and were showing rapid progress as players. Sharsig felt each Delahanty was a good batter, and Joe, like big brother Ed, looked to be a "natural-born" hitter.[40]

It is doubtful that the brothers' schedule allowed them to get to Philadelphia, other than on Sundays, to see Del and his family. Ed was very proud of his siblings and could not get over how three Delahantys were starting players on the same team. Although he rarely had a chance to watch the trio, he did compete against Tommy in a preseason exhibition game in Newark. The Phillies won 15 to 3, and Tommy went hitless, while Ed scored four runs on three hits.[41] For Delahanty, the satisfaction of his brothers' progress helped relieve the pressure of salvaging something positive from another lackluster Philadelphia baseball season.

Delahanty and his teammates had to pick up the pace over the next six weeks if they were to capture a spot in the first division and earn Colonel Rogers' prize money. With the help of Delahanty, the Phillies made a 16 and 10 run in September. Ed hit safely in 21 out of 26 games for a .376 average. More than half of his hits were for extra bases. Underlying Del's success was his switch to a lighter bat. A stifling heat wave in early September and the strain of the season had slowed his swing to the point where he forsook his usual 50-plus-ounce bat. Using the lightest bat he could find, he regained his hitting stroke.[42] Delahanty also kept his lead in base stealing, doubling his total from 1897. More than individual titles, though, he wanted to finish in the first division.[43]

What the Phillies needed was a prolonged winning streak and a serious run against the better teams. Frustrated by a lack of success, the ball club whined about prejudiced umpiring. They believed that other teams intimidated umpires unfairly and that officials took it out on the retaliatory Phillies.[44] Another distraction was a $300 lawsuit by former Phillie Lave Cross for his good-behavior playing bonus. After months of wrangling, Delahanty and several other players were called to testify before a St. Louis justice of the peace. Loyal to his friend, only Delahanty supported Cross, providing testimony that he heard former manager Stallings say he could not contradict John Rogers' judgment and authorize a bonus. It took three years before Lave Cross won a judgment, but his case was another distraction for Philadelphia's season-wearied ballplayers.[45]

In the end, the Phillies went 8 and 6 in October, with eleven of their last games against the tail-end Brooklyn and Washington ball clubs, to slip quietly into the first division (fifth place) for the first time in three years. Delahanty did not make much of an offensive contribution. He had only 13 hits and batted .288 for the last two weeks of the season. Philadelphia finished 24 games behind Frank Selee's repeating champions from Boston, and the Phillies were 59 and 44 under Billy Shettsline.

Reach and Rogers were pleased with Shettsline's performance and his handling of the team. Pitcher "Red" Donahue said that Billy Shettsline understood how to get good work out of his players without "bossing them in an offensive way."[46] Captain Dick Cooley seconded this opinion, relating how Shettsline was in a class by himself in "handling men without friction."[47] Both manager and captain were reengaged for 1899, and the money that had been promised for good behavior was dispersed to the players.

Delahanty was somewhat satisfied with his inconsistent season. Philadelphia sportswriters felt he played excellent all-around baseball despite his dramatic decline in batting, a 46-point drop to .330. Willie Keeler, who lost 53 points in his average, again led an array of contact hitters, such as Hamilton, Burkett, McGraw, and Fred Tenney, in the batting race. But when the *Sporting News* calculated hitting success over the last six seasons, Delahanty at .377 led the pack by seven points.[48] The question asked by many pundits was, why the 1898 decline?

Many hitters complained about the quality of the ball, improved fielding, and power hitters of the Delahanty-Lajoie-Jimmy Collins mold trying too hard to slug the ball. Baseball's reigning sage, Henry Chadwick suggested that fewer extra-base hits would have led to higher averages. Chadwick also attributed the slump to better pitching. He declared that pitchers were varying their selection and were getting better at disguising what they threw. He added that pitchers benefited from catchers crowding closer to home plate.[49] Without ignoring any of these factors, the decline was probably affected more by a rule change that no longer gave a hit for certain forced outs.[50]

Whatever the cause, Delahanty's subpar season would have pleased most major league players. He finished fourth in slugging (.454), second in doubles (35), and led the league in stolen bases (66). Ed also had the highest average on a team that hit .280. Only Napoleon Lajoie rivaled Delahanty's numbers, leading the league in doubles (40) and RBIs (127). Rookie Elmer Flick pleased everyone with his 81 RBIs, 8 home runs, and .302 average. In the pitching department, Al Orth had a 3.02 ERA and 15 wins, and Wiley Piatt won 24 games and gave up 3.18 runs per contest.

Delahanty would have preferred a first-place finish but was pleased that the team appeared to be moving in the right direction. This success was important to Del as he approached his thirtieth birthday. It bothered him that he had no championships to show for his great years in Philadelphia. He was also upset that he would make less money in 1899 than players at the beginning of the decade. These feelings fed postseason speculation that he wanted to be traded to better-paying contending teams, such as Chicago.[51]

To think of Delahanty leaving Philadelphia at this time was still premature. Ed was busy working on two things that would tie him to the Quaker City. Delahanty and his wife had made the decision to sell their home in Cleveland and settle year-round in Philadelphia. Norine wanted to be near her sister and family, and Ed, who had never held an off-season job, was looking to open a downtown cafe. It was reported that Del had worked out terms and drawn up papers with his partner, Billy Shettsline. Everyone believed they would make a "great pair of kings to draw to," but the enterprise never materialized.[52] This failure was unfortunate because if Delahanty had succeeded in a business, he might have been better able to handle the problems and temptations that beset the rest of his career.

The troubles that destabilized Delahanty's life gathered momentum during the 1898 season. The suffering economics of the National League were not remedied by the arrogance and greed of the magnates. Their failures rekindled union and alternate league solutions, reminiscent of the Players' League experience. These conditions, for a young player beginning a career, were unsettling enough, but for frustrated, veteran players such as Delahanty, they kindled desperate expectations.

The underlying factor inciting these circumstances was the financial consequences of declining attendance figures. In 1898 only half of the league's ball clubs benefited from an extended 154-game schedule. Playing twenty-one more games, the league drew a half-million less fans. The Phillies saw their attendance drop for the third straight year, a 210,000 decline since 1895. Colonel Rogers also asserted that the team's revenue of $49,000 was $10,000 less than the previous season.[53] These losses were significant when considering the expenses of running a National League franchise. The *Sporting News* advertised that the average annual operating costs of a National League baseball club was about $106,000 per season.[54] More than 40 percent of these expenses went for salaries. To remedy this condition, ticket prices could be raised or salaries cut. But escalating prices with attendance falling, or cutting salaries that were at a decade low, made no sense.

The question that troubled the owners was what was keeping attendance down. Magnates and columnists blamed it on the war, the weather, the new 154-game schedule, and rowdy baseball.[55] A closer look exposed a sport run solely for the benefit of grasping, bickering, and short-sighted owners. The league had become a closed shop, run down to the point where franchises were polarized to "haves" and "have nots." Only three teams won championships in the 1890s, interest in Philadelphia and New York was fading, and a twelve-team league did nothing to stimulate pennant rivalries or the league's economy. Under the caretaker reign of "Uncle Nick" Young, the National League president since 1884, the owners ran their organizations as they wished. One historian has called it baseball's "feudal era," a time when individual magnates operated their personal fiefdoms to suit themselves.[56] In this contentious arena, owners aligned themselves with issue-driven cliques. Prominent baseball lords, such as the irritating John Brush of Cincinnati, stifled change and promoted the integrity of the twelve-team league. Often he spoke for the "little seven," small-market, status quo franchises (Baltimore, Brooklyn, Cincinnati, Cleveland, Louisville, St. Louis, and Washington). At the other extreme was New York's Andrew Freedman. He favored a form of centralized syndicate that strove to reduce league membership, pool the best players, and select a strong league president. John Rogers appreciated Freedman's notions but was content to play the role of a self-centered mediator, solely concerned with the well-being of his own investment. Star players of the stature of Delahanty, Keeler, and Rusie had no input into these dealings. Without union support or competing organizations, they were pawns to the sport's feudal barons.

In the search for remedies, it was ironic that the fate of Delahanty and his sport would be shaped by the Robison brothers of Cleveland. Enterprising streetcar entrepreneurs, the brothers dealt obstinately with labor and league troubles. When attendance fell in Cleveland, the Robisons turned their back on their one-time supporters and scheduled thirty-eight games on the road. By this maneuver, Robison's Spiders, now termed the "Exiles" or "Wanderers," irreparably alienated their fan base. The Robisons' salvation was the financial misfortunes of Chris von der Ahe, the owner of the St. Louis Browns. Von der Ahe, suffering from bad investments and a costly divorce, put his team in receivership. Not one to overlook an opportunity, Frank Robison finagled with his fellow owners to purchase the St. Louis franchise. With brother Stanley remaining in Cleveland, Frank Robison shifted players between the two ball clubs, creating a strong St. Louis club and a poor Cleveland team.[57] Termed "pooling," this practice became the league's way of using ailing franchises to make money elsewhere.

The precedent also inspired wealthy brewer and Orioles owner Harry von der Horst and his manager-president, Ned Hanlon, to make a similiar deal with Brooklyn. With Hanlon getting $10,000 of Baltimore's $39,000 payroll, there was not much for the Orioles to cut. Instead they focused on their attendance that had fallen by 120,000. Unable to draw with a contending team, von der Horst and Hanlon saw an opportunity when Charlie Byrne, the president of the Brooklyn Bridegrooms, died. With a chance to move into the ailing New York market, von der Horst and Hanlon purchased 50 percent of Brooklyn's stock, while Brooklyn's minority partners, Frank Abell and Charlie Ebbets, bought shares in the Orioles. Like the Cleveland–St. Louis deal, this arrangement took better players, such as Joe Kelley, Willie Keeler, and Hugh Jennings, and created a Brooklyn super team, nicknamed the "Superbas." John McGraw remained in Baltimore and did what he could to salvage the once-proud Orioles.

While these actions were being set in motion, the owners attended to more mundane decisions. At the December league meetings, they voted to keep the twelve-team format, the new 154-game schedule, and debated John Rogers' admission scale. The thorniest issue to reconcile was the disposing of John Brush's controversial behavior code. It was only after these matters were settled that Rogers and Reach gave attention to postseason personnel questions.

Boston again made a pitch for Delahanty, offering a multiplayer package for the Philadelphia stalwart. Another Delahanty–Billy Lange trade also resurfaced at the league meetings. In each case, the offers were dismissed. "Trade Delahanty," Billy Shettsline remarked, "not on your life, Del suits us all right. He can play just as good all around baseball as Lange [a superb defensive outfielder] and has better habits."[58] What the Phillies wanted was another dependable pitcher. After much bartering, they purchased Louisville's erratic 20-game loser, Chick Fraser. Reach and Rogers hit the jackpot, however, when they signed the former University of Pennsylvania star outfielder, Roy Thomas. It was hoped that the speedy 24-year-old from Norristown, Pennsylvania, would become a successful leadoff batter, something the team had been lacking since the Billy Hamilton trade.

Everyone in Philadelphia was optimistic that 1899 would be the turn-around year for the franchise. Delahanty looked forward to redeeming himself, but he had no idea that the machinations in Baltimore and Cleveland were about to change the course of his life.

12

Captain Ed, Batting Champ

The 1899 season was pivotal for Ed Delahanty. He and his team-mates anticipated a formidable year, but economic tensions would derail the franchise and eventually drive Delahanty from Philadelphia and to ruin. The groundwork for this turmoil was precipitated by the Cleveland and Baltimore transfers and the mistreatment of small-market ball clubs by self-possessed, vindictive owners. Their jockeying for position was intensified by the anticipated end of the ten-year, poststrike National Agreement (1891). In his Sunday column for the *Philadelphia Inquirer,* Frank Hough took the owners to task. He rebuked the magnates for overreaching themselves, predicting their greed would come back to harm them like a boomerang. Hough likened them to a "coterie of doormat thieves, second-story men . . . and pocketbook snatchers." These owners, he remarked, were "as devoid of sporting blood as an egg is shy of hair." He spoke of their distrust for each other, and said they deluded themselves when they labeled their most "dexterous thief [John Brush]" as the "Moses of the League." Hough warned that the sport could only afford so much asininity.[1]

For Delahanty and his mates, the immediate financial issue was the franchise's gate-receipt policy. Since 1893 Colonel Rogers had operated the club by dividing his grandstand and twenty-five-cents general admission charges with visiting teams. Using "incontrovertible" figures, accumulated over sixteen years, Rogers presented his case for maintaining this arrangement at the baseball meetings. At these gatherings he resorted to his tactic of trading off his support. But this time he awkwardly involved himself in the St. Louis and Brooklyn deals and the plight of the Louisville and Washington franchises. In his attempt to bargain with Frank Robison, Rogers angered James Hart, Chicago's president and the league's schedule-maker. Hart accused Rogers of bartering his vote, and in the heat of an argument, it was alleged that Rogers pulled out a pistol and had to be restrained by his associates. John Rogers countered this report, asserting he was reaching for his eyeglass case.[2] In the end, Rogers worked out higher individual admission prices with each of his colleagues.

The mounting expenses and controversies of the Philadelphia ball club were wearisome to a successful businessman such as team president Al Reach. He faulted Rogers for many of these problems. Most disturbing to Reach was Rogers' violation of an agreement to keep their stock shares balanced. Rogers ignored the pact when he went behind Reach's back and bought out Harry Wright's widow, making him the majority stockholder. From this point forward, Rogers ran the team and accrued expenses without consulting the club's president.[3]

Colonel Rogers' ballplayers had no inkling of these festering tensions. Delahanty was busy in Cleveland, selling his home and shipping everything to Philadelphia. This move forced him to miss the first days of training camp in Charlotte, North Carolina. Billy Shettsline learned of this situation in a wire from Rogers, informing him that Delahanty was house hunting and expected to be in camp when he got his family settled. Three days after spring practice began, Delahanty arrived at the training site. "Smiling like a basket of chips," Ed was warmly greeted by his teammates. He was impressed with the new white and green uniforms, particularly the sweaters with their "patriotic" emerald hue that "has never been seen this side of Ireland."[4]

Delahanty took it easy the first couple of days, as the team prepared for their initial intersquad game. He did his usual long-distant runs and workouts in an effort to trim down to 190 pounds.

Meanwhile, the somber Charlotte community opened their local lodges to Delahanty and his teammates. One reason for the players' popularity was the melodious voices of some of the ballplayers. Led by Dick Cooley's piano playing, groups of singing players tried to outperform each other at evening functions. The only activities more popular than these song-fests were trainer Scanlon's post-practice, alcohol rubdowns and the "clearing tables," as Delahanty called the meals. Billy Shettsline said his players were not interested in *haute cuisine*. "Take Delahanty, for instance," Shettsline said, "He would no more think of eating a *pate de fois gras* before his berries than he would of wearing a high hat with a sack coat."[5] Other than these pastimes, the Phillies went about their regular training routines.

Captain Cooley insisted on two daily practices and held nightly study sessions, working on signs and simulated game tactics. He also stressed bunting. Cooley was especially concerned that Delahanty and Lajoie master this fine art before the team returned home.[6] Overall, the training camp progressed well. Roy Thomas and Bill Douglas looked settled at their new positions, and the lanky young hurler Bill Bernhard impressed everyone with his poise and speed. After a series of southern exhibition games the team arrived home to a large welcoming crowd. But hungry ballplayers and an overeager Ed Delahanty, anxious to see "how much Miss Delahanty had gained in his absence," had no time for John Rogers or the team's supporters. They hurriedly made their way out of the station, taking their hand-luggage with them.[7]

In the week before the season began, Delahanty busied himself with his newly rented home, a two-story row house at 2614 North 18th Street. Situated three blocks west of the ballpark, below Lehigh Avenue, Delahanty easily became a part of that North Philadelphia community. After participating in a number of preseason games, Delahanty and the Phillies opened the season on the road against Art Irwin's Washington ballclub.

The Phillies took four of five games from Washington. In the concluding game Delahanty went 5 for 6 with a home run and a double. His 400-foot-plus home run aroused the crowd as it soared over the left-center field fence. The day before, with his power stroke in a groove, he had pulled a towering foul ball over the Freedman's Colored Hospital beyond the left field stands.[8] His heavy batting continued against Hanlon's restocked Brooklyn Superbas. While the owners haggled over the gate receipts, Philadelphia split the four-game series with Del going 9 for 20. That Sunday the *Inquirer*'s magazine section featured a pictorial display of an early morning workout, the centerpiece being a picture of Delahanty taking batting practice against the backdrop of an empty stadium. With his teammates waiting their turn, Del, with his bat cocked, was shown leaning back on his powerful right leg, his left foot raised to step into a pitch. The caption said that young boys excitedly chased after his long hits.[9]

By mid-May, after sweeping four games from New York, the Phillies were in second place behind Frank Robison's retooled St. Louis "Perfectos." Leading the offensive charge was "King Del." Sports columnists said that Delahanty was playing the best ball of his career. His prowess was noteworthy considering that he was one of only twenty-five players from the 1880s still performing in the National League.[10] His fielding was described as outstanding, and his baserunning suprised his teammates. But Delahanty was still the consumate batter, leading the league with a .450 average. In his first twenty-five games, he went hitless only twice. He had six three-hit games, two four-hit games, and one five-hit game during this early season stretch. In one of his four-hit games, he stroked four doubles against Tom Colcolough of New York. The *Sporting News* said that Delahanty was setting a pace for his fellow players and was having a strong effect on the moody Napoleon Lajoie.[11]

Although the Phillies were still not in first place, people talked about the awesome nucleus of their batting order—Delahanty hitting third followed by young Lajoie and his .440 average. It was a unanimous sentiment around the league that these two batters were the most feared duo in baseball history. The Phillies believed that as long as both players stayed healthy, the team was not likely to go into a prolonged batting slump. With Cooley and Thomas hitting ahead of Del, Lajoie, and Flick, the Phillies could ignite a game-winning rally at any moment. But what made Delahanty and Lajoie unique was their successful powerful slugging. Unlike Keeler, Burkett, and McGraw, they were hard-swinging batters who rarely punched out their hits. Many observers said the twenty-four-year-old Lajoie was the league's best player. Lajoie took exception. He asserted that Delahanty was the "greatest batter of his age."[12]

One of their shared feats happened in Philadelphia on May 13, the day Ed hit four doubles. In the third inning, with Roy Thomas on second base, Delahanty hit a mighty double, scoring the runner and loosening the seams on the ball. Lajoie followed by hitting a towering triple that ricocheted off the brick clubhouse in left center field. When the ball was returned to the infield, Kid Gleason was astonished to see the ball cracked and misshapened, with the yarn hanging out. He said he had never, in his eleven years in the league, seen a "ball knocked to pieces." Gleason declared, "I guess no ball was ever hit so hard as Lajoie and Delahanty banged that one."[13]

The hitting of Delahanty and Lajoie could not overcome problems created by injuries or personnel troubles. The Phillies lost pitcher Al Orth for several months because of illness. Bill Lauder played third base with a sore shoulder and Delahanty was slowed by a badly pulled groin. Ed missed ten games but was 2 for 3 as a late-inning pinch-hitter. During the seventh game of his absence, Flick and Lajoie collided in the outfield, injuring both players. Without Delahanty and Lajoie, the Phillies' offense stalled. On June 1, with both men ailing, they returned to the lineup. Lajoie had two hits, including a home run, and Delahanty had three hits as the Phillies beat Chicago 7 to 1. Eight days later, Lajoie, still bothered by his injured chest, sat out five games.

When Delahanty and Lajoie reappeared the team was in fourth place, 6½ games behind Hanlon's Brooklyn Superbas. Their return was accompanied by a prolonged heat wave that oppressed the east coast. The humidity was so intense that regular every-inning players like Delahanty worried constantly about dehydration. Talk in the locker room also revolved around the upcoming heavyweight championship bout between Australian Bob Fitzsimmons and his American challenger, Jim Jeffries. On June 10, at the Coney Island Athletic Club, Jeffries surprised the Phillies and the sporting world by upsetting the champion with an eleventh-round knockout. Other clubhouse gossip concerned the future of Brooklyn's Hughie Jennings. The former Baltimore shortstop hurt his arm and had come to Philadelphia to see a specialist for treatment. His appearance set off reports that he would captain and play first base for the Phillies. Shettsline salivated at this prospect, but Ned Hanlon had no desire to give up on one of his mainstays. In the wake of these stories, the public lost track of Ed Delahanty's remarkable batting streak.

Unlike today's sports coverage, hitting streaks did not attract much attention. If a hitter was doing well, he was highlighted in the daily press, but rarely was a streak scrutinized. On June 4, Delahanty went 2 for 4 against Pittsburgh's Billy Rhines and Jim Gardner. Eighteen games later, after going 28 for 70, Delahanty went hitless against Bert Cunningham of Louisville. The next day Del was 2 for 4 and, for twelve games, batted 14 for 51. After this consecutive streak was halted, Delahanty hit safely for the next thirty-one games. During this time he went 53 for 128. Over a ten-week period, Delahanty hit safely in 61 of 63 games. He had 106 hits in 255 plate appearances for a .416 average. Even in hostile Brooklyn, Ed was a "royal favorite" and was greeted as if he was a member of the home team.[14] In New York after his streak, "the mightiest slugger of them all . . . the very drum-major . . . of batters in the league," brought the crowd's hearts to a "thumping halt" every time he came to bat with his "mighty cudgel."[15] The enthusiasm for Delahanty's progress and the team's success did not endure.

For the first time in Delahanty's career, his team was in the late summer pennant hunt. Excited by this prospect, John Rogers again proposed a financial incentive. In a letter to the Philadelphia players, Reach and Rogers offered the team $5,000 for a championship and $2,500 for a second-place finish.[16] The ball club was thrilled by this prize and had a chance to finish in the money if the pressures and sufferings of past seasons did not revisit them. Unfortunately, their propects were spiked by a near season-ending injury to Lajoie and the controversial suspension of Captain Dick Cooley.

On July 15, the first day of Delahanty's thirty-one-game streak, Lajoie hurt his knee in a collision at second base. Lajoie was assisted off the field, and ordered to stay in bed for a week. His badly swollen knee could not bear any weight. With the exception of a few games at the end of the season, Lajoie was out of the lineup.[17] That same morning, during practice, Captain Cooley was struck in the mouth by an errant ball—the second time in a two-week period. He required stitches and sat out three games. Cooley's mishaps were symptomatic of his failing fortunes and inconsistent play. The question was whether Cooley's condition was the result of, or was caused by, his drinking. The situation festered early in June after it was decided to move the fleet-footed Roy Thomas to center field and shift the veteran captain to first base. Thomas, later known as the "walking-man," eventually took over Cooley's leadoff spot.[18]

Cooley's biggest problem was being a highly visible, thinned-skin team captain. Like Lave Cross and Billy Hamilton before him, Dick Cooley was a popular target of "incompetent critics" who voiced their opinions from the stands. Popular among the players and esteemed as team captain, there was nothing Cooley could do to pacify the hometown "cranks" and their taunting commentaries.[19] It was only a matter of time before the "roasting of [the] bleacherites" and the meddling of management took its toll on the vulnerable team captain. Outwardly, he shrugged off the jeers, but he was upset that his presumed off-field activities were being reported to Reach and Rogers. Cooley denied these charges and inevitably got into a bad argument with Rogers, who suspended and removed him from the team. Newspaper accounts said that Cooley had violated the club's temperance policies and was charged by Rogers for setting a bad example for his teammates. Unwilling to let his former captain go to another ball club without getting full value, the vindictive Rogers let him finish the season without pay or affiliation.[20] Cooley's demotion also thrust Ed Delahanty back into the dilemma of accepting the team's captaincy.

No one on the Phillies had the experience, respect, and popularity of Ed Delahanty. The captaincy had always been his for the asking, but he was uncomfortable with the demands and responsibility of command. Ed never made decisions easily and often went out of his way to avoid upsetting situations. He wanted to be liked and admired and never took criticism well. He obviously dreaded the kind of scrutiny that drove Cooley and other Philadelphia captains from the city. Initially, during home games, he shared the captaincy with shortstop Monte Cross. It was not until the team was on the road that Delahanty was comfortable enough to take charge.[21]

The change inspired the team's play, but the pressure on Delahanty detracted from his hitting. He continued to lead Cleveland's Jesse Burkett for the league's batting honors, despite a mild slump and an injured ankle. Nevertheless, when the Phillies, under their new captain, returned from a successful western road trip, expectations were high. The team was only a game and a half behind second-place Boston, and with the Quaker City decorated for a grand military review for President McKinley, flags and banners were on display at the railway station. Impressed by the setting, Ed Delahanty remarked tongue-in-cheek, "I know the cranks would be tickled to death over the way we trimmed the western gazabels [dashing young men-about-town] but I never thought they would enthuse in this way. I tell you it is great." At that moment, a teammate playfully tossed a bat bag at "Captain Ed" which sent the laughing players scurrying out of the station.[22] The optimism and all the levity were premature. Turbulent rip tides were threatening National League baseball, forces that would disorient the great batsman and leave him far from safe shores.

These disruptive conditions were set in motion by the "pooling practices" of Cleveland. By June 1899, baseball attendance in Delahanty's hometown had fallen to a few hundred per game. National League owners complained that they could not clear $25 a game in Cleveland, a situation which moved the Robison brothers to play all their games on the road. Their fate was shared by the Louisville franchise, whose president, Barney Dreyfuss, claimed losses of $200 per day. In a three-game series with Delahanty's Phillies at the end of August, Louisville took in only $300. Dreyfuss reacted with an announcement that he would follow Cleveland's example and finish the season on the road. These crippling trends also affected the weakened Baltimore and small-market Washington franchises. Speculation posed that the National League would become an eight-team league. These prospects played into the hands of opportunistic men, such as Ban Johnson, the president of the Western League. A former sportswriter, the thirty-five-year-old Johnson saw an opportunity to expand his franchise base by moving into former or failing National League cities. If successful, Johnson could create a rival major league that could ignite the conditions and temptations that ensnared Delahanty a decade ago.

◔ While events that were to shape Ed Delahanty's destiny were developing, his brothers pursued their baseball dreams in Allentown, Pennsylvania. Although their team enjoyed good attendance in their new ballpark, the financially troubled Atlantic League closed its doors in August. Until the league's demise, the hard-playing Delahantys performed well when they were healthy and not injured.

THE BASE BALL FAMILY OF DELEHANTYS.

JAMES DELEHANTY — FATHER

JIM DELEHANTY

FRANK DELEHANTY

WILLIAM DELEHANTY

TOM DELEHANTY

JOE DELEHANTY

ED DELEHANTY

FAMILY OF BALL PLAYERS.

Without question the greatest base ball family in the country is the Delehanty family. James Delehanty of Cleveland is the father of more good players than any man in the United States. Six of his sons have won fame on the diamond, four of them in the big leagues.

Ed Delehanty was the greatest of them all. He was with the Philadelphia club in

State team, and is one of the hardest hitters in the league.

Frank Delehanty got his start with the Montgomery team, played in Syracuse and was with the New York Americans before being traded to the Cleveland club.

Jim Delehanty began with the Little Rock club, went to the Chicago Nationals, then to Boston, then to Cincinnati and this year was sold to the St. Louis Browns.

Tom Delehanty played with Toronto, Atlanta, Detroit and Seattle, and last year was with the Williamsport team of the

Delahanty men. *Washington Star*, June 9, 1907.

JAMES DELEHANTY —FATHER

James Delahanty, Ed's father. *Washington Star*, June 9, 1907.

Ed Delahanty standing behind George English, 1887 postcard.
Courtesy of Randall Papers, Mobile, Alabama.

Detail of 1887 Phillies team picture (*left to right*):
unknown, George Wood, Jimmy Fogarty, Harry Wright, John Clements.
Courtesy of J. Casway and New York Public Library.

Ed Delahanty, 1888.
Courtesy of Randall Papers,
Mobile, Alabama.

Al Reach, Phillies
president. *Reach
Baseball Guide*, 1890.

John Rogers,
Phillies treasurer.
Courtesy of J. Casway.

Phillies at spring training, Jacksonville, Florida, 1890. Delahanty seated on step next to a young boy. Courtesy of J. Casway.

Ed Delahanty, from detail of 1892 Phillies team photo. Courtesy of National Baseball Hall of Fame Library.

Wedding portrait of
Ed and Norine
Delahanty, October
1894. Courtesy of
Randall Papers,
Mobile, Alabama.

Norine Delahanty,
c. 1894–95.
Courtesy of
Randall Papers,
Mobile, Alabama.

Florence Delahanty,
c. 1902. Courtesy of
Randall Papers,
Mobile, Alabama.

Delahanty family,
c. 1896
(left to right):
Tommy, Jimmy,
Ed, Kate, Florence,
Bridget, Norine.
Courtesy of
Randall Papers,
Mobile, Alabama.

Baltimore Orioles
players, mid 1890s
(left to right):
Willie Keeler,
John McGraw,
Joe Kelley, and
Hugh Jennings.
Courtesy of National
Baseball Hall of Fame
Library.

Ed Delahanty
and Bill Shettsline,
detail of 1899
Phillies team
picture.
Courtesy of
National Baseball
Hall of Fame
Library.

WAITING THEIR TURN. DELAHANTY AT BAT

Ed Delahanty at morning batting practice. *Philadelphia Inquirer*, April 23, 1899.

Tommy Delahanty.
Courtesy of Randall Papers,
Mobile, Alabama.

Jimmy Delahanty, 1909.
Courtesy of Randall Papers,
Mobile, Alabama.

Frank Delahanty, 1909.
Piedmont cigarette card.

Joe Delahanty.
Courtesy of Randall Papers,
Mobile, Alabama.

William Delahanty, 1907.
Courtesy of J. Casway.

DELAHANTY AND LAJOIE
The $30,000 Stars of the Base Ball World

These Wonderful Batters of the "Phillies," for Whom the Most Extravagant Offers Have Been Made and Refused, Unite in Praising the Value and Efficacy of

STUART'S DYSPEPSIA TABLETS

"Stuart's Dyspepsia Tablets are a powerful digester, preventing acidity and discomfort of any kind after eating. Keeping the stomach in prime condition. I would not be without them. If you have stomach troubles try one or two after meals, you'll be delighted."

E. J. DELAHANTY.

"It has been my experience that Stuart's Dyspepsia Tablets never fail to cure all stomach troubles such as Gas and Fermentation, Sour Stomach, Biliousness, Sleeplessness, Constipation or in fact any kind of stomach trouble. I heartily recommend them to travellers as a help to perfect health on the road."

N. LAJOIE.

STUART'S DYSPEPSIA TABLETS are for sale at all Druggists at 50 cents a box.

Ed Delahanty–Napoleon Lajoie advertisement.
Philadelphia Inquirer, June 20, 1900.

Delahanty family house on Phelps Street, Cleveland, Ohio. *Cleveland Press*, July 8, 1903.

Ed Delahanty and family, c. 1900. *Cleveland Press*, July 8, 1903.

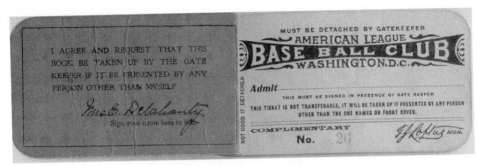

Norine Delahanty season ticket book, no. 26, 1903.
Courtesy of J. Casway.

Envelope addressed by Ed Delahanty to his wife, April 14, 1903.
Norine wrote on corner, "This your father hand writing here."
Courtesy of J. Casway.

Ed Delahanty, Washington Senators, 1903.
Courtesy of Randall Papers, Mobile, Alabama.

International railroad bridge, looking south toward the United States.
Courtesy of J. Casway.

Early in May, Tommy hurt the middle finger of his left hand and had surgery. A month later, he reinjured the finger and had part of it amputated. Tommy returned to Cleveland after the mishap, having played in only 54 games. He batted .333 and did well enough again at second base to attract the attention of a few National League clubs.

Before Tommy's season-ending injury, brother Jimmy badly sprained his ankle and was out of the lineup for about a month. The young Delahanty, noted more for his fielding, earned the praise of Manager Billy Sharsig. He declared that Jimmy was the best young shortstop he had seen. Most everyone raved about his arm, and one columnist said he covered "as much ground as a circus tent." Despite hitting .250 in 59 games, he was showing improvement at the plate.

The brother coming closest to be "made of almost as good material" as "Big Ed" was Joe Delahanty. Playing without his brothers for long stretches of the season, Joe performed like an "old leaguer." His defense in left field was excellent, and he led the team in batting, finishing sixth in the league with a .344 average. He also played in every game and hit an astounding number of triples. In one stretch of twenty games, he connected for twenty triples, and ended the year with 30 three-base hits in 86 Atlantic League games.[23] His performance attracted the attention of at least four National League teams. But Joe's chances of advancing were impaired by the anticipated availability of players from soon-to-be disbanded National League franchises. Unwilling to risk his fate on the faltering fortunes of the National League, Joe chose to stay the following season with his brothers and the paternal Sharsig in a reorganzied Atlantic League. With the boys committed to returning to Allentown, a fifth brother, the seventeen-year-old Frank, decided on a baseball career.

The signing of Frank Delahanty did not sit well with his mother. Mrs. Delahanty still hoped that her remaining sons would pursue more respectable occupations. But as in Jimmy Delahanty's case, Bridget relented and let Frank play ball closer to home. Mother Delahanty's conflicted attention may have been affected by Tommy's decision to open a "wet-goods" emporium (liquor store) in Cleveland. It was evident that Bridget could not impede the lure of baseball or the hype her sons attracted in the sporting press. Newspapers heralded the inherited talents of her boys, and to their way of thinking, one or more of the brothers could follow in the footsteps of her celebrated oldest son, the new Philadelphia team captain.[24]

◯ Delahanty's Phillies remained competitive despite the loss of Lajoie and the disruption of Cooley's discharge. By Labor Day, Philadelphia and Boston were battling for second place, 7 games behind Hanlon's Superbas. The Phillies had twenty-one home games left and were hopeful of earning Colonel Rogers' prize money. Ed Delahanty shared this confidence. He had worked hard to restore the team's harmony and altered his batting to meet the club's needs. Without Lajoie or Sam Thompson hitting behind him, and Elmer Flick sidelined by a bad ankle for twenty-seven games, Del knew he would get fewer pitches to hit. He adjusted by "dumping" the ball over the infield. Ed said if outfielders were going to play him deep, he would take advantage of his reputation as a heavy batter and do more place-hitting.[25] During the last thirty games of the year, Delahanty batted .434, stroking 37 singles out of 49 base hits. He had a fourteen-game hitting streak in mid-September and batted safely in 26 out of 30 games. Ed Delahanty also moved ahead of Jesse Burkett and Willie Keeler in the race for the batting championship.

Delahanty's successes were again tempered by off-field distractions. His business venture with Billy Shettsline did not materialize after the property deal fell through. Ed was also affected by the tragic death of the wife of his good friend John McGraw; she died from a ruptured appendix. The suddenness of her passing and McGraw's subsequent melancholy were unsettling to Delahanty and many of John McGraw's associates.

Delahanty also was playing with a bad ankle when the Phillies took on the Beaneaters in a struggle for second place. After taking two games, the Phillies were tied with Boston just as ill-timed injuries and John Rogers' obstinacy impeded their progress. With Delahanty and Flick playing on tender ankles and Lajoie still limping, the Phillies next suffered the loss of Roy Thomas. Injured by a undisclosed off-field "accident," Thomas could not play in the rest of the Boston games. Shettsline and Delahanty favored reinstating a healthy and sober Dick Cooley. The plan was for the former captain to play center field and resume his old leadoff spot in the lineup.

But Rogers would have none of these stratagems. The lame Lajoie went to center field and Pearce "What's the Use" Chiles played first base. At the cost of his team gaining second place, Rogers would not allow Dick Cooley to play again for the Phillies.[26] The result was a 6 to 0 loss. Delahanty had a single and triple in four at-bats; Lajoie managed only a single. With the Beaneaters back in second place, the concluding four games moved to Boston.

In this decisive series, the vaunted Phillies' batters failed to hit. Earlier in the season, Willie Keeler reminded people that, when Philadelphia was not hitting, their play was weak.[27] This evaluation proved correct, as the Phillies split the series with two closely contested shutout losses. In these critical games, Lajoie went 3 for 15, Chiles batted 1 for 17, and Delahanty hit 8 for 16. With no offensive support behind him, Captain Delahanty's Phillies finished third and lost their chance for Rogers' $2,500 second-place prize money. What should have been Delahanty's most satisfying year, turned into another sour and disheartening season. The Phillies had moved from sixth place to within a game of second. They ended the year at 94 and 58, their greatest total of season victories, 9 games behind the restocked champions from Brooklyn.

The loss of money was offset by an exhibition series with Hanlon's pennant-winning Superbas. Six games were arranged by team captains Ed Delahanty and Joe Kelley. Delahanty's ankle was bothering him, and he missed the last two games. Since the clubs split the series, no one was entitled to the 75 percent share of the gate receipts. The money was to be divided and awarded at a planned post-season celebration.[28]

At Brooklyn's Academy of Music on Saturday night, October 21, both teams attended an Irish-studded gala. In between the entertaining vaudeville acts, such as William Cahill's reciting of "Casey at the Bat" and James Byrne's singing "Off to Philadelphia," awards and acknowledgments were presented. The champion Superbas were lauded by former heavyweight champions John L. Sullivan and James J. Corbett, and Hanlon presented Joe Kelley a $2,500 check for the players to divide. A similar amount, the size of Rogers' second-place prize money, was given beforehand to Ed Delahanty. Hanlon did not neglect the Philadelphia players, who occupied their own front box. He said the Phillies had great players and would be a team to reckon with in 1900. He followed these words by introducing the league's batting champion, Ed Delahanty. Del came to the front of the box and bowed politely to the excited audience. It was a fitting tribute to the end of Delahanty's brilliant season.[29]

The year 1899 was Ed's greatest campaign. With the exception of home runs, he exceeded all his feats of 1893–95. Del led the league in batting with a .416 mark and he topped baseball in slugging average (.582), hits (242), doubles (54), RBIs (137), and total bases (335). In runs scored, he was five behind (135) league-leading John McGraw. His stolen bases dropped to 30, but defensively Delahanty played a brilliant left field. He made only 10 errors and had 26 assists. Often playing hurt, Delahanty missed only six games.

Some critics gave Ed his due reluctantly because he was an "old-fashioned slugger," who was not a "brainy worker of pitchers" such as Burkett, Keeler, McGraw, or Duffy.[30] League President Nick Young said Delahanty's championship "beggars belief" since he clearly out-distanced bunters and slap-hitters like two-time leader Willie Keeler.[31] Some detractors went so far as to remind the baseball public that Burkett's malaria and Keeler's bad ankle affected their performances.[32] But *Sporting Life* marveled at Delahanty's achievement of breaking the Burkett-Keeler string of batting titles.[33] Drawn into the debate, Delahanty acknowledged how difficult it was to compete against the so-called "scientific batsmen" and confessed that his concessions to place-hitting helped earn him his first batting crown.[34]

During Delahanty's amazing season, he used only two bats. One broke in early July, and the other lasted the season. Del prided himself about the selection and care of bats. He preferred hardwood bats of the "old school" and, like Lajoie and Wagner, wanted his slugging tools to be long and heavy-barreled. These bats were turned and made for him by a Cleveland carpenter. His batting clubs, each weighing between 45 and 50 ounces, contrasted with the light and smaller types used by Burkett and Keeler.[35] With his favorite bats in hand, Delahanty had done what he could to keep the ill-fated Phillies' offense productive.

Boston's manager Frank Selee regarded the Phillies as a very dangerous and potent ball club. Their strength, he said, came from batting, sparked by their "two artillerymen," Delahanty and Lajoie. Selee remarked that both men "take a [Jim] Jeffries lead at the ball."[36] Lajoie's injury, he felt, was the critical blow to a team that

dismissed Cooley, lost Orth to illness, and had suffered the untimely absences of other key players. Captain Delahanty was the
Phillies' one assured batter, who defended his team by saying that
no one could fault this ball club for not playing as a unit. In Delahanty's estimation the players worked hard and put aside individual
goals during an injury-riddled year.[37]

Delahanty did have a supportive cast in 1899. Rookie Roy
Thomas had an exceptional first year. He missed only the last two
games in Boston and batted .325. He scored 137 runs, walked 115
times, and stole 42 bases. Elmer Flick hit .342 and had 98 RBIs,
while shortstop Monte Cross played every game and kept the changing infield together. Napoleon Lajoie played in only 76 games and
hit .378 with 70 RBIs and 70 runs scored. On the mound, Piatt,
Donahue, and Fraser each won 20 games, and Al Orth finished
with a 14 and 3 mark and a 2.49 ERA. Young Bill Bernhard won
12 games and held the opposition to 2.65 runs per game.

The Phillies' successes and travails paled when compared to
what first-year manager John McGraw experienced in Baltimore.
His ball club, having lost its Irish nucleus of Keeler, Kelley, Jennings, and pitchers "Doc" McJames and Jim Hughes to Hanlon's
Brooklyn Superbas, finished 6 games behind the Phillies. McGraw's
Orioles were in the pennant race until the end of August, when his
wife died. Playing in only 117 games, McGraw led the league in
runs scored (140) and base-on-balls (124). He also finished third
behind Delahanty in batting with a .391 mark. But McGraw's successes, and the instability of the Baltimore franchise, propelled the
young manager into the maelstrom of baseball's pending wars. His
actions also affected the course of Ed Delahanty's remaining career.

◯ The turbulence that set Delahanty and McGraw on their fateful orbit took shape at the end of the 1899 season. Although league
attendance totals increased by almost 200,000, eight of the twelve
franchises lost patronage. The largest increases were the reconstituted teams from St. Louis and Brooklyn and the Phillies, whose
attendance rose by 120,000.[38] At first, it was reported that all franchises made money, and Cleveland broke even. This prosperity
was immediately challenged by disclosures that most ball teams finished in debt, collectively losing over $100,000. John Rogers' Phillies

allegedly made $65,000, more than a half of the league's total profit.[39] Such figures did not bode well for the future of major league baseball.

Behind the flagging attendance and revenues was the growing disenchantment with National League baseball. People were upset by the callous management of interlocking teams and the acceptance of uncompetitive ball clubs. As the decade drew to a close, the well-being of baseball and the course of Ed Delahanty's career would come down to decisions made in the closed-door boardrooms of the National League. Into this conflicted realm of failing franchises and growing deficits came the challenges of reorganization, new rival leagues, and another players' association. It was a full buffet of indigestible problems.

The most immediate issue was the financial state of the National League. Throughout the season, rumors had been circulating about the downsizing of the league. At the December league meetings, the Committee on Reduction recommended that four clubs (Cleveland, Washington, Louisville, and Baltimore) be bought out. Their players were to be auctioned to the surviving franchises. The magnates also took steps to secure these baseball territories until the two-year buyouts were complete. The details of this absorption would be finalized in the spring meetings. In the interim, the sport's autocrats, with their petty vanities, battled over compensation, jurisdictions, and ballplayers. An example of their manipulations was the demise of the Louisville Colonels. Their director was thirty-four-year-old Barney Dreyfuss, a German-Jewish immigrant, who prospered in his cousins' liquor business. Unwilling to be bought out of baseball, he was allowed to purchase the floundering Pittsburgh club. Soon after the December meetings, in anticipation of the league's reductions, he transferred the rights of his star players—Honus Wagner, Rube Waddell, Fred Clarke, Tommy Leach, and Bert Cunningham—to Pittsburgh.[40]

Colonel Rogers supported the proposed realignment but tried to resolve the pending consolidation scramble. In a rare burst of ingenuity, he recommended adding new franchises, thereby creating two eight-team leagues. In this way, the expenses of travel and the turmoil of discord could be eliminated.[41] Al Reach concurred with Rogers and openly voiced his support for New York's Andrew Freedman and his changed stand against syndicate baseball.[42] The urgency of reform was heralded by the appearance of two rival leagues and the leverage they offered to ballplayers.

Challenging the National League was Ban Johnson's Western League that coveted the midwestern cities of Cleveland, Chicago, and St. Louis. Following Johnson's lead was a group of disaffected baseball men, Chris von der Ahe, Cap Anson, and John McGraw. The latter group wanted to re-create the old American Association. At first, the two proposed leagues tried to work together, but a failed consolidation in October moved Ban Johnson to broaden his appeal by renaming his organization the American League. Reacting to this threat, the National League made a fateful mistake. They initially believed Johnson and his supporters were more accommodating and saw the American League as a buffer to the more intrepid new American Association.[43]

Thanks to the action of Cap Anson and John McGraw, the Phillies were alerted early to the association's actions. The American Association had targeted disaffected star players and held out large advances and $3,000 salaries to players such as Napoleon Lajoie and Cleveland's Jesse Burkett. When Ed Delahanty was asked about the new association, the old "triple jumper" said he only knew what he read in the newspapers. Content for the moment with his position in Philadelphia, Del commented that he was "not much interested anyway."[44]

As team captain, Ed Delahanty kept silent and distanced himself from these proceedings. He was occupied with domestic matters and could be seen about town in the company of his family and new little terrier dog. While visiting his family in Cleveland, Delahanty was interviewed in a home furnishing store. The batting champion said he was in town for a short while and intended to return to Philadelphia before the holidays. He remarked that he enjoyed living in Philadelphia and believed next year's team would make a serious run for the pennant.[45] At the same time he was unhappy with the new wording of his unsigned 1900 contract and distraught that his former teammate and friend Jack Taylor, his health and career broken by excessive drinking, lay dying of kidney failure in his Staten Island home. But concerning his team, Ed Delahanty had every reason to be optimistic and upbeat. His team had talented ballplayers, and the prospect of strengthening their club in a new eight-team league appealed to the Phillies' captain.[46]

13

The "Hoodoo" Season

The end of the century excited the imagination of people who were stirred by changing calendar dates. Some welcomed the new era with optimism, and others greeted the twentieth century with ignorant foreboding. The centenary year of 1900 would have its share of trauma: the worsening condition of the Boer War in South Africa, the violent outburst of the Boxer Rebellion in China, and a devastating hurricane that decimated towns along the Gulf of Mexico. In contrast, the Paris Exposition and the second Olympics opened, a new presidential election year began, and Queen Victoria's visit to Ireland raised hopes for political reform.

Baseball, too, was divided between the poles of hope and despair. The national pastime was entering a new and turbulent period. After a decade of monopolistic self-indulgence, the secure world of the old league was shattered. The next few years saw ballplayers scattered to new franchises in a rival league, changes that set in motion events that eclipsed the Emerald Age of Baseball.

Captain Delahanty was not truthful when he said that he had no interest in the upstart leagues. Ed followed their dealings closely and avoided the pitfalls that embarrassed him a decade ago. Del was unhappy with Colonel Rogers' meddling and tight-fisted finances.

He knew the Phillies were a profitable organization and could afford to pay their star performers more than the $2,400 league maximum. In the eyes of Delahanty and his teammates, Rogers was a petty and self-righteous tightwad. Rogers saw things differently. He believed his players were spoiled and overindulged. After more than a decade of dealing with Rogers, "the only Del" welcomed the bargaining leverage of the new leagues.

Both the American League and the new American Association looked covetously on Philadelphia and its ballplayers. At the head of their shopping lists were Delahanty and Lajoie.[1] Both players denied interest, but their behavior exhibited contrary motives. At the association's meetings held in Philadelphia from January 30 to February 2, the curious gathered like bees to flowers. In the lobbies and hallways of the Continental and Hanover Hotels, Delahanty and his teammates circulated. Joining Del and his friends were former Philadelphia captain Bill Hallman and Delahanty's old brotherhood mates, Cub Stricker, Art Irwin, and a sober John Clements. Unlike Delahanty, many of these men were not everyday visitors. Del claimed he was using the conference to renew his acquaintances with Anson, McGraw, and Tommy McCarthy. The real intent of the players was the discovery of their market value. Delahanty's former manager George Stallings, who now managed Detroit in Ban Johnson's American League, had warned that if the leagues went to war, Delahanty and Lajoie might be worth $3,000 a year.[2] Coincidentally, neither man had signed their new contracts.

The reason for this omission reflected the manipulative arrogance of John Rogers and his peers. Following the lead of Boston club president Arthur Soden, contracts were not sent out before March 1, as required under Article 22 of the National Agreement. Instead, players were notified that they were still bound by their former contracts. This premise was based on Rogers' "renewal option" clause, stating that players could be held over from season to season by simply telling them before October 15 of their intended renewal.[3] This tactic bypassed or, as Rogers indicated, superseded the more controversial and legally unreliable "reserve clause." To the magnates' way of thinking, this strategy kept players in tow during the protracted struggle with the new leagues by binding players through their previously signed contracts.[4] These maneuvers were debated in the press,[5] but their implementation soured ballplayers toward their National League employers and encouraged men such as Ban Johnson that ballplayers might listen and perhaps accept rival offers for their services.

Two of the targeted players, Delahanty and Lajoie, were spending a great deal of time together in the off-season. If the Phillies' front office believed that Del might temper the headstrong Lajoie, they did not fully appreciate Delahanty's character. Ed was not always the most prudent or strong-willed man and needed some supervision of his own. Often, his young wife provided this support, when she accompanied him on short road trips.[6] Another concern was that Delahanty never worked in the off-season, and after his unrealized business venture with Billy Shettsline, Ed had time and a volatile Lajoie on his hands. This was a troublesome combination because Lajoie was one of the city's most eligible bachelors and had a taste for hard liquor. At first, things went well. For example, both players joined Shettsline in a local chapter of the Fraternal Order of Eagles, an organization dedicated to civic and community relief.[7] By February, Delahanty and Lajoie turned their attention to getting into shape by playing handball at the Pythian and Caledonian Athletic Clubs in downtown Philadelphia.[8]

Both men were expecting productive seasons and believed their team could finally make a serious run at the league championship. As in past years, the problem for Delahanty's Phillies was management's roster decisions. Their immediate concern was the status of the repentant former captain, Dick Cooley. Then Cooley's replacement, Bill Goeckel, retired to attend to his new law practice in Wilkes-Barre, Pennsylvania. His departure was followed by third baseman Bill Lauder's announcement that he would rather coach at Brown University and sell jewelry than play again for Colonel Rogers. Another dissenter was shortstop Monte Cross, who was upset with Rogers for not giving him what he believed was a well-deserved bonus.[9] Like many of his teammates, Cross reported to spring training without a new contract. Faced with these uncertainties, Shettsline and Captain Delahanty considered their alternatives.

The immediate solution was to go to spring training and again try Delahanty at first base.[10] Many questioned this move. Barney Dreyfuss of Pittsburgh said it would spoil another good man and predicted Del would be "put on the run the same as Cooley."[11] The *Sporting News* concurred and reminded readers that Delahanty had "a mortal fear of injury" and with his hot temperament, the infield was not a good place for him.[12] The *Inquirer*'s Frank Hough thought otherwise. He was confident that Ed Delahanty could make the shift, a choice made better because he believed it was wiser than moving Lajoie back to first and looking for a new second baseman.[13] Delahanty had mixed feelings about going to first base. He looked forward to playing alongside Lajoie and placing himself, as team captain, closer to the action. But the switch disrupted a productive outfield and brought with it the pressures of infield play.

Ed Delahanty's choice for filling his spot in left field was his old Phelps Street neighbor, young Tommy Leach of Pittsburgh. The Pirates turned down any offer for Leach, and the Phillies settled on the fleet-footed Jimmy "The Rabbit" Slagle from the defunct Washington baseball team.[14] Resolving the third base vacancy, the Phillies tried for John McGraw, who had gone to the St. Louis Browns from Brooklyn after Hanlon and his partners closed out the Baltimore franchise. Unable to secure McGraw, the Phillies waited until after the season started and purchased Chicago's regular third baseman, Harry Wolverton.[15] These roster moves also reflected the changing condition of the national pastime.

Following the National League's buyout of their four failed franchises, Ban Johnson's American League, after promising to abide by the National Agreement, expanded into Chicago and Cleveland. Meanwhile, two of the militant supporters and franchise-brokers of the still-born American Association, John McGraw and Wilbert Robinson, were assigned to St. Louis. These transfers and other postcontraction schemes agitated the well-being of major league baseball.

Ed Delahanty had a bad feeling about the start of the season, and it had nothing to do with the typhoid outbreak in the city wards bordering on Fairmount Park. Like most ballplayers, Del was superstitious and uneasy when he learned that the ball club was scheduled to leave Philadelphia at 1:13 P.M. from track 13. Train #13 would have them in Charlotte, North Carolina, on March 13. Delahanty said it was a "hoodoo" that could not be ignored.[16] He and Lajoie, both still unsigned, gave the ball club a fright when they failed to show up at boarding gate #13. Instead, they greeted Shettsline and their teammates on the platform, having gotten on the train at an earlier stop.[17]

With the exception of the St. Patrick's Day celebrations that saw the Irish players dressed in green and Delahanty sporting a large Irish harp on his lapel, things did not start out well for the "hoodoo" training camp. Some of the equipment, including the new uniforms, had not arrived, and the cold, wet, and blustery weather upset the team's training schedules. Shettsline and Delahanty had to search out alternate workout sites. They made arrangements with the local YMCA, and with the support of the police chief, Delahanty obtained the use of the large assembly room at City Hall. A carpenter boarded up the windows, and Delahanty had his handball court. The Phillies also had to regrade and sod the ball field and, on a few occasions, practiced on an unused school lot.[18] To his credit, Captain Delahanty worked hard in running his first spring training camp. He maximized good weather conditions by practicing game situations. Players participated in unison and bunting was emphasized.[19] On his own, Delahanty worked on taking ground balls and relearning first base movements. At the plate, the batting champion picked up where he had left off. Playing against a nearby college team and the Phillies subs, Delahanty had two six-hit games and one seven-hit contest. But on too many mornings, it was so raw that Delahanty and his teammates could hardly move with all the clothing they wore. It was no wonder that they were anxious to leave Charlotte and get back to Philadelphia. Unfortunately, coming home brought with it a new round of problems and distractions.

Before the Phillies headed north, Samuel Gompers and the American Federation of Labor announced they would assist baseball players in organizing a protective union. From Washington, D.C., Gompers declared that if ballplayers were willing to affiliate with his union, he would do everything to support them against the "caprices of the magnates."[20] Delahanty and his teammates spent many an hour discussing the ramifications of Gompers' invitation.[21]

This situation was set in motion in the summer of 1899 when Chicago labor leaders were approached by unidentified ballplayers. One of the teams said to be ripe for organizing was the Phillies. A core of Philadelphia players were unhappy with Rogers' ploys and his "renewable option" tactic. Others were distressed by the way he treated the popular Dick Cooley. But the critical catalysts were the opportunities provided by the rival major leagues. In the weeks before the season opened, Ed Delahanty became a focus of discontent, a position unbecoming the captain of a John Rogers' team.

Delahanty's notoriety and predicament revolved around the machinations of fellow-Irishmen Ned Hanlon and John McGraw. Hanlon, manager of the champion Brooklyn team, knew that Hugh Jennings could no longer play shortstop and was growing suspicious of his dealings with John McGraw. Jennings and McGraw were equally upset with Hanlon's Brooklyn syndicate and his treatment of the Baltimore franchise. The sore-armed Jennings wanted to play first base and saw an opportunity to be a playing-manager in Philadelphia. Hanlon refused to sell Jennings to the Phillies, but offered to trade him for Delahanty or Lajoie. No one took the offer seriously. A few days later, Hanlon reversed himself and proposed $10,000 for Lajoie.[22] Not to be outdone by Brooklyn, Andrew Freedman of New York said he would buy either Lajoie or Delahanty for $15,000. Eventually, both teams shifted their offers and bid $8,000 for each player. The *Inquirer* said if the Phillies sold Delahanty for that figure, they should go out of business.[23] Rogers declared that the offers were "too ridiculous to even merit consideration."[24]

Although the deals were never likely, they inspired new personas. Delahanty and Lajoie were depicted in the *Philadelphia Press* as the "$15,000 Stars."[25] More than a month later, a full-page advertisement in the *Inquirer* had the "$30,000 stars of the Baseball World," Delahanty and Lajoie, endorsing Stuarts Dyspepsia Tablets for upset stomachs.[26] These expressions of value did not sit well with the expectations of trade unionism. Stirred by their inflamed senses of worth, the two star players took advantage of the confusion over Rogers' contracts and held out for more money.

Not to be overlooked as a backdrop to these dealings were the unprecedented bargaining stances taken by John McGraw and Wilbert Robinson. Although the specifics of their deals with St. Louis were not yet known, it was evident they were asking for terms that far exceeded those sought by Delahanty and Lajoie. If later disclosures are to be believed, the contracts of McGraw and Robinson exceeded the league's maximum and had no option clauses. These agreements did not endear intransigent National League owners to their ballplayers,[27] particularly dissatisfied unsigned players and the two striking Philadelphia superstars.

Eight days before the start of the regular season, Flick, Thomas, Douglass, Cross, Bernhard, Lajoie, and Delahanty had not returned their contracts. Colonel Rogers brashly asserted that all players knew about the three-year renewal clause in the 1899 contract. Rogers said no player could play more than five games unless their contracts were turned back. "We want only men on our team who are good, loyal, honest and honorable. Only when we find they are traitors will we consent to sell them and we don't believe we have any of this class. Any man who went south at our expense and would strike would be in the position of receiving money under false pretences." Rogers said Lajoie and Delahanty have no serious grievances and was optimistic that everything would work out well.[28]

Al Reach was not as rhetorical. He related that Delahanty needed only to work out his compensation as team captain.[29] In management's eyes, a great deal of attention was unnecessarily focused on the renewal terms of the contracts and the financial arrangements of the behavior postscripts.[30] Delahanty acknowledged he was okay with the new clauses and wanted a "straight National League contract," but hinted that the ball club knew what he wanted—a larger guaranteed salary. "I'm so disgusted that if I could get a good-paying position in any other business I'd quit baseball altogether, and what's more I'd give a guarantee never again to put on a uniform or even see another game."[31] Frank Hough, in his Sunday sports column, disclosed that Delahanty and Lajoie wanted and deserved $3,000 salaries.[32]

With the contract deadline approaching, every Phillie, except Delahanty and Lajoie, relented and signed their 1900 contracts. Their teammates' actions did not dissuade Delahanty and Lajoie from their holdout. Captain Delahanty would not practice and said the team should not look for him on opening day. An *Inquirer* editorial took the position that a salary dispute was not ordinarily a matter of public concern. But ballplayers were public figures who were important to the economy and disposition of the community. The editor urged both sides to settle their differences amicably.[33]

As opening day approached, it was inevitable that the conciliatory Billy Shettsline would intercede. A close friend of Delahanty, Shettsline assumed direct talks with his ballplayers. He knew Delahanty had already turned down two separate contracts, $2,400 for the season and $600 for the captaincy. Delahanty told his manager that the $600 was not guaranteed if he was replaced as captain. Shettsline told Delahanty he would assure both contracts. But Del replied that Shettsline might not be the manager for the entire season, and therefore regardless of his captaincy, he wanted a regular $3,000 National League contract. The Philadelphia manager also received the same $3,000 demand from Napoleon Lajoie.[34] Rogers countered with the threat of a trade, and with Ned Hanlon in town, speculation erupted.[35]

It was not reported how the controversy was resolved, but Delahanty and Lajoie rejoined the team and boarded the train for the Boston opener. It was learned sometime later that Delahanty got his $3,000 guaranteed contract, and Lajoie signed for $2,600. The story that emerged behind these signings was inconsistent, and it was obvious all the parties were not being truthful. Delahanty got his $3,000, but that total included his guaranteed captain's stipend. If Rogers or Shettsline told Lajoie he received the same money as Delahanty, they were lying.

According to testimony given in a 1901 lawsuit against Napoleon Lajoie, the dispute was settled when Shettsline met with the players at Delahanty's home. The question remains that if both players agreed on terms, as Shettsline indicated, why did Delahanty sign his contract immediately, and Lajoie wait until he got to the ballpark? The answer may be that Lajoie was signing a supplemental contract for $200 that he believed put him on par with Delahanty. When Lajoie was asked whether he read or had a copy of these contracts, he answered negatively. He said that every request for copies was ignored. It was only after Lajoie saw Delahanty's first paycheck that he confronted Rogers about more money. Lajoie later contradicted himself. He swore that he was not aware that Delahanty was team captain or that Del's salary was larger than his. In the end, Delahanty received the team's top salary, and Rogers, having refused Lajoie's demands, set in motion discord that would undermine the franchise.[36]

Delahanty's role in these proceedings is not very clear. He was never called to testify, and it is doubtful he was part of any conspiracy. Ed got his $3,000 salary in a form that satisfied him, but it is doubtful that he knew of Shettsline's promises to Lajoie. Since there was no evidence of a rift between the players, it was likely each party tolerated the others' interests and agenda. The events and claims of the following season verified that all parties had not been above-board in these negotiations. Neither was management's credibility enhanced by John Rogers' mean-spirited treatment of Dick Cooley. It was a public relations disaster and an intimidating message at a time when the National League owners needed to be attentive to the sentiments of their players.

Having not received a contract, Dick Cooley reminded Colonel Rogers of the yearly obligations of the "option clause." He believed he was still part of the club and asked Bill Shettsline whether he should report for spring training. Told that his presence was not required, Cooley waited on the pleasure of John Rogers.[37] The Phillies entertained offers from other teams, but Rogers would not move Cooley unless he could get fair market value.[38] The former Phillies captain finally rested his case and appeal on the three-year renewal clause of his former contract.[39] As the Delahanty-Lajoie episode ended and the season began, the Cooley case exploded into editorial diatribes.

The *Philadelphia Inquirer*'s sports editor, Frank Hough, an ardent supporter of players' rights, said that Rogers acted in an autocratic and "czar-like manner." His treatment of Cooley was un-American and went against Thomas Jefferson's "self-evident truths." The Phillies "admit they do not want him. They won't release him and yet they won't pay him the salary named in his last year's contract. And all of this in the name of sport!"[40] He asked how working men who support baseball could accept a situation where a man is denied the privilege of earning a living at his trade.[41] The *Sporting Life* entered the fray and said Cooley was being handled like a Russian or Italian contract laborer.[42] But with no National Agreement magnate willing to go against the Cooley ban, the Phillies stood their ground. Hough ultimately appealed to club president Al Reach and asked how he would have tolerated this kind of treatment.[43] Within a day of Hough's entreaty, Dick Cooley was sold to the reconstituted Pittsburgh club for $1,000. Meanwhile, as each one of these self-imposed dramas unfolded, the Phillies opened the season in Boston, winning with two runs in the ninth inning, 19 to 17.

The new baseball year brought with it significant changes. Two of these reforms affected the structure of the league, and two influenced how the game was played. The league changes were motivated by the financial shortfalls of previous seasons. After the league reduced itself to eight teams, they cut their schedule to 140 games. But neither of these alterations had the desired effect. The loss of traditional baseball cities—Washington, Baltimore, Louisville, and Cleveland—had two unsettling consequences: it attracted ambitious new league prospectors and incurred debts that outweighed the anticipated benefits and cost reductions.

As for reforms of how the game was played, the return to a one-umpire system proved a step backward. Magnates blamed this action on a lack of competent officials, but it was more a product of miserly owners trying to save a few dollars. The experiment alienated fans and overworked the umpires. The introduction of a five-sided home plate, however, did promote better officiating and tightened the strike zone. It was the only action taken in 1900 that benefited baseball.

Competing under these changes and conditions, Delahanty's Phillies got off to an impressive start. Philadelphia returned home for the second game in the Boston series, and before 14,000 fans, triumphed 5 to 4 in eleven innings. Playing first base, Delahanty had twenty-one putouts and one assist without committing an error. After the first thirteen games, the Phillies headed the league with a 10 and 3 mark. But Ed Delahanty played with a swollen thumb that hampered his hitting. Against Brooklyn and New York, he recaptured his batting stroke, batting 17 for 37 with four doubles and a triple. This hitting spree was the beginning of a nineteen-game streak, during which he batted .476. By the time his streak ended, the Phillies were 16 and 7, two games ahead of Brooklyn.

Although Ed did not make his first error until his eighth game, it was debated among the fans and press whether his move to the infield would be a "profitable experiment." One admirer believed that, since Delahanty "owns the town," his supporters would view his work "charitably." Another writer said that if columnists were not "kicking" about his play, he must be doing a good job.[44] Frank Hough commented that one could not teach "old dogs new tricks," but said Del could be a suitable and valuable member of the infield.[45] Shettsline concurred and said that it was doubtful that Delahanty would ever again see the outfield. Delahanty's assessment was a bit more apprehensive. "Well sometimes I like it and sometimes I don't. When things are coming easy and I am not in trouble down there I sort of like the job, but when things get mixed up at first base I wish I was in the outfield. I am really not throughly accustomed to the position. . . . Perhaps after I have played it awhile I will get stuck on it."[46]

Also in question was Delahanty's role as team captain. Ed initially proved to be more dutiful than was first imagined. No one confused him with John McGraw, Hugh Jennings, or John Montgomery Ward for spontaneous and clever leadership, but with front-office Billy Shettsline as manager, Del assumed responsibility for on-field decisions. Delahanty pleaded calls, developed strategies, and set the tone for a ballgame. Delahanty's problems did not come from his lack of baseball knowledge or experience, but rather from his style of play and disposition. Delahanty's temper, sulking, and affability were not a constructive combination. He had a tendency to overmanage and be too aggressive when less direction was necessary. On several occasions, his leadership came under question and rebuke.

Contesting calls and intimidating umpires were part of late nineteenth-century baseball. Often the protests of a "kicker" led to his ejection from a game. But artful antagonists such as John McGraw were calculating, and rarely was he expelled when his presence was required. This strategy sometimes was lost on Delahanty, especially when his explosive batting was needed in tight ballgames. After one of his ill-considered exits, a columnist lectured Delahanty that a leader had to be more circumspect in his conduct and should not let his actions weaken the team. "Keep in bounds, Ed," the commentator warned.[47]

Delahanty was sometimes reproached for his ill-advised game tactics. In the eleventh inning of a June 22 home game against Hanlon's Superbas, Delahanty's behavior was called "childish and disgusting."[48] It started after Ed hotly disputed an umpire's call. After his futile objections, Del returned to first base and seethed about the play. Two hits later, with Brooklyn in the lead, Delahanty decided to stall, hoping that darkness would end the game before the inning was complete. The Philadelphia reliever was directed by Del to walk the next three batters, who freely ran the bases and scored without any resistance. The next Brooklyn hitter deliberately swung and missed at three pitches above his head, but catcher McFarland dropped the third strike and threw the ball into right field. With protests coming from the Brooklyn bench, umpire Hank O'Day had enough of Delahanty's tactics and declared the game a forfeit. A riot almost ensued, and O'Day, not the Phillies captain, needed police protection. A local sportswriter described the stratagem as "inexpressively stupid and tactless," and reminded his readers that there was at least forty-five minutes of daylight left. The columnist called the tactic "baby playing," and suggested that it would not have been tolerated if Al Reach was in attendance.[49] Ed Delahanty never commented about the incident, and no fine or censure from the league or the club was forthcoming.

In the midst of Delahanty's misadventures, the Phillies suffered a debilitating setback, for which Ed bore some responsibility. On Decoration Day, the Phillies had returned from a successful western road trip comfortably in first place. The Quaker City was thrilled by the team's performance, and almost 30,000 people turned out to see their "pets" take two games from Chicago—5 to 2 and 15 to 3. The satisfaction of victory was short-lived. Sometime after the games, in a dispute over a baseball bat, Napoleon Lajoie bullied the "inoffensive" Elmer Flick. The big French-Canadian cursed his teammate and grabbed the bat from him. Before the players realized what had happened, a fight broke out. Punches were thrown, and Flick suffered bruised eyes. Ed Delahanty rushed over and separated the combatants. Unfortunately, Lajoie continued his ranting and lashed out again at Flick. The Phillies' right fielder ducked away from Lajoie's errant left hand which landed on a wooden washstand. When the ruckus was over, Lajoie had a broken thumb. He would miss five weeks of play.[50]

Delahanty was not to blame for Lajoie's assault. The Phillies' captain, however, was responsible for tolerating Lajoie's bullying behavior. According to clubhouse sources, Lajoie was like a "king pin among his teammates, much after the fashion of the biggest boy in the school who uses his superior strength to overawe his smaller associates."[51] Flick said Lajoie had been picking on him since last autumn, and many players confided that they would be relieved if the slugging second baseman played elsewhere.[52]

At first, the team reported that the players collided in the morning practice.[53] But the truth eventually emerged, and the impact of the scuffle was immediate and far-reaching. The incident left the surging Phillies in an unsettled position. Flick missed four games, and without Lajoie in the lineup, opposing teams pitched around Ed Delahanty. At the time of the clubhouse brawl, Lajoie was batting .401 and Delahanty was not far behind at .384.

Lajoie's damaging outburst coincided with reports out of China describing militiamen, known as Boxers, who attacked foreigners and Christians. The western countries acted swiftly to quell the crisis. But the Boxer Rebellion never distracted the imagination of the Philadelphia public like the Spanish-American War, which was unfortunate, because after Lajoie broke his thumb, injuries mounted, the team's performance declined, and Delahanty succumbed to the very pressures that unseated Dick Cooley.

Ed Delahanty had a great deal on his mind. In addition to the weighty burden of captaining a John Rogers team, Del was distracted by a rash of personal matters. One of Norine's sisters was terminally ill, his three brothers were soon to be displaced by the collapse of the Atlantic League, and a new Players' Protective Association was scheduled for a June 10 organization meeting in New York. Incredibly, Captain Delahanty was to be the Phillies' chief delegate; the other representatives were pitcher "Red" Donahue and seldom-used catcher Morgan Murphy.

The most important decision of the new Players' Association was whether they would affiliate with Samuel Gompers' American Federation of Labor. The union had given the players moral support and guidance, but ballplayers, even in an era that distrusted the "robber barons" of big business, were not ready to take a strong union stance. They hesitated about alienating the owners with A.F.L. craft union talk, a threat of strikes, and a new philosophy of "workplace democracy." Players, instead, saw the association as a potential bargaining chip in the forthcoming new league struggles. They wanted higher pay and better job security. Hugh Jennings, the secretary of the Protective Association, said the players desired "justice and fair dealing."[54]

It was ironic that the Phillies' team captain would be the club's representative at these proceedings. Despite his outward support for the status quo, Ed Delahanty remained a self-serving casualty of the brotherhood wars. He wanted a larger guaranteed salary commensurate with his on-field achievements and believed he could play off a union and the new leagues for his own advancement.

As in the old brotherhood conflict, Irish baseball players made up the largest constituency of the twenty-three representatives. More than half were Irish, and that number did not include John McGraw and Jimmy Ryan, who could not attend the proceedings. Among these ballplayers, only Delahanty and the absent Ryan had been active brotherhood members who performed in the Players' League. The players set their course by selecting Pittsburgh catcher Charlie Chief Zimmer president, Chicago pitcher Clark Griffith vice-president, and Jennings from Brooklyn as secretary. Annual dues and initiation fees were settled, and Gompers' offer to affiliate with the A.F.L. was politely rejected. The players decided to meet again in July to decide on a specific platform.[55]

Coinciding with the development of the Protective Association was the demise of the Atlantic League. Under the steady direction of Billy Sharsig and his Allentown backers, another attempt had been made at reestablishing the defunct league. With eight teams, one newly located in Philadelphia, it was hoped that a compact and solvent organization would avoid the pitfalls of the old league.[56] Each ball club put a $1,500 limit on their monthly payrolls and worked hard to promote community interest in their teams. Sharsig, who was starting his twenty-first year as a manager, believed Allentown, led by the charming and popular Delahanty brothers, would draw well and compete for the pennant.[57] But Allentown did not get off to a good start; and with inclement weather, attendance around the league slumped. The ball clubs tried to attract interest by hiring former heavyweight champion Jim Corbett to umpire games or play first base for home-playing teams. These promotions did little for the failing Atlantic League. By the first week of June, two clubs folded, a players' strike was narrowly averted, and the Philadelphia franchise relocated to Harrisburg, Pennsylvania.[58] On June 14, two more teams failed, and the remaining four clubs, including Allentown, approached the Eastern League for admittance.

Allentown tried to salvage its investment by selling the contracts of their best ballplayers. Tommy Delahanty, after hitting .317 in nineteen games, found himself back in Cleveland. Tom served a few games as a utility infielder for the new American League club in Cleveland, before joining up with a team in Youngstown, Ohio, in the Interstate League. After five games, the team was bought out and moved to Marion, Ohio, where he finished the season with a

.270 average. Jimmy Delahanty fared better. He was sold to Worcester, Massachusetts, in the Eastern League. The young Delahanty played 80 games at third base and shortstop and hit .281.

When Allentown went under, Joe Delahanty was leading the league in average [.469], triples [11], and hits [67]. After hearing nothing from Cincinnati in the National League, Joe returned with Tommy to Cleveland and stayed there until he got a position with Montreal in the Eastern League. Upset by his Allentown experiences, Joe did not regain his earlier form. In 54 games at Montreal he batted only .248. The breakup of the "Delahanty brotherhood"[59] capped a disappointing season for Ed Delahanty's siblings. But their disillusionment paled in comparison to what was in store for their famous older brother.

During the five weeks of Lajoie's absence, the Phillies went 12 and 17 and dropped into second place, 4½ games behind Brooklyn. Not even the excitement of the Republican National Convention in Philadelphia, which nominated Delahanty's friend, William McKinley, and young Theodore Roosevelt, could ignite the spirits of the Quaker City. Mediocre pitching and injuries to Wolverton, McFarland, and Douglass, coupled with unimpressive bench play, took their toll on the club's performance. Nevertheless, Delahanty remained productive and carried the brunt of the offense. It was only after the embarrassment of the forfeit game that things unraveled.

After the forfeit, the team went on an exhausting eighteen-game western road trip in a sweltering, oppressive Midwestern heat wave that made train travel unsettling to a team struggling to right itself. In the first ten games, the Phillies played listlessly and were shutout twice. They were 2 and 8 before Napoleon Lajoie, with a small plaster cast on his thumb, returned to the lineup. When the team arrived in Cincinnati after a two-day trip from St. Louis, Ed Delahanty took a step from which he never fully recovered.

It was reported that Captain Delahanty missed two games because of illness,[60] but it was apparent that Del had been drinking. No one can say for sure how temperate Delahanty had been over the last decade. There were no indications that he had a problem, and his name was never linked with the heavy liquor-drinking Phillies of the past. On the contrary, newspapers usually spoke of his moderation and good habits. Billy Shettsline, his manager and supportive friend for many years, asserted that Del rarely drank and added, "and then only under stress or some trouble real or imaginary."[61] However, his wife later said that Ed was a "spree" drinker. Norine Delahanty was never specific about whether this was a chronic problem that plagued his career or something that developed over the last few years of his life.[62] Binge drinking was not apparent in any pattern of Ed Delahanty's daily batting record up to the summer of 1900. Delahanty might have gone on "sprees" when the season was over, but nothing before the Cincinnati "illness" suggested sobriety problems.

It can only be conjectured that, by the time Delahanty got to Cincinnati, liquor had become an escape from the pressures of the stressful season. Billy Shettsline maintained the team's stance that Delahanty had not violated the curfew and was just feeling under the weather. The club reported that Del had been suffering from "colic cramps" on the trip from St. Louis. An attending doctor over-prescribed him with a remedy of brandy and herbs that worsened his condition. At this point, Delahanty allegedly went to bed around midnight, a "little the worse for his indiscretion." The next morning, stories circulated that Del had been thrown out of a local beer saloon. These reports greatly disturbed the Phillies' captain. In a lame apology for Delahanty, Charles Dryden, the reporter for the *North American*, who traveled with the club, wrote that not once in Ed's long career had the great batsman "side-stepped the path of rectitude nor sought the flowing bowl in business hours." Dryden went on to speak about Del's state of mind, the old gag of a "cramp colic," and the fact that Delahanty was "entitled to a great deal of consideration." The "real gripe . . . at the bottom of all of Del's woes" was never identified. Instead, the column was introduced with a Delahanty-inspired limerick:

> Not for me the ruby wine, in the goblet gleaming.
> Defeat is in its hue divine, sorrow in its beaming.
> From the clear and sparkling rill, nector freely flowing.
> Tra la la
> There my brimming cup, I fill, life and joy bestowing.[63]

The *Philadelphia Press* took a harsher stand on the Delahanty binge. They criticized the "me too" selfishness of Delahanty and Lajoie. In their eyes, Delahanty's intemperance and the recent behavior of Lajoie, especially after their threatened strike, were responsible for undermining the team's composure and well-being.[64]

With Lajoie sitting out a few games because of an injury to his other thumb, Delahanty returned to the lineup for the last two games of the Cincinnati series. The Phillies lost both contests, the latter by a no-hitter thrown by Frank "Noodles" Hahn. In both games, Delahanty struck out at critical times to the delight of the fans. The final stop on the road trip, Pittsburgh, demonstrated the Phillies' erratic play. They bombarded three Pittsburgh hurlers for 23 runs and 24 hits. Delahanty went 1 for 6, but his last at-bat was a noteworthy one. With the Phillies ahead 20 to 4, Manager Fred Clarke brought in right fielder Honus Wagner to pitch the last three innings. Noted for his powerful throwing arm, Wagner enjoyed the challenge. In the eighth inning Wagner faced Ed Delahanty and pretended to shake his knees together in fright. Everyone was delighted by the scenario, but the outcome was not to Ed's liking. He popped up to the infield.[65]

The Phillies returned to the Quaker City after a 5 for 13 road trip. Delahanty's club was now in fourth place, 7 games behind Brooklyn. The *Philadelphia Press* ran drawings of Delahanty, Lajoie, and Shettsline with bandages over their heads. The caption read, "Home again, Home again from a ???."[66]

Ed Delahanty was not totally responsible for the Phillies' collapse, but it was apparent that Del was suffering from more than a batting slump. The lack of reports of drinking bouts did not mean, however, that Delahanty was dealing well with the problems, pressures, and situations that ensnared him. In nineteen games, from the Lajoie fight to his embarrassing forfeit against Brooklyn, Delahanty hit .419. In the next 10 contests, he batted .294 and during the sixteen games after his Cincinnati "spree," Ed Delahanty crashed to 9 for 63 for a .143 average. It was the worst hitting performance of his twelve-year, major league career. At the time of the forfeit, Captain Delahanty was hitting .406, five weeks later, he was at .334.

Whatever sporting interest remained in Philadelphia was focused on the exploits of successful American athletes at the Paris Olympics. At the Broad and Huntingdon ballpark, fans expressed displeasure at their tarnished heroes. Lajoie was booed by his one-time supporters, and Delahanty again heard disturbing jeers from his bleacher critics. Writers covering the Phillies felt the team had become "corpse-like," perhaps a reflection of their slumping team-captain, who again was distracted by the reconvening of the Players' Protective Association.

While the Phillies traveled to Pittsburgh, Delahanty led the club's delegates to a meeting in New York. Harry Taylor, a Buffalo attorney and former Louisville player, presented a constitution to the players' representatives. Of the fifty-two ballplayers present, thirty were of Irish descent. No segment of these assembled players objected to the ratified document that called for the end to farming, selling, or trading players without their prior consent or compensation. The by-laws also opposed unfair pay cuts and fines and favored a limited reserve clause. A grievance committee was set up, and players were asked not to sign next year's contracts without a lawyer's approval. John Rogers said he was not against his players joining a protective organization that conducted itself properly. He did object to professional baseball seeing itself as a labor organization.[67] The players did not respond to Rogers. They agreed instead to send delegates to the winter league meetings in December. By that time, Delahanty and his fellow players hoped a rival association would weaken the resolve of the National League. Confident of success, Delahanty rejoined his struggling team with a renewed faith that better times were on the horizon.

These expectations were too much for a season that was "hoodooed" from the start. Delahanty and his peers could muse optimistically about their pending opportunities, but the sport, and what remained of the season, had ruinous symptoms. Delahanty never recovered from his dreadful July, and Lajoie played with two bad thumbs and nagging injuries, all of which sapped the Phillies' competitive edge. Most unsettling were the bad feelings on the ball field. With a lone umpire, fighting and spectator violence grew more commonplace.

On their western road trip, the Phillies endured two fights in St. Louis at the expense of Harry Wolverton. Five days later, Roy Thomas was sucker-punched by a Cincinnati pitcher who objected to his fouling off too many pitches. Captain Delahanty threatened to take the Phillies out of the Protective Association if something was not done.[68] Faced with this challenge, the Players' Protective Association president, Chief Zimmer, cautioned that the association could not take any action against individual players because the organization did not exist to protect players from each other. Their purpose, he said, was to deal with the relationship between players and management.[69]

Delahanty's captaincy appeared to be out of sync. His leadership was inconsistent and too volatile for the floundering Phillies. By September, Philadelphia was one game above .500 and tied with Boston for third place, 11 games behind Brooklyn. Manager Shettsline remained confident that his team would recover, but his captain was more philosophical. On the topic of worrying about the club's chances, Del said:

> Worry never won many ball games. . . . it has helped to lose a lot. I'm a hard loser and feel bad when I can't win and am not hitting, but when it comes to worrying I cut that out and let other people do that. If people would only look upon base ball in a more rational way they would be happier and the sport better. Eight teams are out to do their best. They are all paid to win and that is an impossibility. All that any team can do is to play its best.[70]

These sentiments revealed Delahanty's detachment from reality. His attitude, given the circumstances of the season, were more apologetic than convincing. He avoided the issues troubling his team and ignored the fact that his performance and that of his ball club were disappointing.

The Phillies' desperation and the league's credibility were soon exposed by the discovery of the Morgan Murphy signal system on the same day as a devastating hurricane struck the city of Galveston, Texas. The disclosure of this elaborate signaling method used to tip off Philadelphia batters was much less shocking than the hurricane's death toll of 5,000 and $40 million in damages, but it raised some embarrassing questions about how the game was played.

Every ball team sought ways to get the upper hand against its opponents. The most successful ball clubs stole signs and looked for mannerisms that disclosed pitching tendencies. Once the signs were detected, it was only a matter of transmitting the information to a batter or baserunners. The Morgan Murphy System allegedly took this practice to a new turn-of-the-century technical height. Murphy, using binoculars, would steal the catcher's signs and relay the information on to a coach who passed it on to the batter. Murphy's innovation was that instead of a visual signal, he relayed the information by an electronic signal.

Never more than a weak-hitting backup catcher, Murphy was a keen student of the game, wise to the idiosyncracies of players and managers. He learned much about finagling from Charlie Comiskey, who managed him for three years in Cincinnati. Another one of Charlie's disciples was Tommy McCarthy, the league's "sign detective." It was said that McCarthy's system helped Frank Selee's Beaneaters win their pennants.[71]

In many respects, McCarthy and Murphy were the stereotypical Irish players in the Emerald Age of baseball, affable goodfellows who knew how to get and use information for a competitive edge. For Murphy, this ability evolved into a role as a nonplaying bench coach, working with front-office man Billy Shettsline. Before long, Murphy moved to better vantage points, such as apartment or clubhouse windows, where he would steal the catcher's signs and use a newspaper, window shade or drapery to convey his message. Other teams attempted this tactic, but no one rivaled Murphy's skill or ingenuity.[72]

As the third-string catcher, Murphy only got into twenty-five games in 1898 and hit only .198. On some days, the clever Murphy worked the gates, making sure ticket receipts were accurate. In 1899 he did not appear in a single game and earned his full salary. It was not until mid-July of the following season that Louisville and Chicago discovered that Murphy was routinely stealing and signaling signs. They complained and changed signals to no avail. Newspapers reported that even John McGraw failed to thwart Murphy's activities.[73] *Sporting Life* wrote that without ever playing a game, Morgan Murphy "was worth all he cost to keep."[74]

During the 1900 season, former teammate Dick Cooley got back at John Rogers by alerting his new team to Murphy's deceptions. Initially, Cooley changed the pitching signals so often his own hurlers were throwing the wrong pitches.[75] When that failed he appealed to the league with little or no effect. Their inaction emboldened "Irish" Murphy to take his system on the road. Bill Magee, who pitched briefy for the Phillies in 1899, said Murphy rented a room across the street from the right field fence in Brooklyn and operated his system with a newspaper wave. When his view was obstructed, as in Boston, the system was impaired.[76] Morgan soon devised a more brazen approach.

Former Philadelphia captain Bob Allen, the manager of Cincinnati, was alerted by Art Irwin to Murphy's new system. Allen was told that the Phillies had installed a box with an electronic vibrating buzzer under the third base coaching area with wires to Murphy's hiding place. Before a September 17 game, Allen visited Shettsline in the center field clubhouse looking unsuccessfully for the wires. When the game began, Cincinnati captain Tommy Corcoran started nosing around Pearce Chiles' third base coaching spot. By the third inning, Corcoran's "scratching" alarmed Shettsline, Chiles, the groundskeeper and a police sergeant, who had all rushed to the digging site. Upon their arrival, Corcoran discovered and lifted a board, exposing a "snuggly fitted electronic apparatus."[77] Players from both teams gawked at the hole, until umpire Tim Hurst ordered the game resumed.

Sporting Life referred to Morgan Murphy as the "Edison of base ball,"[78] and most coverage of the discovery was humorous and damning. The league had no rule about stealing signs, and most teams at one time indulged in the practice. John McGraw confessed that one of his teams relayed stolen signs, and thanks to Dick Cooley, Pittsburgh awkwardly mimicked the Murphy system. But the sharp-eyed Morgan Murphy, an accomplished lip-reader, was one of a kind.

Colonel Rogers, the league's self-proclaimed conscience, was in Europe when the buzzer container was uncovered. He denied its intent and asserted that the buzzer was a joke played on Bob Allen. Rogers explained that the box was something left over from a circus that had used the grounds that summer. Rogers acknowledged knowing of Murphy's binoculars and meekly confessed that they did not work very well. Rogers further indicted himself when he asserted: "It is ridiculous, but so far as being fair or legitimate is concerned I can find no fault with it. It is a game that both sides can play and surely a club may take advantage of whatever brains it may possess. If it is fair to use your naked eyes to discover signals there can be no objection to the use of glasses."[79]

The lasting question was the effect of Murphy's information. John McGraw said many batters were not comfortable with pre-knowledge of a pitch. It took away from their concentration, making them dependent on an external sign. He declared that only "lay back and swing batters" such as Delahanty and Honus Wagner appreciated knowing when a fastball was coming.[80] Arlie Latham, coaching for Cincinnati the day of the incident, loudly proclaimed, "Ah, discovered—Delahanty's batting average."[81] Former Phillies pitcher Bill Magee said Murphy helped Delahanty win the batting championship.[82] Long-time Phillies shortstop Bill Hallman asserted that Delahanty was the major beneficiary of these tips. When the signals were decoded, Hallman said Ed always went on a hitting tear.[83]

There was no question the Phillies hit better at home with Morgan Murphy and his binoculars in the center field clubhouse. The question is, how did signaled information affect hitters such as Delahanty, Lajoie, and Flick from 1899 until September 1900?

Examining Delahanty's daily hitting record for this period reveals a noteworthy disparity. In 1899, Ed batted .461 at home and .366 on the road. He went hitless five times in Philadelphia and failed in thirteen instances in away games. But with thirty-five less road at-bats, Delahanty also hit more triples and home runs than he did at home. During his grand batting streak of 61 out of 63 games, Ed Delahanty hit .455 (61 for 134) in Philadelphia and .372 (45 for 121) on the road. In 1900, up to the uncovering of the box (September 17), Del hit .371 at Broad and Huntingdon and .291 in away games. His totals during the alleged life of the Morgan Murphy Signal System was .422 at home and .335 on the road. Comparisons with full-swing batters such as Napoleon Lajoie and Elmer Flick (1899 until September 17, 1900) bore interesting results (see table 2).

There is no doubt John McGraw was correct that sluggers such as Delahanty profited from Murphy's tips. But does his complicity discredit Del's great 1899 season? Knowing when a fastball was coming was the only apparent advantage to Murphy's signal. Location and the type of off-speed pitch were not disclosed to the batter. No doubt Delahanty was fooled less often at home, but on the road he still batted almost seventy points above the era's relative batting average.

Table 2. The effect of the Morgan Murphy Signal System as reflected in the hitting records, 1899–1900

		H	AB	2B	3B	HR	AVG
1899 Delahanty	(h)	141	306	35	3	4	.461
	(a)	101	276	19	6	5	.366
1899 Lajoie	(h)	59	146	9	4	3	.404
	(a)	60	162	11	6	2	.370
1899 Flick	(h)	83	257	12	5	—	.323
	(a)	83	222	7	7	2	.374
1900 Delahanty	(h)	91	245	18	6	—	.371
	(a)	71	244	10	5	—	.291
1900 Lajoie	(h)	78	201	10	5	4	.388
	(a)	61	195	16	5	1	.313
1900 Flick	(h)	99	255	17	6	3	.388
	(a)	77	212	7	5	7	.363

In retrospect, with Napoleon Lajoie missing 116 games over the last two seasons, Delahanty welcomed any opportunity to get a pitch to hit. Moreover, Del also was a thirty-three-year-old veteran who was becoming too complacent and arrogant about his career. He knew every team tried to alert their batters to oncoming pitches and believed he had earned the right to know whether a fastball was coming his way. One can imagine him salivating at the prospect of not being caught off stride at the plate. It was part of an emerging pattern in Delahanty's life. Spoiled by adulation, Delahanty felt he should not be constrained by the rules and standards that guided others. Stealing signs was not cheating, it was a competitive advantage in an age where survival of the fittest reigned.

⚾ The stigma of Murphy's signal box was the capstone on another disappointing Philadelphia baseball season, one in which they finished in third place, 8 games behind the Hanlon-led Brooklyn Superbas. Captain Delahanty did not contribute much after the Murphy incident. He hit only .271, including four doubles and three triples and joined Lajoie on the sideline for the last seven games of the "hoodoo" year. Both players, bound by friendship and their preseason holdout, were put out of action in the same game. Against New York, Delahanty split his finger on an errant throw to first base, and Lajoie was hit on the elbow by a wayward fastball. That at-bat was Lajoie's last as a Phillies ballplayer.

Lajoie missed almost forty games in 1900 and his batting average dropped forty-one points to .337. He did knock in 92 runs and, despite numerous hand injuries, still led the league in fielding his position. Delahanty's record was more the result of self-inflicted pressures. He hit at an eight-year low of .324, with 32 doubles and 10 triples. He was second in the league in RBIs (109) and finished eighth among first basemen in fielding. Elmer Flick slumped at the season's end and finished second in batting (.367), behind Pittsburgh's Honus Wagner. Flick did lead the league with 110 RBIs and was second in slugging (.545). Roy Thomas led the National League in walks (115) and runs scored (131). On the mound the Phillies' problems persisted. The staff had the highest ERA (4.12) in the league.

This disillusioning season contributed to a further decline in attendance. After the Lajoie fight, the team's quality of play fell off and fan support dropped considerably. The franchise lost 87,000 fans at the gate. League totals were more ominous, with a loss of about 700,000. Only three teams in the reconfigured National League, among them Philadelphia, made any money. With John Rogers bemoaning this condition, the *Cincinnati Times Star* commented on Rogers' ever-suffering attitude. The paper said that no franchise whined so much about its circumstances and was as cheap as the Philadelphia club.[84] At an end-of-the-year meeting of owners and Players' Association representatives, Rogers blamed the season on the nonchalant demeanor of his players, "taking the field like a lot of tired day laborers, tired before the game began." When quizzed about the responsibility for this condition, he blamed his manager for being "too popular with the players to enforce any rules . . . for fear of hurting their feelings."[85] The *Philadelphia Press* was more direct when it declared that the Phillies needed a "never-say-die spirit and first-class coacher like [Hugh] Jennings or [Joe] Kelley."[86]

With the congenial Shettsline and the affable Delahanty running the club, the Phillies saved money and hoped that talented players alone would guarantee a championship. But it was Rogers, the majority stockholder and the only person not responsible to President Reach, who set the tone for the franchise. His vindictive and tight-wallet ways alienated Billy Lauder, Monte Cross, Dick Cooley, and Bill Goeckel and led him to pass up an opportunity to get pitching prospect Joe "Iron Man" McGinnity. Rogers also encouraged the breakup of the team's outfield when Delahanty moved to first base, and who else was accountable for not disciplining Lajoie's disruptive behavior? By the end of the year, the people of Philadelphia were more excited about the victorious McKinley-Roosevelt presidential campaign than they were about the chances of the 1901 Phillies. Little did they know that the failed season had also derailed Ed Delahanty and undermined the fabric of John Rogers' team.

14

The New League

Nursing his injured hand and a tarnished reputation, Ed Delahanty remained in Philadelphia with his family until after the holiday season. Distressed by the outcome of the year, he knew that off-field distractions and his inconstant leadership contributed to his troubling season. Regrettably, his disappointment never focused on the greater problem, his failed sobriety. Like many of his ballplaying peers, he was in denial. He saw the Cincinnati episode as an intemperate lapse, not a regular indulgence. This repudiation was troubling because there were too many disquieting elements in his life. Delahanty feared his skills might be slipping, and without prospects or savings for life outside of baseball, he was dependent on Philadelphia's unchanging salary scale. He also knew that after a remarkable twelve-year career with the Phillies, the best he could wrangle from management was getting his captain's stipend included in his regular contract. But Ed did not have the temperament to run a John Rogers team, with its urgency on winning. Neither was he immune from the erupting labor tensions that swirled around baseball. Instead, he blamed last season's failures on his move to first base and the swelling pressures that occupied his attention. Delahanty hoped if Billy Lauder returned and played third base, Harry

Wolverton could move over to first, and he would resume his position in left field.[1] If this switch cost him the captaincy, Del was undeterred because he believed his stipend was guaranteed.

Waiting to see what management and the new leagues had in store for baseball, Delahanty removed himself from the fray. With a negotiated preseason advance in hand, Ed, Norine, and young Florence departed for the inviting swirl of New Orleans. Traveling first class by train, Delahanty and his family stayed in the South until the opening of spring training. The lifestyle of New Orleans, with its glittering nightspots and long racing season, was intoxicating to the high-living Delahantys.[2] Over the years, gambling had become a popular off-field entertainment for Del. He prided himself on being an astute handicapper and, like most racing enthusiasts, believed he had devised an unerring system of wagering. According to league gossip, the Phillies were "a hotbed of horsey-boys, with Captain Delahanty the ranking chief."[3] To Del's way of thinking, success at the horsetrack, and the prospect of a contract war among the rival leagues, gave him a false sense of security and prosperity. Delahanty had no idea that he was setting a course that would make him the victim, not the master, of his fate.

While Delahanty indulged himself in New Orleans, his future was being shaped by the successes of Ban Johnson. In 1900 Johnson's "not-yet" major league prospered thanks to the driving spirit of Charlie Comiskey and the financial support of Charles Somers, a wealthy Cleveland coal dealer. Initially, Comiskey, Johnson's long-time mentor, had him appointed commissioner of the Western League. Working together, Johnson and Comiskey enlarged their league, moving it east into the domain of the big market National League cities. This opportunity was made possible by the older league's contraction of four franchises. Having gained Cleveland, the American League also occupied Detroit, Milwaukee, Minneapolis, Kansas City, and Indianapolis, and with Charles Somers' backing, Comiskey wormed his way into Chicago's National League territory. Comiskey's White Stockings became the pivot and expansion model for going into Philadelphia and Boston and the vacated ball towns of Washington and Baltimore.[4]

By 1901, Johnson and Comiskey had seized the momentum. They proclaimed themselves a major league and refused to pay the required fees of an affiliated minor league. They also asserted their right to expand without the permission of the senior circuit and distanced themselves from the lame-duck National Agreement. The National League magnates countered this militancy by supporting a revitalized American Association, now called the National Association. The intent of this move was to use the lesser of two evils, the retitled National Association, in the same way the National League had used the new American League against the 1899–1900 American Association threat. Without any accord among the contending leagues, Philadelphia faced the prospect of having three ball clubs for the 1901 season. This possibility saw baseball agents scouring the Quaker City for backers and playings grounds.

As early as September 1900, two Milwaukee businessmen, August Koch and Harry Quinn, put in a bid for the National Association Philadelphia franchise. Eventually, they were displaced by backers favored by Colonel Rogers: Frank Richter, the editor of Al Reach's *Sporting Life,* and Hezekiah Niles, a minor league baseball speculator and the owner of a New Mexico silver mine.[5] Holding the lease on a large, well-situated lot at 29th and Columbia Avenue, the National (formerly the American) Association had a big advantage over their American League rivals. This obstacle did not deter Ban Johnson and his supporters, because the manager of his Western (and later American League) Milwaukee franchise, Connie Mack, was already in Philadelphia evading National League detectives and downplaying his intentions.[6]

As this baseball drama unfolded, Ed Delahanty prospered in New Orleans. He won money at the track and kept himself in shape by playing baseball twice a week with a local club.[7] He was also thrilled to hear that his kid brother, Jimmy, had been secured from the Eastern League by the Chicago National League club.[8] Ed's peace of mind was soon disrupted by events in Philadelphia that gave life to Ban Johnson's new league.

Although American League advance men, like Connie Mack, were nurturing other east coast cities, Rogers and Reach set in motion the course baseball would travel for the next two years. It began when hardline owners John Rogers, John Brush, and Arthur Soden met with officers of the Players' Protective Association. These representative owners stalled the players, claiming they had no authority to agree to the union's demands. Capitalizing on this tactic, disaffected players from the Protective Association, Clark

Griffith, Connie Mack, and John McGraw among them, began so-liciting ballplayers for the American League. Johnson advanced his campaign by supporting the union against farming out players, salary caps, and the National League's reserve clause contracts. By the time the old league's owners revisited the Protective Association, it was too late to bargain. Their concessions were inadequate, and players were quietly committing to the American League.[9] Frank Hough, anticipating this breach, said the National League got what they deserved, and every player had the right not to sign his con-tract "until he sees just how the cat is going to jump."[10]

John Rogers' other contribution to the American League was indirect. It came in the form of his support for the renamed Na-tional Association. In an effort to control his sporting environment, Rogers indebted his nominees, Niles and Richter, by insisting the new franchise lease the Broad and Huntingdon grounds for $5,400 per year. Rogers argued that Niles and his partners would save the expense of erecting and maintaining a new ballpark. However, he never anticipated this move would permit Connie Mack and his prospective backers the opportunity to get the association's unde-veloped lot at 29th and Columbia. National League owners Arthur Soden of Boston and Andrew Freedman of New York were furi-ous with Rogers' greed and lack of foresight.[11]

Because of this opening, the persistent Connie Mack, supported by Johnson and Somers, secured a primary investor for the Phila-delphia baseball franchise. Benjamin Franklin Shibe was a backer of the old American Association Athletics, who had come to base-ball when his family's horse-carriage leather goods business began producing sporting and gymnastic equipment. Shibe's development of a machine that automatically wound baseballs made him a rival and later a business associate of Al Reach. By the end of the 1880s, the partnership prospered with the selling of the retail side of their sporting goods business to their competitor Al Spalding. The part-ners, however, continued on as manufacturers. Their principal prod-uct, major league baseballs, was a virtual monopoly. The two men were further linked in 1894 when Al Reach's only son, George, mar-ried Ben Shibe's only daughter, Mary.

Most puzzling about Delahanty's employers was understand-ing Al Reach's role in the Shibe-Rogers competition. The *Sporting News* reported, "Politics make strange bedfellows, but baseball gave politics a furlong handicap and beat that game a hundred yards in a mile run."[12] From the first, Reach denied he had any stock or interest in the American League. He said it would be a conflict of interests to do business this way,[13] but the actions of the Phillies president were very suspect. Reach and Shibe were like brothers and always consulted the other, making it hard to believe that Reach had no input into Ben Shibe's decision to fund a rival team in the Phillies' own backyard.

Another motivating factor was the Shibe-Reach baseball, the official ball of Ban Johnson's original Western League and the new American League. Building on this existing relationship, it was more than a coincidence that Reach, weeks before the announcement of Shibe's selection, met with Ban Johnson in Chicago for two days of private talks. It can only be inferred that the baseball production contract talks were extended to include Shibe's investment in the Athletics.[14] But underlying Al Reach's actions was his relationship with John Rogers.

Ever since Rogers violated the gentleman's agreement with Reach about not seeking a majority ownership of the Phillies, their partnership had deteriorated. He believed Rogers did not understand the operation of a baseball franchise. Al Reach knew that a new league and higher expenses were inevitable, and rather than overspend in an inflationary, nonreserve contract marketplace, it was best to reevaluate his baseball assets. If this meant selling the Phillies, keeping the ballpark, and capitalizing on supplying both leagues with baseballs, so be it.

Colonel Rogers was stunned by this chain of events. The appointment of Connie Mack as Shibe's manager and Bill Sharsig as the Athletics' business director meant his competitors would be well led. His more immediate concern came from within his own league and team. Rogers was being attacked by fellow owner John T. Brush, and many of Rogers' players were positioning themselves to jump leagues.

Brush of Cincinnati had been the owner of a large Indianapolis department store before moving into baseball. A strong-willed and calculating businessman, Brush had authored a plan to create a National League trust scheme as a way to combat financial and new league threats. He was also disturbed by Colonel Rogers' meddling and attacked him for undermining the National League's new surrogate, the National Association. Indignant over the turn of events, Rogers called Brush a liar and a coward, and said it was small and petty for "the chief marplot" of the association scheme to blame him for its collapse.[15] These accusations served no purpose, for the threat of a third league was over, and the way was clear for Ban Johnson and his associates.

It was reported that 111 out of 182 American League players in 1901 had previously played in the National League. The new league attracted an impressive array of ballplayers: Jimmy Collins, Cy Young, John McGraw, Joe McGinnity, "Buck" Freeman, Clark Griffith, Mike Donlin, and young Roger Bresnahan. The most coveted player sought by the American League was Delahanty's teammate, twenty-six-year-old Napoleon Lajoie. His jumping to Connie Mack's Athletics gave the new league instant credibility. In the final tally of first-year jumpers, John Rogers' Phillies lost only Lajoie and pitchers Chick Fraser, Bill Bernhard, and Wiley Piatt. The Athletics also signed three former Phillies, including Delahanty's old friend Lave Cross. In the midst of these desertions and speculated moves, Ed Delahanty departed from New Orleans.

By the end of February, Delahanty and his family arrived in Cleveland to visit his parents. He was reported to be in excellent shape and in good spirits. He was looking forward to a redeeming season and was encouraged when Chicago offered three players for his services.[16] The Phillies had no interest in letting their veteran star leave, especially in the wake of Lajoie's desertion. What was remarkable about the movement of Philadelphia ballplayers was that Delahanty's name was never mentioned as a possible jumper. Given his Players' League experiences and his recent disagreement with the Phillies' management, his omission was surprising. The answer according to John McGraw was that American League clubs were wary of Delahanty because he "went wrong" in 1890. Whatever the answer, Manager Shettsline was greatly relieved when Delahanty telegraphed him from Cleveland asking for his new contract.[17]

Delahanty's commitment to the 1901 Phillies was most likely his uncertainty as to whether the American League would be a viable option, and he had already bound himself to Philadelphia.[18] Unlike his bachelor friend Larry Lajoie, Delahanty did not want to revisit the problems and uncertainties of 1890 as a husband and father. He could have reneged on his contractual obligations, like

Lajoie, but the prospect of Colonel Rogers' legal wrath did not appeal to Delahanty or his wife. The intimidation and expense of drawn-out lawsuits such as the Lave Cross case and the uncertainty of the new league's success were unappealing to the Phillies' captain. Del already had a $3,000 guaranteed salary and accepted an advance in October when he received his option clause notice. Needing the money for his trip to New Orleans, Delahanty bound himself with a cash advance he could not afford to refund. So before the contract war heated up, Ed Delahanty was legally out of the initial bidding.

The American League signings began in earnest some time after President McKinley started his second term. The key figure was Lajoie. Newspaper accounts initially said "King Larry" signed for $3,600, but Lajoie and Connie Mack put the amount at $4,000.[19] Whatever the figure, Lajoie got his money from a special bank account that was held by his landlord and the sports editor of the *Inquirer*, Frank Hough. His salary was also secured against default or the legal actions of John Rogers and the National League.[20]

Ignited by Lajoie's signing, Manager Shettsline said the club would not get into a bidding contest, and following Colonel Rogers' lead, he publicized the legitimacy of the renewable option clause contract. On March 12, he wrote to Connie Mack about tampering with ballplayers who were legally bound to the Phillies. Shettsline said his players were given notice of renewal on October 15, 1900, and their new contract ran for six months, beginning on April 1, 1901. He advised Mack about violating contractual rights, warning him that he could no longer plead ignorance of breached contracts.[21]

As the expenses of the contract war heated up, the Phillies, to save money, held their preseason training at home, at Broad and Huntingdon. Captain Delahanty was especially anxious to get everyone together. He wanted to know what players intended to return to the fold and what positions needed restaffing. Del already knew that Lajoie and half of the Phillies' pitching staff had jumped leagues, and the "buzzer collaborator," Pearce Chiles, was in a Texas prison for embezzlement.[22] But Captain Delahanty was relieved that many of the suspected jumpers decided to stay with the Phillies rather than chance their salaries on a new league venture. Delahanty scheduled games against college and local semipro teams, but his greatest task was replacing lost players.

The Phillies hoped that the signing of "Frosty Bill" Duggleby, "Doc" White, and Delaware-born Jack Townsend, together with returning veteran Al Orth and Red Donahue, would sustain the Philadelphia pitching staff. Another option was the availability of Brooklyn's Hugh Jennings, who had moved over from shortstop to first base to conserve his ailing arm. If the Phillies could get Jennings, then Delahanty could return to left field. The Jennings' negotiations progressed until June and were as important as filling the hole left by Lajoie at second base. Delahanty and Shettsline resolved the latter by re-signing former Phillies' captain and malcontent, the thirty-four-year-old Bill Hallman. These preseason decisions, however, were very much affected by what was going on in the league's front offices and in a Philadelphia courtroom.

A popular Chicago sportswriter, Hugh Fullerton, commenting on the situation in Philadelphia, said he was anxious to see Colonel Rogers "writhe as Mack tears the silver lining out of his trouser's pocket."[23] But cynics such as Fullerton were mistaken if they believed Rogers would not address this attack on his franchise. In Rogers' eyes, if New York offered $15,000 last season for Delahanty or Lajoie, why should one of these players be stolen by interlopers without any compensation? Critics responded that he created the problem by paying his two star players a fraction of their market value.[24] Rogers' remedy for these raids was his renewable option clause, which he conceived and felt duty-bound to defend.[25]

Reacting to Ban Johnson's claim that a Rogers-inspired injunction against Lajoie and other jumpers would not hold up in court, the Colonel consulted the "camp of the [former] enemy," John J. Johnson, the Philadelphia attorney who had represented ballplayers in the old Players' Brotherhood. Johnson told him that the grounds upon which Judge Thayer had refused the 1890 injunction "does not arise under the present contract." He praised the skill and care of the wording of the renewable clause contract, and said it appeared appropriate for the "limited period" designated by the contract. In Rogers' mind, the obligation was a "perpetual one." Frank Hough, an American League investor, attacked Rogers by declaring that there was a wide difference between Johnson's "limited period" and Rogers' "perpetual" time frame. For Hough, the option clause restrained a ballplayer like the reserve rule, and was thus inequitable.[26]

American League vice president Charles Somers countered Rogers with a contrary opinion. The league's lawyer, Charles Higley of Cleveland, said the legality of the contract had never been questioned, but it had to be equitable and just in all of its parts, not one-sided and harsh in its provisions. An injunction, Higley remarked, was unlikely to be used in "this enlightening age to drive a man into the performance of an unconscionable bargain." Higley believed each case had to be judged on its own merits, and that Colonel Rogers was not entering a court of law "with clean hands."[27] This position was seconded by the former brotherhood president John Montgomery Ward, and by the dean of the University of Pennsylvania's law school.[28] Undeterred by these opinions, John Rogers, on March 26, 1901, went to the Common Pleas Court in Philadelphia with a bill in equity to restrain his players from taking part in American League games. Codefendants in the suit were Ben Shibe, Connie Mack, Frank Hough, and the four ballplayers.

The underlying issues of these personal contracts were the mutuality of the Phillies' "ten-day clause," and the notice required by a ball club to terminate a ballplayer's services. Another key point was the "irreparable harm" to the plantiff's business from the loss of these players' services. These factors were bantered about in the sporting press while the team prepared for the regular season. Neither Captain Delahanty nor any Phillies player openly voiced their opinions. They quietly went about their business and watched with great interest the unfolding developments of the lawsuits. It was a day after the Lajoie-less Phillies lost their home opener to Brooklyn, 12 to 7, that testimony began in Common Pleas Court #5.

On the following day, Lajoie, through his attorney, filed his answer to the Phillies' injunction. His statement alleged that he signed his 1900 contract believing it had no option clause and his obligations expired at the end of last season. He went on to say that he would have never consented to a contract that reserved his services beyond 1900. Lajoie said he took Shettsline's word about the terms of the contract and never read it or received a copy of the said agreement. He also related that the Phillies lied about him being the team's highest paid ballplayer. Lajoie disclosed that John Rogers in February had offered to pay him the difference if he signed his 1901 contract. The second baseman's statement concluded with a denial that he was "induced or persuaded by his co-defendants" to sign a contract with the Athletics.[29]

When the court reconvened, Rogers and John Johnson questioned Lajoie on the witness stand. The second baseman identified his two 1900 agreements, one for $2,400, and a supplementary one for $200. Lajoie recalled that he never received the latter sum. Johnson contradicted his memory by presenting him with a signed receipt. "King Larry" claimed that he had signed it before he got paid. When confronted that Delahanty's extra money was a captain's stipend, Lajoie lied and played dumb. He remarked that Del was "supposed to be captain. I heard it said that he was captain." Johnson immediately asked Lajoie directly whether Delahanty was the team captain. Lajoie replied no, "Shettsline seemed to manage and captain from the bench." Johnson later remarked that the second baseman dodged questions like they were ground balls. The defendant ended his testimony by saying that he did not recollect Manager Shettsline ever referring to a reserve clause contract.

Ed Delahanty was never called to testify. He was in Brooklyn at the time and made no effort to appear at court. Billy Shettsline, however, followed Lajoie with his own testimony. He negated most of what Lajoie said and concentrated on the value of the great second baseman to the team's success. Cross-examined by the defense counsel, Shettsline confessed that he would like to have Lajoie back on his team. The defense asked Shettsline how indispensable Lajoie was to the Phillies if they had never won anything in the franchise's history. Shettsline never responded to these inquiries, leaving it up to Rogers to summarily defend the team's case. Rogers reiterated what had been said and concluded by charging that the stability of the sport depended on binding contracts. He addressed the "ten-day notice clause" with a question about how was a team expected to deal with indifferent or unproductive ballplayers.[30]

Surprisingly, six National League teams had nothing to do with Rogers' suit, and only Brooklyn sanctioned it, in the hope of getting Lave Cross back. While the verdict was being decided, the baseball season progressed. The American League drew well, but a looming apprehension hung over Ban Johnson's grand experiment. On May 17, with the Athletics outdrawing the Phillies, and with both teams under .500, the verdict came down from the three presiding Common Pleas judges. Their decision said Lajoie's contract with the Phillies lacked "mutuality" and denied Rogers' injunction. Pitchers Fraser, Bernhard, and Piatt were also covered by the Lajoie ruling. The decision, written by Judge Ralston, held that no court of equity would enforce the specific performance of a contract, or enjoin the breach of it, where one party was bound by a series of years, while the other could annul it at any time upon giving ten-days notice. The justices, having never seen Lajoie play baseball, also said that the second baseman's services were not "unique or extraordinary" and that his position could be filled by another player.[31]

Ban Johnson was elated and declared that the decision "clears the atmosphere in the American League wonderfully and gives us renewed strength." Andrew Freedman said it was a major mistake taking the National League contracts to court on the mutuality issue.[32] Frank Hough felt vindicated, and Ben Shibe and Connie Mack were relieved and gratified. Shibe said he expected the decision and said nothing further. Manager Mack related that he had had enough of lawsuits and would not use the Lajoie case to restrain young Christy Mathewson, who reneged on his contract with the Athletics and returned to New York and the National League.[33] On the Phillies' side, Al Reach was nowhere to be found, and Rogers, who was out of town, was incensed by the decision and took the setback as a personal affront.

Phillies players, such as Ed Delahanty, remained aloof and quietly evaluated their 1902 options. For his part, Delahanty never responded to Lajoie's allegations and statements about his salary or captaincy. Rather than be angry over Lajoie's assertions, Delahanty had a few laughs about his friend's imagination and convenient loss of memory. After the verdict was given, sports coverage returned to normal, as the reverberations of the lawsuit rippled through the baseball community. Behind the scenes, Rogers made preparations for an appeal to the Pennsylvania Supreme Court, and the 1901 baseball season settled in for the long summer months.

The Lajoie lawsuit was not the only sign of the uneasy times. John McGraw, seeking to improve his new American League Baltimore club, tried to sign a black second baseman, Charlie Grant. McGraw hoped to pass Grant off as a Cherokee Indian, Charlie Tokohama. But Charlie Comiskey challenged McGraw by saying Grant was "fixed up with war paint and a bunch of horse feathers."

If Baltimore stood by this ruse, Comiskey threatened to find a "Chinese third baseman or whitewash a colored player."[34] Exposed by this influential spokesman of the Emerald Age, Grant quietly left the Orioles to play in a Chicago "negro league."

Had Grant been allowed to play in the major leagues, he would have seen new rules for speeding up the game with advantages going back to the pitchers. Beginning in 1901, the catcher had to be positioned "under the bat at all times," and each foul ball became a strike until the batsman had two strikes. The pitcher also could not hold the ball for more than twenty seconds, and a batter hit by a pitch got a ball-count rather than taking first base.[35] The American League postponed the foul-strike rule until 1903 as pitchers in the senior circuit regained some of the competitive edge lost when the pitching distance was lengthened in 1893. For Delahanty's Phillies, weakened by player defections and distracted by court rulings, out-of-ordinary things became menacing omens.

Troubled by bad weather and twenty-two conflicting dates, attendance at Philadelphia games was down. It was so alarming that National League owners gave in to Rogers' pleas and reduced their inclusive seventy-five cents admission demands.[36] The fans also responded to the Phillies' improved play. Batting third or second, Delahanty won a number of games with extra-base hits in the late innings. It was apparent to the most vocal "bleacher-crank" that Delahanty had recovered his batting stroke. But the Phillies knew that Delahanty alone could not bring fans back to the ballpark. Rogers needed on-field attractions and a pennant-contending team. With this in mind, the Phillies pursued one of the better "inside men" of baseball, Hugh Jennings, and publicized events like the visit of Chicago's young Jimmy Delahanty. In the City of Brotherly Love, the curious looked forward to seeing the Delahanty brothers oppose each other on a major league baseball diamond. This opportunity fascinated local baseball cranks and awakened memories of the brothers' Atlantic League play.

Chicago got the twenty-two-year-old Jimmy Delahanty by outbiding three National League teams.[37] Manager Tom Loftus was impressed with Jimmy's strong arm and cool on-field demeanor. But Jimmy Delahanty's play at third base fell off because of a sore knee and the symptoms of malaria. These maladies kept the "young Del" out of the lineup until the third game of the Chicago series.

During that game, Ed played the part of the big brother by encouraging Jimmy during timeouts. Jimmy went hitless in four at-bats and stole second base after getting on base on a fielder's choice. "Big Del" had a double and a single in three plate appearances and knocked in three runs as the Phillies took the game, 5 to 2. Chicago also dropped the final game. Jimmy went hitless after again flawlessly fielding his position. Ed Delahanty had a single and double off of Rube Waddell and made an exciting running catch on a foul ball.[38]

Jimmy Delahanty played a few more games before he was displaced. Hobbled with a swollen knee and racked with chills and an intermittent fever, Jimmy's season was over. On June 27 the youngster got his ten-day notice. Ailing and dejected, he returned to Cleveland and the care of his mother. When the 1902 season opened, Jimmy Delahanty began his quest anew with his old Worcester team.[39]

While Jimmy was struggling in Chicago, his brother Joe re-signed with Montreal in the Eastern League. Having played uninspired ball after the Allentown breakup, Joe Delahanty did not draw much attention. In 1901 he did play a full season and had a productive year: batting .292, with 31 doubles and 13 triples, and scoring 78 runs in 131 games. Brother Tommy, on the other hand, was twenty-nine years old and knew that his best playing years were behind him. Separated from Joe and Jimmy, he signed to play for Grand Rapids in the Western Association. After the franchise went under, Tom was purchased by Wheeling, West Virginia, and finished the year playing in Columbus, Ohio. He appeared in a total of 61 games at second base and batted .313. Concerned about the solvency of the Western Association, Tom finished 1901 by going out to Colorado and playing a few games with Denver in the new Western League. He stayed with Denver for the next two seasons. Ed, meanwhile, continued to follow his brothers' careers through game summaries in the weekly sporting press. He also kept in touch with the convalescing Jimmy in Cleveland, but "Captain Ed" was more preoccupied with his own changing status and well-being.

Delahanty's stay at first base and his captaincy hinged on the status of Hugh Jennings. Born and raised in a Pennsylvania coalmining town, Jennings fought his way out of the mines to stardom on the ball field. A fierce competitor, he worked hard at mastering his skills and was considered, along with his friend and former teammate John McGraw, one of the best "inside men" in major league baseball.[40] Like McGraw, Jennings' ambitions went beyond baseball. He joined McGraw as a student-coach at a small Franciscan school, Allegheny College in Pennsylvania. His eventual success with the Baltimore and Brooklyn clubs was matched by his academic progress. After an arm injury and a falling out with Ned Hanlon, Jennings enrolled at Cornell University. He signed to coach baseball and take courses toward a law degree. Using this sabbatical as leverage in his contract negotiations with Brooklyn, it was obvious Jennings intended to capitalize on the interleague bidding war.[41]

The Phillies had been interested in Jennings for a number of years. Although Jennings was committed to be at Cornell until June, there was no lack of interest in his services. As early as March 1901, Connie Mack and Billy Shettsline competed to sign the recovering Jennings. Their efforts were complicated by John McGraw's desire to be reunited with his former teammate. Ban Johnson, the American League president, intervened and asserted that Connie Mack had first claim to Jennings. This bickering prevented Jennings from signing with the new league. A delighted Rogers paid Brooklyn $6,000 for his contract and on June 21 Jennings signed for $3,500.[42]

Jennings' real value was that he brought Philadelphia what Art Irwin, Billy Nash, and George Stallings could not. He was the "right man in the right place," a "first-class manager," who would provide "snap and dash," "brains and ginger" and all-around smart hustle to the ball club.[43] With Hugh Jennings on board, Delahanty could return to left field, and within a few weeks, the team was playing inspired baseball. The greatest adjustment to Jennings' presence came from Captain Delahanty.

Jennings' signing occurred in the midst of an oppressive three-week heat wave that drove temperatures into the triple digits. The same intensity and discomfort brought on by the weather was apparent in Delahanty's reaction to Jennings. The Phillies' captain found himself torn between feelings of relief and outright sullenness. He was happy to return to the outfield without the burdens of directing every play, but he agonized over his loss of stature and Jennings' large salary.

Delahanty was batting .360, third in the league, when Jennings came on board. The *Philadelphia Press* said that no youngster who received a hobby-horse for Christmas was as happy as Delahanty with the prospect of returning to his "old pasture" in left field.[44] He celebrated the news by going 3 for 5 with a double and mighty home run in a 4 to 1 victory over St. Louis. Delahanty's homer was the talk of the town. It came within a few feet of being the first ball ever hit over the distant 430-foot left field Lehigh Avenue wall. It landed in the upper gallery and was said to be the longest ball hit inside the rebuilt ballpark. On the following day, Delahanty went back to left field and rejoiced by going 4 for 5. Over the next month, Delahanty regained his outfield skills. He may have lost a step and his arm was a little more erratic, but his supporters were pleased with his progress. His contribution to the team's surge to third place was his hitting. Batting fourth, behind Elmer Flick, Delahanty led the league in extra-base hits and, at .384, was just three points behind Brooklyn's Willie Keeler.

The ball club's most obvious change, however, was their style of play. Jennings took over more than first base. He gradually affected how the Phillies competed and approached the game. As a result of his leadership, the Philadelphia team began to play more of a "heads-up" style, reminiscent of the old Browns, Orioles, and Superbas. The "inside" Irish style of baseball, made popular by Comiskey, Hanlon, and McGraw, had finally come to the Quaker City.

Delahanty's greatest adjustment was his changing role and diminishing authority on the Jennings-led Phillies. Delahanty was a respected veteran with a legion of admirers; his presence could not be easily ignored. Jennings knew he could not come on-board and displace a player of Delahanty's stature. Instead, Jennings began his Philadelphia career by working in tandem with Ed Delahanty. Jennings took over the immediate decisions from first base, and Delahanty provided less urgent input and consultation from the outfield. Players and the press still referred to Delahanty as the captain, even when it was apparent that Jennings was running the club. This relationship between a tacit and a ceremonial leader was bound to cause problems. On occasion, Jennings would trot out to left field and confer with Delahanty, who would shout directions to the players. One columnist said Jennings was the captain, and Delahanty was his megaphone.[45] On the surface, there were few outward signs of the brewing discomfort and rivalry. Some observers believed Delahanty was happy to be relieved of the pressures of that "thankless position,"[46] but others said "Del was becoming jealous and resentful."[47] When Jennings was hurt and did not play, Delahanty resumed the captaincy and played first base. A local commentator referred to him as "First Lieutenant Delahanty."[48]

At first, Del welcomed the chance to stand down, but he never expected to be distressed over his loss of status. He always wanted to be seen as an important and successful man of consequence. Jennings, to his credit, tried to be tactful in his assumption of leadership. The difficulty was that Delahanty never resolved personal disputes well. He became overly anxious, sulked, or behaved in a surly manner. Delahanty expected people to defer to his feats and deeds. An unidentified former teammate, probably Billy Lauder, confided that the Phillies would be better off without Delahanty because "he takes baseball too easily" and does not have to overexert himself. This demeanor and attitude, he felt, adversely affected the ball club's performance.[49] What Lauder detected was that Delahanty's matter-of-fact style was not always in keeping with teamwork. Del's world revolved around himself and how he performed on the baseball diamond. Symptoms of Delahanty's discomfort, his brooding upset and petty jealousy were soon evident in his lackadaisical play in the outfield.[50] He was envious of Jennings' success and quick mind. Delahanty wanted to have the same kind of respect the self-made Jennings inspired. Delahanty was also distressed that the Phillies, without any hesitation, paid Jennings $500 more for a half a season than he earned with his guaranteed captaincy stipend. Frank Hough fueled the problem with his campaign against Rogers. The columnist reminded his readers that Delahanty, like Lajoie, had a $15,000 price tag. Rogers, he said, bought Jennings for two-fifths of that amount and paid him at a rate double to what the long-suffering Delahanty was getting. Hough did not blame Jennings. "He would be a sucker not to take advantage of the situation."[51] Distressed by these conditions, the prideful "King of Batters" felt spurned and unappreciated. For Delahanty, Jennings was a reminder of how he had been underpaid for his years of service. But Delahanty's discontent was soon mollified by the team's improved play and his own not-so-secret talks with American League agents.

Battling a fever, Delahanty elevated his play and the Phillies gave chase to Pittsburgh and Brooklyn. The Phillies were getting good pitching, and Jennings' coaching made the team more competitive. In the eyes of many superstitious and racist players, part of the ball club's resurgence came in the form of a popular new black mascot. "Lucky" Williams was a young black itinerant who joined up with the Phillies in Chicago. Tabbed as a good luck charm, "Lucky" became a short-lived celebrity. His good fortune was a product of the era's racism. Most ballplayers, the Phillies notwithstanding, had little contact with the black community. In their eyes, black people carried bags, shined shoes, ran errands, or were the butt of adolescent pranks. "Lucky" Williams was no exception. He became the team's human pet. The players gave him spare change, old uniform parts, and food leftovers. He also traveled with sandwiches or cold pork chops on the roofs of their Pullman trains. After these journeys he was so soot-ridden that Monte Cross, Delahanty, and other players would scrub him down in nearby rivers. Eventually, the pressure of winning ball games and the jeers of hostile crowds drove Williams to drink. After a three-week, 14 and 6 run, the second-place Phillies left their dejected mascot on a New York train platform. The Emerald Age of Baseball reflected the prejudiced society that it entertained.[52]

With the Phillies winning, large crowds came out to the ballpark. For the first time in many years, the club appeared to be picking up momentum at midsummer. It seemed like everyone had forgotten the loss of Napoleon Lajoie and was preparing for a run at the pennant. But this optimism was premature. The two leagues were still far apart, and plans for the 1902 season were quietly being put into place. It was a lull before the baseball war began anew.

Two weeks after Rogers labeled Ben Shibe and Connie Mack "raiders and outlaws,"[53] there were murmurs that Delahanty and other Phillies were being pursued by American League teams. It began with a report that the American League was moving into Pittsburgh and was about to sign Flick, Wolverton, and Delahanty. The players said they knew nothing about this deal, and Delahanty cautioned people not to believe all they read in the newspapers.[54] Another rumor disclosed that Delahanty was targeted by Connie Mack's agents.[55] In reality, Delahanty, Douglass, Flick, and

Wolverton were talking with Jimmy Manning, the manager of Washington. On August 12, the *North American* reported that seven Phillies had agreed to American League contracts. Follow-up stories said that Ed Delahanty had definitely signed to captain and play left field for the Washington Senators.[56] By the end of the month, it was widely confirmed that Delahanty, Wolverton, and Orth were going to Washington, and Flick, Duggleby, Townsend, and possibly Roy Thomas would be with the Athletics.[57] Colonel Rogers said it was the same old story. "It crops up so frequently that I am tired of denying it." He asserted that his players were more concerned with winning the pennant and confessed how he believed the players more than the "sensation-hunting scribes."[58]

These signings did not deter the solid-playing Phillies. They held on to second place and remained a few games behind league-leading Pittsburgh. Delahanty played hard and continued to come through in the clutch. In the month after Del made his American League commitment, he batted .333 and played 38 games without an error, despite a swollen right hand. His play, however, revealed only part of what was happening in his life. Ed Delahanty was putting on weight and appeared to be tense and distracted.[59]

Delahanty's conflicted state of mind tore at his loyalties. His competitive drive to excel remained intense, thirsting for that elusive championship, but his anger with Colonel Rogers moved him to become a league jumper. Unfortunately, the unenviable stigma of being a "revolver" also disserved the reality that he was an aging and underpaid star seeking to maximize his earning opportunities. Fans saw things differently. They felt betrayed by jumping ballplayers and labeled them sporting mercenaries. Rarely did the baseball public hold the magnates in either league responsible for the players' actions. Delahanty had a different perspective. He had gone this route with the old Players' League, and knew if he was to break away again from the National League, he required certain conditions. Del wanted to be on a competitive team and be compensated with a multiyear guaranteed contract. Manager Manning promised him a $1,000 bonus, a multiyear pact at $4,000 a season, and the team's captaincy. This kind of money and security was what Delahanty felt he deserved. But while he waited to see how these machinations played out, Delahanty was struck by a tragedy that touched an entire nation. On September 6, 1901, President William McKinley was mortally wounded by an assassin.

On the same day that the American League threatened to blacklist players jumping back to the National League, McKinley was shot by a young Polish anarchist at the Buffalo Exposition. Delahanty and his Philadelphia teammates joined the nation in prayers for their fallen leader. The vigil went on for eight days. During this anxious time, Pittsburgh came to Philadelphia for a critical three-game series that would determine the pennant. After dropping two of the games, the prospects for a Philadelphia championship dimmed. Delahanty out-hit Honus Wagner, batting 7 for 14 with two doubles. But when it mattered most, the Phillies' pitching was ineffective.

In the wake of this hard-fought series, news bulletins reported that William McKinley had taken a turn for the worse. On Saturday, September 14, the president died. Delahanty, an ardent Republican and long-time friend of William McKinley, was shaken by this loss. He and his fellow players persuaded management to postpone the scheduled game with Brooklyn. Four days later, after Theodore Roosevelt was sworn in as the twenty-sixth president of the United States, McKinley was laid to rest in Canton, Ohio. Delahanty, who was recovering from the effect of a bad bowl of chili, got out of his sick bed, and with some of his teammates, attended a memorial service in a nearby Catholic church.[60] By the time McKinley was interred, the pennant race had been decided and attention was refocused on the interleague competition for players.

Caught in the middle of this free-market frenzy, Delahanty was apprehensive and intimidated by the consequences of his move. Confronted by his dear friend and manager, Billy Shettsline, about joining the Senators, Delahanty confessed to a lucrative offer but disavowed his signing. Wishfully, Shettsline added that he was satisfied with Delahanty's assurances because the newspapers did not always have the correct facts.[61]

For almost two months, reports circulated that Delahanty was secretly acting as an agent for the American League. He encouraged teammates to listen to offers and spoke with visiting players, such as Willie Keeler, about the opportunities of jumping leagues. Colonel Rogers tried without success to catch his once-favored player conducting other teams' business. But players said nothing and refused to implicate Delahanty. Even Del's admirers questioned the integrity of a person under contract with one league acting on the behalf of another organization. One columnist came forward and asked Delahanty to clear his reputation and refute these accusations.[62] It was only after Ed was accused of negotiating with Boston's Kid Nichols that Delahanty publicly responded to his detractors. He declared that he was innocent and swore he could get supporting affidavits from his teammates.[63]

His indignant denials were self-deluding bluster. Delahanty had a history of acting as a player intermediary, and since he had committed himself to the American League, he felt no compunction to restrain himself. He believed Rogers had forsaken him after so many years of service and, like a brooding adolescent, resented the credit Hugh Jennings got for the Phillies' strong 1901 showing.[64] His intention was to leave his mark by undermining an ungrateful franchise. Secure with his proposed Washington guarantees, Delahanty felt that Rogers could keep Hugh Jennings and see whether his new captain could win with what was left of the once-mighty Phillies. But the role of dissembler exposed Del to a new set of pressures.

During the season's last weeks, fans taunted Delahanty about his actions. In Pittsburgh, cranks harassed Del about his American League dealings. "Who are you working for?" they shouted from the stands. Delahanty laughed and tried to ignore their barbs. Before his last at-bat, when he swatted a game-winning double, he shouted back "Both have got money."[65] The question was whether his newfound wealth could insulate him against Colonel Rogers' wrath.

Rogers called ballplayers "ungrateful and deceitful liars" when he responded to the Players' Protective Association's stand against his suspension of the injured Harry Wolverton.[66] Out with a broken collarbone, Wolverton was suspended without pay for his American League dealings. This action was part of Rogers' bullying tactics. Intent on finding out who was negotiating with Ban Johnson's agents, Rogers questioned each of his ballplayers. At every meeting, he heard denials and disavowals. His most heated exchanges were with Harry Wolverton. But as long as no incriminating evidence surfaced, Rogers could do little more than rant and threaten. Wolverton's injury, and his refusal to admit or deny his actions, made him expendable. Wolverton had crossed Colonel Rogers, and like Dick Cooley, he would be punished. The difference was the existence of an alternate major league.

The strange thing about the Wolverton case was Ed Delahanty's complicity. It was Delahanty who introduced Wolverton to Washington's Jimmy Manning. Wolverton and Delahanty met with an American League agent, the *Inquirer's* Frank Hough, and traveled together to the nation's capital to discuss terms. Wolverton would say nothing about these actions and simmered over losing his last 1901 paycheck ($525).[67] The Philadelphia third baseman countered that he was hurt playing baseball and threatened to take Rogers to court. The Colonel alarmed everyone when he announced that all players would lose their final paycheck unless they signed an affidavit about not contracting themselves to an American League team.[68] Clark Griffith, an officer in the Players' Association and captain of Comiskey's Chicago ball club, said that Rogers' legal claims had no validity and threatened a strike.[69]

Rogers went on the "warpath" over these allegations and threats. "I defy the . . . Protective Association to order a strike. The days of anarchy and revolution are over in America and I would prosecute anyone concerned for conspiracy." He promised he would meet any strike by hiring "a team of schoolboys, if necessary, to finish off the season."[70] In this atmosphere, Delahanty kept his silence, Wolverton continued to report to the ballpark, and the association's grievance committee favored a player walkout. Fortunately, the pocketbook won out over the heart. Players such as Hugh Jennings, Red Donahue, and even Delahanty believed a strike would hurt ballplayers more than management. To their way of thinking, the season was almost over and the owners would save the players' much-needed wages if they struck. Moved by this logic, the Phillies stayed out of Rogers' way.[71]

Cautioned by his attorney, Louis Hutt of Philadelphia, Ed Delahanty said little about these events. His teammate and friend Ed McFarland disclosed that in spite of his silence, Delahanty had been "gobbled up as early as August 10."[72] Years later, details about Del's contract were disclosed. It was reported that Delahanty, concerned about a sore throwing arm, was not sure how many more years he could play major league baseball. He wanted Hutt to get him a lucrative "ironclad" contract, whereby he "would have to die in between seasons to lose any part of the $8,000."[73] The specifics of this pact were worked out during Delahanty's denial period. It was only after the Wolverton strike was averted that Delahanty disclosed the terms he expected from Washington to Billy Shettsline. Up to this point, Delahanty believed if he kept quiet and did not sign a contract, it would be difficult to prove his disloyalty.[74] These conclusions may be inferred from a postseason interview with Delahanty. Accompanied by John McGraw and Clark Griffith, Delahanty was questioned by a reporter on a New York street. Del said that if John Rogers wanted him for 1902, Rogers "has got to come up to the price I quote." He reiterated that he had not signed any contract, but "I don't mind saying that I am out for the money, and shall go where I can get the most." Delahanty concluded by saying that he was still listening to offers.[75]

On October 5, in a home game against Boston, Delahanty, filling in for an injured Hugh Jennings, played first base and captained the team. It was his last appearance in a Philadelphia uniform. The Phillies lost 7 to 3, with Del going 0 for 3 against Vic Willis. After thirteen years, 1,555 games, 2,213 hits, 1,286 RBIs, and 1,369 runs, the Irish batsman from Cleveland finished his remarkable career in the Quaker City. Few of the 1,853 spectators who braved the cold were aware of this circumstance. The significance of the moment was not lost on Delahanty and other Philadelphia jumpers. They continued to listen to belated offers from Rogers, but they knew their careers at Broad and Huntingdon were over. In a sentimental moment, the team gathered together and gave a tearful Billy Shettsline an inscribed gold watch, chain, and locket.

Shettsline knew that nine of his players were not returning. Delahanty's roommate, young Jack Townsend, his close friend Al Orth, and Harry Wolverton joined Ed in Washington. Elmer Flick, Bill Duggleby, and Monte Cross went to Lajoie's Athletics. Red Donahue signed with St. Louis, and Ed McFarland inked a contract with Comiskey in Chicago. In one year, Rogers' ball club lost twelve quality players, including three future Hall of Famers, to Ban Johnson's league. No other National League team came close to matching Philadelphia's losses. Only Roy Thomas, among the regulars, remained loyal to Rogers and the Phillies. The pity was that these jumpers, together with Hugh Jennings, might have produced a championship team.

The Phillies' last contending team for more than a decade finished second (at 83 and 57) to Pittsburgh. In the first foul-strike rule season, Ed Delahanty placed second in batting (.357), slugging (.533), and RBIs (108), and was fourth in home runs (8). He led the league in doubles (39), swatted 16 triples, and scored 106 runs. Flick, Wolverton, Thomas, and Jennings each hit over .300. Donahue and Orth won twenty games, and Duggleby finished with 19 wins. Each of the three had an ERA below 3.00. Under Jennings' guidance the Phillies were 59 and 33 for a .620 percentage.

Across town, Connie Mack's Athletics finished fourth with a 74 and 62 record, and Napoleon Lajoie, batting against less-seasoned pitchers under the old strike rule, won the triple crown. He hit .422 with 14 home runs and 125 RBIs. He also led the league in slugging (.635), hits (229), doubles (48), and fielding percentage.

On the ledger side of baseball, the Phillies outdrew the Athletics 234,937 to 206,329. But their attendance had dropped by 68,000, to a ten-year low. Rumors circulated that the National League was anxious to rid itself of John Rogers. The owners held him responsible for the Athletics entry into Philadelphia and believed his obstinacy had wrecked his franchise.[76] They stopped short of censuring him because it might further weaken the league in this time of crisis. It was ironic that at a time when Guglielmo Marconi was sending the first wireless messages across the Atlantic Ocean, major league owners had trouble communicating in the same room.

These troubles did not bother Delahanty. He was pleased by his performance, and the prospects for 1902 looked bright. When the season was over, Del did not barnstorm with the Phillies. Instead, he took his family to New York and spent his afternoons at the Aqueduct race track. He and National League batting champion Jesse Burkett "hit the bookmakers quite hard" with their American League bonus money.[77] Delahanty did well at the races and followed the racing circuit to Washington to conclude his baseball business. Arriving with his family on November 10, the Delahantys stayed at the Oxford Hotel. Although he continued to deny his signing, Delahanty checked on the progress of his contract and commented about the criticism of jumpers. He said newspaper accounts were unjust and also acknowledged the liberal salaries of the American League: "and I can not see where any blame can be attached to a man who desires to secure the largest amount of money for his services. The courts have decided that the reserve clause is not binding and that clause is the only tie that is broken when a National League player goes over to the opposition." He sidestepped other inquiries about his doings in Washington by saying he was there to see the horse races at the Benning track.[78] His explanations and grievances gave him little credibility. In the eyes of his supporters, Delahanty had abandoned them, and they lamented that Philadelphians would no longer see their "sturdy stake horse . . . thundering down the stretch in a ding-dong finish."[79] Ed Delahanty now ran toward a new finish line.

15

Cresting in Washington

The *Sporting News* described Ed Delahanty as the most startling example of professional ballplayers who were "out-for-the-stuff-stars."[1] What the paper overlooked was that ballplayers, after the cutbacks of 1892 and 1893, had a rare window of opportunity to maximize their worth. Unfortunately, Delahanty's ambition whetted an appetite that exceeded the expanding pace of the major league bidding war.

Delahanty saw the interleague struggle as a unique offering. But rather than use the war to enhance his estate and future security, he squandered his money on a siphoning lifestyle. He believed there was no limit to what a star player could extract from complying magnates. This attitude was a hazardous one for an improvident, aging ballplayer. Instead of nurturing his good fortune, Del succumbed to heedless intemperance.

Following his accustomed annual routine, Ed Delahanty and his family left for New Orleans, after spending the holiday season with relatives and friends in Cleveland. The move coincided with the Crescent City's 100-day racing season. His daughter, Florence, recalled these exciting times, the Pullman trains, the very best hotels and a life full of "ease, luxury and fun." A hired nurse tended to

Florence's daily needs, while her parents indulged themselves in the swirl of social activities. Only after the Mardi Gras festivities and the races were over would Delahanty start his northern trek to spring training.[2]

Much of Del's stay in New Orleans centered around the Crescent City Jockey Club. Attired in expensively tailored suits and stylish hats, Delahanty posed the figure of a wealthy celebrity with his gold watch and chain, rings, and diamond stickpins. With an expensive cigar in his mouth and a large roll of cash in his pocket, Delahanty hung around the paddock area studying his little racing notebook, where he kept a detailed record of betting odds and the paid results of each race.[3] At the track, Delahanty was at ease. He enjoyed the fast and savvy racing crowd and was alert for any tips or insights. Billy Shettsline said Delahanty's one weakness was his love of horse racing. According to Shettsline, Del bragged about his successes and big payoffs. Privately, he confided that Delahanty sometimes suffered significant losses. Shettsline would later say that Ed's losing days made him "an easy prey for American League agents."[4]

These problems did not plague Delahanty during his current stay in New Orleans. Flushed with success, attention, and swelling pockets of bonus money, Ed believed he could do no wrong. Reports out of Louisiana spoke of his "cleaning up" at the race track. It was said that he won between $5,000 and $6,000, and would be paying off his mortgages and looking for investments.[5] But winning the equivalent of two of his 1901 contracts only reinforced Ed's sense of invincibility. He was on a roll, and the prudent path for ensuring safe returns on his money was ignored. Delahanty believed he only had to play baseball for the highest bidding franchise and stake his bankroll on the seductive annuities of the race track, and all would be well. With a full money-belt, Delahanty set off for training camp in Washington, D.C., and the beginning of the new racing season at the Benning Jockey Club.

The nation's capital that greeted Ed Delahanty and his family was smaller than Cleveland, and had a million less people than the Quaker City. Washington was unlike the industrial northern cities. It was a political and administrative center with a transient and seasonal population. The smallest of the major league markets, the city was distinctly southern and rural in character. Termed a "regular sleepy hollow," the District practically closed down in the hot summer baseball months. Unlike most major league towns, it did not have large and varied immigrant communities. In this regard the nation's capital was alien to Delahanty. Only 7 percent of Washington was Irish and about 15 percent of the population was Catholic. Both groups were dwarfed by the black community that made up 31 percent of the capital's inhabitants. When Delahanty reported to his new seasonal home, Washington had two marked distinctions: the District had the largest "colored" population of any city on earth, and four out of every five native American whites living in the capital were born below the Mason-Dixon Line.[6]

Despite these characteristics, Washington had a rich baseball tradition that dated from after the Civil War. But never once in the seventeen years before Delahanty signed with Washington did the city's major league ball clubs ever have a winning season. Playing in a segregated Jim Crow society, without a traditional large Irish-German baseball spectator base, attendance was poor. Only once (1896) did a Washington team draw more than 200,000 fans. People, nevertheless, were excited by the prospect of Delahanty and his Philadelphia teammates playing for the year-old American League Senators. For the thirty-four-year-old Delahanty, it was to be an ill-suited experience.

The Senators had been created in December 1900, when Ban Johnson relocated a number of Western League franchises to former eastern National League cities. The manager was Jimmy Manning, an astute and experienced baseball man, who learned his craft from the indomitable Ted Sullivan and the wily Johnson. Manning had run the Kansas City franchise in Johnson's Western League, and together with club president Fred Postal, a Detroit hotelman, oversaw the new franchise. But both men were minority stockholders, and like other American League teams, were directed by Ban Johnson under a syndicated league operating scheme. When the 1901 Washington ball club took the field for the inauguration of the new league, the club was made up of many of Manning's Kansas City regulars. Their disappointing play and a sixth-place finish soured local supporters.

Manning tried to strengthen his club by attracting players from the struggling National League. For him, there was no better place to shop than John Rogers' discontented Philadelphia franchise.

Using money from the American League's reserve fund, Manning signed Delahanty, Al Orth, Jack Townsend, and Harry Wolverton. The key was Delahanty. He gave the Senators a popular drawing card and credibility with other players. When Jimmy Manning was finished, he had spent nearly $14,000 on four contracts. These outlays disturbed Ban Johnson, who refused Washington more reserve money to pursue Brooklyn's Willie Keeler. Some months later, Manning would resign as manager and be replaced by Johnson's close friend Tom Loftus. Only three pitchers and two everyday players remained from the 1901 ball club.[7]

The months before Delahanty's Senators assembled for spring training were desperate ones for the scheming owners of both leagues. It was Delahanty's misfortune that his aspirations were shaped by the prohibitive actions of these petty sporting lords. On the American League side, everything revolved around the single-minded Ban Johnson. It was his guile and dogged determination that propelled the American League into its second and decisive year. Against Ban Johnson, the National League had no singular leader or unified front. Some blamed Colonel Rogers of Philadelphia for their American League troubles and threatened him with expulsion. Other owners approached the National League's former savior Albert Spalding, hoping he might lead them out of their desperate state.

A critical problem dividing National League owners was how to organize themselves in this time of crisis. One faction, led by Andrew Freedman and Cincinnati's overbearing John Brush, sought to subordinate their franchises into a single interlocking trust. Their opponents turned to Spalding. Initially, the victor of the brotherhood war tried to buy out Freedman and spoke with Ban Johnson about settling interleague strife. But Spalding had no official league position or constituency. His only opportunity was to wrest the National League presidency from the inoffensive Nick Young.[8]

The campaign for Young's reelection configured itself around Freedman's organizational compact. The Red Bank Plan, as it was termed, was named for Freedman's New Jersey estate where Brush, Soden, and Robison worked out their project. Their scheme strove to create a large baseball holding company. The National League clubs were to become part of a syndicate whose chosen officials made all operating and personnel decisions. Preferred stock would be issued with two-thirds of it held by Freedman and his supporters. The remaining owners, Rogers, Hart, Dreyfuss, and Ebbets, dissented and rallied around the candidacy of Albert Spalding. Although Spalding had formerly favored a syndicate scheme for baseball, he now supported the integrity of the sport in the "active struggle to protect the game from enemies in its own household."[9] In his eyes, "Freedmanism" had become the "incarnation of selfishness supreme,"[10] and the league presidency became his vehicle of redemption.

After a number of failed ballots, the Freedman group left the meeting room. In their absence, Rogers was elected chairman pro-tem, and Spalding was chosen as league president. Freedman and his associates condemned these actions and filed an injunction against Spalding's election. Spalding left New York and had no communication with his allies. In the months that followed, the National League was rudderless. It was only after Spalding failed to override the injunction that he resigned his miscarried presidency. In his place, the National League owners set up a three-man executive committee made up of Brush, Soden, and Spalding supporter James Hart. But the damage had been done, and the spectacle of feuding owners encouraged Ban Johnson and his supporters. It was not the way the National League wanted to start the new season.[11]

For major league baseball and Ed Delahanty, 1902 was a critical year. The National League attended to their self-inflicted wounds, the American League strove to expand their immediate advantages, and Delahanty carried the burden of proving his worth to Washington's investors. As for the prospects of Delahanty's Phillies, their fate was not difficult to predict. The team lost its best ballplayers and any chance for being a contender. Delahanty never acknowledged his role in the team's demise, but a vindictive Napoleon Lajoie bragged that Rogers had more to work with "than I would have done if I had my whole say about it."[12]

In the nation's capital, cranks were brimming with confidence and high hopes. Outside observers saw things differently. One Philadelphia paper said that for Delahanty and his friends, "their room is better than their company," and the ball club was better off without them.[13] Another columnist questioned Washington's logic of building a team around veterans such as Delahanty and the newly signed, thirty-nine-year-old Jimmy Ryan of Chicago. Ryan and Delahanty were good friends and welcomed the opportunity to play together in the Washington outfield. The concern was whether two players with thirty years of major league baseball experience between them were capable of a full productive season.[14] Tom Loftus never doubted their capacities. He was more alarmed over rumors that Delahanty was being courted by the National League.

Ed Delahanty's problem was his reputation as an inveterate jumper. Whenever he appeared with a major league agent, suspicions were raised. His denials were no longer creditable. Nevertheless, he asserted that any National League approach was useless, because "I want no contract breaking in mine."[15]

As the 1902 Senators arrived at the capital, Manager Loftus was busy organizing local training exhibition games and renovating their ball field, a small 6,500–seat stadium erected in 1901 on the grounds of the Washington Brick Machine Company at Florida Avenue and Trinidad Street, Northeast. It was during the park's makeover that Loftus was notified that Ed Delahanty's bats had arrived from New Orleans. Relieved that Delahanty would soon follow his five "wallopers," Loftus, acting on Del's directions, stored the bats in the team's strong-vault. Delahanty, it was said, "would rather meet a cross-eyed woman or miss a load of hay over his right shoulder than lose his bats."[16] Assured of his commitment, the city of Washington waited on the appearance of the great Delahanty.

Finally, on Monday, April 7, team captain Delahanty and his family arrived at the newly opened Union Station. Loftus put aside his displeasure with Delahanty's lateness and beamed at the sight of his star slugger. Delahanty said he was feeling well and related that he had dropped twenty pounds working out over the last two weeks.[17] His first task was to meet with the players and observe their workout. But when the following day's practice was interrupted by rain, Captain Delahanty led his cronies Orth, Ryan, and Wolverton to the Benning Race Track.[18] The next day, playing in ankle-deep mud, Delahanty directed an exhibition game against a Jersey City traveling team. An admiring reporter described Delahanty as "[b]ig, raw-boned, broad shouldered [and] savage-looking." At the plate, the Irish slugger, he wrote, squared off at the pitcher "as if he was going to throw the bat at him and strike at the ball like a man chopping down a tree."[19] The Delahanty era in Washington had begun.

Ed Delahanty's early preseason games were played with enthusiasm, but within a few weeks, his performance was criticized. He and Harry Wolverton were accused of "playing a lazy and listless game." Delahanty's fielding was described as "rather yellow" and he was "painfully slow" returning the ball to the infield.[20] This performance was not atypical of Delahanty. Believing he was ready for the season, Del did not overextend himself in meaningless games, especially with a sore throwing arm. The Washington captain also had his mind on other matters. He was adjusting to a new club, setting up his family in a suitable hotel, and keeping his eye on the Supreme Court of Pennsylvania, where a decision in the Lajoie case could disrupt Delahanty's content little world.

Although they were playing on different teams, Ed Delahanty's fate was tied to the action of his former teammate. Their 1900 walk-out and its controversial settlement cast a long shadow. It fueled Lajoie's rebellion, led to the interleague bidding war, and provoked Colonel Rogers' injunction. Having ridden the crest of these crises to Washington, Delahanty again found himself swept up in another set of Lajoie-inspired actions. The first came out of New York after Spalding's resignation and involved reports that a National League war fund was established for inducing players back to the senior circuit. Rogers and fellow owners denied its existence and said their case would be vindicated in a court of law.

Five days into the new baseball season, the appellate court unanimously overturned the Lajoie case. This action meant that John Rogers' injunction against Lajoie could be enforced, and players such as Delahanty were suddenly liable to their former ball clubs. Overnight, Lajoie legally became a "unique and extraordinary" ballplayer, one who knowingly signed, and then rejected a three-year contract with his original employer. The repercussions of the new ruling reverberated throughout the major leagues.

On the issue of "mutuality," the court said that the Phillies had lived up to their side of the original contract and the exclusive agreement was written in understandable language. If Lajoie's three-year service contract met the court's legal criteria, then the second baseman should be restrained from playing for any other team during the life of his Phillies' contract. Not everyone agreed with this interpretation of "reasonableness and fairness." What was indisputable was its far-reaching and immediate impact.[21]

Colonel Rogers was elated by the decision and wired the good news to his fellow National League magnates. They congratulated him on his victory and remarkable persistence. Ban Johnson was stunned by the reversal. He called it a fatal blow and quickly set out to oversee damage control. Lajoie did not know what to say and declined comment until he spoke with his attorneys. The most eloquent response came from the usually reticent Ben Shibe.

> Of course we will fight it to the bitter end, and will make our final appeal to the people—the plain people. . . . If the court declares that a club may prevent a ball player from reaping the benefit of his skill when he is in his prime, and may discard him like a sucked orange when he has outlived his usefulness, we must abide by that. . . . But I believe that the laborer is worthy of his hire—that a ball player is worth the value of his drawing capacity.[22]

In the wake of these reactions, a telegram was sent by Phillies manager Billy Shettsline to Lajoie, Delahanty, and other Philadelphia "jumpers." The message informed the players that the Supreme Court had ruled that their original contracts were binding, and therefore, "You are hereby ordered to report forthwith to me at Philadelphia Ball Park for performance of duties under your contract. Refusal to do that will be at your peril."[23]

Ed Delahanty was distressed by this turn of events. Before the reversal, he was convinced that he was worth more than the value of his new Washington contract, and in the free market climate of baseball, he could hand-pick his next club. Ideally, he envisioned himself signing a Lajoie-size, New York contract and playing in a city whose lifestyle suited him. Unfortunately, his dreams were shattered by the Pennsylvania decision. Del feared he would lose the leverage of his remaining productive years or be forced by a Rogers' injunction to return to Philadelphia. Such an order would void his Washington contract and require him to play one more year at $3,000.

When Delahanty, Orth, Wolverton, and Townsend received Shettsline's telegram, they took it to Loftus. He consoled them and said he foresaw no problems. With that assurance, Delahanty and his mates played their last exhibition game against Georgetown College. Delahanty homered over the center field fence, but reports said that the former Phillies wore "ghastly smiles" and tried to put on a swell front. Each player boastfully declared he would not return to Philadelphia even if it meant never playing ball again.[24] In support of his players, club president Fred Postal and his attorneys secured a restraining order from the Supreme Court of the District of Columbia. This directive, in place by opening day, warned the National League not to interfere with Delahanty and his teammates.[25]

Delahanty and the Senators beat Boston in his inaugural game, 7 to 3, before 6,000 spectators. Del went 2 for 4 with a double and three runs scored, and Al Orth got the win. The next day was a different story. With twenty-five policemen present to prevent anyone from arresting or interfering with Delahanty and his teammates, Cy Young shut down Washington 11 to 3.[26] Safe for the moment, the question for Ed Delahanty and the former National Leaguers was how the Pennsylvania decision could be applied. The National League declared the matter was between the players and the Phillies, and had no idea how the Philadelphia club intended to enforce their "alleged equitable rights."[27]

Colonel Rogers reacted quickly and got a five-day injunction against Lajoie, restraining him from playing baseball for the Athletics. In the meantime, the Philadelphia Common Pleas Court agreed to hear the case and decide whether to extend Lajoie's injunction and apply it to Bernhard and Fraser. Although newspapers rekindled the well-worn themes of ballplayers as "human chattel" and "white slavery," on May 6 the judges enforced the injunctions. The complicating problem was the ruling of other state courts who said the Pennsylvania decision was applicable only to the Keystone State. This pronouncement meant players, such as Delahanty, signed by non-Philadelphia teams, could play anywhere except in the jurisdiction of Pennsylvania. The question was what to do with Philadelphia Athletics' players—Lajoie, Bernhard, Duggleby, Fraser, and Elmer Flick.

Each player was filled with apprehension. Flick, nervous about being caught up in Rogers' equity suits, eluded the commonwealth's jurisdiction and returned to his Cleveland home. The American League ensured his presence by brokering a deal between the Cleveland Blues and Connie Mack's Athletics.[28] Pitchers Chick Fraser and "Frosty Bill" Duggleby were less resilient. They returned to Shettsline's "uncle Tom's cabin" with raises in their salaries.[29] Napoleon Lajoie was a different matter. Detroit, New York, and even Washington pursued him. Tom Loftus met Lajoie in Philadelphia and asked him to rejoin Delahanty in the nation's capital. Captain Delahanty followed with a telegram, entreating his friend to get out of the Quaker City.[30] Looking out for his best interests, Lajoie came out to the Phillies' ballpark and met with Rogers. Unable to grasp the importance of securing Lajoie for the National League, Rogers refused to give his former second baseman the $500 difference that separated their negotiations. Later, Rogers lamely excused his failure on Lajoie's refusal to accept salary contraints on his behavior.[31] A week after this meeting, Lajoie and Bill Bernhard joined Elmer Flick in Cleveland.

The National League owners, including Phillies' president Al Reach, were furious with Rogers' obstinance. For the sake of a few hundred dollars, Lajoie was lost and court battles and salaries escalated. Connie Mack and Ben Shibe recognized the importance of keeping Lajoie in their league and accepted his transfer to Cleveland. These moves strengthened the faltering Cleveland franchise and repaid Charles Somers for his early financial support. Lajoie signed a three-year, $25,000 contract and was named team captain. These maneuvers hamstrung the stubborn Rogers. He could not extract compensation from American League ball clubs and his restraining orders did not extend to Ohio and other jurisdictions. When Cleveland played in Philadelphia, the three players would not accompany the team; they spent their days in New York or the Jersey shore. These same restrictions held true for Delahanty and the former Phillies who played for Washington.

Well before the Lajoie reversal, Delahanty's return to Philadelphia as a Senator was greatly anticipated. But Loftus and club president Fred Postal, expecting Rogers' restraining order, decided Delahanty, Orth, Wolverton, and Townsend should not go with their team for the four-game series. The Athletics' opening game drew nearly 12,000 fans. Neither Delahanty nor Lajoie played. Lajoie watched the game in street clothes from behind the players' bench. Ed Delahanty and the other Washington "jumpers" got off the Philadelphia train at Wilmington, Delaware, and made their way to Camden, New Jersey, before going on to New York City.[32] This bizarre state of affairs continued throughout the 1902 season.

Commenting on this situation, Delahanty said the Phillies had no right to order him about or keep him from playing with someone else. He remarked that his former team should comply with the federal restraining order.[33] For the moment, Delahanty put baseball and his legal problems aside. He had four days in New York before he rejoined the Senators on their road trip in Boston. As a "confirmed plunger on the ponies,"[34] Delahanty's attention was on the New York racing season. At the big Metropolitan Handicap race at Morris Park, Del wagered $20 on a horse named Arsenal and won $500.[35] On another day, when Delahanty, Orth, and Wolverton were at the track, Townsend ran into Billy Shettsline, whose Phillies were playing in New York. After a congenial greeting, Shettsline jokingly told his former pitcher that, having found him, he intended to kidnap him that evening. The remark unnerved the impressionable Delaware farmboy. Townsend told Shettsline that he would be safe with his roommate, Delahanty, who had been acting as the young man's mentor "since he [Townsend] entered fast company." The youngster warned Shettsline that Delahanty carried a gun, and the Phillies' manager should watch his step. The amused Shettsline later recounted this incident to Delahanty, who played along with the threat. Townsend spent the entire night on the "verge of nervous prostration" waiting for a break-in. For many days, Delahanty and his teammates kidded Townsend about his panicked behavior.[36]

The levity of Delahanty and his "fast-paced" companions did not conceal their concern about the appearance of sheriffs or process-servers. Any travel near Pennsylvania required extensive detours and careful planning. When Delahanty's wife and child were visiting family in Philadelphia, the recognizable former Phillies star could not travel to see his in-laws. In one incident, Lajoie and Bernhard, now playing for Cleveland, clandestinely made their way back from Atlantic City to rejoin their team in Washington. Their ordeal reminded people of the days of the underground railroad.

The players snuck around the Delaware Valley, hiding in woods waiting for trains and a tug boat. They bolted their hotel doors and contemplated disguises to avoid the "clutches of Simon Legree Rogers."[37] A Quaker City columnist who knew Delahanty and the Washington jumpers ridiculed their skulking endeavors. He reported that Delahanty and his pals once hid in a bale of hay and were shipped in the hold of a steamer "consigned to Tom Loftus as a bunch of bananas." Another commentator remarked, "What some people will endure in order to play baseball surpasses all belief."[38]

With or without Delahanty, the Senators were not a very good team. By June 1, Washington was six games under .500, and well secured in seventh place. But the club's disappointing performance did not detract from the cranks' fascination with Delahanty's play. The kids of Washington adored him. Attentive to their adulation, Del even sponsored a local team called the "Young Delahantys," who played throughout the late summer months.[39] On the field, he was not the same dominating outfielder who played for the Phillies. His greatest success, as expected, came at the plate, where he benefited from the American League's continued rejection of the new foul-strike rule. Ban Johnson, hoping to give the fans more offense, carried the rule over from the 1901 season. With former National League batsmen such as Jesse Burkett, Jimmy Collins, Elmer Flick, and Napoleon Lajoie competing with Delahanty for hitting honors, the 1902 offensive nature of the new league produced 565 more hits, 931 more runs, 160 more home runs, and a .16 higher batting average.

Delahanty's productivity drew attention again to his brothers' careers. The Delahanty boys, having gone their separate ways after the Atlantic League folded, had more opportunities for advancement with the new major league. Since 1901, attention on the siblings was largely focused on Jimmy Delahanty. The previous season, Jimmy had his brief introduction to the National League aborted by an injury and illness. He began the new year by returning to Worcester, but before long the New York Giants signed the twenty-three-year-old to play the outfield. *Sporting News* remarked that

Jimmy was a "wonderful straight-away batsman" and a hard-working and obliging young ballplayer. Jimmy's stay in New York, however, was not a long one. He was not in peak playing form and was fielding an unfamilar position. He appeared in only seven games and batted .231 before he was released in early May. He quickly signed to play third base for Little Rock in the Southern League.[40] He played in 101 games, hit .328, and led the league in triples (19). After the season, it was rumored that Jimmy would follow his brother Tom and join the Western League and play for Colorado Springs.[41] It was only after much discussion that Jimmy returned to Little Rock, embarking on his own path to the major leagues.

While playing for Little Rock, Jimmy Delahanty persuaded his nineteen-year-old brother Frank, or "Pudgie," to try out for the Southern League. With mother Delahanty's permission, Frank stayed near home and played semipro ball in Warren, Ohio.[42] But he played so well, Frank was scouted and signed by Birmingham in the Southern League. The Iron Barons saw in young Frank a raw, talented kid with a drawing-card surname. The youngster played third base and the outfield in 71 games, batting 10 triples with a respectable .269 average.[43] It was an auspicious beginning.

The middle brother, Joe, whose career looked so promising, remained in the Eastern League, where he was sold from Montreal to Worcester. Joe took over Jimmy's spot at third base. Not familiar with this position, he had trouble charging and fielding bunted balls. His strength, it was noted, was batting "like the head [brother Ed] of the family."[44] Overall, most observers felt Joe Delahanty was "pretty near ready for advancement."[45] In a league considered just a step below the majors, Joe performed well. He played in every game, had 24 doubles, 13 triples, and 8 home runs, and batted .277.

At the time that Joe Delahanty was reestablishing his baseball credentials, his older brother Tommy was sparkling with Denver in the Western League. In 1902 Tommy played second base exclusively. He fielded his position well without missing a game. For a thirty-year-old journeyman, Tommy's career was at its peak. He batted .350, scored 118 runs, and stroked 194 hits.[46] Even so, Tommy's age was against him making it back to the major leagues. Meanwhile, his sixteen-year-old kid brother William followed the dream sparked by Ed Delahanty more than fifteen years before.

Ed Delahanty's prowess as a great batsman continued to draw attention to his siblings. But the feats of the senior Delahanty could not offset his team's shortcomings or insulate him from baseball's pending crisis. While newspapers reported on the peace terms ending the Boer War in South Africa and the devastation wrought by the massive eruption of the Mont Pelee volcano on the French island of Martinique, repercussions of Lajoie's case were congesting the corridors of major league baseball.

National League players such as the young Christy Mathewson and the veteran Willie Keeler were being targeted by Ban Johnson's agents. At the same time, as threats circulated about expelling ballplayers, the Players' Protective Association was weakened to the level of a toothless advocate by the actions of players and owners. Contributing to this evolving malaise were a number of contentious actions. Jim "Deacon" McGuire, a long-time catcher and Delahanty friend, had a Brooklyn injunction against his playing with Detroit in the American League overturned, and the talented Rube Waddell successfully jumped to Connie Mack's American League Athletics. Waddell's exploits were crowded off the Philadelphia sports pages by recriminations that wounded Delahanty's former team. President Al Reach openly criticized John Rogers' decision-making and dogmatic management style. Reports abounded during the summer of 1902 that Rogers would be ousted and the team sold. This friction paled in contrast to the split between Ban Johnson and his American League nemesis, Baltimore's player-manager, John McGraw. Their conflict not only disrupted the new league's momentum, it dragged Delahanty into its turbulent wash.

Ban Johnson and John McGraw had many things in common. They were competitive, hard-driving men with large egos, who used the national pastime for their own betterment. At first, McGraw worked with Johnson, Comiskey, and Charles Somers for the right to resurrect an American League franchise in the abandoned baseball market of Baltimore. But the two strong-willed autocrats clashed over personnel issues, organizational matters, and the style of ballplaying. It was obvious by the 1902 season that the establishment of an American League team in New York would finish their deteriorating relationship. McGraw knew that Johnson wanted to move the disappointing Baltimore franchise to New York. He also believed that Ban Johnson no longer appreciated him and wanted him out of any New York deal. John McGraw feared Johnson would abandon Baltimore and leave him "holding the bag." McGraw justified his suspicions by accusing Johnson of trying to undermine his team with harassing penalties for rowdy baseball. The Baltimore manager was convinced that the frequent suspensions and disciplining of McGraw and his players were crippling the club's chances of winning.[47] In his autobiography, McGraw said he sidestepped Johnson's actions by legally negotiating his release from Baltimore. "I did not jump . . . neither did I deceive the stockholders." They knew, he asserted, "that I acted in good faith. I had simply protected myself as any businessman would do."[48] What John McGraw did was to extricate himself from a doomed franchise by opening negotiations with the National League's Andrew Freedman of New York.

On July 8, 1902, McGraw left Baltimore and went to New York, where he agreed to manage the floundering Giants. He became the highest paid person in baseball, signing at $11,000 a year for four years. McGraw also had complete authority over the ball club and an unlimited budget. At his New York press conference, John McGraw attacked Ban Johnson and the Chicago-Philadelphia-Boston cartel. Ban Johnson charged that McGraw's comments were "the muttering of an insignificant and vindictive wasp."[49] The *Baltimore Sun* wrote, "Loyalty and gratitude are words without meaning to ballplayers and especially to McGraw."[50]

Once in place, McGraw assured reporters that he would not interfere with the Orioles, but in less than ten days Baltimore had to forfeit a game because of a lack of ballplayers. Financed by Andrew Freedman and Cincinnati's John Brush, McGraw and Joe Kelley's father-in-law, John T. Mahon, took over and savaged the Orioles franchise. Not even the actions of Delahanty and Lajoie in Philadelphia could rival what these schemers did to the Orioles. Joe McGinnity, Roger Bresnahan, Dan McGann, and Jack Cronin were released to the Giants and Cy Seymour joined his Baltimore teammate and new manager Joe Kelley in Cincinnati. With only five players under contract, Ban Johnson assumed control of the Orioles and restocked the team with players from other American League clubs. Almost a month after these dealings, Brush sold his Cincinnati stockholdings, and for $125,000, bought out Andrew Freedman's controlling shares in the Giants.

The once-hated rivals, Freedman, Brush, and McGraw, had choreographed a baseball *coup d'état*. Even by nineteenth-century standards it was an extraordinary series of skullduggery. If McGraw was the catalyst of this revolution, then the muscle-impaired John Brush was its pilot and major beneficiary. Years later, the *Sporting News* remarked, "Chicanery is the ozone which keeps his [Brush's] old frame from snapping" and his "dark-lantern methods [are] the food which vitalizes his bodily tissues."[51] Brush, like Freedman, believed McGraw was the person to restore New York to its winning ways. At twenty-nine years of age, the combative Irishman, whom critics called "Muggsy," turned the tide in the major league baseball war. When asked what he needed to rebuild his new ball club, McGraw listed Kid Elberfeld, George Davis, and Ed Delahanty.[52]

It was evident by mid-July that the Senators would not be contending for a pennant and were mired in the second division. The strain of the season took its toll on Del and his fellow jumpers. Harry Wolverton could not bear the pressures of lawsuits and threatening arrests. He became depressed, and his overall play deteriorated. Eventually, he asked Loftus for a few days off to compose himself. In a hotel in Cape May, New Jersey, he made his peace with Rogers and agreed to return to the Phillies and the National League.[53] The Phillies also opened talks with Al Orth and young Jack Townsend, evoking speculation that they might join Wolverton in the Quaker City. Another report said it would not take much to entice Delahanty back to the Phillies' outfield. These stories were vigorously denied by Delahanty and Tom Loftus.[54] But Delahanty was not immune to these distractions. Del already had missed two series in Philadelphia and was drained by the alarms and alerts of his East Coast road trips. The illness of his wife that brought him back from Cleveland did not soothe his outlook.[55] It seemed Ed Delahanty was only at peace when he took his bat to home plate.

Delahanty and former teammate Napoleon Lajoie dominated the 1902 American League batting race. By midsummer, both were hitting over .400. Del kept the pressure on Lajoie by starting a twenty-game hitting streak. During this feat, he batted .380 with four doubles, three triples, and three home runs. It was sometime during this streak, around July 4th, that the ever-scheming John McGraw and his agents tried to lure Delahanty to jump leagues and play for New York.

McGraw made his first offer through Delahanty's old friend, former Philadelphia sportswriter and short-lived New York manager Horace Fogel. The columnist went to Delahanty's Oxford Hotel hangout and asked Ed what it would take for him to break his Washington contract. According to *Sporting Life*, Fogel's proposals met with "such a frost that it queered the gaft effectively." Delahanty was disturbed by the proposition, and a local columnist said that president Freedman should "keep his fingers out of the Washington sugar bowl."[56]

Fogel's failures did not deter John McGraw. Supported by Brush's money, McGraw confidently enticed coveted ballplayers. In his mind, contacted players were like uneasy husbands confronting temptation. They were alarmed by their excitement and aware of their windows of opportunity. Susceptible to McGraw's persuasive charm and persistence, players like Delahanty listened until their resolve weakened. McGraw wanted a power hitter. He knew that Lajoie and Flick were unlikely to leave Cleveland, but he suspected that the way Delahanty lived, the Washington captain would eventually put himself in jeopardy. For this reason, he came to the nation's capital and telephoned Delahanty. Del reportedly laughed at McGraw's offer of $5,500 a year for two years plus a $2,000 advance. He commented, "Do you think I am any cheap man?" McGraw was not put off and asked Delahanty if the price was "sweetened" could they talk about next year? Delahanty replied that he was well fixed and comfortable in Washington and was opposed to making a change. McGraw suggested the "mighty King of Swat" should come to New York and listen to another offer. Delahanty flippantly responded, "Oh, I'll probably get up there before the snow flies. . . . I have an appointment to take tea with Colonel Rogers . . . at the close of the American season, and if you care to join us we'll have green tea served."[57]

Following on McGraw's heels was Brooklyn's president, Charlie Ebbets. From his suite at the new Willard Hotel, Ebbets sent "perfumed pink notes to Delahanty, Orth, and [Bill] Coughlin." The *Post* ran a cartoon depicting Tom Loftus, with a revolver, protecting a ballplayer from a contract-wielding agent.[58] The Senators' official line was that Ed Delahanty rebuffed John McGraw and signed no contract. Del told the press that he would not do business with the Giants' manager and would rather play ball in Washington for $1,000 a year less "than go to any other city in the country."[59] Loftus equated McGraw's actions to "a fellow trying to pick up a lot of feathers on a windy day."[60]

The ensuing contention incited popular opinion. In Boston, while coaching third base, Delahanty was given a telegram. The delivery caused the local cranks to shout, "How much are they offering you to jump? Gimme your old job Del!"[61] One columnist compared Delahanty to a "Peoria Dutchman" innkeeper, who overbooks his rooms. He said Ed Delahanty was "honor bound" to live up to his Washington contract that his Philadelphia attorney had drawn up. The ballplayer was also chided for his old brotherhood actions.[62] For the moment, he had nothing to hide, but McGraw's courtship had just begun.

These distractions did little to affect the performance of Delahanty or the Senators. Washington finished the season in sixth place with a 61 and 75 record, 22 games behind Connie Mack's Athletics. Despite the loss of Lajoie, Flick, and others, the "Mackmen" led by the pitching of Eddie Plank and Rube Waddell, and the captaincy of Lave Cross, brought the Quaker City the championship so coveted by Colonel Rogers. In the nation's capital, the fans could only celebrate the batting of Ed Delahanty. He led the American League in doubles (43) and slugging (.590), stroked 14 triples and 10 home runs, and knocked in 93 runs. His greatest achievement was another hitting title. Del won the honor in a heated race against Lajoie. Delahanty put himself in front by going 21 for 36 in his last nine games. This meant that Ed Delahanty became the only player to win a batting title in each league. Although the averages of Delahanty and Lajoie have been disputed, a detailed study of both batters revealed Ed won the title with a .380 mark to Lajoie's .366 batting grade.[63] It is doubtful Delahanty appreciated this honor. He complained about a stiff neck and did not play in the last three games of the season. Delahanty knew these games meant nothing to his club's finish and was anxious to get his family ready to move to New York City for the opening of the new racing season. With $600 captain's money in hand, the Delahantys, accompanied by Jack Doyle,[64] boarded a train, unaware of how their lives were about to change.

16

Get the Money

Despite the attraction and performance of the "great Delahanty," Washington's season frustrated their supporters and it showed at the gate. The team drew about 188,000 fans. In the American League, only the pillaged, last-place Orioles attracted fewer people. Delahanty's former club, the Phillies, fared worse. They finished seventh, 46 games behind Honus Wagner's Pirates, with the lowest attendance in both major leagues. The suffering circumstances of his current and former teams meant nothing to Delahanty. He again excelled at the plate and enjoyed the fruits of his successes. But the cranks of Washington saw things differently. They knew that Delahanty was no longer a great outfielder, a swift base runner, or an effective field captain.

Delahanty's faltering leadership was a matter of inattention and disposition. Ed was much too casual and not assertive enough to lead a baseball team.[1] He lacked the drive and focus of fellow Irishmen John McGraw, Hugh Jennings, Patsy Tebeau, or Charlie Comiskey. Neither could he inspire the quiet confidence and direction of Connie Mack or Ned Hanlon. For him, the sport remained an outlet for an adolescent ego that filled him with a false sense of importance. He did not see the game as a vehicle for betterment.

Del gave his attention to the schedules of the racing seasons and the issue of whether his salary was commensurate with his status as a dominant player. Tom Loftus understood Delahanty's priorities and remembered the player's broken pacts in 1890 and 1901. But the Washington manager had few alternatives. He put his faith in Delahanty's word and the binding nature of his captain's contract. Regrettably, the strength of Ed's resolve was scripted by his New York trip.

Jack Doyle and Delahanty were in high spirits and looking forward to making the New York "bookies look like the proverbial 30 cents."[2] And while the city of Philadelphia prepared for a grand parade to celebrate the Athletics' championship, Billy Shettsline plotted ways to meet up with his friend and former player. Aware that Delahanty would avoid Pennsylvania on his way to New York, the Phillies manager intercepted his train at a small station in New Jersey. Delahanty was surprised to see Shettsline and was impressed that the Phillies were anxious to match John McGraw's offer. Shettsline showed the "king of Swatville" a newly printed contract for $5,500 a year for two years. He informed Del that he could draw on it at any time. Delahanty sighed and allegedly told his old pal that he was tied up with Washington and had taken advance money from Loftus. Shettsline told a different story. He recounted that Delahanty said if he could get his release, he would be happy to return to Philadelphia. After Shettsline departed, Delahanty covered himself and wired Tom Loftus with details of Philadelphia's proposition.[3]

This incident confirmed Delahanty's conflicted position and vacillating nature. By October 1902 Ed was still uncomfortable with these approaches and found it hard to reject offers carried by long-time friends. When the Senators' stockholder Michael Scanlon asked about these overtures, Delahanty said the stories about him leaving Washington for a better offer were quite upsetting.[4] This sentiment, remarkable as it may appear, was probably close to the truth. Delahanty was troubled by his reputation as a contract jumper and knew his current agreement was not contestable. But the situation changed once his handicapping fell from the "high stool" of the race track. The more he lost, the more he bet to make up for his previous setbacks. Locked into an addictive gambling cycle with its accumulated debt, a desperate Delahanty became prey to the renewed National League's bidding frenzy.

John McGraw, a passionate gambler in his own right, made it a point to be with Delahanty on many of these losing Aqueduct afternoons. Having already lost his bankroll, Ed Delahanty needed instant cash to break out of his losing streak. Fred Postal responded with an additional $600 and stopped payment on another check when he suspected something was amiss.[5] But Del's difficulties were a boon to McGraw, "who had lost sleep to get the line on Delahanty."[6] With the support of his new boss, John T. Brush, a long-time admirer of Delahanty, McGraw was ready to ensnare his hard-luck and coveted companion. Accompanied by his wife, Delahanty signed a guaranteed contract with New York for $6,000 a year for three years, including a $2,000 cash advance. One story said that Ed took this step because he could no longer draw on his Washington salary. Whatever the case, when Del returned to Washington about November 9 for the Benning race season, reports said that prosperous-looking Delahanty had many a "big killing as a chaser" at Aqueduct.[7] From his appearance, nothing seemed to be wrong. Delahanty struck a dashing and successful presence at the lavish opening of the Benning season. It was a grand façade and spectacle. Delahanty, surrounded by local well-wishers and baseball cronies, Ned Hanlon, Joe Kelley, John McGraw, and Wilbert Robinson, stood out at the newly renovated Washington Jockey Club.[8] For the moment, the anxiety of what he had done was eased by the heat of the action. Unfortunately, Del could not outrun "dame rumor," and soon the festivities were marred by persistent stories that McGraw had affirmed Delahanty's signing. One afternoon at Benning, Eugene Cochran, a Washington stockholder and local tobacconist, confronted Delahanty with these allegations. The Senators' captain flatly denied their accuracy and reminded Cochran that he had two more years on his Washington contract.[9]

Surprisingly, some fans still took Delahanty at his word and were convinced that he would again appear in a "senatorial toga." One writer reported that Ed has been measured for his robe which was "to be cut something like a horse blanket, the taste of the big un [sic] having an equine tendency at all times."[10] Michael Scanlon, who had gotten an earlier denial from Delahanty, surmised that Del had signed with New York. His theory was that Delahanty would stay in Washington if he could repay McGraw from recouped winnings at the Benning or New Orleans race tracks.[11] These speculations troubled Senators' president Fred Postal. He naïvely commented that Delahanty was "one of the last men on earth whom I would suspect of treachery." He said Delahanty had already taken a large advance on his 1903 salary and, knowing his captain as well as he did, could not conceive of him again stooping to contract-jumping. If he left Washington, Postal lamented, "I don't believe I will ever trust the word of a baseball player again."[12] On December 5, 1902, the new Giants owner John T. Brush confirmed McGraw's news leaks by publicly presenting Delahanty's three-year contract.

Once Delahanty's actions were exposed, Washington spokesmen asserted that they intended to hold their captain to his contract. The *Washington Post* spoke of McGraw and his signees as "men-of-no-word"—worthy of the "Garbage Collectors Association."[13] In Philadelphia, Colonel Rogers declared that Delahanty was obligated to him and would not waive his rights to the American League batting champion. Rogers also pronounced his willingness to go to court to ensure that Delahanty played for no other National League team.[14] The irrepressible Brush, countered that he had no intention of surrendering Delahanty and believed that future peace negotiations favored his position.[15] As one reporter commented, Delahanty was in "a pretty pickle sure enough."[16]

Now in New Orleans, Ed Delahanty continued to deny the stories of his desertion. He insisted that he would not return to Philadelphia or to any other National League team.[17] In spite of this stance, Delahanty allegedly told an interviewer, "of course I may sign elsewhere than with Washington, but to date McGraw and I haven't come to any agreement. . . . No, there is nothing in it."[18] The public's skepticism was captured by the *North American,* who regretted that owners continued to quarrel over the Delahantys, McGraws, and Matthewsons. "They are not worth it. For the good of the game they should be barred, no matter how great their skills as players."[19] Paul Eaton, covering Washington for *Sporting Life,* was more understanding. He said that Delahanty was a "good-natured chap, who always intends to do right." Unfortunately, his value as a ballplayer, Eaton warned, was set by men like Brush and McGraw, who establish temptations that players such as Delahanty find difficult to resist. To Eaton's way of thinking, "The people who tempt players to break contracts are often more to blame than the players." These men, he wrote, created the environment that everyone condemned.[20]

These sentiments struck home in the Delahanty affair. Ed Delahanty's gambling made him vulnerable and desperate. His would-be benefactors knew what they were doing and used the baseball war to justify their actions. McGraw pressured Del with well-placed stories and was at his side in New York, Washington, and New Orleans, feeding on Ed's addiction. The conspiring John McGraw even advanced him another $2,000. Ensnared by the narcotic cycle of gambling, Delahanty did not try to correct his compulsion. Surrounded by other free-spending athletes such as "Broadway Aleck" Smith, Honus Wagner, Napoleon Lajoie, and McGraw himself, Delahanty was deluded by their camaraderie and a false sense of security. Only his wife, Norine, expressed concerns about her husband's mounting debts. But she was reminded by him that everything he did was to ensure his family's well-being.[21] In the end, Delahanty had been advanced $4,000 by New York and $1,600 by Washington and was contractually tied to three different teams in two competing leagues.

Although the reckless Delahanty later rationalized that he was taking advantage of the renewed bidding war, neither his runaway addiction nor his inflated ego excused his disdain for contracted law. The underlying factor was that the hustling John McGraw had conned Delahanty into believing that he had no reason to fear American League reprisals and that the National League magnates would not allow Colonel Rogers to thwart him from rejoining his old league. Delahanty's only response was that he was sorry to "cut loose" from a good fellow like Tom Loftus, who treated him so well.[22] To protect himself, Delahanty again had his Philadelphia attorney, Louis Hutt, draw up an "ironclad" contract that exceeded the certified safeguards of his existing Washington pact. In this new contract, Delahanty was to be paid regardless of injunctions, disbarment, or injuries. The money was to be deposited in a New York bank and was subject to Del's checks at dated intervals. "I am in no way concerned which way the wind goes. I get the money . . . no matter what proceedings may follow. . . . When my contract wears out I will be satisfied to quit the game and follow the turf to campaign a string of racers."[23] Armed with his new contract and the assurances of the scheming Brush and McGraw, Delahanty readied himself for whatever settlement the two leagues concocted.

Both leagues were uneasy about the 1903 season. The National League was in disarray, and the American League was stretched to its limits. The older organization, reeling over the Brush-Freedman maneuvers, tried to right itself under new leadership. With attendance in decline and New York about to be invaded by Ban Johnson, the National League elected a compromised, proactive league president: Pittsburgh's secretary, Henry Clay "Harry" Pulliam. The thirty-three-year-old Pulliam was a former Louisville newspaperman whose selection signaled the shift from Brush and the hard-line old guard to moderate owners ready to bargain. It was not a coincidence that a preliminary meeting of a "Peace Commission" at New York's Criterion Hotel greeted Pulliam's election. The representatives of both leagues agreed to meet in Cincinnati in early January to work out a permanent accord. The future of baseball and the career of Delahanty rested on their decisions.

After much posturing and compromise, four men from each league convened in Cincinnati on Friday, January 9, 1903. Ban Johnson was accompanied by Charles Somers of Cleveland, Charlie Comiskey of Chicago, and Henry Killilea of Boston. They engaged the National League's Harry Pulliam, Frank Robison of St. Louis, James Hart of Chicago, and August "Gary" Herrmann of Cincinnati. The key figure was Herrmann, the newly named president of the Cincinnati ball club. He was a lifelong friend of Ban Johnson and a confidant of John Brush.

The issues of organization and territorial rights were not an obstacle to the executives. They rejected an association of sixteen teams, as suggested by Brush, in favor of two leagues. The magnates agreed to cooperate in scheduling games and adopted National League rules, such as the foul-strike regulation. The old league even accepted Johnson's entry into New York after he dropped plans to move into Pittsburgh. Both organizations also recognized the reserved rights of every team, and a new contract was perfected. In anticipation of future cooperation, plans were made for an executive commission to govern major league baseball. This three-man committee, two league presidents, and a third member chosen by them, would rule baseball until after the 1919 World Series scandal.

The most controversial obstruction, threatening their progress, was the ownership of ballplayers.[24] Central to the debate was the status of Ed Delahanty.

Up to the time of the Cincinnati conference, Delahanty was financially bound and emotionally committed to playing with McGraw's Giants. He expected problems over his contract, but believed Brush and McGraw would somehow exact concessions from the negotiators. Unfortunately, his expectations were premature. Brush and McGraw had alienated many of the conferees, especially Ban Johnson, who had not gotten over McGraw's actions in Baltimore. Delahanty's future, therefore, would be determined by unsympathetic owners with larger agendas. In their eyes, McGraw and Delahanty were untrustworthy troublemakers in need of punishment. Before the Cincinnati conference, the commissioners went on record that New York's pact with Delahanty would not be permitted to upset the reconciliation.[25]

Delahanty's attitude and broken contracts alarmed too many baseball people. In their eyes, Del's actions testified to the game's need for reserve contracts.[26] Ban Johnson and the American League Senators asserted that Ed was under contract for two more years, and the issue of his obligations was beyond debate.[27] G. Hector Clemes, a Washington stockholder and close friend of Johnson, declared that he had a picture of Delahanty on his wall with an inscription calling for the shooting of all contract jumpers. "Yes," he said, "Delahanty will play in Washington or he will not play ball at all next season. The public is too well informed of the facts in this case to go over the ground again."[28] John Brush saw things differently. He believed Delahanty was committed to New York and was confident he would retain the services of the great Irish slugger. But Delahanty, the "human grasshopper," had become a symbol to Ban Johnson: we intend to stop the contract-jumping evil if we have to continue the war to a case of extermination."[29]

As Johnson and Brush postured over Delahanty, Colonel Rogers in Philadelphia reminded everyone that Ed Delahanty was still his ballplayer. Rogers made Delahanty an issue at a preliminary owners meeting in December. In a letter to President Pulliam, Rogers asserted that Delahanty signed a Philadelphia contract through the 1903 season and that New York was violating every pledge and agreement of the league. The Pennsylvania Supreme Court, he said, supported this contract with an injunction against Delahanty.[30] As usual, Rogers also threatened legal action against New York and demanded just compensation if Delahanty was allowed to play with the Giants. With the last word in mind, Rogers charged that "The idea of a club in your own organization outbidding you for your own player is absurd. New York claimed it was done as a war measure. But now that the war is practically over, I will fight the Delahanty case to the finish."[31] The conflicting positions on Delahanty collided on the second day of the Cincinnati conference.

Altogether, there were sixteen contested players. These ballplayers and their contracts were to be judged by the 1902 season. Other players, who jumped after the start of the new season, were to be returned to their old clubs. Each case was bargained and settled individually. It was obvious that New York and Brooklyn, who resisted the peace talks, were the big losers. Brooklyn lost the claims to Willie Keeler and Bill Donovan, and New York failed to get George Davis, Kid Elberfeld, Dave Fultz, and Delahanty. The Giants did retain the rights to contract-jumping pitcher Christy Mathewson.

Thanks to Gary Herrmann's diplomacy and Barney Dreyfuss's proddings, Pulliam and Johnson got their long-awaited peace settlement. The accord was achieved at the expense of John Brush and the National League's hard-liners. Although Ban Johnson and the American League appeared to be the big winners, the benefits to all parties, including dissidents Brush and Rogers, were so obvious that they grudgingly ratified the pact. Brush later lamented, "You can make me swallow it, but you cannot make me like it."[32] This attitude was in keeping with Brush's maverick nature. One columnist wrote that Brush was like a "shipwrecked Irishman" who told his rescuers, "If you have a government I'm agin it."[33]

Despite Brush's disposition, under McGraw the Giants survived these setbacks and eventually became one of baseball's most successful franchises. Events took a different turn for John Rogers and his Phillies. His dream of a championship ball club was shattered by his own shortsightedness. One detractor lamented that John Rogers "knew too much about the law and not enough about baseball."[34] By his own admission, he became disgusted by the events of the last two years and was ready to join Al Reach in selling the ball club. In March the Phillies were sold for $170,000 to a syndicate led by socialite James Potter. Within a few months of the sale, the Phillies dropped their injunction against Lajoie and Bernhard. Ed Delahanty was not as fortunate. He was ordered to repay his New York advance money and was directed back to Washington. But Del got off easy because he was almost blacklisted.

Delahanty's future in baseball was in doubt when Ban Johnson launched a tirade against contract jumpers. Johnson singled out Delahanty for punishment. By the time he was finished talking, seven out of eight magnates were in favor of banishing the "only Del" from the major leagues. The holdout was Charlie Comiskey of Chicago. An alleged supporter and spokesman for the ballplayers, Comiskey argued that Delahanty should not be made a scapegoat. He spoke instead of the owners who enticed players to abandon their contracts. He reminded his colleagues that if ballplayers were to be punished, what about complicitous owners? Although Comiskey appreciated the severity of his charges, he had ulterior motives. He knew that Delahanty's blacklisting would not be popular with Chicago's southside Irish fans, nor could he overlook how it affected his claims on his contract-jumping shortstop, George Davis. After a heated debate, Comiskey, with the support of Gary Herrmann of Cincinnati, prevailed, and the owners dropped their drastic position.[35]

Delahanty was in New Orleans with his family when his baseball fate was being decided. Johnson notified him by telegram that he was under contract to Washington and needed to return the $4,000 advance money to John Brush. Delahanty agreed to play for the Senators but balked at reimbursing the Giants. "My contract was a special one," he said, "which provided for a certain sum a year even if prevented from playing by injunction or unforseen debarments."[36] In an interview, Delahanty proposed to do his best for Tom Loftus and reiterated that he had no problems with the Senators. "I left to better myself not because I was dissatisfied." He confessed, "I wanted the money and got it. I will not return [it]. . . . the advance money is in my kick to stay."[37] Less than a week before these comments were made, Delahanty worsened his position when he reputedly lost $4,000 at the race track.[38] Months later, the *Philadelphia Press* said Delahanty believed in his "system" and had become a reckless "plunger." His friends, when they heard that he lost another $1,000 wager, lamented, "his race track fever was hopeless."[39]

Torn between his addiction and his deteriorating financial condition, Delahanty was deaf to the debate going on around him. Before the contract storm erupted, *Sporting Life* reported that Washington losing Delahanty, the "king of sluggers," was like Britain without their new monarch, Edward VII.[40] This attitude gave way to feelings of resentment and abandonment. Many of Delahanty's friends and supporters were disheartened by his "treacherous conduct."[41] Some accused him of playing for records and being a disruptive and distractive presence on the ball club—a team captain looking for excuses to go to the race track.[42] One editorial said that his days of usefulness were over, and "just as soon as he loses his batting eye he will not be worth a cent to any ball club."[43] Other opinions went further. Delahanty, one commentator said, either abides by the league's rulings or is out of baseball. Another called him a "goldbrick," who was not "entitled to a bank president's salary."[44] Washington director Eugene Cochran acknowledged Delahanty's shabby treatment of the Senators but took a more understanding position. He believed Delahanty would return to Washington and give a good account of himself. He also felt the peace and the interleague guidelines would make Delahanty easier to handle. The problem was that whichever course Delahanty took, he would owe some team a great deal of money.[45]

Delahanty may have had a preference where he wanted to play, but the matter rested in the hands of the Washington club. The Peace Commission acknowledged the Senators' contract with Delahanty, and said he would remain their property unless they moved him to another team. In a revealing interview, Washington president Fred Postal gave assurances that should have put Delahanty's mind at ease. He spoke of his captain's "unpleasant notoriety" and reiterated how Delahanty's financial condition gave John McGraw his opening. Postal, willing "to let bygones be bygones," declared that Ed was a great batsman and terrific draw around the league. He said many ball clubs were interested in dealing for him, but Postal preferred to keep the "king of swat" in the nation's capital. Postal was so infatuated with Delahanty that he promised to help fix "the financial end all right," and "make good any amount he may have received from the New York club."[46]

The contract-jumping debate, centering on Delahanty and Davis, became intense in the winter of 1903. The *Washington Post* spoke of Delahanty and Davis as "specimen of the genus contract jumpers," whose reinstatement was conditional on the repayment of advance money.[47] The paper agreed with the *Sporting News* that yielding to either player would wreck the peace conference. In the commentator's eyes, the "bulking form" of Delahanty should be "swept aside . . . to baseball oblivion," and there should be "no dearth of physic in the case of Delahanty."[48]

Another feature in this ongoing drama was the salary benefits of playing in Washington or New York. With the advance money Del owed, he was better off being idle for the year, provided that the New York contract guarantees were fulfilled. Otherwise, any reimbursal would mean that Delahanty would be playing for an unacceptably low salary.[49] If Ed sat out the year, however, Washington would get no compensation for their captain. The solution was to trade Delahanty to New York for a couple of pitchers and a few young prospects. McGraw, who was also courting George Davis, said he would deal for Delahanty and pay the player's debts to Washington. The only ballplayer not available for trade was young Christy Mathewson. "I would not trade Mathewson for a team of Delahantys," McGraw barked.[50] Washington also got feelers about Delahanty from Detroit and the new American League club in New York.[51] These inquiries forced McGraw to redouble his efforts while Brush applied official pressure on Harry Pulliam and his supporters.[52]

Reactions to Brush and McGraw were immediate. Gary Herrmann of Cincinnati said that his team would not take the field against the Giants if Delahanty and Davis played for New York and warned McGraw to stop encouraging these players "in this hallucination."[53] President Pulliam reinforced Herrmann's position. He declared that Delahanty and Davis must fulfill their contracts with Washington and Chicago unless they were released from their obligations.[54] These responses, and the accompanying pressures, took their toll on the hopeful Delahanty. He needed the money, and time was running out on his off-season. With spring training about to start, Delahanty wired Fred Postal that he wanted to meet with manager Tom Loftus.[55]

One story from New Orleans suggested that Delahanty was doing well enough at the racetrack to sit out the year but concluded that a season layoff for a player his age would likely lead to permanent retirement.[56] Delahanty did not want to stop playing major league baseball, nor had he recouped his gambling losses. He was being squeezed by his receding alternatives and was at the point where he examined every conceivable option. His sincere and desperate message to Postal quickly found its way to Tom Loftus. The Washington manager said he had directed Delahanty, like the other Senators, to report to training camp on Monday, March 22. Loftus also asserted there was little chance of Ed being dealt to New York or any other National League club. He related that Delahanty got himself into this mess, and now it was up to him to work his way out of it. "There is nothing else for him to do except quit altogether."[57]

Another opinion came from an ethnically charged editorial in the Sunday *Washington Post*. The column said that if Delahanty and Davis did not play baseball for a "princely salary" then a "policeman's uniform was about all they were fit to wear." The paper said little John McGraw deserved to be spanked for what he had done, and Delahanty was out of touch with reality. The article further stated that the "fat fielder [Delahanty]" was deluding himself if he felt he would get a "sunny Jim parade" to New York. The paper accused McGraw of intoxicating Delahanty with expectations and predicted that Del "will hang on until the last plank is pulled from under him."[58] These venomous sentiments troubled the anxious Delahanty, who was starting to realize that no one was about to cave in to his demands. What Del wanted was to work out a deal that would pay off his debt with prorated deductions from his paychecks. Loftus was willing and waited to see if the big Irishman was coming to Washington.[59]

The 1903 Senators had neither the money nor the players to be a pennant-contending team. The team's strength, its outfield, impressed no one. Without Delahanty, it revolved around the forty-year-old Jimmy Ryan, who batted .320 in 1902. With Ryan in center field, Washington put its hopes on the thirty-two-year-old "Kip" Selbach from the defunct Baltimore ball club and the thirty-four-year-old Jim "Ducky" Holmes, purchased from Detroit. The undermanned infield was not well served by the recyled Eugene DeMontreville, the new team captain. On the mound, Washington relied on Al Orth and the 1902 regulars. The team could not even afford to go south for spring training. They scheduled their practices at Georgetown College's ball field and hoped their only legitimate star, the defiant Delahanty, would show up.

Delahanty sent his wife and daughter to his in-laws in Philadelphia while he settled affairs in New Orleans. His intention was to be in Washington when Loftus called his ballplayers together. On his way north, Delahanty stopped in Atlanta on Saturday, March 20, to meet with New York's American League manager, Clark Griffith. Delahanty, still anxious to play in New York, tried to persuade Griffith to work out a deal with the Senators.[60] It was not until March 24 that Del arrived at Union Station, where he was besieged with questions about his status.

The ballplayer who disembarked from the train did not resemble the 1902 batting champion. Delahanty weighed about 230 pounds, which confirmed that he "enjoyed eating better than even playing the horses." The "king of hitters" also showed the strain of his last few months. He appeared as a weary, out-of-shape, middle-aged athlete. Questioned about his situation, Delahanty confirmed he would like to finish his career in New York. However, he was reporting to the ball club as directed and looked forward to meeting with Loftus. Later in the day, Delahanty said he hoped Loftus could work something out with McGraw, and if nothing happened he would play ball in Washington. "I do not intend to remain idle for ballplaying is a good profession and I will do the best I know how here. It is up to . . . Loftus."[61]

The Senators' manager told Delahanty that he wanted him back and advised Ed that his situation revolved around his New York debt. Alarmed by Loftus' stubbornness, Delahanty promised to be at practice, and adjourned to the Benning Race Track, where he hoped to recoup some of the $4,000.[62] But while Delahanty was anguishing over his choices, George Davis, on the advice of his attorney and with the consent of John McGraw, ignored Comiskey and Pulliam's warnings and started working out with the Giants in Savannah, Georgia. Davis's actions contrasted with Delahanty's more conciliatory stance. Ed lacked Davis's audacity and felt put out by the sudden willfulness of Tom Loftus, who was about to give Del a taste of his own medicine when the ballplayer reported in uniform for spring practice.

Delahanty was delighted to be working out with his old team-mates. They were pleased to have him back, and no one spoke ill of his contract dealings. Some players were sympathetic and questioned why their captain had to repay money for an invalid contract.[63] Del fielded balls in the infield and took his turn with the "willow." Everyone agreed that he looked fit in the batter's box. The same could not be said for his outfield play, where he labored to catch up with fly balls. He repeated this routine for a few days and, with aching muscles, confessed that he "felt about forty years old."[64] The problem was that Delahanty was beginning to look that age. A formal studio picture taken at the start of the 1903 season portrayed a jowly, untoned, and overweight middle-age man with dark, hollowed eyes and thinning pomaded hair.[65] But Delahanty's biggest shock came with the Senators' first exhibition game. He expected to be in the lineup and was stunned when Loftus refused to play him until the compensation issue was settled. It was obvious that Loftus and Postal knew they had Delahanty beaten and took the position that Del pay the money out of his own pocket. Loftus also wanted his former captain to mull over his relationship with Washington, "which looked so unimportant six months ago." Delahanty confessed that his "tail feathers had been plucked."[66]

With his baseball future in limbo, Delahanty played his last two futile cards. Responding to the advice of his brother Tommy, Del made inquiries about the unaffiliated California League. Most observers felt this was a desperate move because it would take Delahanty away from the "real thing race tracks."[67] Loftus saw it as a bluff. A more serious matter was Tom Delahanty's representations to the Western League. When news of this negotiation broke, it was terribly embarrassing to Ed Delahanty. The season had already started, and Del vehemently denied anything that went beyond his brother's inquiry.[68] Exasperated by this complication, Delahanty declared, "I have no more idea of deserting the Washington club then I have of jumping off the Washington Monument."[69] But while the Denver ploy was being played out, Delahanty, who was still banned from playing ball, stopped coming to the grounds and spent his time at the Benning race track.

Unable to gamble his way out of debt, Delahanty called on Tom Loftus and told him he was ready to settle the dispute. On April 11, Delahanty worked out an agreement whereby the Senators agreed to pay the Giants $4,000, with Del reimbursing the team from his salary over each of his remaining two years in Washington.[70] The "king of Swatville," the American League batting champion, would be making a thousand dollars less than John Rogers had paid him before his 1902 jump. It was a bitter pill for the self-absorbed Delahanty to swallow. To his credit, he took it graciously and was relieved that the problem seemed to be resolved. Those who saw him at the Georgetown grounds said he was like "a small boy with a new pair of red-topped boots."[71]

Before Delahanty gave his attention to getting into playing shape, he addressed his disappointed supporters. Del admitted that he never intended to offend anyone, especially Loftus and Postal. He said he had not approached other teams and reminded reporters that last season was a "jumping period." He confessed to newsmen that it was not easy to turn his back on a huge guaranteed salary and a contract that promised immunity from any trouble. Ed finished his remarks by saying that he would let his bat and field-play win back the confidence and affection of his admirers.[72]

Loftus supported Delahanty's sentiments. He said his former captain was a "royal good fellow at heart," and it was a pity he got himself involved in such a harmful transaction.[73] Loftus remarked that Ed Delahanty was "not as bad as pictured." He told the press that Del took advantage of the new bidding war because he needed the money. He also reminded his listeners that Ed reported to training camp "without a murmur."[74] Loftus told anyone within earshot that Del was still a premier batter and was worth whatever it took to put him in the lineup. One enthusiastic crank boasted, the "king has decided to don his armor."[75]

Delahanty and his teammates nervously anticipated the season opener. On a windy afternoon, 11,590 fans turned out to see former National League spitballer Jack Chesbro take on Washington's reliable off-speed ace, "smiling Al" Orth. The ball clubs paraded through the nation's capital to old League Park, where ropes restrained the overflow opening-day crowd. The fans saved their loudest cheers for their prodigal "king," Ed Delahanty. During batting practice, Del brought the spectators to their feet with hard-hit drives to the deep outfield. The bleacherites, it was said, yelled themselves hoarse. Delahanty played left field and batted third. When he came to bat for the first time, he was presented with a "gigantic horsehoe of American Beauty roses." It was like old times, and everything seemed to be forgiven. Delahanty went 1 for 3 and drove in the winning run.[76] The Senators went on to split the four-game series with Clark Griffith's New Yorkers. In the third game, Delahanty had three singles, and in the fourth contest, he showed his old spark by chasing balls all over left field in an 11 to 1 loss. He made seven putouts and delighted the crowd with a few eye-opening running catches. For the moment, Delahanty believed the contract crisis was behind him.[77]

These feelings did not last long. Delahanty lapsed into an angst when the story about his Denver inquiry hit the sports pages. Angered and embarrassed by the disclosure, he apologized and reconfirmed his loyalty to the Senators, but the story kept the contract controversy alive.[78] A casualty of Delahanty's plight and later problems was his sobriety. A short time after the Denver revelation, Delahanty stumbled into an old friend, New York sportswriter William Rankin, while roaming the streets of Manhattan after an evening on the town. Rankin warned and comforted the intoxicated ballplayer, who compliantly returned to his hotel.[79] This incident was precipitated by many factors. Del was upset over the unresolved case of George Davis and the owners' threat to go to court to settle their disputes. He was also concerned about his wife's health. On Sunday, May 3, he left the Senators and journeyed to Philadelphia to be at her side. He rejoined the ball club in Boston for its Monday game.[80] The fans in Boston were not as understanding and scoffed at his contract-jumping. In a *Boston Herald* cartoon, shivering bleacher cranks taunted a portly Delahanty, shouting, "say Del, lend us some of that four thousand dollars to burn—it's cold up here!"[81] If not too personal, Delahanty enjoyed trading quips with local fans. But Del wanted to turn the page on his preseason crisis and looked forward to a three-game series with the champion Athletics in Philadelphia.

These contests marked his first baseball appearance in the Quaker City since October 1901. He was nervous about his reception and came to the park early before the crowds arrived. Del was quite relieved when he was warmly greeted like a returning hero. He walked around the park shaking hands and getting pats on the back. Facing three of baseball's best pitchers, "Chief" Bender, Rube Waddell, and Eddie Plank, Delahanty showed flashes of his former self. He went 4 for 12 with three extra-base hits in three lopsided losses to the Athletics.[82] In each game, Delahanty tipped his cap to loud and sustained ovations. When Delahanty took leave of Philadelphia for the last time, the Senators were 5 and 10 and he was hitting .280.

After splitting the next road series with St. Louis, Washington's prospects worsened. The team suffered a number of injuries that decimated their infield. Tom Loftus compensated by moving players out of their natural positions. But the club's situation worsened when Delahanty, already suffering from back spasms, hurt his right ankle running in the outfield. Unable to play, Loftus sent the overweight Delahanty to a health spa in Mt. Clemens, Michigan. For the next eleven games, Kip Selbach replaced Delahanty in left field. During that spell, the Senators were 2 and 9, on their way to losing 18 consecutive games. On May 29, when Delahanty returned to the lineup, the team was seven games into their winless streak.

Delahanty was supposed to meet the Senators in Detroit but was again called back to Philadelphia to attend to his ailing wife. A few days later, he rejoined the club at Boston and walked into a situation that threatened his career. Del objected to going back into the lineup as the right fielder. Kip Selbach, who was acquired as a replacement if Delahanty sat out the year, complained that he was not comfortable playing in the right field sun, and Ducky Holmes, the right fielder, was needed for the patched-up Washington infield. Delahanty balked and lost his temper discussing the switch with his manager. Loftus, fearful of losing control of his sinking club, suspended Delahanty. Ed did not take the threat seriously. It was only after club secretary Walter Hewitt came to collect his uniform and refused him a train ticket to Washington that Delahanty realized the severity of the censure. Having no alternative, Delahanty gave in and went to right field.[83]

Up to this point, Loftus and the Senators did everything to make things "agreeable" for Delahanty, but they were running out of patience. His critics asserted he was playing without enthusiasm and pouting about his predicament. It was said that the moody outfielder, playing on a bad ankle, failed to give his all on every play. He did not charge balls hit to the outfield, and he threw late and erratically to the infield.[84] More troubling were rumors that he was neglecting his weight and drinking heavily.

Underlying most of his problems was his growing disillusion-ment of playing for a hapless team. One story recalled that a funeral hearse parked beyond the scoreboard fence made people wonder whether it had come for some of the players.[85] Delahanty did not see much humor in the story. He craved the opportunities he envi-sioned in New York—the limelight and winning. Obligated to two more years in Washington, his prospects looked bleak. McGraw and Brush were forever in his thoughts, and the hope that George Davis could pave the way for him to play in New York loomed large.

The Davis case revolved around his two conflicting contracts. His lawyer, John Montgomery Ward, the former brotherhood president, argued that the reserve clause in his client's original 1901 New York contract superseded his recent pact with Charlie Co-miskey. It was an ironic position for attorney Ward, but Davis, McGraw, and Brush were determined to shove their interpretation down major league baseball's throat, even if it meant toppling the Cincinnati peace accord. In the meantime, Davis worked out a compensation package with the Giants and waited to see what Brush and McGraw could do. He spent his days losing money at the race track and kept himself in shape playing semipro baseball in Rhode Island.[86]

The Davis situation and the Delahanty dilemma were reignited by Detroit's trading of Kid Elberfeld to the American League Highlanders of New York. This move affected Davis and Dela-hanty because McGraw's contracts with all three were invalidated by the National Commission. Brush could not believe that Elber-feld had been dealt to his crosstown rivals. The Giants' new presi-dent declared the trade violated the peace settlement and maneu-vered to barter the Elberfeld breach for the rights to George Davis.[87] This scheming incited Delahanty with visions of escaping Wash-ington for New York.

These wishful expectations did not mean that Delahanty gave up on his playing. Running on a bad ankle, Delahanty performed as well as an overweight and bewildered ballplayer could. Even the "only Del" in his prime could not salvage the woeful Senators. From May 14 to June 25, Washington was 6 and 28 and mired in the American League basement. It was no wonder Delahanty was en-couraged by Clark Griffith's renewed inquiries and excited by John Brush's recent orchestrations. But Delahanty needed to show the owners that he was still a valuable commodity and that his bad fielding games were more a symptom of his condition than his attitude. The proof came with his regained batting stroke.

Adjusting to the foul-strike rule, and motivated to prove his worth to the New York teams, Delahanty returned to his 1902 form. From June 1 to his final game on June 25, Delahanty was 28 for 72 for a .390 average. Riding the crest of a sixteen-game hitting streak, Del's .340 average put him fourth in the league. The *Washington Post,* delighted with Ed's batting, commented, "shipped to New York by mistake, McGraw sent it back."[88] To Del's dismay, his production backfired because it alerted Washington to his real value.

The Senators' financial state complemented their ballplaying. Washington's stockholders could not afford to overlook any revenue-making opportunity, and Delahanty was a proven box office draw. In their desperate condition, they would look foolish to let their resurgent batsman go to another team.[89] Annoyed that his batting had evoked the wrong results, Del's play again deteriorated.

Although he would hit safely in his remaining eight games, his overall hustle was lacking, and his faulty defense cost the lowly Senators precious wins.[90] It seemed like every dysfunctional part of his life was striking him at one time. His poor physical condition, his desperate finances, a distraught and ailing wife, and his thwarted ambitions were breaking him down. The great batsman found himself in a position where even his mighty bat could not save him. He had exhausted his options and contracts, and was torn as to what to do about the unfolding events in New York over George Davis. Undoubtedly, McGraw and Brush were applying pressure on the bewildered ballplayer. The only solace for his anxiety and stress was drinking.

The Senators took pride that they were a ball club that followed the "water wagon." Management accommodated the city's Anti-Saloon League and removed whiskey advertising signs from the outfield walls. It was quite a decision for a team worried about their revenue,[91] but Ed Delahanty's life was on a different track. Alcohol had never been a good tonic for the great batsman. It brought out the dark and sullen side of the good-natured, weak-willed ballplayer. Drinking for such a person heightened his adversity and incited aggressive behavior. For pathological gamblers like Delahanty, liquor was self-destructive. In a few documented instances, in less stressful times, Delahanty demonstrated that he could not handle the effects of his binges. His wife said he would become "boisterous, devilish . . . very ugly" and break things. She testified that he would act in an "insane way." Norine confided that he never hurt anyone and was soothed with "kindly talk."[92] Unfortunately, she could not always be there for him, and was not well enough to accompany her troubled husband on a long western road trip.

From the few surviving accounts of Del's last days, it can be surmised that Norine saw her husband for the last time on June 17. She had attended a ball game and put her purse and season ticket passbook #26 in his black leather satchel. After two innings, with Detroit ahead 7 to 1, the game was rained out. Norine met her husband outside the dressing room, retrieved her bag, and went home to help him pack for his two-week road trip. Sometime that evening, before Delahanty departed for Union Station, he and his wife had an emotional conversation over her concerns: their debt, his drinking, and the situation with John McGraw. The discussion stirred Delahanty's fears that his anxious wife was disappointed in him as a husband and a provider. Imagining that his behavior was upsetting his young wife was too much for Delahanty to bear. Her immediate reassurances calmed him, but erupting tensions dwelled on his conscience. Relieved for the moment, he tried to placate his wife by telling her about a $2,000 consignment of jewelry he was taking to sell on the road trip. He also told her that his drinking was under control. She, in turn, promised to write and assured him that everything would work itself out. Undeterred by her sentiments, a disquieted Delahanty boarded the midnight train. On the long journey to St. Louis, Delahanty comforted himself with playing cards and drinking. His wife's alarms, and his troubling circumstances, were momentarily forgotten. As the Pullman train traveled westward, Ed's solace came from a bottle of whiskey.

17

The Fall

Relaxing in the lobby of Detroit's Oriental Hotel, Jimmy Ryan, Delahanty's old friend and current teammate, sipped lemonade and told a story about the saloon venture of Boston's "Heavenly Twins," Tommy McCarthy and Hugh Duffy. Their relationship, he said, soured when Duffy "got the temperance bee." According to Ryan, Duffy wanted to sell soft drinks, and McCarthy swore he would have "smote him [Duffy] right there" if they had not been long-time friends and partners. McCarthy bought out his friend and vowed he would never take another partner for fear of a second conversion.[1] Ryan laughed about his anecdote, but there was nothing funny about drink and baseball. It was a bad combination. Too many athletes had their careers and lives ruined by overindulgence. The most combustible mixture, the *Chicago Tribune* wrote, was liquor and the race track. The paper called it "the most destructive curve" to great batsmen.[2]

Before Delahanty departed for St. Louis, he purchased a twenty-four-hour travel insurance policy naming his daughter, Florence, as the beneficiary. He would buy similar policies before his trips to Chicago and Cleveland. In his wife's notebook, written after his death, Norine mentioned how her husband arrived "safe,"[3] suggesting that she was alert to her Ed's state of mind.

By the time Delahanty and the Senators arrived in St. Louis, the players were travel-weary and anxious to get settled. For Delahanty it meant returning to reality. His body felt the effects of his drinking, and his mind rediscovered its former turmoil. The three games against Jimmy McAleer's Browns exposed the troubling conditions of Delahanty and his ball club. The Senators dropped each of the closely contested games. Del was 4 for 12, with a double in the series, but his field play was described as "half-hearted." He labored around the bases and seemed to lumber, not run, after fly balls. In the first game, he allowed three routine balls to drop for hits.[4] Red Donahue, who pitched the second game, had been a Phillies teammate of Delahanty for four years. He was startled at his friend's condition and overall play.[5] The Donahue game also revealed Washington's cursed fortunes. Tom Loftus, the Senators' well-liked Irish manager, was increasingly despondent over the team's failures and may have come to the park intoxicated. From the bench he verbally badgered his old nemesis, the thin-skinned and volatile Jesse Burkett. Called "the Crab" because of his sour disposition, Burkett took offense at Loftus's cutting comments about his lineage. "The Crab" rushed to the Senators' bench and began pummeling the Washington manager. Umpire Tom Connolly kicked Burkett out of the game, and Ban Johnson fined him $50. Loftus was later suspended for five games. A local editorial condemned the attack and mockingly declared that only the disappointed fans of Washington would be justified in erupting so.[6] The episode marked Delahanty's last multiple-hit game.[7]

In the third contest, Jimmy Ryan was hit on the hand and catcher Lew Drill was beaned by errant pitches. Delahanty fared better, but struggled against veteran pitcher "Wee Willie" Sudhoff. He knocked in Washington's only run with a line drive single, but let in the winning run when he misplayed a ball into a two-base hit. One newspaper asked whether Del's bat was worth what he gave up in the field.[8] After the series, Delahanty was sure that his bad fielding and poor conditioning would get him suspended.[9] The dismissal never came. Washington was so desperate for healthy players that an out-of-shape, discontented outfielder who could hit .300 had a place on the club.

With the St. Louis experiences behind them, the ailing Senators moved on to Chicago, where the players looked forward to entertaining good times. It was here in the Windy City that Delahanty hoped to sell some of his consigned jewelry. Unfortunately, Delahanty was not much of a salesman. He had already let third baseman Bill Coughlin wear a diamond ring and loaned a gold pocket watch given to him years ago by admirers to a hard-pressed young utility player.[10] Obviously, Delahanty's generosity had not yet succumbed to his wasting intemperance. On the field, Delahanty and the Senators continued to fare poorly. They lost both games to Comiskey's White Stockings, as Del continued his hitting streak. From Chicago the club traveled to Delahanty's hometown of Cleveland, unaware that their fading star was about to implode.

On Thursday, June 25, Delahanty's family and friends came to League Park to see Ed play in what would be his last ball game. Before the game, Del greeted his well-wishers and visited with former teammates Napoleon Lajoie, Elmer Flick, and Bill Bernhard. Before a crowd of 2,582, the Senators faced the popular youngster Earl Moore, the first pitcher in the American League to throw a no-hitter. Because of injuries and his poor outfield play, Delahanty started at first base for the only time in the season. It was not a memorable game. He struck out once, and in the fourth inning slugged a single to left field, the 2,597th hit of his sixteen-year career. Washington got only five singles and was shut out by Moore, 4 to 0.[11] That evening, Delahanty took a teammate to Phelps Street for one of Bridget Delahanty's renowned "Irish turkey" (corned beef and cabbage) dinners. Friends stopped by, and a good time was had by all.[12] Few suspected how distraught the pride of Cleveland had become. By the next day, family, friends, and teammates dealt with an entirely different person.

On the following morning, when Delahanty read the morning paper, all of his anxieties rose to the surface. The newspapers reported that National League president Harry Pulliam, without the consent of the owners, relented to John Brush's appeals. The fair-minded Pulliam was convinced that the Giants had not been treated fairly, and the trading of Elberfeld to the Highlanders contradicted the intent of the Peace Commission. Following Brush's logic, Pulliam believed George Davis's original 1901 New York contract was valid and allowed him to play for McGraw. Davis was named team captain and was scheduled to be in the lineup that afternoon for a game against Pittsburgh at the Polo Grounds. Pulliam declared,

> Elberfeld occupies the identical position that Davis and Delahanty occupied and there is no question in my mind but what the New York club of the National League has a just case of complaint. . . . The spirit, if not the letter of the Cincinnati Agreement has been violated . . . the only sufferer has been the New York club, therefore, I am [allowing] the said New York club to exercise its legal right and make disposition of the services of George Davis.[13]

Ban Johnson and Charlie Comiskey were furious with Pulliam and accused him of being taken in by Brush's warped logic. Gary Herrmann, the Cincinnati president and the commission's major mediator, also repudiated Pulliam's actions. Herrmann contended that the Elberfeld trade did not violate the accord and reminded reporters that Brush had acknowledged, in front of his fellow owners, that he had no legal claim to the Detroit shortstop.[14]

Unlike George Davis's claim, Delahanty's 1902–03 National League contract reserved him to Philadelphia, not New York. This distinction was lost on the agitated Delahanty, who was already upset that he had not received a letter from his disquieted wife.[15] The Pulliam announcement pushed him over the edge. He ranted about his situation and began drinking. As the time came to go to the ballpark, Delahanty was not in condition to play. He stayed behind at the hotel. The newspapers related that Delahanty's "enforced retirement" was due to illness. With Ryan and Delahanty out of the lineup, the Senators managed only three singles and lost 1 to 0.[16]

Returning to the hotel, the forlorn Senators did not find Delahanty. In a city with old drinking haunts, Delahanty eluded his family and teammates. When he finally appeared, a mean-spirited Delahanty proved difficult to handle. Confused and angry, he lashed out at everyone. Only the timely intervention of his mother and family got him settled. They left him at the hotel under the watchful eye of Jimmy Ryan and Bill Coughlin.

The next morning, the cycle began anew. The blaring headlines in the *Cleveland Press* declared "Baseball War Is On Again." The

Davis case, it said, was the "opening gun," and Brush and Dreyfuss were preparing to raid the American League. The same paper reported that Davis played his first game with the Giants without incident.[17] Delahanty was in a quandary. He undoubtedly wired John McGraw for advice and was given directives about what to do. Whatever the specifics, Delahanty's conscience was being pulled in two directions. Torn by guilt and indecision, he lapsed into a panicked hysteria. Fueled by alcohol, Delahanty turned violent. He stormed around the hotel and barged into other players' apartments. He frightened his teammates by brandishing a penknife. On a few occasions, he "grieved" about not hearing from his wife and "proceeded to do a sensational tank act . . . making several scenes and threatening other players and himself with a knife."[18] After much cajoling, Delahanty calmed down and settled into a hot bath. In the remaining evening hours, his teammates watched over him, "fearing a disastrous termination."

The following day, the exhausted and ailing Senators had a Saturday doubleheader. They split the games, losing the first 8 to 0 and winning the second 5 to 2 against a twenty-three-year-old sensation, pitcher Addie Joss. The weary Senators did not have time to dwell on their rare success. They had to check on Delahanty and prepare for a steamboat trip across Lake Erie to Detroit. The injured Jimmy Ryan had stayed behind and looked after Delahanty. Ryan did everything he could to get Ed ready to travel. He convinced Del that a boat trip and fresh air would revive his spirits and get him back to normal. With the overwrought Delahanty in tow, the Washington ball club set out that evening for their last road stop, Detroit.[19]

On the boat, Delahanty was able to stretch his legs and walk off the effects of his binge. Thanks to Jimmy Ryan's care, Delahanty was sober and shook off his demons. Perhaps a reassuring letter or wire from his wife helped calm his frenzy. Whatever happened, Delahanty responded well to the lake cruise. On Sunday morning, after the Senators disembarked, they registered at the Oriental Hotel, owned by Fred Postal. Here the players ran into a local reporter who spoke with Del and commented on the ballplayer's good condition. The newsman later recalled that Delahanty was in a "rational frame of mind" and did not smell of liquor. He said Ed blamed his layoff on being overweight and claimed it was "an injustice."[20] Unable to deal with the terms of his benching or infirmity, Delahanty was bound to repeat the Cleveland episode.

No sooner had his teammates left for their game at Bennett Park than Delahanty started drinking. What led to this new spree cannot be determined. The newspapers carried stories of the pending baseball war, and there may have been a distressing telegram from the Giants. The *Detroit Times* also exposed his condition. The paper commented tongue-in-cheek that Delahanty looked "pale as a ghost, suffering from an attack of cholera morbus—caused by drinking water out of the Cleveland tunnel."[21] By the time the club returned from their 3 to 0 loss, Delahanty was in a state of "delirium tremens." On the verge of a breakdown, Ed Delahanty began hallucinating and imagined his teammates were conspiring against him. He took out his pocketknife again and threatened some young players. To imagine the great batsman reduced to a knife-wielding madman testifies to the depth of Delahanty's suffering. It was only after he exhausted himself that his teammates got him under control. His body shaking and his clothes soaked with perspiration, Del needed external help and support. The frightened players responded by calling a doctor and sending off a telegram to the Delahanty family in Cleveland. That evening Bridget Delahanty, her seventeen-year-old son, William, and a matron cousin, Mary Barnes, took the steamship to Detroit.[22]

Throughout this crisis, nothing was said about the intentions or whereabouts of Delahanty's father. His absence was peculiar, or perhaps like Del, he, too, found it hard to confront personal traumas and found solace in a whiskey bottle. Throughout his thirty-five years, Ed Delahanty took his life cues from the male arenas of the firehouse, ball field, and racetrack. As one commentator related, Delahanty was "nothing but a big overgrown boy by nature,"[23] an immature and spoiled adolescent man who depended on the strong women in his life: a dominating mother and a manipulative and aspiring wife. He probably resented this dependence, but in time of need he required his mother's attention and his wife's comfort.

When Bridget Delahanty arrived at the hotel on Tuesday morning, she was shocked by her son's condition. He was fatigued by his ordeal and ashamed of his situation. He listened passively to her counsel on the dangers of alcohol. She reminded him of his responsibilities and encouraged her son to have faith in his ability to overcome his intemperance. Being a devout Catholic, Bridget Delahanty looked to the church for her son's immediate salvation. After he cleaned himself up, and had some solid food, she hustled him to a nearby church. She believed that if he swore off drinking, he would be able to cope with his other pressing problems.

Counseled by a local parish priest, Del and his mother prayed and the remorseful ballplayer signed a "be-good document." In this pledge Del promised to treat Manager Loftus and his Washington teammates "on square" and swore to "leave the 'red eye' [whiskey] alone."[24] The repentant Delahanty returned to the hotel and tried to put things back in order. His first task was to let his wife know he was okay and to tell her when he would be returning to Washington. He wired her in Philadelphia, where she was staying with her sister, but he confused the arrival date. He asked her to meet him on Friday rather than on Saturday.[25] The emotionally spent Delahanty passed the rest of the day quietly with his family. It was hoped that keeping him calm might restore his peace of mind. This priority was not easily accomplished. On the first page of Wednesday morning's *Detroit Times,* there was a picture of Delahanty under the headlines, "DEL MIGHTY HITTER, SIGNS PLEDGE." It was followed by the lead: "Confronted by his mother, wife and child here, Big Fellow decides to cut out the booze."[26] The misleading story was humiliating for the proud Delahanty. It demeaned the great "king of swatville" and made him look like a misguided adolescent scolded by his mother and a priest. All day, the story festered inside of him. He paced the hotel corridors and craved a drink. With his family and teammates on shift, Delahanty overcame the difficult day and stayed sober.

On Thursday, July 2, Delahanty awakened to no new problems or newspaper exposés, just a small item that Charlie Comiskey had received an injunction to prevent George Davis from playing with New York. Delahanty had no idea how this might affect his conflicted ambitions. Anxious about Davis's status, Delahanty likely wired John McGraw and attended to his mother while he waited for a reply. He assured his mother and cousin Mary that he was feeling much better and would not need them. Convinced of his sincerity, the women went to the Mt. Clemens spas for the day. His brother, William, accompanied Jimmy Ryan and the players to the ballpark for the final game of the Senators' western road trip.

Delahanty appeared to be in good spirits, and everyone wanted to believe that he could take care of himself.

On his own, Delahanty did not stand much of a chance against the mounting pressures. He remained troubled by the disclosures in the *Detroit Times* and was provoked by some kind of reply from New York. He was probably told that McGraw was about to take the Giants on a western road trip, and if Del did not quickly get to New York, Brush would have to look after him. Delahanty did not have much time to make up his mind, and this indecision wreaked havoc on his dispirited conscience. As the pressure built, Delahanty reneged on his day-old pledge. Depressed and terribly confused, Delahanty did two things that shed light on his state of mind and intentions: he sent a letter to his wife, and he bought a train ticket for New York.

In the letter to Norine he enclosed one of the lapsed accident insurance policies. He also confessed that he hoped the train he was taking would jump the tracks and "end his career." Another version said he wished the train would be "dashed to pieces and he with it." After mailing the letter, he returned to his room and packed his suitcase and satchel. He had $200 in his pocket and the jewelry, including the ring and watch he had lent his teammates. Del never paid his mother's hotel bill and left no money for his family to get back to Cleveland. His uniform and cap remained in his room. He did not speak to anyone and went to the train station where he purchased a ticket on the Michigan Central Railroad. His overnight journey would take him to Buffalo, New York, from where he would proceed to New York City. Ed boarded train #6 at 5:25 P.M. His trip took him across Ontario, Canada, north of Lake Erie, to the village station of Bridgeburg, the crossing of the Niagara River to the United States. His arrival in Buffalo was scheduled for 11:00 P.M.[27]

Delahanty had a Pullman sleeping berth, which entitled him to the buffet car that served tobacco and drinks. At first, the troubled ballplayer attracted very little attention. He silently fretted about his fate in the smoking compartment of the Pullman car and ordered whiskey to ease his frayed nerves. He was so inconspicuous that the head conductor, John Cole, had no recollection of Delahanty when tickets were clipped. Two hours into the trip, sometime after the train stopped at St. Thomas, Ontario, notice was taken of the large, brooding passenger.

He was settled at the rear of the lavatory compartment of the Pullman. He smoked incessantly and was warned by the porter that smoking was not permitted in the Pullman when the buffet car was operating. Delahanty ignored the porter, and conductor Cole was fetched to resolve the problem. He told his sullen passenger about the restrictions, and without arguing, Delahanty put out whatever he was smoking. A few moments later, the electric service bell, much to the annoyance of the passengers, began ringing. Delahanty had become agitated that the porter, who was already upset with his smoking, was not answering the bell. One witness commented that the porter refused to serve Delahanty any more liquor, and Del responded by pushing the button.[28] When the sleeping car conductor could not calm Delahanty, John Cole was again summoned. Rather than create a disturbance, Cole had the electric bell disconnected. This frustrated Delahanty. On his way to the buffet car, Delahanty stumbled into and broke the glass front of the emergency tool cabinet. Startled by the accident, Delahanty returned to his seat in the smoking compartment. Informed about the broken glass, Cole confronted Delahanty. He lectured Ed about his behavior and demanded $3 for the damages. Running out of patience, the conductor warned Delahanty that he was still in Canada and was subject to Canadian law. The flustered Delahanty blurted out that he "did not care whether he was in Canada or Hell." Cole tried to calm the ballplayer, whom he did not know, by telling him that there "was no use feeling that way."[29] Delahanty defused the situation by conniving the conductor, "I will be good if you give me a drink."[30] In hope of quieting Delahanty, Cole okayed the order and a glass of whiskey and a small, corked sampler bottle were delivered.

Forty-five minutes later, when Cole was making his rounds, he had another encounter with Delahanty. This time, the ballplayer, on his way to the buffet car, stumbled into a wooden partition. Cole testified that Del deliberately tried to shove the partition down, and shouted after Delahanty, "Here, none of that." Delahanty grinned out of embarrassment and returned to his seat in the Pullman car. From then until the scheduled stop at Bridgeburg, Delahanty sulked and dozed in the smoking compartment. It was only after the train stopped to change engines at the Bridgeburg crossing station that Delahanty began to stir.

Bridgeburg was the border stop before the train crossed the International Bridge. Once over the Niagara River, the next station was the city of Buffalo. The sleeping Delahanty must have believed the train had reached his destination because he got up and walked down the aisle to the sleeping berths to fetch his bags. But in the dimly lit aisle, Delahanty went to the wrong berth. He pulled the curtains back from a lower sleeper and awakened a male passenger. The man berated the confused Delahanty, who was now trying the upper berth. A startled woman awoke and joined in the tirade. Baffled by the commotion he had aroused, Delahanty lost his patience and tried to pull the woman out of her compartment. This action intensified the shouting. Some reports alleged that Delahanty threatened someone with a straight razor, but no evidence or testimony confirmed such an attack.[31] According to eyewitnesses, Del seemed agitated and became annoyed by the disruption. An observer remarked that Delahanty appeared to be stunned by the cursing of the disturbed occupants. Delahanty did not become violent or unmanageable. He was disoriented and bewildered. One passenger did not remember Delahanty saying anything more than, "I don't think much of you."[32]

While this fracas was erupting, conductor Cole was in the Bridgeburg station signing clearance papers. When he was alerted to the problems in the Pullman car, he quickly finished his business and attended to the disturbance. By the time Cole arrived, he found Delahanty in the grasp of the porter and two conductors. Del was not resisting, and no struggle ensued. The foursome guided Delahanty up the aisle, away from the tumult. Tired and weary of his troublesome passenger, Cole took the advice of his staff and ordered Delahanty off the train.

Delahanty was upset by his ejection but allowed himself to be directed to the side rail in front of the Bridgeburg Station in Fort Erie, Ontario. As the new engine completed its coupling, Delahanty was given his Christy derby hat. His valise and satchel remained on the Pullman. Moments later, the train departed across the bridge for the United States. Left unattended with the lights of his destination faintly visible in the night, Ed Delahanty lamented his situation and pondered his options.[33]

It was a moonless and lightly clouded evening with the temperature in the mid-sixties. The harbor of Black Rock, on the American side, was five minutes away by train. Fifteen minutes beyond was the city of Buffalo. Facing east toward the bridge, the Bridgeburg depot was on Delahanty's right. Later court testimony stated that no one appeared to assist him from the one-story platformed building. To his left, about 700 feet from the entrance to the bridge, was a guardhouse where an elderly bridge-tender, Samuel Kingston, was on duty. The old man had no idea that train #6 had left a passenger at the station platform. Kingston only heard Del's train depart and checked his watch. In the meantime, the stranded Delahanty could only stare at the crossing in disbelief. Dazed and distraught, the "king of swat" watched the train disappear from sight. Perhaps remembering he had to get to New York before McGraw left the city, Delahanty followed the Michigan Central train over the darkened bridge.

Built in 1873, this single track bridge was owned by the Grand Trunk Railway Company of Canada. No pedestrian traffic was permitted. The bridge had no side railings, the planked footing was treacherous, and the only illumination came from summer marine lights. The structure was not the place for an unfamiliar traveler, especially one who had been drinking.

Delahanty ignored, or did not see, the wooden sign warning pedestrians to keep off the bridge. As he passed under the foreboding iron-framed archway, he resisted the frightening reality of his venture. With his vision greatly reduced, the 3,600-foot span would have appeared before him like a shadowed passageway over an unseen and swiftly running river. Shrouded in darkness, Delahanty trod warily on the timber ties that abutted and cradled the track on the north side of the twenty-foot-wide bridge. In a matter of about ten minutes, Delahanty made his way to the third span when the track ahead of him became illuminated by the headlights of an oncoming freight train which had waited at the Black Rock Station for the Michigan Central to pass.

With the freight train bearing down on him, there was little the befuddled ballplayer could do. The only escape was the double iron chord girder at the side of the bridge. Two-foot wide and latticed on top, the edge chord was five inches above the timber tie. Delahanty must have stepped from the wood frame onto the chord and braced himself against the vertical truss that linked the bridge to its external frame. As he got set on the chord, the freight train passed within a few feet of the frightened intruder. After some terrifying moments, Delahanty tried to steady his nerves and balance in a new veil of enveloping darkness.

Just as the freight train exited the bridge, a small light appeared to make its way toward the unmoving Delahanty. The bridge watchman had seen someone go on the span. He knew nothing about the abandoned passenger but was attentive to smugglers along the river. With his bull's-eye lantern in hand, he set out to investigate the situation. Samuel Kingston, who had worked on the bridge since its opening, moved steadily toward the third span. He later testified that he put his light on a large man standing on the chord against the first upright column. The recovering Delahanty, stunned and upset by his discovery, cried out, "Take that light away or I will knock your damned brains out." The old watchman claimed that Delahanty threatened him with a rock or large piece of coal. Standing on the rail, three feet away from Delahanty, Kingston asked why the stranger was on the bridge. Del repeated his former threat. Kingston said he thought the man was drunk or crazy and was afraid he would "jump into the river." Acting quickly, the watchman tried to grab Delahanty. He said he "threw his arm over his and caught him by the collar of his coat and pulled him down." Both men tumbled onto the track and Kingston got his foot stuck between the ties. Lying astride the tracks with his lantern light out, the old man struggled to his feet when he heard a splash. He ran to the side of the bridge and saw Delahanty's head above the water hollering for help. The ballplayer called out several times until he vanished from sight. Shaken by this calamity, Kingston ran back to the station to awake Paul Colclough, the bridge foreman, who ordered a tugboat to search the water below the International Bridge. The rescuers found no body. Only a derby hat was recovered by the watchman from the top of the iron chord.[34]

Explaining what happened to Delahanty perplexed investigators because every party had a stake in contrary conclusions. The Michigan Central and Grand Trunk Railways were occupied with liability issues, the Delahanty family had religious and personal concerns, and Sam Kingston and conductor Cole were wary about their responsibilities. As a result, each person had his own interpretation. To unravel the mystery, the agendas and explanations of each party have to be weighed and taken into account.

Foul play was the most convenient and tolerable explanation for Delahanty's tragic demise. If proven, the actions of the railway or Delahanty's behavior would not be open to judgment. Everything could be explained and questions resolved if someone waylaid the finely attired ballplayer, took his money and jewelry, and pushed him off the bridge. Kingston and the Grand Trunk Railway Company would be off the hook, and the Delahanty family would be relieved of the religious stigma of suicide and Del's shameful dissipation.

Initially, conductor Cole suggested Del might have been robbed in Detroit because he could not recall any jewelry on his troublesome passenger.[35] However, most robbery opinions took their cue from Ed's angry and disbelieving twenty-year-old brother Frank. The younger Delahanty, who played for Syracuse in the New York State League, was one of the first people on the scene. He told reporters in Buffalo that stories of suicide or intemperance had no foundation. He spoke of foul play and suggested his brother was held up and murdered.[36] His view was supported by the talk of smugglers and crimes along the Niagara border. One story in particular created confusion. It told of a wealthy farmer from nearby Tonawanda who was robbed and thrown into the river sometime after Delahanty's disappearance.[37] During the investigation of Ed Delahanty's death, no evidence of a crime was ever uncovered. As for the ballplayer's valuables, if his clothes were washed off his body, then anything he was carrying would be scattered along the course of the Niagara River or was at the base of the Horseshoe Falls.[38]

The issue of suicide was the most controversial and sensitive scenario for the Irish Catholic Delahantys. They and many of Del's friends refused to acknowledge that Delahanty's pyschological distress might have pushed him to such a desperate act. No one was more steadfast than his mother. In her heavy Irish brogue, Bridget Delahanty told Cleveland reporters, "I am confident that he had not taken his own life, unless he did it while rendered insane by heat [whiskey], for he was in the best of spirits when with me. No, he was not despondent. He had no reason at all to be so."[39]

Mrs. Delahanty's remarks were part of her denial and inability to appreciate the severity of Ed's emotional crisis.

The talk of suicide owed much to the prejudiced assessment of Sam Kingston, who spoke of the troubled man looking out over the river from the bridge's girder.[40] His description fitted Delahanty's behavior in Cleveland and Detroit. As reported by the press, the "king of batters" suffered from depression and panic anxiety. The question remained whether his vocal and frequent threats of self-harm were whiskey-induced pleas, a way of reaching out for help and relief, or statements of intention. For example, his remarks to his wife about not surviving a train wreck might well be an appeal for her confirming love and support.[41] Delahanty could have been saying that he regretted what he had done to upset his wife and, though he could not take his own life, maybe a train crash would do it for him. This threat was not his first. He alluded to hurting himself throughout his latest tirades. There was even an unverified story that Delahanty's teammates once stopped him from turning on the gas in his Washington hotel room when he became despondent about his marriage.[42]

All of these accounts confirm Delahanty's pained state of mind. They do not, however, prove he committed suicide on the International Bridge. The fact that he made these intoxicated threats around people who could look after him should tell us something. Perhaps the only way to appreciate whether Delahanty wanted to die is to put this presumption into the context of his flight from Detroit.

Delahanty's disappearance and death followed the much publicized suicide of the popular Detroit pitcher, George "Winnie" Mercer. Troubled by family problems and the loss of thousands of dollars in gambling and racetrack debts, Mercer, on January 12, 1903, wrote letters of farewell and apology before putting a rubber tube from the gas jet into his mouth. The last writings of the twenty-eight-year-old pitcher included, "Beware of women and a game of chance."[43] Mercer's suicide stunned the sporting world and became a gauge for explaining Delahanty's disappearance.

Another factor was the association of the International Bridge and Niagara Falls with suicides. On the afternoon of the Delahanty incident, an electrical engineer, attending a local conference, took his life by going over the falls. Part of the confusion surrounding Del's vanishing was identifying the dead engineer.[44]

But the critical point dispelling suicide talk was Delahanty's intentions. Distraught over professional and personal problems Delahanty was intent on going to New York. His coupon ticket was for Manhattan, where he intended to meet with his manipulating benefactors, McGraw and Brush. Although neither man ever acknowledged their scheduled rendezvous, it was widely believed that they were in contact with Delahanty throughout the Davis affair. The *Washington Post* reported that most people believed that Delahanty was in touch with the New York ball club and expected to play there.[45] Fred Postal, Washington's president, publicly stated that Brush was responsible for Delahanty's death. He asserted that the Giants' president was always tampering with the big outfielder and never let him get satisfied with his situation. "Brush and McGraw," he said, "do not know . . . the baseball war is over."[46] President Herrmann of Cincinnati endorsed these sentiments. He asserted that Delahanty would be alive, and appearing in his outfield, if New York had not obstructed his trade efforts.[47]

Overlooked in the confusion was the fact that Delahanty left his Washington uniform in Detroit and had his spiked baseball shoes in his leather satchel.[48] In other words, Delahanty took leave of the Senators and believed McGraw and Brush would find a way for him to play in New York. It was this corroboration that Delahanty was waiting on before he took the Michigan Central train to Buffalo. And though he did not mention his New York destination to his wife, he did ask her to meet him in Washington. In other words, Delahanty had a plan and intent for his trip. These designs and incentives were not the actions of a man bent on self-destruction. As a *Sporting News* editorial related, "Delahanty's death was due to dissipation and not design."[49] Nor does a lapsed insurance policy mean anything. It was customary to forward these indemnities ahead and he must have overlooked its deadline.[50] When sober and rational, the Catholic Delahanty also had an opinion on suicide. Speaking with his teammates, he declared that "no one but a coward would ever drown himself."[51] If Delahanty did not take his own life, then what happened on the International Bridge?

According to news reports of interviews with Sam Kingston and railroad officials, Delahanty either jumped into the river or ran east toward the United States and an open drawbridge. In his original statement, the shakened watchman said the draw was operative to allow a steamship to pass. This story put the blame on Delahanty for running up the unlit bridge to the waiting chasm. The problem with this version was that the drawbridge was at least two spans away and Kingston would have had to go some distance to see the struggling Delahanty in the swirling water. Nor could he explain away the automatic gate that guarded the opening.[52]

Kingston, distressed with the notion that he had a role in Delahanty's death, promoted the drawbridge story.[53] But his description of the fall did not endure the police investigation or the family's lawsuit against the railroad. In sworn testimony, Sam Kingston eventually asserted that after he fell on the tracks, with his foot wedged between the ties, Delahanty "got away . . . and went some little distance further on."[54] He also confessed he did not know whether Delahanty was running or how he got into the river. Kingston did relate that the man on the bridge went to the other [south] side of the span and then recrossed the track and fell in on the north side where he had originally been standing.[55] With the drawbridge defense eliminated, the question is narrowed to how Delahanty fell off the bridge.

There were two possibilities worth considering. One had Delahanty losing his footing when Kingston lunged at him; the other was that he tripped on the raised tie or chord in his effort to elude the elderly watchman. Both explanations were plausible given Delahanty's physical condition and the darkened state of the bridge. Of the two, the latter met the criterion of the incident. The footing was unstable under the best of circumstances and no side rail or rope existed along the bridge's edge. A person stumbling over the tie or the chord would be less than a body length from the precipice. Had both men fallen on the tracks in a scuffle, the befuddled athlete could have easily slipped or staggered over the unprotected side. Evidence for this was the fact that both men lost their hats on the bridge. If Delahanty had fallen when Kingston grabbed him on the chord, his Christy hat would have likely followed him into the Niagara. Instead, each man lost his headpiece on the bridge. The crushed watchman's hat was found between the ties, and Delahanty's derby was mistakenly picked up and worn by Sam Kingston.[56] The only reasonable conclusion was that the fleeing Delahanty lost his balance and tumbled over the unsecured side.

Ed Delahanty fell about twenty-five feet into the blackened void of the chilled, fast-moving river. The treacherous mid-stream current flowed as rapidly as 8 miles per hour. It was a capturing torrent that ensnared anything in its midst, even a strong and accomplished swimmer like Delahanty. Bill Hallman, Ed's former roommate, found it hard to believe that Del, "a miraculous swimmer," could succumb to drowning. Hallman boasted that no one in baseball could outswim Delahanty. He recalled Delahanty's long swims in the Delaware River and his challenge of the turbulent surfs of the Atlantic Ocean.[57] What Hallman never comprehended were the overwhelming conditions of Delahanty's plunge—the surprise and jolt of the fall, the cold water and the darkness, and the strength of current. The greatest handicap was his intoxication. Drunk people, who fall into water often get disoriented when water enters the inner ear. They become confused and swim downward, instead of up toward the surface.[58] But Delahanty did not stumble out of a boat; he toppled twenty-five feet into a surging river in the darkness of night. He never had time to right or compose himself before being overwhelmed by the elements and his panic. Shouting for aid, he was unaware that Squaw Island was a few hundred feet to his right. The current quickly carried him forward to the river's widest expanse, below Grand Island, before taking him west into the Chippawa Channel. He probably drowned before the confluence, north of Navy Island. Ahead lay dangerous rocks and rapids that began Delahanty's twenty-six mile journey to Niagara Falls.

In the early morning hours following Delahanty's accident, another Michigan Central train, carrying the Washington Senators, crossed the International Bridge. The sleeping players had no idea that their teammate had tried to pass this way and would never again meet them on the ball field. They were returning to Washington after their long road trip. The club had a doubleheader on July 4 with Lajoie's Cleveland Blues and did not imagine that when they arrived at Union Station they would be met by a frantic Norine Delahanty.

Norine had come to the station, as directed, expecting to meet her husband. Vainly she searched among the crowd of ballplayers and passengers for Del, until she realized that something was amiss. Jimmy Ryan and Al Orth inquired whether she had any word from her spouse. Taken aback by these queries, the young woman became upset when she learned about her husband's troubled road trip and his flight from Detroit. Ryan calmed her fears with assurances and escorted her back to the Oxford Hotel. Norine's comment throughout the first troubling days was that it was unlike her husband not to let her know his whereabouts, even on his sprees.[59] To ease her mind, the young woman sent out telegrams to her sister in Philadelphia and to her in-laws in Cleveland.

Alarmed by her son's disappearance, mother Delahanty wired her brother, J. F. Croke, in Buffalo, New York, to see if he had heard from his famous nephew. Even manager Loftus made inquiries along the major league circuit for his missing player. But each passing hour made the situation more ominous. By the evening of July 4, newspapers had stepped up their speculations. Some reports believed Delahanty had joined brother Tommy in Denver. Others had him going back to the Mt. Clemens spa. His mother suspected he had gone fishing with an old friend. Del's teammates believed he went to New York to play for McGraw and attend the races. Each day another lead or probe came up empty. These failures did not deter Norine Delahanty. She maintained her vigil at the Oxford and was consoled daily by players and friends. What she found most distressing were his teammates laments that they should have never left her husband unattended. Mother Delahanty, growing more alarmed, added, "He is not the boy to let his family worry for nothing, and if he had gone to New York he would have let us know."[60]

While the frenzied search intensified, the police investigation of the mysterious bridge accident progressed. Under the direction of Chief Griffin of the Ontario Police and his assistant, C. J. Metcalf, the events of that fateful night were reconstructed. They searched the waters north of the span, walked to the drawbridge and interviewed Kingston and Colclough. By the end of the weekend, they discredited the drawbridge theory and identified the high-crowned hat, worn by Kingston, as the one belonging to the missing stranger. They learned from the label that the derby came from Washington, D.C. Determining the victim's identity and recovering his body would take a while longer.

On Tuesday morning, as the world was reading about the condition of the dying Pope, Leo XIII, Elmer Hayes, a sportswriter for the *Cleveland Press,* learned from sources in Buffalo that Delahanty had purchased a ticket in Detroit for New York. He related that the ballplayer was put off the train in Fort Erie, Ontario, because of an "altercation" with the conductor. Hayes said Delahanty tried to cross the bridge, got into a scuffle with the watchman, and fell off the structure. Reporters could not confirm the story with the Washington ball club or the Delahanty family.[61]

The major break in the investigation came from John K. Bennett, Pullman's Buffalo district superintendent. On July 6, Bennett examined two unclaimed pieces of luggage. He suspected this baggage from the Michigan Central #6 belonged to the nameless accident victim. In the black leather satchel, he found a pair of laced high-topped baseball spikes made by the Clafin Company of Philadelphia. The suitcase contained a suit of clothes and a Washington baseball season blue ticket book #26. Ed Delahanty's name was on both items. Rather then prematurely reveal his discovery, Bennett telegraphed Loftus asking him to identify the holder of the #26 "blue book." He informed the ball club that the pass book was found in the baggage of the man who fell from the International Bridge. Using the suit's label, Bennett and the Buffalo police also contacted the Washington clothier and got Delahanty's address. They notified Norine about their discoveries and received back a wire asking for her husband's belongings. It was not until late Wednesday night that Loftus located club secretary Walter Hewitt and verified that the coupon booklet belonged to Edward J. Delahanty.[62] Shakened by this disclosure, Loftus and Hewitt roused Jimmy Ryan and went to Norine Delahanty's room. To their surprise, Norine Delahanty was already distraught with the news from Bennett about her husband's death.

Not knowing where to turn, Norine telegraphed the Delahanty family in Cleveland. Immediately, a wire was sent to the ballplayer's uncle, J. F. Croke, in Buffalo, asking him to inspect the unclaimed baggage. After his confirmation, Bridget Delahanty wasted no time mobilizing the family. She sent her son-in-law, E. J. Maguire, an attorney, to Buffalo and notified her sons. Young Frank "Pudgie" Delahanty, playing in nearby Syracuse, took leave from his team and joined Maguire, Croke, and detectives hired by Norine Delahanty. Their first task was to reexamine the luggage and investigate the circumstances of Del's disappearance. Hoping for an early start on Thursday morning, their plans were altered by news that a body was recovered below the Horseshoe Falls.

On the Canadian side of Niagara Falls, across the gorge from Prospect Point, is an inlet where steamships take sightseers to the foot of the Horseshoe Falls. The area is called "Maid of the Mist" after an old Seneca Indian legend about a beautiful native princess who rises out of the spray and mist. At about 8:30 on the morning of July 9, William Le Blond, a worker from nearby Drummondville, spotted a body floating in an eddy beyond the boat landing. He and a few others roped the corpse and pulled it to shore. The body was in ghastly condition. It had been in the water for a week and had been swept into ragged-edged rocks of the cascades before being carried over the 170-foot falls. It was also suspected that the body had been struck by the propeller of one of the tourist boats. The once muscular athletic body was now a bloated, disfigured, and badly decomposed corpse. Delahanty was naked, except for a slate-colored, white dotted necktie, a pair of low-laced shoes and black work socks held up by garters. The top of his head was bald due to the action of the water. His face and head were almost black, and his trunk and broken legs were badly discolored. The ballplayer's left leg was nearly severed at the thigh, and his stomach had been torn open, exposing bulging entrails. The undertaker said the body's dreadful state of decomposition was intensified by his intoxication, a condition verified by the alcohol found in his stomach.[63]

The Morse Funeral Home in Drummondville, now Niagara Falls, Ontario, was summoned, and the body was transported by wagon to their morgue. The corpse was examined by Mr. Morse, who waited for an identification and directions.

M. A. Green, a stockholder in the Washington ball club, was in Buffalo when the story of Delahanty's accident broke. Having been a close friend of the ballplayer and his family, Green took it upon himself to be an on-site contact for the family and the team. In this role, he went with a local reporter to Bennett's office and affirmed the unclaimed baggage belonged to Delahanty.

On the morning the body surfaced, another reporter came to the Genesee Hotel and told Green what had happened. Both men quickly set out on a farm wagon for the Drummondville undertakers. Green was shakened by what he saw. He said Del's features were not discernible, but he knew it was his friend because of a gold-crowned front tooth, his two disfigured "baseball fingers," and his surviving necktie. Green turned away in tears and verified that the corpse was indeed Delahanty. Upon leaving the funeral home, he telegraphed his corroboration to Loftus.[64]

When Frank Delahanty heard about the body, he collected his uncle and brother-in-law and took a train to Drummondville. They arrived at the Morse Funeral Parlor sometime after Green's departure. The men recognized that the corpse on the examination table was their beloved Eddie, but carefully went over the body for confirming private marks.

This inspection, and its accompanying identification, weighed heavily on the men's emotions. The strain of the last few days and the acceptance of Del's death surfaced in an outburst of accusations and anger. Speaking for the family, young Frank questioned the accuracy of the published accounts. Talk of suicide or his brother's intoxication were not acceptable explanations. He suggested his big brother was the victim of a robbery and tried to fit a crime into every rendering of the accident. Their suspicions were not dispelled either by visits to the bridge or by meetings with Kingston and Cole. Frank Delahanty and his brother-in-law were actually taken aback by the guard's age and size and wondered how he could have gotten the better of Delahanty in a scuffle. As the evidence shifted toward an accident, Frank began to take out his grief and wrath on the railroad. He and his relatives blamed the Michigan Central and asked how conductor Cole could leave a man unattended in such a vulnerable spot when his destination was minutes away.

These questions were put to John Cole when he was approached at a stopover at the Buffalo station. Frank Delahanty reminded Cole, "It seems to me that insomuch as you took care of my brother in Detroit, you could have brought him across the bridge. If you had done that, Ed would probably be alive today."[65] Delahanty's comments disturbed Cole. It was only after he composed himself that he reverted to the railroad's official stance. The conductor confessed that if he had known that Delahanty was going to jump from the bridge, he would have taken the agitated passenger to Buffalo. Cole reiterated that he had no idea of the ballplayer's intentions.

"God knows I tried to take care of that man," Cole replied. He repeated that he watched over Delahanty and tried to keep him calm, but when Delahanty began to disturb people in the Pullman car and drag them from their berths, he had to take action. Cole went so far as to say that Delahanty was brandishing an open razor. "Suppose it was your mother or your sister" in those berths, Cole asked, "What would you have me do in a case like that?" Neither Frank Delahanty or Maguire replied.[66]

Cole's comments did not temper the indignation of the Delahanty family. Frank said the Michigan Central was responsible for Del's death because they had acknowledged selling him whiskey and then punished him for his behavior. Maguire, the attorney, reminded reporters that Cole earlier had denied that Delahanty was drunk. He also repudiated the alleged razor attack, saying that his brother-in-law owned a safety razor. By the time Delahanty's body was ready for shipment to Cleveland, the family began talking about a lawsuit against the Michigan Central.

Another area of concern for the Delahantys was the nature of Ed's marital problems. The family was disturbed by stories of how Del was jealous of his wife and that his despondency stemmed from these obsessions. Relatives and friends reacted defensively. They said Norine Delahanty was an "estimable woman, who gave him no cause for suspicions."[67] No one spoke about her flirtatious and manipulative nature or about her excessive lifestyle. Instead, the family gave a traditional account of the relationship. Frank said the couple was very much "attached to each other," and it was "his anxiety to see his wife that caused Ed to rush across the bridge to catch his train and nothing else."[68]

Norine Delahanty was inconsolable and spoke bitterly about Cole and Kingston. She felt betrayed by this tragic mishap and fretted over how she would handle her daughter's grief and the Delahantys' decision to bury her husband in Cleveland. Anxious to leave Washington, Norine wired her sister in Philadelphia who made arrangments for the trip to Ohio. She brought her five-year-old niece, Florence Delahanty, to the Market Street Station, and after a tearful reunion, the two women and the child boarded a Pullman train for Cleveland.

Delahanty's teammates and legions of fans and friends were stunned by the news of Del's unexpected death. Long-time mates

Jimmy Ryan and Al Orth and Jim "Deacon" McGuire (who was in Washington with the visiting Detroit Tigers) publicly grieved for the loss of their esteemed friend. Most ballplayers, however, were strangely silent about Delahanty's death. Flags around the two leagues were flown at half-mast, and the Senators wore black mourning arm bands. In Drummondville, Ontario, Morse and his son worked through the night getting the corpse and its casing ready for the journey to Ohio. A metal-lined container with extra handles and a carrying crate with a cooling board were assembled. The body was embalmed and disinfectant was applied. Frank Delahanty and E. J. Maguire paid $125 for mortuary expenses and $75 in shipping costs.[69] Early on Friday morning, the tenth of July, Delahanty was taken on the Michigan Central Railroad to Buffalo, New York, on the way to Cleveland, Ohio. Frank Delahanty and his brother-in-law accompanied the body. Once in Cleveland, Delahanty's remains were taken to the Flynn and Froeck Funeral Home. Thomas Flynn transferred the body to a casket that remained closed during the service at the Church of the Immaculate Conception.

Monsignor J. P. Thorpe said a Requiem High Mass the next morning before a full gathering of mourners and well-wishers. He spoke of Ed's "admirable disposition and his unstained character." The hymn "Lead, Kindly Light" was sung as the casket was carried from the church.[70] The Delahanty family bore their grief in tears and shocked silence. Frank Delahanty, in a remembrance, said the whole episode "nearly killed my mother."[71] Bridget Delahanty sat next to her stoic husband and tried to console her pained daughter-in-law and disbelieving granddaughter. The brothers (except Tommy, who was playing in Denver, Colorado) were in attendance. Joe had come from Birmingham, Alabama, and Jimmy returned from Little Rock, Arkansas. Jimmy sat silently with his arm in a tight-fitted sling. He had broken his shoulder and was coming home to Cleveland to recuperate when he learned of his brother's death. The youngest brother, William, with the Detroit spree fresh in his memory, sat among relatives, long-time friends, and neighbors. All mourned the premature death of a beloved husband, father, son, brother, and friend. He left a void in their lives and an unfinished page in the annals of the national pastime.

Because the family wanted to bury him quickly, most of Delahanty's teammates and friends across the country could not be on hand to pay their final respects. But their presence was obvious from the floral tributes that took up two carriages. The Cleveland baseball team, which was playing in Philadelphia, sent a wreath of lillies, roses, and white carnations. The American New York club and the Phillies ordered floral baseball displays. Tom Delahanty's Denver team sent flowers, as did the firemen at Engine House #5 on Phelps Street. The floral display from the Washington Senators arrived too late for the funeral.

The hearse was followed by a long line of mourners and carriages. The people of Cleveland stopped and removed their hats as the cortege passed. They remembered Ed Delahanty as one of their own, an Irish-American boy who had given them pride and enriched their lives with his athletic feats. They saw only his successes and were blind to his abuses. They worshiped his accomplishments on the ball field and ignored his improvident ways. Perhaps the sorrow in Cleveland over how he died made people mindful that their hero was a casualty to the fame and fortune he sought.

At the Calvary Cemetery, Ed Delahanty and his dreams were interred at the family's burial site. The grave was covered with flowers as the assembled mourners heard the final prayers and benedictions. The pallbearers quietly stood by. They were old friends and prominent Irishmen who had known Delahanty most of his life, men such as Sheriff Ed Barry. Ironically, the only ballplayer in attendance was New York's John McGraw. He came from Cincinnati, where his Giants were playing, to be a pallbearer[72] and pay his last respects to a dear friend and competitor whose life he had tragically altered.

Epilogue

Baseball in the Emerald Age provided no significant benefits for ballplayers. The responsibility for nonplaying expenses generally fell on the athletes. There were no pensions or retirement plans, no relief funds or insurance policies, and no guaranteed medical coverage from ball clubs. If a player's career ended unexpectedly without any plan for the future, it was not the team's concern. A few prominent players might be remembered with coaching positions or ball park jobs, but most players went from baseball back into the general workforce. On occasion, indigent or suffering players and their families received collected money from active players and benefit games. Some provident ballplayers traded on their fame, invested wisely, and capitalized on the opportunities afforded professional athletes. For every Comiskey, Ward, McGraw, and Mack, however, there were hundreds of players who stumbled and fell from prominence. Intemperate ballplayers such as Ed Delahanty squandered their money on celebrity lifestyles. An editorial in the *New York Journal* commented, "he [Delahanty] never grasped the idea that the game afforded a field for improvement and betterment of habits and character that could have firmly established him in life as a prosperous and successful man."[1] As a consequence, Norine Delahanty and her five-year-old daughter, Florence, were left with debts, pain, and pity.

Delahanty's widow was not yet twenty-five years old when she lost her husband. Norine had never worked, but was accustomed to the comforts of better living. She had no intention of moving to Cleveland and being a ward of the Delahantys. Instead, Norine took Florence and returned to Philadelphia, boarding with her unwed older sister, Nettie. The child adapted much better than her mother. Florence made her newfound chores into games of fantasy while Norine mourned and waited on events.[2]

At that point, Norine had few prospects. Delahanty's estate amounted to his last paycheck. All his cash and jewelry were lost in the Niagara River. His road trip insurance policies had lapsed and the benefits from his Fraternal Order of the Eagles Lodge #42 of Philadelphia were not forthcoming because of arreared dues.[3] For the moment, Norine was reliant on the generosity of her husband's teammates and the players and fans from around the two major leagues. Washington's Jimmy Ryan assumed the role often borne by Ed Delahanty, that of soliciting money for a needy player and his family. Unfortunately, the collections were disappointing. Some speculated that the Delahanty family would take care of the widow. Others attributed the restraint to resentment brought on by Delahanty's contract jumping.[4] A benefit game between the Senators and the White Stockings was suggested, but a spokesman for Washington bemoaned the club's "endangered" financial condition and offered only to organize the addressing of letters to ballplayers around the country. The club's justification was that it already had lost about $5,300 on Delahanty.[5] Washington's policemen, however, did not forsake their hero. They staged a Saturday afternoon benefit game at the Senators' park for the widow and her child.[6] Another effort came from the Phillies, who raised a subscription during a Sunday game in Cincinnati. The Chicago White Stockings donated $150, and Charlie Comiskey sent Jimmy Ryan a personal check for $40.[7] More reassuring were news stories that the Delahanty family were holding the Michigan Central Railroad responsible for Ed's death.

Ten days after Del's body was recovered from the falls, Frank Delahanty charged the railway with serving his brother alcohol and putting him off the train for being intoxicated.[8] The legal obstacle for Norine and her brothers-in-law was one of jurisdiction. Alleging negligence in Delahanty's death, the claim against the Michigan Central had to be filed and heard in Ontario, Canada.[9] For this reason, Norine Delahanty, through her attorneys in Cleveland and Philadelphia, retained the law firm of German and Pettit in Welland, Ontario. As a convenience, a local Philadelphia attorney, one recommended by Del's local baseball friends, took the widow's deposition. In her testimony, she claimed her husband was "physically sober" when he left Detroit. Norine accused the railroad of illegally selling him liquor while he traveled in Canada and then left him unattended in sight of his destination. According to the widow, "We are advised that no liquor can be sold on the train in Canada and that it is positively prohibited."[10]

One of her Canadian solicitors believed he could establish "actionable negligence" against the railroad. But he cautioned Norine that the Michigan Central was not ready to entertain a settlement and recommended giving them time before filing the lawsuit.[11] The railroad discounted the "imputed liability" of serving alcohol or the "violation of any at-present unknown statutes" concerning Del's removal from the train. Delahanty, the brief said, was "fighting drunk" and hence it was an "urgent necessity to eject a threatening passenger." To their way of thinking, the ballplayer was neither "senseless or stupid," nor was the drop-off area "particularly dangerous." Delahanty, they asserted, put himself in jeopardy by trying to cross a bridge not meant for pedestrians in the dark.[12]

By mid-February 1904, the lawsuit was docketed, and on May 4, a jury decided in favor of the plantiffs, Norine Delahanty and her daughter. It was the jury's contention that the conductor left Delahanty in a "physical and mental condition which made him entirely incapable of looking after or taking care of himself." With no one watching out for him, the deceased, "unconscious of what he was doing," followed the departing train over a dangerous rail crossing. The court awarded Norine $3,000, and Florence was directed to receive $2,000.[13]

The relief and vindication for Norine Delahanty and her in-laws were short-lived. The railroad appealed the judgment to an appellate court in Toronto. The Michigan Central questioned whether there was sufficient evidence to find a verdict for the plantiffs. Their attorneys argued that there was no proof of negligence fit for a jury's consideration. They asserted that negligence was a breach of some duty owed to another. The conductor and the stewards, they said, had acted responsibly and were preoccupied on preparing the train for its Buffalo stopover. They had no time to "guard a violent man." The defendants took the position that Delahanty's argument with the bridge guard showed how useless it would have been to leave him with someone. They believed the ballplayer was physically capable of caring for himself. Their conclusion was that Delahanty went on the bridge under his own power and "fell over the girder accidently or threw himself over deliberately."[14] On June 29, 1905, the five judges of the Court of Appeals overturned the lower court's decision. Norine was shattered when she heard the verdict. Her solicitors advised her that she could appeal the ruling to the Supreme Court of Canada.[15] But the shakened young widow was put off by the $500 security required for the final hearing, particularly when $200 was already being held from her first appeal.[16] Although she received a time extension to make up her mind, in the end Norine Delahanty could not risk further debt. After court costs were deducted from her original deposit, Norine had little choice and went on with her life.

The months that followed were restless ones for Norine and Florence. They moved several times to different North Philadelphia apartments, and at one time thought was given to putting Florence into a convent.[17] Norine's outlook improved in 1906, when she met Louis Lerio, a plumber and inventor with ambitions of starting his own business. They married before the year was out and together with Florence, relocated to Mobile, Alabama. Here Norine began a new life. Her husband made money from his patents and opened a manufacturing company that produced copper and galvanized cornices and blow piping. In 1910 Norine gave birth to twin boys; only one, Louis Jr., survived. With two children and a prospering family business, Norine settled into a comfortable southern lifestyle, nurturing pretensions of being a southern gentlewoman.

The Lerio home was not a placid one, though. Norine was "insane[ly] jealous" of her husband and arguing was commonplace. Florence, however, was treated well by her stepfather and was spoiled by her mother. Stubborn and strong-willed, the self-possessed daughter of Ed Delahanty dropped out of school at the age of fourteen and went to work for the phone company. Courted by many young men, Florence was smitten with a prominent socialite, seven years her senior, who was "long in manners and short on cash." J. K. Randall embodied everything that Florence wanted. He came from the "right society" of Mobile and deferred to her spousal lead. They married in 1919 and within a year, Florence gave birth to a girl named for her mother. The family also moved into a home bought by her stepfather.[18]

Life for Norine Delahanty's family remained unsettled. Norine's troubled son committed suicide in 1937, and her granddaughter and namesake inherited the autism that afflicted Del's younger sister. Both women were overly attentive and protective of the precocious child. With the passing of her mother (in 1945), stepfather (1942), and husband (1954), Florence was left alone to look after her daughter. When she passed away in 1967, close family friends assumed responsibility for young Norine, who lived in her parents' house until her own death in June 1993. On a bureau in her living room she kept a picture of her grandfather in his Washington baseball uniform. When questioned about him, she asked why the railroad put him off the train.[19]

Ed's family felt the same despair. They knew there was little they could have done to relieve his demons and had little understanding of the severity of his emotional state of mind. The family met their adversity with prayer and denial. Bridget Delahanty took the death of her favored child the hardest, blaming it on her maternal failings. She had been with him in Detroit and had seen him through his drinking crisis. But Mrs. Delahanty, believing Ed was okay, left him alone on what proved to be his fatal last day. Grief and guilt tore at this devout, strong woman. She never understood how her faith and strength had failed her flawed and troubled son. For years, she dressed in black and lit candles in the privacy of her local church. By the end of Bridget's life, her mourning became part of her matriarchal bearing.

Her husband's response, on the other hand, can only be assumed. James Delahanty was never mentioned in any account or reporting. He appears to have again let his wife deal with their son's anguished behavior. But James' absence cannot be seen as an indication of how this stoic and detached man felt. He seems to have suffered in silence and immersed himself in his daily labors, or perhaps in a neighboring saloon. When James died in March 1919 at the age of 83, he was interred next to his baseball-playing son in Calvary Cemetery.

Bridget Delahanty lived until November 1926. Her last years were troublesome for her family and friends. Mrs. Delahanty's health and state of mind required constant attention. It became so compelling that her daughter Katherine Maguire took Bridget into her home. Leaving the Phelps Street hearth was difficult for the failing Delahanty matron. The move immediately incited family frictions over the cost of her care and the management of her estate. Fueled by old sibling tensions, the family was consumed by suspicions and recriminations. The brothers were upset by Katherine's controlling manner, the spiraling expenses, and their mother's discontented dotage. They would not speak with their sister or visit their mother at Katherine's home. Eventually, Joe Delahanty became her guardian, which created a new set of problems because the brothers did not trust his wife's intentions.[20] The bickering over Bridget's $10,000 estate persisted after her death. When all debts and costs were settled, each of Bridget's children and Florence Delahanty received $1,336.77.[21] The acrimony tore the family apart and left it dysfunctional.[22]

Ed Delahanty's brothers never fully resolved the circumstances of Ed's pointless death. Nearly sixty years after the accident, Frank Delahanty still found it difficult to explain his brother's demise.[23] To the boys in the family, Ed was a model and inspiration for their youthful ambitions. With Ed and their father as primary male figures, it was not surprising the Delahanty boys had shallow outlooks and took refuge in the game they learned from their big brother. They also found life without baseball a difficult challenge.

Tom Delahanty, the most withdrawn of the brothers, knew Ed the best. Five years younger than Del, Tommy grew up with Ed still living at home. At the time of the accident, Tommy was living out west and had not seen Ed in about two years. As such, he did not get a chance to say goodbye to his brother. Apparently, his bereaved family, not wanting to prolong their anguish, rushed to bury Ed without waiting for Tom to return from Denver. Tommy never forgave the family's decision and for a long time had trouble accepting that Ed's death was not the result of foul play.[24] Nevertheless, he played through his grief, batting .310 for the 1903 season before returning to the still-grieving Delahanty household. When not on the ball field, Tommy worked in a boiler shop. In the years that followed, he continued to play ball out west with Seattle and Colorado Springs and for a short while managed his old Denver club. In 1906 he played briefly with his brother Joe at Williamsport in the Tri-State League before retiring from baseball at the age of thirty-four. Tommy Delahanty appeared in only 19 major league games and hit for a .239 average. His best seasons were his twelve years in the high minor leagues where he compiled a .295 lifetime batting mark.

The third brother, Joe, was playing for New Orleans in the Southern League at the time of Ed's death. He did not linger to console his bereaved family after the funeral, but rather returned to the Crescent City and finished out the year in Memphis. In the off-season, Joe, a bachelor, lived at home and found work as a lithographer. The following seasons, he performed well with Buffalo in the Eastern League and Williamsport in the Tri-State League. His continued good play over the next two years earned the thirty-two-year-old his long-awaited call to the major leagues. For two seasons Joe was the regular center fielder and part-time first baseman for St. Louis. But age was getting the best of Joe Delahanty and by 1910 he was playing for Toronto in the Eastern League. Two years later he was out of professional baseball. He played in only 269 National League games and had a .238 lifetime average. Like brother Tommy, Joe was an outstanding minor league ballplayer. In fourteen years, performing with fourteen teams, he competed in 1,423 games, hit 170 triples, and batted .303.

Brother Jimmy was the closest to Ed Delahanty in both temperament and athletic skill. He learned of his brother's death on his way home to convalesce from a cracked shoulder blade. Less than a week after Ed was interred, Jimmy returned to Little Rock with his arm still in a sling and scouted for his ball club.[25] Jimmy still led the Southern Association in batting and in 1904 he joined Boston in the National League. For two seasons he filled in at every position and did some spot pitching for the Beaneaters. This versatility caught the attention of the new Cincinnati manager Ned Hanlon. In 1906 Jimmy hit .280 for the Reds[26] and was sent the following year to the American League, first to St. Louis and then to

Washington. Over the next three seasons, performing primarily at his favored, second base position, Jimmy appeared in 282 games for the Senators.[27] The turning point in Jimmy's career was 1909 when Detroit manager Hugh Jennings traded for him. Unlike his brothers, Jimmy now had the chance to play for a contending champion, a team led by players such as Ty Cobb and Sam Crawford. Teammate Davy Jones recalled that Delahanty gave the club a "big lift." He described Jimmy as a "tobacco-chewing tough guy" with a great sense of humor. Without him, Detroit "would not have won the pennant."[28] Jimmy played in 46 games and batted only .253, but he saved his best efforts for the World Series against Honus Wagner's Pittsburgh Pirates. Although Pittsburgh took the series 4 games to 3, Jimmy out-hit everyone, including Cobb (.231) and Wagner (.333). He collected 9 hits and batted .346. The following season, Delahanty dislocated his chronic bad knee. He still appeared in 106 games and hit .294. In 1911 Jimmy had his best year in baseball. He batted .339 and knocked in 94 runs.

This success did not last. During the 1912 campaign, Jimmy's play was undermined by nagging injuries and a damaging controversy. League president Ban Johnson blamed Jimmy for a players strike over Ty Cobb's suspension for attacking an abusive fan. Despite vigorous denials, Jimmy was marked as a dissembling troublemaker. At the age of thirty-three, Delahanty was waived out of the league.[29] He had participated in 1,186 major league games and batted a respectable .283. Delahanty moved on to Minneapolis in the American Association and stayed with them until 1914 when he signed on with Brooklyn in the new rival Federal League. After the new league challenge failed, Delahanty joined Hartford in the Colonial League and took the batting title with a .379 average. In 1916, hitting .306 with Beaumont in the Texas League, Jimmy retired to manage the ball club. But he lacked the patience to coach "know-it-all youngsters" and quit at the end of the year. His retirement closed the Delahanty era that began in 1887 when brother Ed signed to play with Mansfield in the Ohio League. "When I go," Jimmy declared, "there is no one to take my place."[30]

William Delahanty was the youngest of the siblings, born nineteen years after Ed. Like brother Tommy, Willie was smaller than the other Delahanty boys. According to family lore, "when God made them He ran out of material when He got to him [Willie]."[31]

William was the wide-eyed, seventeen-year-old brother who accompanied Jimmy Ryan and the Senators to the ballpark on the day Ed Delahanty took the train to Buffalo. It was William who returned to Cleveland with his mother to wait for news about his vanished brother. And it was William who remained at home in the summer of 1903 and dealt with a grieving household. Two years later, William followed his brothers into professional baseball.

Over the next five years, William performed as an infielder for teams in the Ohio and New York State Leagues. The reason given for his lack of progress was that he suffered some sort of head injury. His brother Frank recalled that a firecracker damaged his eye.[32] Other stories said he was badly beaned while waiting for his call-up to Brooklyn.[33] Whatever the reason, William was out of baseball by 1912.

The last living brother was Frank Delahanty. Three years older than Willie, it was Frank who left the Syracuse ball club to help investigate Del's disappearance and later identified the mutilated body. Like his older brothers, Frank took leave of the family after the funeral and returned to finish out the year in the New York State League. The next two seasons, he played for Montgomery and Birmingham in the Southern Association before being sold to the American League New York Highlanders. At the age of twenty-two he got into 9 games as an outfielder and first baseman. In 1906, while Jimmy was playing in Cincinnati, Frank appeared in 92 games with New York and batted .238. The next year he was sold to Cleveland and played for Napoleon Lajoie. Competing in his hometown, Frank learned that "too many friends" and "too much stepping around" affected one's performance.[34] He returned to New York the following year, and after 37 games was released. He ended the season on brother Joe's former New Orleans team. Over the next five years, Frank played for a variety of ball clubs in the American Association, never hitting higher than .276. With the advent of the Federal League, he followed Jimmy into that ill-fated organization. After the league folded, he had a brief stay with Erie in the Inter-State League, before he retired.

Out of baseball, the brothers returned to Cleveland and lived off their athletic reputations. Tommy never married. He moved to Florida and worked as a boat mechanic. He died in 1951 and was buried in Sanford, Florida. Joe, Jimmy, and Frank took patronage jobs with the city and William worked at a local aircraft company. Personally, Joe was plagued by gambling problems, Jimmy struggled with intemperance, and fraternal harmony was torn by petty family discord. Joe died first in 1936. Jimmy passed on in 1953, William in 1957, and Frank, the "Last of the Ballplaying Delahantys,"[35] in 1966. Only Frank and William were buried near Ed in the Delahanty family plot. When the last brother died, a fascinating sports story was closed. Five sons of Irish postfamine refugees played in 3,596 major league baseball games and knocked out 4,214 base hits.

> There's Frank and Jim, Tom and Bill
> And another one called Joe,
> But the greatest batsman ever
> Passed away some time ago
> . . . .
> Their appearance on the diamond
> Bring us back to other days
> When their big and famous brother
> Heard the robin sing its lays
> But glory waxes and wanes
> Much like the silvery moon
> So look out, you Delahantys
> That you don't go back too soon.[36]

Major league baseball as played by the younger Delahantys was a product of the strife and instability that existed at the time of their brother's death. Fearful of another costly bidding war and the impending injunctions from the Davis and Elberfeld cases, the owners provided their leagues with a new presiding executive, the National Commission. The commission consisted of a three-man board, comprised of the presidents of each league—the weak-willed and brooding Harry Pulliam of the National League and the hard-driving and dominating Ban Johnson of the American League—and a chairman, Gary Herrmann, the president of the Cincinnati ball club. Operating under this new governing body, both leagues agreed to be separate but equal organizations. Stability was built on the old reserve clause, territorial rights, shared playing rules, and complementary schedules. The casualties of this new monopsony were the bargaining positions of ballplayers and the large salaries and contracts of past years. Players again found themselves without mutuality or appeal. Average salaries in the century's first decade regressed to 1900 levels.[37] Only such players as Cobb, Wagner, Mathewson, and Lajoie were making the kind of money that Ed Delahanty was denied.

The commission also kept their fellow magnates in check, disciplined players, mediated disputes, defeated the Federal League challenges and cleared up the rowdy side of baseball. The most apparent changes were how the game was played. The National Commission adopted the foul-strike rule, elevated the pitching mound, and set a minimum fence distance of 235 feet. The result was a pitching-dominated, "dead ball" game that saw home runs and batting averages decline and pitcher's earned run averages fall to record lows. Between 1904 and 1910, the combined batting average for both leagues was .246 and ERAs shrunk to 2.62. In 1905, only two American League hitters batted over .300. Complementing these innovations were the two-umpire system, a 154-game schedule, and a postseason, interleague World Series. The sport's new identity was expressed by the adoption (in 1907) of the Doubleday myth of baseball's native origin and the public's embrace of the song, "Take Me Out to the Ball Game." The game's appeal also reflected the nation's unprecedented growth and vitality. With attendance rising and salaries controlled, profits were reinvested in large, fireproof, steel and concrete stadiums such as Philadelphia's prototype, Shibe Park (opened in 1909). The good fortune of the National Commission era lasted until the World Series scandal of 1919 and the appointment of Judge Kenesaw Landis as baseball's first commissioner.

The national game after Delahanty's death also changed in other ways. New faces and personalities dominated the playing fields. Only thirteen ballplayers, who competed with Ed Delahanty in the late 1880s, were active after his death.[38] Most of Del's peers left the game with little to show for the years of adulation and success. For the franchises and players that were a part of Delahanty's turbulent career, the results were mixed.

For the Phillies' original triumvirate, Reach, Rogers, and Shettsline, the post-Delahanty years were bittersweet. After selling the franchise, Al Reach turned his attention to the family's sporting goods business and spent most of his time living in Atlantic City,

New Jersey. His contact with the national sport revolved around the manufacturing of major league baseballs. After a long illness, the grand old man of Philadelphia baseball died on January 14, 1928. Reach's estate was valued at more than a million dollars.

John Rogers left baseball with a great deal of bitterness. He was disillusioned by his setbacks and upset by his fallen reputation. His remaining years were occupied with his law practice and scholarly research. An active outdoorsman, the sixty-six-year-old Rogers suffered a fatal heart attack in March 1910, while hiking in Colorado. His passing drew little attention from major league baseball.

Billy Shettsline, Rogers' protégé and Delahanty's close friend, remained with the Phillies until 1926 in a variety of capacities. After serving briefly as club president (1905–8), he worked as the team's all-purpose, front-office man. When he left the Phillies, he was employed by the Philadelphia Highway Department. After a short illness, Billy died on February 22, 1933. The popular figure, who looked after three generations of Phillies ballplayers, was mourned by players and fans alike.

John Brush, on the other hand, had a difficult time recovering from his interleague setbacks. Neither he nor John McGraw ever spoke publicly about Delahanty's death. Both ignored any charges of responsibility.[39] Brush did have to accept the loss of George Davis, the advent of the American League Highlanders, and the ascendancy of his dreaded adversary Ban Johnson. But Brush's discomfort with the authority and policies of Ban Johnson and the National Commission was intensified by his crippled and failing body. Worn down by the pace of his demanding life, on November 25, 1912, John T. Brush died on a California-bound train. The man whose attitudes and ambitions drove the National League during Delahanty's career was neither missed nor easily forgotten.

The passing of an influential sports magnate or dominating ballplayer did not usually attract a great deal of discussion or attention beyond obituary notices. Ed Delahanty's death was different. Its mysterious circumstances were difficult for the sporting press to ignore. The fascination with the abrupt and tragic demise of the game's dominant batsman had the qualities of a popular morality play. His self-destructive ways and his humiliating decline exposed the pitfalls of an intemperate life and the corrupting impact of the baseball war. His death also had a sobering effect on how professional baseball was conducted. Less obvious was the eclipse of the sport's Emerald Age.

Delahanty's death did not mark the end of the Irish dominance of baseball as much as it signaled a transition to a new era of ballplayers. Ed Delahanty was a renowned link to the dynamic and celebrated Irish players of the late nineteenth century, an era when Irish ballplayers outnumbered and often outplayed their contemporaries. Delahanty was the age's ultimate explosive Irish power-hitter. He would have no successors. Decades after his death, his feats were reverently recited. Not even the exploits of Willie Keeler and his generation of catalytic contact hitters could compete with the excitement generated when Delahanty strode to the plate. But the notoriety of his passing and the changing nature of the post-merger game obscured his achievements and the evolving ethnic character of those who played the sport.

As the proportion of Irish players declined, other nationalities were drawn into baseball by the same factors that had attracted the Irish decades before. These emerging second-generation American ballplayers grew up in a baseball-playing society without regard for Old World sporting traditions. These young men honed their batball skills and competitive instincts in America. Their models were Delahanty and the players of the Emerald Age. The formula, therefore, was already in place when native-born sons of later European refugees took advantage of the opportunities provided by two major leagues.[40]

Even though the National Commission years belonged to players named Cobb, Mathewson, Alexander, Wagner, Speaker, Lajoie, Bender, and Jackson, the Irish influences were carried on by Joe McGinnity, Rube Waddell, Jimmy Collins, Willie Keeler, Joe Kelley, and the arrival of Ed Walsh, Eddie Collins, and Johnny Evers. Former ballplayers of Irish lineage moved on to managerial and front office positions. Among the prominent managers were John McGraw, Connie Mack, Hugh Jennings, Bill Joyce, Jimmy Collins, Roger Bresnahan, Kid Gleason, Pat Moran, Jimmy McAleer, Joe Kelley, and Irish-born Patsy Donovan. These men bore the traditions inspired by Ted Sullivan, Charlie Comiskey, Ned Hanlon, and Patsy Tebeau. From 1900 to 1922, including non–World Series years, fourteen champion ball clubs had Irish managers. In addition to Mack and McGraw, running the operations of successful franchises were sporting entrepreneurs like Charlie Comiskey, Frank Farrell, and Charley Murphy. In 1913, 44 percent of the leagues' team presidents were of Irish descent.[41]

Professional baseball in the decades after Delahanty's death was also played by a greater number of athletes from white collar backgrounds, young men who learned the sport away from the vacant lots and fields of the congested inner cities. By the end of the First World War, one-fourth of major league players attended and played ball in college.[42] Unfortunately, baseball's changing character did not embrace ballplayers of African descent. They continued to be shut out by the lingering prejudices of Delahanty's era.

The wake stirred by baseball's Emerald Age endured for another half-century. Connie Mack, who contributed so much to the break-up of Delahanty's Phillies, survived the interleague battles and made the Athletics the dominant team in the Quaker City. From 1905 to 1914 Mack's club went to the World Series five times, winning three championships. Ensuring that Connie Mack remained in Philadelphia, Ben Shibe refinanced his franchise to enable his manager to buy a full half-share interest in the ball club. Mack's Athletics returned to prominence again in 1929 with three consecutive appearances in the World Series. After the last Shibe son died in 1936, Connie Mack took over the franchise. He was elected to the Hall of Fame in 1937 and managed the Athletics until 1950. Over his career he collected 3,731 victories, 9 American League pennants, and 5 world championships. At the age of 94, he died quietly in Philadelphia on February 8, 1956.

Charlie Comiskey never duplicated the successes of his American Association St. Louis Browns. And though his influence on others changed how the game was played, Comiskey redirected his drive to front office business. His early support of Ban Johnson and his new baseball league got him the attractive Chicago American League franchise. Over the next two decades, his White Sox were a profitable and successful club. He won five pennants and two World Series. In 1910, with attendance booming, this son of an Irish immigrant built a new ball park that bore his surname for more than ninety years. His post-1915 White Sox led by Joe Jackson, Eddie Cicotte, and Eddie Collins brought Comiskey again to the top of his profession. Unfortunately, his players did not enjoy the fruits of the owner's publicized generosity. The resulting player discontent paved the way for the fixed 1919 World Series. The "Old Roman" never came to terms with the Black Sox scandal. Neither did his White Sox recover from the stigma of that association. When Comiskey died at the age of 72 on October 26, 1931, he was better known for the shame of 1919 than he was for his contributions in St. Louis. Eight years after his death, his importance was recognized by his induction into Cooperstown.

Ned Hanlon, one of the most successful heirs of Comiskey-style baseball, was to the 1890s what the "Old Roman" had been to the previous decade. But Hanlon was never in a position to perpetuate his string of Baltimore-Brooklyn league championships. He was undermined by American League raids and interfering team presidents. At the end of the dismal 1905 season, Hanlon was forced out of Brooklyn, and after two mediocre years in Cincinnati, he retired to Baltimore. It was his disciple John McGraw who upheld the legacy of the Emerald Age. Like Comiskey and Mack in the American League, McGraw was the decision-maker for his ball club. Settled in John Brush's newly built Polo Grounds, the New York Giants under McGraw's direction became the model of a successful baseball franchise. In his thirty seasons as the Giants manager, McGraw won ten pennants, three World Series, and finished in second place eleven times. McGraw managed the Giants until midway through the 1932 season. He remained as a team vice-president until his death from prostate cancer on February 25, 1934. McGraw was inducted into Cooperstown in 1937, the year Hanlon died. Almost sixty years later, Hanlon followed his protégé into the Hall.

Eight years after McGraw's induction and 42 seasons after Delahanty's death, the "only Del" took his rightful place with the legends of the sport. In the original "old-timers" vote in 1936, familiarity cost Delahanty and other nineteenth-century stars a first-round admission. In the next six ballots, Delahanty lost out to more contemporary ballplayers. Only nine of his peers preceded Delahanty to Cooperstown, and five of them, Anson, McGraw, Spalding, Comiskey, and Mack, were influential managers and front-office men. It took the Centennial Commission of 1945 to select nine more nineteenth-century ballplayers, including Delahanty. His class was made up of Roger Bresnahan, Dan Brouthers, Fred Clarke, Jimmy Collins, Hugh Duffy, Hugh Jennings, King Kelly, and Jim O'Rourke. The fact that eight of the nine were Irish and five of the previous nine inductees shared the same ancestry said something about the ethnic character of late-nineteenth-century baseball.

The influence of Delahanty and his fellow Irishmen did not go unnoticed in the popular sporting press. And though their backgrounds were sometimes slurred, commentators generally gave them their due. Baseball had become too important a cultural totem and pastime to be ignored or deprecated. As one commentator begrudgingly wrote, "Who build our jails? The Irish. Who fill our jails? The Irish. And it might also be said the Irish do their share toward building up the national game."[43] When the fabled baseball promoter Ted Sullivan in 1897 was asked how players in the Emerald Age had changed since the 1870s, he replied that the ballplayers "use their heads now instead of playing mechanically, and have attained a higher degree of efficiency in team work."[44] Such was the legacy of Irish-American ballplayers.

Delahanty's legacy as a man and ballplayer, however, posed sharp contrasts. He lived for immediate gratification and trusted everything to his athletic skills. Del believed his triumphs on a baseball diamond entitled him to special preferments and compensations. He lived conspicuously with little regard for tomorrow. But all his base hits and adoration could not insulate him from the responsibilities and burdens of life. As one obituary bluntly said, "Personally, Delahanty lacked the ability to pick up the culture which he might have, as a constant associate of educated people in base ball. . . . He never made any claim to refinement. He was absolutely lacking in the sense of obligation and cared not how many contracts he signed, so long as he was permitted to play with the club which would give him the most money."[45]

Del's place as a ballplayer is more difficult to determine. No one now alive saw him play the field or hit a baseball. There are no films or videos of his feats. The last of his contemporaries died decades ago. For many of today's baseball enthusiasts the nineteenth-century game is archaic history, something that is revered but seldom esteemed. Performances more than a century removed are beyond their knowledge and imagination. Cross-generation comparisons are also tainted by the variables and the idiosyncrasies of the nineteenth-century game. This sentiment is unfortunate because, while some rules and conditions differ from today's play, the sport is remarkably familiar and germane.

These obstacles can be bridged by comparisons with more familiar athletes and assessments of peers who crossed over multiple generations of ballplaying. Following these guidelines, the feats of Ed Delahanty take on a more meaningful perspective.

Harry Wright told an interviewer, "Batters are born, not made."[46] Fourteen years later, the *Sporting News* echoed Wright's sentiments when speaking about Delahanty.

> As for Delahanty . . . he was among the greatest batters the game ever produced. Great batters, like poets, are born, not made . . . [like] a handful of really great hitters, such as Dan Brouthers, "Del," Lajoie and men of that class.[47]

Frank Hough of the *Philadelphia Inquirer,* who covered Delahanty throughout his career, said Del "will occupy a conspicuous place . . . among the games' most distinguished exponents."[48] Another longtime columnist, Sam Crane, wrote in 1912 that "as a natural hitter . . . baseball never produced a heavier slugger than Big Ed Delahanty." He went on to lament that Delahanty's record would have been much better had he "taken the game more seriously."[49] The *Detroit News Tribune* called Ed "one of the most remarkable batters which the National League had ever known."[50] In Del's full-page obituary in *Sporting Life,* it was said, "With the exception of Anson, Delahanty was probably the finest natural batsman ever in the game."[51] Napoleon Lajoie, after his triple-crown 1901 season, commented that he considered Delahanty to be "the greatest batter of that age."[52]

Baseball men with more than a half-century in the sport compared Delahanty to dominant players they had seen. Al Reach, writing in the 1920s, asserted, "Both Ruth and Delahanty represent the greatest hitters baseball has ever known." He said Del was a "surer hitter" and never went after bad balls. Connie Mack called Delahanty "this Atlas, who for a time carried the baseball world on his shoulders."[53] In 1939 the grand old man of baseball selected Delahanty as one of the few nineteenth-century players on his "Best of All-Time" team.[54] More emphatic was the opinion of John

McGraw. In his 1923 memoirs, McGraw chose Delahanty for center field on his All-National League ball club. In retrospect, McGraw announced that "Ed Delahanty was the Babe Ruth of his day. Though a right-handed hitter, Ruth did not have a great deal on him when it came to smashing the ball out of the park."[55] As a boy growing up in Philadelphia, the sportswriter Fred Lieb remembered Delahanty and admitted that the dead ball of the era kept Delahanty from matching home runs with modern-day sluggers.[56] The *North American* of Philadelphia, whose scorecards Lieb sold as a youngster, called Delahanty "perhaps the greatest batsman the game of baseball ever produced." In the paper's estimation, Delahanty "had a shade" over Brouthers, Anson, and Lajoie.[57] Patsy Tebeau of Cleveland, who had seen all the great nineteenth-century hitters, proclaimed Delahanty "the hardest hitting batter of his time."[58] Tom Loftus, Delahanty's manager in Washington, boasted that "there is no doubt in the world that Del was the greatest batter that ever went to the plate and the game will never see his equal."[59]

Despite these ringing endorsements, Del was not seen as a "free batsman." Delahanty had a "faultless eye" and a "world of patience" in the batter's box.[60] Del also avoided Lajoie's style of first-ball hitting and cured himself of "Brouthers' mania for hitting every ball out of the lot." Delahanty learned to be deliberate. He enjoyed guessing at pitches and taking "the nerve out" of opposing hurlers.[61] Jack O'Connor, who spent twenty years catching in the major leagues, said, "If Del had a weakness at the bat I could never discover it."[62] Once he made contact, it was dangerous to be in the way of his smashes. Third basemen and pitchers shuddered at the thought of being in front of a Delahanty line drive. He even had the distinction of splitting a baseball with a mighty swing. One pitcher, who compiled notes on every National League batter, had no comments opposite Delahanty's name. He explained, "When you pitch to Delahanty, you just want to shut your eyes, say a prayer and chuck the ball. The Lord only knows what'll happen after that."[63]

Contrary to popular belief, Delahanty was not a one-dimensional ballplayer. The people who knew him best said he was a smart and versatile player, an excellent baserunner with "the speed of a hundred-yard sprinter."[64] Frank Hough said Delahanty studied pitchers and rarely got a bad jump. He knew instinctively when the pitch was going to be delivered and "was under full sail before it [the ball] had left the pitcher's hand."[65] Hough also agreed with John McGraw that Delahanty was a great outfielder.[66]

Delahanty might have failed in the arena of life, but on the ball field his feats cannot be overlooked. Sportswriter Grantland Rice was more philosophical about a ballplayer's accomplishments:

> When the game is done and the players creep
> One by one to the League of sleep
> The way of the fight, the fate of the foe
> The cheer that passed, and applauding hands,
> Are stilled at last—but the record stands. . . .
> So take, my lad, what the Great Game gives,
> For all men die, but the Record lives.[67]

Upon learning of Del's death, Frank Hough wrote, "Poor old Del has been called out by the inexorable Umpire, but his deeds on the diamond will long be remembered."[68] In his prime, there was no better all-around outfielder and dominating athlete in baseball.

Appendix

Delahanty's achievements are shadowed by the circumstances of his death. To remove this distraction, his career should be put in an appropriate comparative context with the great hitters of later generations. *Sports Illustrated* and the Elias Sports Bureau addressed this problem when they computed for San Diego outfielder Tony Gwynn a batting differential average of .0789 between his lifetime mark and the hitting average of his era. When compared to the differentials of other great batsmen, he ranked sixth historically, behind Cobb, Williams, Hornsby, Lajoie, and Keeler. In eighth place was Ed Delahanty with a .0752 differential ("*Sports Illustrated,* 28 July 1997, p. 44). To further demonstrate Delahanty's prowess, the same model is applied to how Ed hit against the top 25 pitchers of his era.

In tables 3 and 4, the 25 pitchers are grouped into two categories: those pitching from the pre-1893, 55–foot distance and those who threw from the new 60–foot, six-inch interval. In the old pitching era, the young and impetuous Delahanty batted .245 as compared to the league average of .244. Under the longer distance, Del batted .359 against these pitchers, as opposed to the league's .271 average. The difference is higher than Delahanty's *Sports Illustrated* historical differential standard.

If one factors in Delahanty's total batting against all hurlers (see table 5), his average would be .343 to the league's .273. In both career and post-1893 categories, Delahanty rates above the .07 barometer of excellence. Only fifteen players in the history of baseball, when batting against all pitchers, reached this level.

Table 3. Delahanty versus Era's Top Pitchers

Pitcher	Batting average to 1892	Batting average from 1893	Career totals	Pre-1893 league average	Post-1893 league average	Total
Clarkson	17–83 .205	10–23 .435	27–106 .259	.239	.288	.253
Galvin	16–46 .348	—	16–46 .348	.271	—	.271
Keefe	7–48 .146	—	7–48 .146	.244	—	.244
Welch	14–53 .264	—	14–53 .264	.237	—	.237
Radbourn	12–37 .324	—	12–37 .324	.259	—	.259
Rusie	11–43 .256	26–76 .342	37–119 .310	.226	.249	.241
King	18–78 .231	12–25 .480	30–103 .291	.240	.297	.269
Weyhing	9–29 .310	14–38 .369	23–67 .343	.263	.329	.316
Killen*	3–14 .214	33–91 .363	36–105 .343	.246*	.292	.281
Nichols	13–47 .277	47–162 .290	60–209 .287	.237	.257	.253
Young	12–45 .250	51–156 .327	63–201 .314	.223	.265	.260
Kennedy	1–7 .142	38–98 .388	39–105 .372	.248	.273	.270
Hawley	1–4 .250	47–123 .382	48–127 .378	.243	.279	.274
Mullane	8–55 .146	12–27 .445	20–82 .245	.218	.271	.244
Stivetts	4–12 .333	18–47 .383	22–59 .373	.245*	.298	.285
Cuppy	6–19 .316	28–72 .390	34–91 .374	.267*	.280	.277
Griffith	—	36–87 .412	36–87 .412	—	.284	.284
Meekin	—	39–90 .433	39–90 .433	—	.280	.280
Chesbro	—	15–53 .283	15–53 .283	—	.257	.257
Waddell*	—	18–48 .375	18–48 .375	—	.259	.259
McGinnity	—	16–51 .314	16–51 .314	—	.269	.269
Mathewson	—	5–20 .250	5–20 .250	—	.230	.230
Plank*	—	3–15 .200	3–15 .200	—	.261	.261
Bender	—	4–8 .500	4–8 .500	—	.237	.237
Joss	—	2–11 .181	2–11 .181	—	.228	.228
	152–620 .245	474–1321 .359	626–1941 .327	.244	.271	.262

* Left-handed
* Only National League Seasons

Table 4.   Comparative Batting Averages of Delahanty and the League against the Top 25 Pitchers

	Delahanty, pre-1893	League, pre-1893	Differential	Delahanty, 1893–1903	League, 1893–1903	Differential
Delahanty	.245	.244[a]	+.01	.359	.271[b]	+.88

Table 5.   Batting Averages for Delahanty and the League against All Pitchers

Delahanty, pre-1893	League, 1888–1892	Differential	Delahanty, 1893–1903	League, 1893–1903	Differential	Delahanty, 1888–1903	League, 1888–1903	Differential
.274	.255[a]	+.19	.372	.281[b]	+.91	.343	.273	+.70

[a] For 1890, average is from the Players' League.
[b] For 1902–3, average is from the American League.

Notes

INTRODUCTION

1. *Washington Evening Star,* 1–5 July 1903, passim; *Washington Post,* 5 July 1903.

2. *Washington Post,* 6 July 1903. *Washington Evening Star,* 4–7 July 1903, passim.

3. *Washington Evening Star,* 6 July 1903.

1. BASEBALL'S BEGINNINGS

1. For a background on the evolution of baseball, consult: John Bowman and Joel Zoss, *Diamonds in the Rough: The Untold Story of Baseball* (New York, 1989), 39–64; Robert Burk, *Never Just a Game: Players, Owners and American Baseball to 1920* (Chapel Hill, N.C., 1993), 1–21; Jeffrey Haven, "Baseball: The Origins and Development of the Game to 1903" (Ph.D. diss., Brigham Young University, 1979), 26–42; George Kirsch, *The Creation of American Team Sports: Baseball and Cricket, 1838–1872* (Chicago, 1989), 21–59; Harold Seymour, *Baseball: The Early Years* (New York, 1989 ed.), 1:3–30; Albert Spalding, *America's National Game* (Lincoln, Nebr., 1992 ed.), 3–74; *Spalding Scrapbooks,* Reel 1, 2, 1887, 7 and 108; 2, 1888, 115 and 120; 2, 1889, 111; and 3, 1892, 96; 3, 1894, 131, 3, 1895, 154; 5, 1905, 74 and 92; David Voigt, *American Baseball: From Gentleman's Sport to the Commissioner System* (Norman, Okla., 1966), 1:3–13.

2. Delmonico Speech, 8 April 1889. *Philadelphia Inquirer,* 9 April 1889; *Spalding Scrapbooks* (1889), 1:117.

3. Spalding, *National Game,* 270.

1. Computations are derived from surnames on rosters reproduced in Rich Westcott and Frank Bilovsky, *The New Phillies Encyclopedia* (Philadelphia, 1993), 9–32; *The Baseball Encyclopedia* 8th ed. (New York, 1990), 63–150; David Nemec, *The Great Encyclopedia of 19th-Century Major League Baseball* (New York, 1997).

2. For an examination of ethnicity and baseball, consult: Melvin Adelman, "Baseball, Business and the Work Place: Gelber's Thesis Reexamined," *Journal of Social History* 23 (Winter 1989): 285–301; Bowman and Zoss, *Diamonds in the Rough*, 115–25; Burk, *Never Just a Game*, 1–32; Steven Gelber, "Working at Playing: The Culture of the Workplace and the Rise of Baseball," *Journal of Social History* 16 (1983): 3–20; Kirsch, *Creation of American Team Sports*, 91–108, 111–37, 145–72; Steven Reiss, *City Games: Evolution of American Society and the Rise of Sports* (Chicago, 1991), 14–22, 90–105; Steven Reiss, "Race and Ethnicity in American Baseball, 1900–1919," *Journal of Ethnic Studies* 4 (Winter 1977); 39–43; Steven Reiss, *Touching Base: Professional Baseball and American Culture in the Progressive Era* (Westport, Conn., 1980), 184–92; John Rossi, "Glimpses of the Irish Contributions to Early Baseball," *Eire, Ireland* 23, 2 (Summer 1988), 116–21; Voigt, *Baseball*, 1: 80–119; Ralph Wilcox, "The Shamrock and the Eagle: Irish Americans and Sport in the Nineteenth Century," in G. Eisen and D. Wiggins, eds., *Ethnicity and Sport in North American History and Culture* (Westport, Conn. 1994), 55–71.

3. John S. Mitchell, "The Celt as a Baseball Player," *Gael* (May 1902), 151–52.

4. Unidentified clipping, *Randall Papers*, Mobile, Alabama, packet 2.

5. John Ibson, *Will the World Break Your Heart? Dimensions and Consequences of Irish-American Assimilations* (New York, 1990), 10. David Doyle, "The Irish as Urban Pioneers in the United States, 1850–1870," *Journal of American Ethnic History* 10 (Fall 1990–Winter 1991): 53; Kevin Kenny, *The American Irish* (Essex, 2000), 104–5.

6. For background of the urban Irish experience, consult: Charles Alexander, *John McGraw* (New York, 1988), 111–12; Peter Bjarkman, "Forgotten Americans and the National Pastime: Literature on Baseball's Ethnic, Racial and Religious Diversity," *Multicultural Review* 1 (April 1992): 46–48; Ronald Briley, "Baseball and American Cultural Values," *OAH Magazine of History* 7 (Summer 1992): 61–63; Dennis Clark, "Irish Americans," in J. Buenker and L. Ratner, eds., *Multiculturalism in the United States: A Comparative Guide to Acculturation and Ethnicity* (New York, 1992), 77–102; Dennis Clark, "The Irish Catholics," in R. Miller and T. Marzik, eds., *Immigrants and Religion in Urban America* (Philadel-

phia, 1977), 48–61; Dennis Clark, *The Irish in Philadelphia* (Philadelphia, 1984), 61–87; Doyle, "Irish as Urban Pioneers," 36–59; Eric Foner, "Ethnicity and Radicalism in the Gilded Age: The Land League and Irish America," *Politics and Ideology in the Age of the Civil War* (New York, 1980), 150–55; T. W. Gilbert, "The 1890s—Baseball's Irish Decade," *Irish Echo* (March 1989), 77; Bill James, *The Historical Baseball Abstract* (New York, 1986), 41–42; Kenny, *American Irish*, 89–179; Eric Koetting, "Shamrocks on the Diamond: The Irish in Baseball," in Washington D.C. St. Patrick's Day Parade Program (1990), 58–61; Lawrence McCaffrey, *The Irish Diaspora in America* (Bloomington, Ind., 1976), 59–76; Kerby Miller, *Emigrants and Exiles: Ireland and the Irish Exodus to North America* (New York, 1985), passim; Reiss, "Race and Ethnicity," 39–43; Richard Renoff and Joseph Varacalli, "Baseball and Socio-Economic Mobility: An Irish-Italian Comparison," *Proceedings of the Sixteenth Annual Conference of the American Italian Historical Association* (1993), 43–51; Randy Roberts, "On the Field of Struggle: The Irish American Sporting Experience," *American Catholic Newsletter* 18 (Fall 1991): 9–11; Rossi, "Irish Contributions to Early Baseball," 116–21; William Shannon, *The American Irish* (New York, 1963), 16–39; Wilcox, "Shamrock and Eagle," 55–57, 65–71; Carl Wittke, *The Irish in America* (Baton Rouge, La., 1956) 23–31.

7. Marriage Records for the Catholic Parish of Graiguenamanagh, 1832 in National Library of Ireland (NLI). Valuation List #26, County Kilkenny, 1861, in Valuation Office, Dublin. Baptism Records of Graiguenamanagh, in NLI.

8. Kerby Miller and Bruce Boling, "Golden Streets, Bitter Tears: The Irish Image of America during the Era of Mass Migration," *Journal of American Ethnic History* 10 (Fall 1990–Winter 1991): 30.

9. K. Miller, *Emigrants and Exiles*, 570, appendix, table 2.

10. *Cleveland Plain Dealer*, 28 December 1867, 30 December 1867.

11. 1880 National Census, Cuyahoga County, Cleveland, Ohio, vol. 13, E.D. 25, sheet 34.

12. *Cleveland Plain Dealer*, 9 July 1903.

13. For a discussion of male congregating centers, consult: D. Clark, *Irish in Philadelphia*, 38–60; Jon M. Kingsdale, "The 'Poor Man's Club': Social Functions of the Urban Working-Class Saloon," *American Quarterly* 25 (October 1973): 472–89; Michael Isenberg, *John L. Sullivan and His America* (Urbana, Ill., 1988), 39–51; Bruce Laurie, "Fire Companies and Gangs in Southwark: The 1840s," in Allen Davis and Mark Haller, eds., *The Peoples of Philadelphia: A History of Ethnic Groups and Lower Class Life, 1790–1940* (Philadelphia, 1973), 41–83; Reiss, *City Games*, 15–22; Steven Reiss, "The New Sport History," *Reviews in American History* 18 (1990): 311–25; Shannon, *American Irish*, 33–36; Victor Walsh,

"Drowning the Shamrock: Drink, Teetotalism and the Irish Catholics of the Gilded Age Pittsburgh," *Journal of American Ethnic History* 10 (Fall 1990–Winter 1991): 60–65; Wittke, *Irish in America,* 193–201.

14. Frank Delahanty interview, *Cleveland Plain Dealer,* 26 May 1963. Tommy Leach, interviewed by Lawrence Ritter, remarked, "The Delahanty kids used to hang around there [firehouse] alot." Lawrence Ritter, *The Glory of Their Times* (New York, 1966), 29. A *Sporting News* story said that Delahanty "made the engine house his headquarters—he was there morning, noon and night." *Sporting News,* 1 July 1943. In a reminiscence, a stepdaughter of another brother, Jimmy, said that her father spent a great deal of time in the fire station and when he heard the fire bell ring he was off to fight the fire. *Lorraine Journal,* date unknown.

15. Unidentified article in *Delahanty Cooperstown File,* 10 November 1932.

16. *Sporting News,* 1 July 1943.

17. *The Sporting Life* quoted by *Chicago Evening Journal,* 17 July 1888.

18. *Sporting News,* 1 July 1943; unidentified article, *Delahanty Cooperstown File,* 10 November 1932.

19. Unidentified clipping, *Randall Papers,* packet 1. *Cleveland Plain Dealer,* 20 January 1889, 17 March 1889.

20. John F. Herne, "To the Delahanty Family," unidentified clipping, *Randall Papers,* packet 2.

21. Ritter, *Glory of Their Times,* 29.

22. *Sporting News,* 1 July 1903; unidentified clipping, *Delahanty Cooperstown File,* 10 November 1932.

23. Kevin Whelan, "The Geography of Hurling," *History Ireland* 1 (Spring 1993): 27–31; Mitchell, "Celt Baseball," 151; *Sporting News,* 6 November 1946; Wilcox, "Shamrock and Eagle," 69–70.

24. *Philadelphia Press,* 31 January 1900; *Sporting News,* 10 February 1900.

25. E. D. Soden, "The Greatest Baseball Family in the History of the Game," *Baseball Magazine* (September 1912): 18.

26. *Washington Star,* 9 June 1907.

27. Daguerreotype, c. 1896, *Randall Papers,* packet 4.

28. *Sporting Life,* 2 September 1893.

3. MAKING THE MAJORS

1. Picture postcard, *Randall Papers,* packet 4.

2. Unidentified article, *Delahanty Cooperstown File,* April 1914.

3. *Sporting Life*, 19 January 1887, 26 January 1887, 9 February 1887, 23 February 1887, 27 April 1887, 14 September 1887, 12 October 1887, 16 November 1887, 7 December 1887, 14 December 1887, 21 December 1887, 1 February 1888, 15 February 1888, 21 March 1888, 4 April 1888, 11 April 1888; *Sporting News*, 25 February 1888, 31 March 1888.

4. *Sporting News*, 25 February 1888, 31 March 1888; *Sporting Life*, 25 January 1888; 14 March 1888; 28 March 1888. For studies on Irish and black economic tensions, see Noel Ignatiev, *How the Irish Became White* (New York, 1995), passim; Wittke, *Irish in America*, 125–34.

5. *Wheeling Register*, 4 March 1888.

6. *Sporting Life*, 29 February 1888; 21 March 1888.

7. Frederick Leib and Stan Baumgartner, *The Philadelphia Phillies* (New York, 1953), 28.

8. Unidentified clipping, *Randall Papers*, packet 1.

9. Westcott and Bilovsky, *New Phillies Encyclopedia*, 17.

10. Ritter, *Glory of Their Times*, 29. The contract negotiations were reported by the *Philadelphia Inquirer*, 19 May 1888; *Boston Herald*, 12 July 1903; *Wheeling Register*, 19 May 1888, 22 May 1888; *Sporting Life*, 6 June 1888; 26 July 1903; *North American*, 19 July 1903; *Sporting News*, 26 May 1888; 2 June 1888. For Delahanty's picture, see *Wheeling Register*, 19 May 1888.

11. For summaries of how the game was played, see: Burk, *Never Just a Game*, 245; James, *Baseball Abstract*, 22–24, and 38–40; Seymour, *Baseball*, 1:172–82; Tom Shieber, "The Evolution of the Baseball Diamond," *Baseball Research Journal*, 23 (1994): 44–50; Robert Shipley, "Baseball Axiom No. 22," *Baseball Research Journal*, 3–13; Spalding, *National Game*, 475–90; Voigt, *American Baseball*, 1: 204–8.

12. Ted Vincent, *Mudville's Revenge: The Rise and Fall of American Sports* (New York, 1981), 136, 162. For additional information about nineteenth-century baseball, consult: Burk, *Never Just a Game*, 50–81; Seymour, *Baseball*, 1:104–220; Voigt, *Baseball*, 1:99–153.

13. Burk, *Never Just a Game*, 94.

14. John M. Ward, "Is the Base-Ball Player a Chattel?" *Lippincott's Magazine* 40 (August 1887): 310–19.

15. *Philadelphia Inquirer*, 23–26 May 1888. *Wheeling Register*, 19 May 1888. *Sporting Life*, 23 May 1888, 30 May 1888.

16. Unidentified clipping, *Randall Papers*, packet 2. *Sporting Life*, 6 June 1888.

17. For an overview of Harry Wright's career, see: *Chadwick Diaries* (1888), 2:115, (1895) 3:157; *Sporting News*, 23 July 1892; *Sporting Life*, 3 March 1894, 26 October 1895; clipping from *Philadelphia Bulletin*, 6 February 1926, in Urban Archives at Temple University; Seymour,

Baseball, 1:71–72; Darryl Brock, "The Wright Way," *Sports Heritage* 1, 2 (March–April 1987), 35–41, 93–94.

18. *Sporting News*, 1 July 1943, and unidentified clipping, 10 November 1932, in *Delahanty File. North American News*, 1917 clipping, *Randall Papers*, packet 2. *Sporting Life*, 15 August 1888. *Sporting News*, 5 October 1889.

19. *North American News*, 1917 clipping, Randall Papers, packet 2.

20. Unidentified clipping, 10 November 1932, in *Delahanty File*.

21. *Sporting News*, 13 June 1888, 11 July 1888, 25 July 1888. *Sporting Life*, 15 August 1888, 5 September 1888, 12 September 1888, 19 September 1888, 24 October 1888, 1 July 1894.

22. Cited in Bilovsky and Westcott, *New Phillies Encyclopedia*, 124 and Leib and Baumgartner, *Philadelphia Phillies*, 29.

23. Delahanty picture, c. 1888, *Randall Papers*, packet 4.

24. *Sporting Life*, 26 December 1888, 9 January 1889.

25. Ibid., 10 October 1888.

26. Ibid., 16 January 1889.

27. *Philadelphia Inquirer*, 2 March 1889.

28. Ibid., 23 March 1889.

29. *Sporting Life*, 17 April 1889, 24 April 1889, 8 May 1889, 22 May 1889.

30. *Cleveland Plain Dealer*, 23–25 May 1889; *Philadelphia Inquirer*, 23–25 May 1889.

31. *Sunday Item*, 26 May 1889; *Philadelphia Evening Item*, 27 May 1889, 13 June 1889; *Sporting Life*, 5 June 1889; *Cleveland Plain Dealer*, 26 May 1889, 28 May 1889.

32. *Sporting Life*, 5 June 1889; *Cleveland Plain Dealer*, 28 May 1889, 6 June 1889.

33. *Cleveland Plain Dealer*, 25 June 1889.

34. *Sporting Life*, 10 July 1889; *Cleveland Plain Dealer*, 8 July 1889, 14 July 1889.

35. *Sporting News*, 19 November 1898.

36. *Cleveland Plain Dealer*, 11 August 1889.

37. Ibid., 28 August 1889.

38. Souvenir of Baseball, November 1889, in *Sunday Mercury* (B.L. 1997.74), National Baseball Library. Unidentified clipping, [April 1914], *Delahanty Cooperstown File*.

4. TRIPLE JUMPING

1. *Spalding's Official Base Ball Guide* (1884), 42–44. Cited by Peter Levine, *A. G. Spalding and the Rise of Baseball* (New York, 1985), 53; Vincent, *Joy in Mudville*, 188.

2. *Sporting Life,* 18 December 1889.

3. *Cleveland Plain Dealer,* 4 January 1890.

4. *Philadelphia Inquirer,* 16 December 1889.

5. Ontario Court of Appeal Book, June 1904, pp. 31–32, 36. *Randall Papers,* packet V.

6. *Universal Base Ball Guide* (July 1890), 39–40, 30–31; *Philadelphia Inquirer,* 25 November 1889, 22 November 1889; *Chadwick Scrapbooks* (1890), 2:135; Seymour, *Baseball,* 1:222–25; Vincent, *Joy in Mudville,* 190–93; Burk, *Never Just a Game,* 101–2; Voigt, *Baseball,* 1:158–60.

7. *Sporting News,* 11 August 1888.

8. Ibid., 2 November 1889.

9. *Sporting Life,* 30 October 1889.

10. Brotherhood Manifesto, cited in Spalding, *National Game,* 272–73; *Sporting News,* 9 November 1889.

11. *Philadelphia Inquirer,* 22 November 1889, 23 November 1889.

12. "Caylor's Comments," in *Sporting Life,* 3 April 1889.

13. *Cleveland Voice,* quoted in *Sporting Life,* 8 February 1889.

14. *Sporting Life,* 20 November 1889; *Philadelphia Inquirer,* 28 November 1889; *Spalding Guide* (1890), 28–31.

15. *Sporting Life,* 13 November 1889; *Philadelphia Inquirer,* 16 November 1889.

16. *Philadelphia Inquirer,* 16 November 1889; *Cleveland Plain Dealer,* 16 November 1889; *Sporting News,* 22 February 1890; *Spalding's Guide* (1890), 11–26.

17. *Sporting Life,* 31 May 1890.

18. *Sporting Life,* 17 May 1890; *Chadwick Scrapbooks,* 2:137. Spalding, *National Game,* 287–88; *Philadelphia Inquirer,* 13 November 1889.

19. Burk, *Never Just a Game,* 104; *Philadelphia Inquirer,* 11 November 1889.

20. *Sporting News,* 26 October 1889, 4 January 1890; *Sporting Life,* 1 January 1890.

21. *Sporting News,* 4 January 1890, 18 May 1889; *Philadelphia Inquirer,* 11 November 1889.

22. *Sporting Life,* 13 November 1889, 1 January 1890; *Sporting News,* 30 November 1889, 4 January 1890; *Philadelphia Inquirer,* 11 November 1889. Ben Hilt, former financial manager of the Phillies and board member of the Philadelphia Players' League team, said the Phillies cleared $30,000 in annual profits. *Sporting Life,* 13 November 1889.

23. *Philadelphia Inquirer,* 6 November 1889.

24. Leib and Baumgartner, *Philadelphia Phillies,* 33; *Philadelphia Inquirer,* 26 December 1889.

25. *Chadwick Scrapbooks*, 2:140; *Philadelphia Inquirer*, 28 December 1889, 27 December 1889.

26. *Cleveland Plain Dealer*, 22 November 1889.

27. Leib and Baumgartner, *Philadelphia Phillies*, 32.

28. *Sporting Life*, 11 December 1889, 11 September 1889, 2 October 1889, 16 November 1889. *Chadwick Scrapbooks*, 2:126; *Sunday Item*, 3 November 1889; *Sporting News*, 2 November 1889.

29. Unidentified article, *Delahanty File*, 10 November 1932.

30. *Philadelphia Inquirer*, 16 November 1889, 18 November 1889; *Sporting News*, 23 November 1889; *Sporting Life*, 13 November 1889; *Cleveland Plain Dealer*, 16 November 1889.

31. *Philadelphia Evening Item*, 25 October 1889.

32. *Cleveland Plain Dealer*, 3 December 1889; *Philadelphia Inquirer*, 4 December 1901, 11 December 1901.

33. *Philadelphia Inquirer*, 3 December 1889, 24 December 1889. *Sporting Life*, 11 December 1889, 25 December 1889.

34. *Cleveland Plain Dealer*, 21 November 1889.

35. *Sporting Life*, 11 December 1889.

36. *Philadelphia Inquirer*, 19 December 1889.

37. *Sporting News*, 15 February 1890.

38. Ibid., 22 February 1890.

39. *Sporting News*, 15 March 1890; *Cleveland Plain Dealer*, 11 February 1890; 23 February 1890.

40. Unidentified article, *Delahanty Cooperstown File*, 2 April 1890, 6; *Cleveland Plain Dealer*, 13 February 1890, 10 March 1890, 21 March 1890.

41. *Philadelphia Evening Item*, 19 March 1890.

42. *Chadwick Scrapbooks*, 2:133.

43. *Philadelphia Evening Item*, 24 February 1890, 11 March 1890; *Sporting News*, 1 March 1890; *Cleveland Plain Dealer*, 13 March 1890.

44. *Philadelphia Evening Item*, 22 March 1890, 24 March 1890; *Sporting Life*, 5 March 1890, 19 March 1890, 26 March 1890.

45. *Philadelphia Inquirer*, 19 March 1890; *North American*, 20 March 1890.

46. Unidentified article, *Delahanty Cooperstown File*, 2 April 1890.

47. *Philadelphia Inquirer*, 14 November 1889, 20 March 1890.

48. *Sporting Life*, 12 March 1890. *Philadelphia Inquirer*, 16 March 1890.

49. Unidentified article, *Delahanty Cooperstown File*, 2 April 1890; *Philadelphia Inquirer*, 25 March 1890, 2 April 1890; *Philadelphia Bulletin*, 22 March 1890; *Sporting Life*, 2 April 1890, 12 April 1890; *Cleveland Plain Dealer*, 22 March 1890, 23 March 1890, 25 March 1890, 28 March 1890, 29 March 1890.

50. *Philadelphia Inquirer,* 31 March 1890; *Sporting Life,* 2 April 1890; *Cleveland Plain Dealer,* 26 March 1890, 31 March 1890.

51. *Sporting News,* 28 March 1890.

52. *Cleveland Plain Dealer,* 29 March 1890, 3 April 1890.

53. *Philadelphia Inquirer,* 11 April 1890; *Philadelphia Bulletin,* 29 March 1890, 10 April 1890; *Sporting News,* 28 March 1890.

54. *Cleveland Plain Dealer,* 14 April 1890.

55. *Philadelphia Evening Item,* 1 April 1890; *Sporting Life,* 5 April 1890.

56. *Philadelphia Evening Item,* 24 March 1890, 22 March 1890.

57. *Sunday Item,* 23 March 1890.

58. Unidentified article, *Delahanty Cooperstown File,* 2 April 1890; *Philadelphia Evening Item,* 24 March, 1890; *Sporting Life,* 2 April 1890.

59. *Philadelphia Inquirer,* 22 April 1890; *Cleveland Plain Dealer,* 25 April 1890.

60. Leib and Baumgartner, *Philadelphia Phillies,* 34.

61. *Philadephia Bulletin,* 24 March 1890.

62. *New York Tribune,* 8 May 1890, cited in *Philadelphia Inquirer,* 9 May 1890.

63. *Sporting Life,* 5 July 1890.

64. *Sporting Life,* 22 January 1890; *Cleveland Plain Dealer,* 5 November 1890; Vincent, *Joy in Mudville,* 201.

65. *Sporting Life,* 21 April 1890, 26 April 1890.

66. Ibid., 19 April 1890.

67. *North American,* 12 July 1894.

68. Ibid., 3 May 1890, 17 May 1890.

69. Ibid., 1 January 1890.

70. *Philadelphia Inquirer,* 28 November 1889.

71. *Cleveland Plain Dealer,* 11 May 1890.

72. Ibid., 11 March 1890.

73. *Sporting News,* 7 June 1890.

74. *Philadelphia Evening Item,* 23 November 1890. These figures do not include expenses for starting up the Players' League. Philadelphia's costs were said to be about $38,000 and Cleveland's was supposedly about $20,000.

75. *Sporting Life,* 29 November 1890.

5. From Cleveland to Philly

1. *Cleveland Plain Dealer,* 27 November 1890.

2. Ibid., 27 November 1890.

3. Leib and Baumgartner, *Philadelphia Phillies*, 36.

4. *Reach's Official Base Ball Guide* (1891) 25–6. *Sporting News,* 18 November 1890.

5. *Sporting News,* 31 May 1890, 2 August 1890, 27 September 1890.

6. *Sporting Life,* 17 May 1890.

7. Ibid., 19 July 1890, 26 July 1890, 20 September 1890, 27 September 1890.

8. Ibid., 3 May 1890, 12 July 1890, 23 August 1890, 30 August 1890, 11 November 1890.

9. *Sporting News,* 16 March 1895; *Cleveland Plain Dealer,* 15 July 1890; *Sporting Life,* 16 March 1895.

10. *Sporting News,* 6 November 1897, 5 October 1895, 5 February 1898; *Sunday Item,* 29 September 1895.

11. Unidentified article, *Delahanty Cooperstown File,* 10 November 1932.

12. *Cleveland Plain Dealer,* 14 May 1890, 25 May 1890, 27 June 1890, 31 July 1890.

13. *Sporting Life,* 6 February 1897.

14. Unidentified article, *Delahanty Cooperstown File,* 10 November 1932.

15. *Sunday Item,* 25 May 1890; *Sporting Life,* 17 May 1890; *Philadelphia Bulletin,* 22 May 1890, 27 May 1890; *Cleveland Plain Dealer,* 8 April 1890, 15 May 1890.

16. *Philadelphia Evening Item,* 30 June 1890.

17. Ibid., 16 September 1893. An earlier version had Kelly saying, "my mother and father would never look at me again if I should prove a traitor to the boys." Spalding denied the story. *Sporting News,* 1 March 1890, p. 1. *Cleveland Plain Dealer,* 26 February 1890.

18. *Cleveland Plain Dealer,* 24 November 1889.

19. Ibid., 7 November 1890; *Sporting Life,* 6 September 1890, 22 November 1890.

20. *Sporting Life,* 28 December 1890.

21. *Cleveland Plain Dealer,* 13 November 1890.

22. *Sporting Life,* 27 September 1890.

23. *Sporting Life,* 31 January 1891, 28 February 1891, 7 March 1891; *Philadelphia Evening Item,* 28 January 1891, 8 February 1891.

24. *Philadelphia Evening Item,* 20 February 1891; *Philadelphia Inquirer,* 22 February 1891.

25. *Philadelphia Evening Item,* 27 February 1891.

26. *Sunday Item,* 12 June 1892.

27. Leib and Baumgartner, *Philadelphia Phillies*, 37.

28. *Philadelphia Inquirer,* 3 May 1891, 5 May 1891; *Philadelphia Evening Item,* 5 May 1891, 10 May 1891; *Philadelphia Bulletin,* 7 May 1891; *Sporting Life,* 16 May 1891.

29. *Philadelphia Evening Item,* 12 May 1891.

30. *Sporting News,* 23 May 1891; *Philadelphia Inquirer,* 20 May 1891; *Philadelphia Evening Item,* 19 May 1891, 20 May 1891; *Philadelphia Bulletin,* 19 May 1891, 20 May 1891.

31. *Sunday Item,* 21 June 1891.

32. *Philadelphia Inquirer,* 19 July 1891; *Philadelphia Evening Item,* 18 October 1891.

33. *Sporting Life,* 18 July 1891.

34. *Sporting Life,* 22 August 1891, 5 September 1891; *Philadelphia Inquirer,* 16 August 1891, 23 August 1891; *Philadelphia Evening Item,* 19 August 1891.

35. *Sporting Life,* 5 September 1891; *Philadelphia Evening Item,* 2 September 1891.

36. *New York Recorder, Boston Globe* and Philadelphia papers are cited by *Sporting Life,* 4 July 1891.

6. THE EMERGING SLUGGER

1. For an overview of this reorganization consult: Burk, *Never Just a Game,* 119–20; David Nemec, *The Beer and Whisky League* (New York, 1994), 228–35, 242–44; Seymour, *Baseball* 1:257–62. Also peruse *Sporting Life* and *Sporting News* for the months of October–December 1891. The resistance of Reach and Rogers is summarized in *Sporting News,* 6 October 1894, 15 December 1894.

2. *Philadelphia Evening Item,* 3 January 1892, 17 January 1892; *Sporting Life,* 16 January 1892.

3. *Sporting News,* 19 December 1891.

4. *Sporting News,* 24 November 1891; Burk, *Never Just a Game,* 123–25; Seymour, *Baseball,* 1:266–9.

5. *Philadelphia Evening Item,* 17 April 1892. Mike Sowell, *July 2, 1903: The Mysterious Death of Hall-of-Famer Big Ed Delehanty* (New York, 1992), 97.

6. Unidentified Hall of Fame clipping, 6 February 1892. *Sporting Life,* 30 January 1892, 6 February 1892; *Sporting News,* 16 January 1892; *Philadelphia Evening Item,* 31 January 1892.

7. *Philadelphia Evening Item,* 29 February 1892.

8. *Sporting Life,* 26 March 1892.

9. *Sunday Item*, 1 May 1892; *Sporting Life*, 23 April 1892.

10. *Sunday Item*, 12 June 1892.

11. *Philadelphia Evening Item*, 16 May 1892.

12. *Sporting Life*, 18 June 1892.

13. *New York Herald*, quoted by *Sporting Life*, 9 July 1892.

14. *Sporting News*, 25 June 1892.

15. W. N. Pringle, "Freaks on the Fly," *Baseball Magazine* (July 1908): 25–26 in Delahanty packet in National Baseball Library.

16. *Philadelphia Evening Item*, 3 July 1892.

17. *Philadelphia Evening Item*, 12 July 1892, 13 July 1892; *Sunday Item*, 18 July 1892; *Sporting Life*, 16 July 1892, 23 July 1892, 30 July 1892, 16 August 1892; *Sporting News*, 23 July 1892, 30 July 1892.

18. *Sporting Life*, 23 July 1892. *Philadelphia Evening Item*, 19 July 1892; *Sunday Item*, 18 July 1892.

19. *Sporting News*, 20 August 1892.

20. *Sporting News*, 17 September 1892; *Philadelphia Evening Item*, 9 September 1892, 10 September 1892, 11 September 1892; *Sporting Life*, 17 September 1892.

21. *Sunday Item*, 13 November 1892, 20 November 1892; *Sporting News*, 3 December 1892.

22. Baseball Hall of Fame picture collection, BL 4007.76.

23. *Sporting Life*, 5 November 1892, 26 November 1892. The figure 193,731 is given in John Thorn and Peter Palmer, eds., *Total Baseball*, 3d ed. (New York, 1993), 144.

24. *Sporting Life*, 8 October 1892; *Sporting News*, 8 October 1892.

25. *Sporting Life*, 15 October 1892.

26. Burk, *Never Just a Game*, 124–25, 246; Voigt, *Baseball* 1:246; Seymour, *Baseball*, 1:268–69. A more detailed study can be found in Peter S. Craig, "Monopsony in Manpower: Organized Baseball Meets the Anti-Trust Laws," *Yale Law Journal* 62 (March 1953): 579–639. Also consult *Sporting News*, 15 October 1892; *Philadelphia Evening Item*, 18 October 1892; *Sporting Life*, 15 October 1892, 4 February 1893.

27. *Sporting News*, 18 March 1893.

28. *Sporting Life*, 11 March 1893; *Sporting News*, 4 March 1893, 11 March 1893; *Philadelphia Evening Item*, 23 February 1893; *Sunday Item*, 5 March 1893.

29. *Sporting Life*, 8 April 1893.

30. *Sporting News*, 1 April 1893; *Philadelphia Evening Item*, 18 January 1893, 12 February 1893.

31. Burk, *Never Just a Game*, 125.

32. *Sunday Item*, 5 March 1893.

33. *Sporting Life*, 8 April 1893.

34. Craig, "Monopsony in Manpower," 605. Also cited in Seymour, *Baseball*, 1:269, and Burk, *Never Just a Game*, 125.

35. *Sporting Life,* 14 January 1893; *Sunday Item,* 15 January 1893.

36. *Sporting Life,* 1 April 1893.

37. *Sporting News,* 18 March 1893, 11 March 1893, 25 March 1893.

38. For an analysis of this pitching change and its effect on individual pitchers, consult: Shipley, "Baseball Axiom No. 22," *Research Journal* 23 (1994): 44–50.

39. *Philadelphia Evening Item,* 31 December 1892; *Sporting Life,* 7 January 1893.

40. *Philadelphia Evening Item,* 17 November 1893, 15 November 1893, 17 August 1893, 31 July 1893, 20 April 1893; *Sunday Item,* 23 April 1893.

41. *Sunday Item,* 23 April 1893.

42. *Sporting Life,* 20 May 1893.

43. *Sporting News,* 10 June 1893; *Philadelphia Evening Item,* 30 May 1893; *Sporting Life,* 27 May 1893.

44. *Sporting Life,* 17 June 1893.

45. *Sporting News,* 24 June 1893.

46. *Sporting Life,* 24 June 1893; *Philadelphia Evening Item,* 19 June 1893, 20 June 1893.

47. *Philadelphia Evening Item,* 30 June 1893.

48. *Philadelphia Evening Item,* 21 July 1893. Florence Delahanty Randall to E. J. Lanigan, 16 May 1946; Lanigan to F. Randall, 21 May 1946. *Randall Papers,* packet 2. After Delahanty was elected to the Hall of Fame in 1945, his daughter donated the bat to be part of the permanent exhibit.

49. *Sporting News,* 11 November 1893.

50. *Sporting Life,* 1 July 1893.

51. *Sporting News,* 5 May 1893.

52. *Philadelphia Evening Item,* 5 September 1893.

53. *Sporting Life,* 7 October 1893.

54. *Philadelphia Evening Item,* 7 December 1893; *Sporting News,* 16 December 1893.

55. *Sunday Item,* 1 October 1893; *Sporting Life,* 7 October 1893; *Sporting News,* 7 October 1893.

56. *Sporting Life,* 14 October 1893.

57. *Sporting Life,* 7 October 1893; *Sporting News,* 14 October 1893; *Philadelphia Evening Item,* 9 October 1893.

58. Leib and Baumgartner, *Philadelphia Phillies,* 41.

59. *Sporting News,* 3 December 1893.

60. *Philadelphia Evening Item,* 6 October 1893.

61. National Baseball Library, Delahanty Clipping File, 10 November 1932.

62. *Philadelphia Evening Item,* 8 September 1893; *Sunday Item,* 17 September 1893.

63. *Sporting News,* 21 October 1893.

64. *Sporting Life,* 28 May 1892, 8 July 1893, 7 October 1893.

65. *Sporting Life,* 9 December 1893; *Sporting News,* 9 December 1893.

66. *Sporting News,* 16 December 1893.

7. KING OF LEFTFIELDERS

1. *Sporting News,* 17 March 1894.

2. *Philadelphia Evening Item,* 17 November 1893, 26 November 1893.

3. *Philadelphia Evening Item,* 25 February 1894, 27 February 1894; *Philadelphia Inquirer,* 24 February 1894; *North American,* 28 February 1894.

4. *Sporting Life,* 26 August 1893; *Sporting News,* 16 September 1893.

5. *Sporting Life,* 13 Januuary 1894; *Philadelphia Evening Item,* 6 January 1894.

6. *Philadelphia Evening Item,* 18 February 1894; *Sporting News,* 24 February 1894; *Philadelphia Inquirer,* 14 January 1894, 16 February 1894.

7. *Philadelphia Inquirer,* 30 April 1894.

8. *Philadelphia Evening Item,* 21 May 1894, 21 June 1894; *Sporting Life,* 26 May 1894; *Philadelphia Inquirer,* 22 May 1894, 24 June 1894; *Sunday Item,* 15 July 1894.

9. *Sunday Item,* 24 June 1894.

10. *Sunday Item,* 15 July 1894; *Philadelphia Evening Item,* 9 July 1894; *Sporting Life,* 14 July 1894, 21 July 1894.

11. *Philadelphia Inquirer,* 9 July 1894; *Sporting Life,* 7 July 1894.

12. *Philadelphia Inquirer,* 10 June 1894.

13. *Sporting Life,* 19 May 1894.

14. *Sporting News,* 25 January 1894. By July, it was suggested that New York would pay $8,000 for Delahanty. *North American,* 4 July 1894.

15. *North American,* 23 June 1894; *Sporting Life,* 23 June 1894. Andy Leonard was a spectacular outfielder from County Cavan in Ireland, who played for Boston and Harry Wright in the late 1870s.

16. *Philadelphia Evening Item,* 20 May 1894; *North American,* 19 May 1894.

17. *North American,* 18 July 1894, 26 July 1894; *Philadelphia Inquirer,* 18 July 1894; *Sporting Life,* 21 July 1894.

18. The *Baltimore Sun* quoted by the *Philadelphia Inquirer,* 20 July 1894.

19. *Philadelphia Inquirer,* 20 July 1894; *Philadelphia Evening Item,* 18 July 1894.

20. *Sunday Item,* 22 July 1894.

21. *North American,* 19 September 1896.

22. *Sporting News,* 11 August 1894. For details of the fire consult: *Philadelphia Evening Item,* 6 August 1894; *Philadelphia Inquirer,* 7 August 1894, 12 August 1894; *North American,* 7 August 1894, 8 August 1894.

23. *Sporting News,* 18 August 1894.

24. *Sporting Life,* 22 September 1894.

25. *Spalding Scrapbooks* (1894), 3:98, 104.

26. Ibid., 3:119, 137; *Sporting Life,* 6 October 1894; *Philadelphia Evening Item,* 2 October 1894.

27. For Tom Delahanty's background, see: *Sporting Life,* 23 June 1894, 21 July 1894, 28 July 1894, 8 September 1894, 16 October 1894; *Sporting News,* 30 June 1894, 18 April 1896, 6 October 1894; *Cleveland Plain Dealer,* 29 May 1894.

28. *Sporting Life,* 19 October 1895, 30 November 1895, 7 December 1895, 18 January 1896, 1 February 1896, 14 March 1896, 25 April 1896, 9 May 1896, 16 May 1896, 23 May 1896; *Philadelphia Evening Item,* 4 October 1895, 18 October 1895; *Sporting News,* 26 October 1895, 14 December 1895, 18 April 1896, 16 May 1896.

29. *Spalding Scrapbooks,* 3:19.

30. *Sporting News,* 13 October 1894; *Sporting Life,* 13 October 1894; *Philadelphia Evening Item,* 3 October 1894; *Philadelphia Inquirer,* 4 October 1894.

31. For a good summary of 1894's offensive statistics, see David Q. Voigt, "1894," *Baseball Research Digest* 23 (1994): 82–84.

32. *Sporting News,* 24 November 1894.

33. Ibid., and 17 February 1900; *Sporting Life,* 4 May 1895.

34. "Reminiscences of Edward D. Osterhout," an unpublished memoir graciously provided by his grandson Richard C. Osterhout.

35. *Sporting News,* 28 October 1899.

36. *Sporting Life,* 25 August 1900.

37. Ibid., 24 November 1894.

38. Ibid., 1 December 1894; *Philadelphia Evening Item,* 9 December 1894; *Philadelphia Inquirer,* 10 December 1894, 16 December 1894; *Sporting News,* 27 December 1894.

39. *Sporting News,* 28 October 1899.

1. Florence Delahanty's Family History, *Randall Papers,* Mobile, Alabama.

2. Marriage License, Receipt and Consent Form, 10 October 1894, #71887, Orphans' Court Division of Philadelphia County. Certificate of Marriage, St. Charles Borromeo Church, Philadelphia, Pa. Death Certificate, 22 May 1945, #725, Mobile, Alabama. 1880 National Census, County of Philadelphia, Philadelphia, Pa., vol. 77, E.D. 630, sheet 2.

3. Daguerreotype, c. 1896, *Randall Papers,* packet 4.

4. *Philadelphia Evening Item,* 20 September 1894, 24 September 1894, 28 September 1894.

5. For an examination of this challenge, consult: Burk, *Never Just a Game,* 126; Voigt, *Baseball,* 1:231–32; Seymour, *Baseball,* 1:270.

6. Consult *Philadelphia Evening Item,* 7 August 1894; *Sunday Item,* 13 January 1895; *Sporting News,* 12 January 1895, 26 January 1895; *Sporting Life,* 26 January 1895, 4 May 1895; "Invitation Program of Philadelphia Ball Park," 2 May 1895, pp. 1–8.

7. *Sporting Life,* 24 November 1894; *Philadelphia Evening Item,* 17 November 1894; *Philadelphia Inquirer,* 16 November 1894; *Sunday Item,* 18 November 1894.

8. *Sunday Item,* 17 March 1895; *Philadelphia Evening Item,* 14 February 1895, 19 February 1895, 20 February 1895; *Sporting News,* 23 February 1895, 2 March 1895; *Sporting Life,* 2 March 1895, 16 March 1895; *Randall Papers,* packet 1.

9. *Randall Papers,* packet 1; *Sporting Life,* 16 March 1895.

10. *Sporting News,* 13 April 1895.

11. *Sporting Life,* 6 April 1895.

12. *Philadelphia Evening Item,* 14 April 1895, 18 April 1895, 19 April 1895, 29 April 1895, 22 May 1895, 27 May 1895, 22 August 1895.

13. *Sporting Life,* 27 April 1895.

14. For full coverage of opening day activities, see Philadelphia papers for 3 May 1895.

15. *Spalding Scrapbooks,* 3:144; *Randall Papers,* packet 1.

16. *Sunday Item,* 28 April 1895; *Sporting Life,* 27 April 1895, 18 May 1895; *Sporting News,* 27 April 1895.

17. *Sunday Item,* 7 July 1895; *Sporting Life,* 15 June 1895, 29 June 1895, 13 July 1895, 20 July 1895, 27 July 1895, 3 August 1895; *Philadelphia Evening Item,* 6 July 1895, 13 July 1895.

18. *Philadelphia Record,* cited in *Philadelphia Evening Item,* 19 July 1895.

19. *Sporting News*, 20 July 1895; *Sporting Life*, 6 July 1895; 10 August 1895.

20. *Sporting Life*, 29 June 1895.

21. Ibid., 20 July 1895; *Philadelphia Evening Item*, 18 July 1895.

22. *Philadelphia Evening Item*, 16 August 1895.

23. For details of Wright's passing and the erection of a monument in his honor, consult J. Casway, "A Monument for Harry Wright," *National Pastime* (1997) 35–37. The proceeds from exhibition games played in April 1896 were spent on a large bronze statue for the "Father of Base Ball." Engraved on the right side of the pedestal is a quote from Shakespeare's *Julius Caasar*: "His life was gentle, the elements so mixed in him that nature might stand up and say to all the world: This was a man."

24. *Philadelphia Evening Item*, 7 October 1895; 9 October 1895; 12 October 1895; *Sporting Life*, 12 October 1895; *Philadelphia Evening Bulletin*, 18 November 1921 in *Randall Papers*, packet 2.

25. *Sporting Life*, 1 February 1896; *Sporting News*, 23 November 1895, 21 December 1895; *Philadelphia Evening Item*, 11 December 1895; *Sunday Item*, 17 November 1895, 8 December 1895, 29 December 1895; *Philadelphia Inquirer*, 24 May 1898.

26. For an expanded justification of this case, see, J. Casway, "The Best Outfield Ever?" *Baseball Research Journal* 27 (1998): 3–7.

27. *Sporting Life*, 26 October 1895; *Sunday Item*, 27 October 1895; *Philadelphia Evening Item*, 22 October 1895, 23 October 1895, 1 November 1895, 19 December 1895; *Philadelphia Bulletin*, 23 October 1895; *Randall Papers*, packet 1.

28. *Philadelphia Evening Item*, 19 December 1895.

29. *Sunday Item*, 22 December 1895.

30. *Sporting Life*, 14 March 1896; *Randall Papers*, packet 1.

31. *Sunday Item*, 1 December 1895.

32. *Sporting News*, 21 September 1895; 12 October 1895.

33. *Sunday Item*, 15 December 1895; *Sporting News*, 21 March 1896.

9. The Great and Only

1. *Sporting News*, 4 January 1896.

2. *Philadelphia Inquirer*, 11 February 1896. *Sporting News*, 8 February 1896.

3. *Philadelphia Inquirer*, 4 March 1896.

4. Ibid., 27 March 1896; *Sporting Life*, 15 February 1896.

5. *Philadelphia Inquirer*, 26 March 1896; *Sporting News*, 4 April 1896.

6. *Sporting News*, 11 April 1896.

7. *Philadelphia Inquirer*, 12 April 1896.

8. Ibid., 27 April 1896.

9. Ibid., 12 May 1896. *Sporting Life*, 16 May 1896; *Randall Papers*, packet 1.

10. *Philadelphia Inquirer*, 16 May 1896, 18 May 1896. *Sporting Life*, 18 August 1896; *Sporting News*, 10 November 1900.

11. *Philadelphia Inquirer*, 3 June 1896, 10 June 1896.

12. *Sporting Life*, 20 June 1896; 27 June 1896.

13. *Philadelphia Inquirer*, 30 June 1896.

14. *Randall Papers*, packet 2.

15. Ibid., packet 1.

16. [Chicago] *Daily Inter Ocean*, 14 July 1896. Consult local newspapers of 13 and 14 July 1896 for the accounts of the game. See also *Randall Papers*, packet 1; Hugh Fullerton, "Del's 4 Homers" in *Randall Papers*, clippings 2; Robert Sensenderfer, "Ed Delahanty's Big Day," *Philadelphia Evening Bulletin*, 18 June 1942; Sowell, *July 2, 1903*, 105–6. *Sporting Life*, 25 July 1896, 8 August 1896, 17 October 1896; *Sporting News*, 5 December 1896.

17. *Randall Papers*, packet 2.

18. Ibid., packet 1.

19. Ibid., packet 2.

20. *Sporting Life*, 1 August 1896, 8 August 1896; *Philadelphia Inquirer*, 2 August 1896.

21. *Sporting Life*, 1 August 1896.

22. Ibid., 14 July 1896.

23. *Sporting News*, 22 August 1896. *Philadelphia Inquirer*, 18 August 1896.

24. For the fullest background study on Lajoie, J. M. Murphy, "Napoleon Lajoie, Modern Baseball's First Superstar," *National Pastime* 7, 1 (Spring 1988): 7–15. *Sporting Life*, 8 August 1896, 25 July 1896; *Sporting News*, 29 August 1896.

25. *Philadelphia Inquirer*, 30 August 1896.

26. *Sporting Life*, 22 August 1896.

27. *Philadelphia Inquirer*, 28 September 1896, 9 November 1896; *Sporting Life*, 10 October 1896, 9 January 1897; *Sporting News*, 3 October 1896.

28. *Sporting Life*, 12 December 1896, 31 October 1896.

29. Ibid., 12 December 1896, 6 February 1897; *Philadelphia Inquirer*, 25 March 1897; *Philadelphia Evening Item*, 23 November 1896, 8 March 1897; *Sunday Item*, 24 January 1897; *Augusta Chronicle*, 4 December 1896.

30. *Sporting Life*, 17 October 1896, 22 August 1896.

31. *Philadelphia Inquirer,* 10 November 1896; *Sporting Life,* 22 August 1896, 7 November 1896.

32. *Sporting Life,* 13 February 1897.

33. Ibid., 19 December 1896, 21 October 1896, 12 December 1896, 2 January 1897. *Cleveland Plain Dealer,* cited by *Sporting News,* 18 March 1899.

34. *Philadelphia Inquirer,* 1 January 1897; *Sunday Item,* 3 January 1897; 10 January 1897; *Philadelphia Evening Item,* 2 January 1897.

35. Cartoon from *Philadelphia Sunday Press,* 27 December 1896, and accompanying articles are in *Randall Papers,* packet 2. *Sporting Life,* 26 December 1896, 6 January 1897, 9 January 1897.

36. *Sporting Life,* 31 October 1896, 24 October 1896; *Randall Papers,* packet 1.

37. *Sporting Life,* 17 October 1896, 31 October 1896, 3 October 1896, 21 November 1896, 19 December 1896.

38. *Sunday Item,* 17 January 1897.

10. PRINCELY JOLLYERS

1. *Sporting Life,* 19 September 1896.

2. *Sporting News,* 4 December 1895.

3. *Sporting Life,* 10 May 1897. *Sporting News,* 13 February 1897; 20 October 1900.

4. For an examination of Comiskey's St. Louis players and tactics, see: Nemec, *Beer and Whisky,* 97–101; Voigt, *Baseball,* 1:253; and G. W. Axelson, *Commy* (Chicago, 1919), 98–101. *Sporting News,* 9 November 1896, 13 February 1897, 19 February 1898, 8 April 1899, 20 October 1900.

5. *Sunday Item,* 18 July 1897; *Sporting News,* 23 December 1899.

6. *Sporting Life,* 6 June 1888.

7. Ibid., 5 May 1894.

8. Robert Burk contends (*Never Just a Game,* 131) that the Lee Allen notebooks at the National Baseball Library in Cooperstown show that Irish participation in the 1890s dropped 14 percent from 1885 to 1890. Contemporary newspaper accounts and census research indicate the Irish participation remained at the same level.

9. *Sporting News,* 28 December 1895.

10. *Sporting Life,* 19 September 1896.

11. Ibid., 9 April 1892. *Sporting News,* 4 April 1896.

12. *Sporting Life,* 10 April 1897.

13. J. McGraw, *My Thirty Years in Baseball* (Lincoln, Nebr., 1995 ed.), 78; Burk, *Never Just a Game,* 134; *Philadelphia Inquirer,* 5 June 1897; *Sporting News,* 15 August 1896.

14. *Sporting News,* 27 June 1896.

15. *Sporting News,* 27 June 1896. Mitchell, "The Celt," *Gael* (May 1902): 151–55.

16. *Sporting Life,* 1 October 1892.

17. *Sporting News,* 17 August 1895.

18. *Sporting Life,* 6 October 1894.

19. Ibid., 23 January 1889.

20. American Press Association, quoted by ibid., 1 May 1897.

21. *Sporting News,* 20 January 1894; 11 February 1899; 21 December 1901.

22. *North American,* 21 September 1893.

23. *Sporting News,* 11 January 1902.

24. Ibid., 3 July 1897, 8 September 1900, 20 October 1900, 17 November 1900, 15 December 1900.

25. *Sporting Life,* 5 July 1902; 23 May 1903.

26. Ibid., 11 May 1887; *North American,* 2 August 1894. According to Connie Mack researcher Norman Macht, the manager in his early days was a vigorous "bench jockey" and kicker. His teams were noted for alert and aggressive ball playing.

27. Illuminating articles on Hanlon's Orioles can be read in Mike Klingaman's three-part series in the *Baltimore Sun,* 7 July 1996, 8 July 1996, 9 July 1996. *Sporting News,* 28 August 1897. Also consult, Burt Solomon, *Where They Ain't: The Fabled and Untimely Death of the Original Baltimore Orioles* (New York, 1999).

28. *Sporting News,* 27 February 1897.

29. *Philadelphia Evening Item,* 30 January 1897.

30. *Sunday Item,* 14 February 1897; *Sporting Life,* 13 February 1897.

31. *Philadelphia Evening Item,* 15 January 1897, 21 January 1897, 3 February 1897; *Sporting Life,* 23 January 1897; *Sporting News,* 6 March 1897.

32. *Augusta Chronicle,* 17 March 1897, 18 March 1897; *Philadelphia Evening Item,* 13 March 1897, 17 March 1897. See also *Philadelphia Inquirer* and *Philadelphia Press* for spring training coverage.

33. *Philadephia Evening Item,* 22 May 1897.

34. *Philadelphia Inquirer,* 24 May 1897.

35. Ibid., 17 May 1897; *Philadelphia Evening Item,* 17 May 1897; *Sporting News,* 22 May 1897.

36. *Sporting Life,* 29 May 1897.

37. *Sunday Item,* 6 June 1897; *Philadelphia Inquirer,* 3 June 1897; 4 June 1897.

38. *Sunday Item,* 13 June 1897.

39. *Sporting Life,* 7 August 1897.

40. Ibid., 10 July 1897.

41. *Sporting News,* 10 July 1897; *Randall Papers,* packet 1.

42. *Sporting News,* 1 January 1898.

43. Ibid., 5 February 1898.

44. *Sunday Item,* 20 June 1897.

45. *Philadelphia Evening Item,* 17 August 1897.

46. Ibid., 26 August 1897.

47. *Sporting News,* 1 January 1898.

48. *Sporting Life,* 29 May 1897, 5 June 1897, 26 June 1897; *Philadelphia Evening Item,* 22 June 1897.

49. *Sporting Life,* 3 July 1897. An earlier denial was given on 22 June. *Philadelphia Inquirer,* 23 June 1897.

50. *Philadelphia Inquirer,* 21 August 1897, 20 August 1897.

51. Ibid., 21 August 1897.

52. *Sporting News,* 14 August 1897, 21 August 1897; *Philadelphia Evening Item,* 12 August 1897; *Sporting Life,* 21 August 1897; *North American,* 12 August 1897.

53. *North American,* 16 August 1897.

54. *Sporting News,* 4 September 1897, 11 September 1897, 2 October 1897; *Sporting Life,* 4 September 1897; *Philadelphia Evening Item,* 28 August 1897, 31 August 1897; *Philadelphia Inquirer,* 28 August 1897; *North American,* 17 September 1897.

55. *Sporting Life,* 21 August 1897.

56. *Sporting News,* 1 January 1898, 6 November 1897; *Randall Papers,* packet 1.

57. *Sporting News,* 5 February 1898.

58. *Sunday Item,* 29 August 1897. Burial records of the Cavalry Cemetery, lot 15, section 10.

59. *Sporting News,* 1 January 1898, 6 November 1897.

60. *Philadelphia Evening Item,* 25 August 1897; *Sunday Item,* 29 August 1897.

61. Lieb and Baumgartner, *Philadelphia Phillies,* 54–55; D and J. B. DeValeria, *Honus Wagner: A Biography* (New York, 1995), 40; *Sporting Life,* 17 July 1897, 7 August 1897.

62. *North American,* 28 August 1897.

63. Ibid., 12 November 1897.

11. A Season in Wartime

1. *Sporting News,* 15 January 1898.

2. Correspondence of Florence Delahanty, April 1937. *Randall Papers,* packet 4. *Sporting Life,* 27 November 1897, 25 December 1897, 5 February 1898.

3. *Sporting News,* 23 April 1898, 26 March 1898.

4. *Sporting Life,* 5 March 1898.

5. Ibid., 8 January 1898.

6. Ibid., 12 February 1898, 26 February 1898.

7. *Philadelphia Inquirer,* 10 March 1898.

8. *Philadelphia Evening Item,* 17 December 1897; *Sunday Item,* 16 January 1898; *Sporting Life,* 25 December 1897, 12 February 1898; *Sporting News,* 18 December 1897.

9. For the Reach and Rogers 4 April 1898 letter to the league and the position taken by magnates at their St. Louis meeting, see *Philadelphia Inquirer,* 5 April 1898; *Sporting News,* 9 April 1898.

10. Burk, *Never Just a Game,* 136; Voigt, *Baseball,* 1:235.

11. *Philadelphia Evening Item,* 15 February 1898.

12. Ibid., 28 February 1898, 17 March 1898, 10 December 1898. Also see: Voigt, *Baseball,* 1:229–30; Burk, *Never Just a Game,* 133; Seymour, *Baseball,* 1:298.

13. *Philadelphia Inquirer,* 11 April 1898, 18 April 1898, 21 April 1898, 22 April 1898, 25 April 1898, 26 April 1898; *Philadelphia Evening Item,* 11 April 1898, 23 April 1898; *Sporting News,* 16 April 1898; *Sporting Life,* 19 March 1898, 16 April 1898.

14. *Sunday Item,* 27 March 1898, 20 March 1898; *Philadelphia Evening Item,* 24 March 1898; *Sporting Life,* 26 March 1898.

15. *Sporting Life,* 26 March 1896; *Philadelphia Evening Item,* 30 March 1898.

16. *Philadelphia Inquirer,* 18 March 1898, 21 March 1898, 23 March 1898; *Sporting Life,* 26 March 1898, 23 April 1898; *Sporting News,* 26 March 1898, 2 April 1898; *Sunday Item,* 20 March 1898.

17. *Philadelphia Inquirer,* 19 March 1898, 28 March 1898; *Sporting Life,* 2 April 1898, 9 April 1898, 23 April 1898.

18. Letter of Reach, Rogers, and Shettsline, 28 April 1898, cited in *Philadelphia Inquirer,* 30 April 1898; *North American,* 30 April 1898; *Sporting News,* 7 May 1898; *Sporting Life,* 7 May 1898; *Philadelphia Evening Item,* 30 April 1898.

19. *Philadelphia Evening Item,* 30 April 1898.

20. Ibid., 26 March 1898, 4 April 1898; *Philadelphia Inquirer,* 30 March 1898.

21. *Sporting Life,* 30 April 1898.

22. *Philadelphia Inquirer,* 17 April 1898.

23. *Sporting Life,* 4 June 1898.

24. *Philadelphia Evening Item,* 28 May 1898; *Sunday Item,* 29 May 1898; *Sporting Life,* 4 June 1898, 11 June 1898; *Sporting News,* 4 June 1898, 11 June 1898; *Philadelphia Inquirer,* 18 May 1898, 30 May 1898.

25. *Philadelphia Inquirer,* 30 May 1898.

26. Ibid., 6 June 1898.

27. *Philadelphia Evening Item,* 17 June 1898.

28. Ibid., 19 June 1898.

29. *Sporting Life,* 25 June 1898.

30. *Philadelphia Inquirer,* 20 June 1898.

31. *Sporting Life,* 16 July 1898.

32. Ibid., 23 July 1898.

33. *Philadelphia Evening Item,* 16 July 1898.

34. *Philadelphia Inquirer,* 28 August 1898.

35. *Sporting News,* 9 May 1896; *Sporting Life,* 9 May 1896.

36. *Philadelphia Evening Item,* 5 May 1897; *Sporting News,* 6 November 1897, 28 May 1898.

37. *Sporting News,* 9 February 1901, 19 March 1898, 30 April 1898, 28 May 1898; *Allentown Morning Call,* 21 May 1898, 28 May 1898.

38. *Allentown Morning Call,* 16 June 1898; *Philadelphia Evening Item,* 4 June 1898, 11 June 1898, 25 June 1898.

39. These figures came from SABR's *Minor League Baseball Stars,* vol. III (Cleveland, 1992), 62–64.

40. *Sporting News,* 13 August 1898.

41. *Philadelphia Inquirer,* 14 April 1898.

42. *Sporting Life,* 10 September 1898.

43. *Philadelphia Inquirer,* 5 September 1898.

44. *Sunday Item,* 14 August 1898.

45. *Ibid.,* 10 September 1898, 30 June 1900, 13 April 1901, 8 March 1902, 3 May 1902; *Washington Post,* 27 June 1902; *Sporting News,* 10 September 1898, 2 December 1899, 16 December 1899, 23 December 1899, 13 April 1901; *North American,* 14 August 1900.

46. *North American,* 3 September 1898. *Sporting Life,* 5 November 1898.

47. *Sporting News,* 29 October 1898; *Sporting Life,* 29 October 1898, 5 November 1898.

48. *Sporting News,* 15 October 1898. Keeler was not considered because of sparse playing in 1892 and 1893. He would have batted .379. According to figures tabulated by baseball researcher Bill Wagner, Delahanty's average was also .379.

49. *Sporting Life,* 19 November 1898, 5 November 1898, 26 November 1898; *Sporting News,* 12 November 1898; *Philadelphia Evening Item,* 8 November 1898.

50. *Sporting News,* 12 November 1898.

51. Ibid., 3 December 1898.

52. *Sporting Life*, 22 October 1898, 10 December 1898; *Philadelphia Inquirer*, 18 October 1898; *Sporting News*, 18 March 1899, 24 June 1899; *Sporting Life*, 24 June 1899.

53. This data is drawn from *Sporting Life*, 24 December 1898; *Sporting News*, 22 October 1898, 28 January 1899; Burk, *Never Just a Game*, 135; Voigt, *Baseball*, 1:232–33.

54. *Sporting News*, 12 November 1898.

55. *Philadelphia Evening Item*, 20 September 1898, 30 September 1898; *Philadelphia Inquirer*, 17 October 1898; *Sporting Life*, 16 July 1898.

56. Voigt, *Baseball*, 1:226.

57. *Philadelphia Ledger*, cited by *Sporting News*, 13 August 1898.

58. *Philadelphia Evening Item*, 12 December 1898; *Sporting Life*, 2 December 1898, 19 December 1898.

12. CAPTAIN ED, BATTING CHAMP

1. *Philadelphia Inquirer*, 29 March 1899.

2. Ibid., 1 April 1899, 27 March 1899, 16 December 1901.

3. *Sporting News*, 2 March 1901, 30 November 1901; *Sporting Life*, 25 April 1896.

4. *Philadelphia Inquirer*, 15 March 1899, 16 March 1899, 17 March 1899, 18 March 1899, 19 March 1899, 20 March 1899, 21 March 1899; *Sporting Life*, 18 March 1899; *Sporting News*, 18 March 1899, 25 March 1899.

5. *Philadelphia Inquirer*, 27 March 1899.

6. Ibid., 31 March 1899; *Sporting News*, 8 April 1899.

7. *Philadelphia Inquirer*, 8 April 1899.

8. *Sporting Life*, 22 April 1899, 29 April 1899; *Philadelphia Inquirer*, 19 April 1899, 20 April 1899.

9. *Philadelphia Inquirer*, Magazine Supplement, 23 April 1899.

10. *Sporting News*, 27 May 1899. Thirty-two players were playing in 1891. Seven of these ballplayers were not in the National League or American Association before 1890.

11. Ibid., 20 May 1899.

12. Ibid., 5 October 1901.

13. Ibid., 27 May 1899; *Sporting Life*, 20 May 1899; 1 July 1899; *Philadelphia Inquirer*, 14 May 1899. Lajoie broke another ball on 22 June. *Philadelphia Inquirer*, 24 June 1899; *Sporting Life*, 1 July 1899. An undated clipping reported that Delahanty also knocked the cover off a ball and the outfielder chased after the unraveling baseball. Unidentified clipping, *Randall Papers*, packet 2.

14. *Philadelphia Inquirer,* 9 July 1899.

15. Ibid., 23 August 1899.

16. Ibid., 20 July 1899; *Sporting Life,* 22 July 1899.

17. *Philadelphia Inquirer,* 16 July 1899, 17 July 1899, 20 July 1899, 21 July 1899, 24 July 1899, 25 July 1899, 26 July 1899, 7 August 1899; *North American,* 26 July 1899; *Sporting Life,* 22 July 1899; *Sporting News,* 22 July 1899, 29 July 1899, 21 October 1899.

18. *Sporting News,* 8 July 1899, 22 July 1899; *Philadelphia Inquirer,* 16 July 1899, 20 July 1899; *North American,* 30 June 1899.

19. *Sporting News,* 17 June 1899; *Sporting Life,* 24 June 1899.

20. *Sporting Life,*22 July 1899; 5 August 1899, 12 August 1899, 19 August 1899, 26 August 1899, 2 September 1899; *Philadelphia Inquirer,* 23 July 1899, 2 August 1899, 6 August 1899, 8 August 1899, 10 August 1899; *North American,* 10 July 1899, 26 July 1899; *Sporting News,* 5 August 1899, 19 August 1899, 10 February 1900.

21. *Philadelphia Inquirer,* 10 August 1899; *Sporting News,* 19 August 1899; *Sporting Life,* 19 August 1899, 26 August 1899, 9 September 1899; *North American,* 10 August 1899.

22. *Philadelphia Inquirer,* 4 September 1899, 6 September 1899.

23. *Sporting News,* 5 August 1899, 9 September 1899, 16 September 1899, 28 October 1899, 25 November 1899, 16 December 1899; *Sporting Life,* 6 May 1899, 27 May 1899, 7 December 1899, 16 December 1899; *Allentown Morning Call,* 24 July 1899.

24. *Sporting Life,* 27 January 1900; *Sporting News,* 16 September 1899, 16 December 1899, 20 January 1900, 14 February 1900; *Philadelphia Inquirer,* 24 October 1899.

25. *Sporting News,* 18 November 1899.

26. *Philadelphia Inquirer,* 12 October 1899, 14 October 1899, 16 October 1899; *Philadelphia Press,* 12 March 1900; *Sporting Life,* 7 October 1899, 21 October 1899.

27. *Sporting Life,* 8 July 1899.

28. *Philadelphia Inquirer,* 12 October 1899, 13 October 1899, 18–20 October 1899; *Sporting Life,* 28 October 1899.

29. *Sporting News,* 28 October 1899.

30. Ibid.; *Philadelphia Inquirer,* 17 October 1899.

31. *Philadelphia Inquirer,* 21 October 1899.

32. *Sporting Life,* 4 November 1899; *Sporting News,* 28 October 1899.

33. *Sporting Life,* 21 October 1899, 28 October 1899.

34. *Sporting News,* 18 November 1899.

35. Ibid., 6 November 1897, 4 November 1899, 18 November 1899; *Sporting Life,* 27 July 1895. A player in possession of one of Delahanty's bats said it weighed 54 ounces. *Sporting Life,* 18 November 1899.

36. *Sporting Life,* 15 July 1899.

37. Ibid., 25 November 1899; *Philadelphia Inquirer,* 16 November 1899; *Sporting News,* 21 October 1899.

38. *Sporting News,* 28 October 1899; Thorn, *Total Baseball,* 144.

39. For the original stories, see *New York World* and the *New York Herald.* Consult: *Philadelphia Inquirer,* 17 October 1899; *Sporting Life,* 21 October 1899, 30 December 1899.

40. *Sporting News,* 16 December 1899.

41. *Sporting Life,* 23 December 1899.

42. Ibid.

43. For more specific accounts of these leagues, consult: Seymour, *Baseball,* 1:302–9; Voigt, *Baseball,* 1:238–41, 270–71; Burk, *Never Just a Game,* 137–42.

44. *Sporting News,* 18 November 1899; *Sporting Life,* 18 November 1899.

45. *Sporting Life,* 25 November 1899; *Sporting News,* 18 November 1899, 16 December 1899.

46. On February 7, 1900, "Whiskey Jack" passed away at the age of twenty-six. *Philadelphia Press,* 8 February 1900, 9 February 1900; *Sporting News,* 4 November 1899, 10 February 1900.

13. The "Hoodoo" Season

1. *Sporting News,* 3 February 1900; *Philadelphia Press,* 6 February 1900; 9 February 1900.

2. *Philadelphia Inquirer,* 13 March 1900.

3. *Sporting Life,* 10 March 1900.

4. *Philadelphia Press,* 14 April 1900.

5. Ibid., 5 March 1900; *Sporting Life,* 10 March 1900.

6. Court Transcript of Norine Delahanty's Law Suit, 1904, p. 37. *Randall Papers,* packet 5.

7. *Sporting News,* 20 January 1900; *Sporting Life,* 3 March 1900.

8. *Sporting Life,* 3 March 1900, 17 March 1900; *Sporting News,* 24 March 1900; *Philadelphia Press,* 20 February 1900.

9. *Sporting Life,* 23 December 1899, 20 January 1900, 10 March 1900, 17 March 1900; *Sporting News,* 20 January 1900, 10 March 1900; *Philadelphia Press,* 2 March 1900, 12 March 1900, 13 March 1900; *Philadelphia Inquirer,* 13 March 1900, 18 March 1900.

10. *Philadelphia Press,* 12 March 1900; *Philadelphia Inquirer,* 12 March 1900, 19 March 1900.

11. *Sporting Life,* 17 March 1900.

12. *Sporting News,* 31 March 1900.

13. *Philadelphia Inquirer,* 12 March 1900, 19 March 1900.

14. *Sporting News,* 27 January 1900; *Sporting Life,* 20 January 1900; *Philadelphia Press,* 16 January 1900.

15. *Sporting News,* 5 May 1900; *Philadelphia Press,* 2 May 1900, 3 May 1900.

16. *Philadelphia Press,* 27 February 1900, 20 March 1900; *Philadelphia Inquirer,* 14 March 1900, 29 March 1900; *Sporting Life,* 7 March 1900, 10 March 1900, 24 March 1900.

17. *Philadelphia Press,* 14 March 1900.

18. Ibid., 15–21 March 1900, 22 March 1900, 27 March 1900; *North American,* 16 March 1900, 17 March 1900, 20 March 1900, 26 March 1900; *Philadelphia Inquirer,* 16–27 March 1900.

19. *Philadelphia Press,* 27 March 1900, 30 March 1900; *North American,* 21 March 1900.

20. *Philadelphia Inquirer,* 1 April 1900; *Sporting Life,* 7 April 1900.

21. *Philadelphia Inquirer,* 3 April 1900.

22. *Philadelphia Press,* 5 April 1900; *Philadelphia Inquirer,* 5 April 1900.

23. *Philadelphia Inquirer,* 5 April 1900, 7 April 1900; *Sporting Life,* 4 April 1900, 7 April 1900; *North American,* 10 April 1900, 11 April 1900; *Philadelphia Press,* 13 April 1900, 14 April 1900.

24. *Philadelphia Press,* 13 April 1900.

25. Ibid.

26. *Philadelphia Inquirer,* 20 June 1900.

27. McGraw, *Thirty Years in Baseball,* 123–24; Alexander, *McGraw,* 70. Reports of the initial signing put the amounts at $4,000 and $3,000. *Philadelphia Press,* 9 May 1900.

28. *Philadelphia Press,* 12 April 1900; *Sporting News,* 21 April 1900.

29. *Philadelphia Press,* 12 April 1900.

30. Ibid., 14 April 1900, 15 April 1900.

31. *Sporting Life,* 21 April 1900; *Philadelphia Press,* 17 April 1900.

32. *Philadelphia Inquirer,* 16 April 1900.

33. Ibid., 19 April 1900.

34. *Philadelphia Press,* 17 April 1900; *Sporting News,* 21 April 1900; *North American,* 17 April 1900.

35. *Philadelphia Press,* 18 April 1900; *North American,* 18 April 1900; *Philadelphia Inquirer,* 18 April 1900.

36. *Philadelphia Inquirer,* 20 April 1901, 21 April 1901, 28 April 1901; *Philadelphia Press,* 20 April 1901, 21 April 1901; *North American,* 19 April 1900. Leib and Baumgartner, *Philadelphia Phillies,* 60; Westcott and Bilovsky, *New Phillies Encyclopedia,* 32–33, 220.

37. *Philadelphia Press,* 13 March 1900; *Sporting Life,* 3 March 1900, 17 March 1900; *North American,* 14 April 1900; *Sporting News,* 10 February 1900.

38. *Sporting News,* 24 March 1900.

39. *Sporting Life,* 21 April 1900.

40. *Philadelphia Inquirer,* 25 April 1900.

41. Ibid., 26 April 1900, 27 April 1900.

42. *Sporting Life,* 28 April 1900.

43. *Philadelphia Inquirer,* 29 April 1900, 30 April 1900.

44. *Sporting News,* 5 May 1900; *Philadelphia Press,* 23 April 1900.

45. *Philadelphia Inquirer,* 21 May 1900.

46. *Sporting Life,* 19 May 1900.

47. Ibid., 26 May 1900; *Philadelphia Inquirer,* 16 May 1900; *Sporting Life,* 26 May 1900; *Philadelphia Press,* 16 May 1900, 21 May 1900.

48. *Philadelphia Press,* 26 June 1900.

49. *Philadelphia Inquirer,* 23 June 1900, 25 June 1900; *Philadelphia Press,* 23 June 1900; *North American,* 23 June 1900; *Sporting News,* 30 June 1900.

50. *Sporting Life,* 9 June 1900; *Philadelphia Inquirer,* 4 June 1900; *North American,* 2 June 1900; *Sporting News,* 9 June 1900; *Philadelphia Press,* 2 June 1900.

51. *Philadelphia Press,* 4 June 1900.

52. *Sporting Life,* 9 June 1900; *Philadelphia Press,* 4 June 1900.

53. *Philadelphia Inquirer,* 1 June 1900; *North American,* 1 June 1900.

54. *Philadelphia Press,* 11 June 1900.

55. Ibid.; *Philadelphia Inquirer,* 9 June 1900, 16 June 1900; *Sporting News,* 9 June 1900; *North American,* 5 June 1900, 9 June 1900, 11 June 1900, 13 August 1900. For a broader examination, see: Seymour, *Baseball,* 1:309–10; Burk, *Never Just a Game,* 143; Voigt, *Baseball,* 1:285.

56. *Philadelphia Press,* 14 February 1900, 9 March 1900, 29 March 1900; *Sporting Life,* 3 February 1900, 31 March 1900; *Sporting News,* 16 December 1899; *Allentown Morning Call,* 17 March 1900.

57. *Allentown Morning Call,* 12 April 1900, 17 April 1900, 18 April 1900, 27 April 1900.

58. Ibid., 20 May 1900, 14 June 1900; *Philadelphia Press,* 16 May 1900; *Philadelphia Inquirer,* 18 May 1900, 19 May 1900.

59. *Sporting News,* 28 July 1900.

60. *Philadelphia Press,* 10 July 1900; *Philadelphia Inquirer,* 10 July 1900; *North American,* 10 July 1900.

61. *North American,* 10 July 1903.

62. Court transcript, 1904, p. 33. *Randall Papers,* packet 5; *Washington Post,* 6 July 1903.

63. *North American*, 12 July 1900, 11 July 1900.

64. *Philadelphia Press*, 11 July 1900. *Philadelphia Inquirer*, 11 July 1900.

65. *Philadelphia Inquirer*, 14 July 1900; *Philadelphia Press*, 14 July 1900; *North American*, 14 July 1900; DeValeria, *Honus Wagner*, 79–80.

66. *Philadelphia Press*, 14 July 1900.

67. *Sporting Life*, 4 August 1900; *Philadelphia Press*, 31 July 1900; Seymour, *Baseball*, 1:310; Burk, *Never Just a Game*, 143–44.

68. *North American*, 14–18 August 1900; *Philadelphia Press*, 15 August 1900, 17 August 1900, 18 August 1900; *Philadelphia Inquirer*, 15 August 1900, 17 August 1900, 18 August 1900; *Sporting Life*, 25 August 1900.

69. *North American*, 20 August 1900.

70. *Sporting Life*, 25 August 1900.

71. *North American*, 20 July 1893.

72. One article alleged that Pearce Chiles came up with the idea of an electric wire. *North American*, 8 October 1900.

73. *Sporting News*, 24 June 1899; *Sporting Life*, 21 October 1899, 17 June 1900.

74. *Sporting Life*, 16 December 1899.

75. *Philadelphia Inquirer*, 3 June 1900.

76. *Sporting Life*, 21 October 1899, 23 June 1900.

77. *Philadelphia Inquirer*, 18 September 1900, 20 September 1900, 27 September 1900, 3 October 1900; *North American*, 19 September 1900, 20 September 1900; *Sporting Life*, 22 September 1900, 6 October 1900.

78. *Sporting Life*, 22 September 1900.

79. *Spalding Scrapbooks*, 4 (1900), 2; *North American*, 3 October 1900, 23 September 1901; *Philadelphia Inquirer*, 3 October 1900.

80. *Sporting Life*, 13 October 1900.

81. *Philadelphia Inquirer*, 20 September 1900.

82. *Sporting Life*, 31 March 1900.

83. Ibid., 10 November 1900.

84. Ibid., 13 October 1900.

85. *Sporting News*, 22 December 1900.

86. Quoted by ibid., 13 October 1900.

14. THE NEW LEAGUE

1. *Sporting Life*, 29 December 1900; 12 January 1901.

2. Ibid.

3. Ibid., 15 September 1900.

4. For summaries of the Johnson, Comiskey, and Somers relationship, see: Alexander, *McGraw,* 73; Axelson, *Commy,* 136–44; Burk, *Never Just a Game,* 138, 147–48; Seymour, *Baseball,* 1:307–9; Voigt, *Baseball,* 1:240–41.

5. *Sporting Life,* 19 January 1901; 26 January 1901.

6. *Philadelphia Press,* 16 December 1900.

7. *Philadelphia Inquirer,* 24 January 1901; *Sporting News,* 9 February 1901.

8. *Philadelphia Inquirer,* 27 January 1901; *Sporting News,* 9 February 1901.

9. See *Sporting News, Sporting Life, Inquirer,* and *Press* for 12/1900 to 3/1901. For good summaries, consult: Seymour, *Baseball,* 1:312–14; Burk, *Never Just a Game,* 148–50; L. Lowenfish, *The Imperfect Diamond: A History of Baseball's Labor Wars* (New York, 1991), 62–66; G. E. White, *Creating the National Pastime: Baseball Transforms Itself, 1903–1953* (Princeton, N. J., 1996), 48–50.

10. *Philadelphia Inquirer,* 21 January 1901.

11. Ibid., 11 February 1901; *Sporting Life,* 2 February 1901; 9 February 1901; 9 March 1901; 16 March 1901.

12. *Sporting News,* 6 April 1901.

13. *Philadelphia Inquirer,* 9 February 1901.

14. *Philadelphia Press,* 8 February 1901; *Sporting Life,* 13 July 1901. For background to the Shibe-Reach relationship, see: B. Kuklick, *To Every Thing a Season* (Princeton, N.J., 1991), 15–16; J. Casway, "Philadelphia's Baseball's Unappreciated Founders: Al Reach and Ben Shibe," *National Pastime* (forthcoming).

15. *Philadelphia Inquirer,* 9 March 1901, 11 March 1901; *Philadelphia Press ,* 9 March 1901; *Sporting Life,* 16 March 1901.

16. *Sporting Life,* 23 February 1901, 2 March 1901.

17. *Philadelphia Press,* 1 March 1901, 16 March 1901; *Philadelphia Inquirer,* 1 March 1901, 25 August 1902.

18. *Sporting Life,* 16 March 1901.

19. Murphy, "Lajoie," 68, 20; *Philadelphia Press,* 31 March 1901; *Philadelphia Inquirer,* 21 March 1901, 21 August 1901; *Sporting News,* 30 March 1901; *Sporting Life,* 30 March 1901; F. Leib, *Connie Mack: The Grand Old Man of Baseball* (New York, 1945), 65; Leib and Baumgartner, *Philadelphia Phillies,* 60. According to Murphy's summary, Lajoie alleged that Rogers countered Mack's offer and he refused it when Rogers denied him the $400 difference in Delahanty's 1900 contract. Lajoie later testified that Rogers offered him $500. *Philadelphia Press,* 21 April 1901.

20. Murphy, "Lajoie," 20; Leib and Baumgartner, *Philadelphia Phillies,* 60–61; Leib, *Connie Mack,* 66; Sowell, *July 2, 1903,* 119.

21. *Philadelphia Inquirer,* 29 March 1901.

22. *Philadelphia Press,* 5 March 1901; *Sporting News,* 30 March 1901, 4 May 1901.

23. *Sporting News,* 4 May 1901.

24. *Philadelphia Inquirer,* 25 March 1901, 29 March 1901.

25. Ibid., 28 March 1901; *Sporting News,* 6 April 1901.

26. *Philadelphia Inquirer,* 12 March 1901; *Philadelphia Press,* 12 March 1901; *Sporting Life,* 16 March 1901.

27. *Philadelphia Inquirer,* 13 March 1901.

28. *Sporting Life,* 30 March 1901.

29. *Philadelphia Inquirer,* 20 April 1901; *Philadelphia Press,* 20 April 1901. During his testimony, Lajoie said that Connie Mack negotiated the contract and Frank Hough witnessed it. Ben Shibe, he related, was not party to the signing. *Philadelphia Press,* 21 April 1901; *Sporting Life,* 27 April 1901.

30. *Philadelphia Press,* 21 April 1901, 28 April 1901; *Philadelphia Inquirer,* 21 April 1901, 22 April 1901, 28 April 1901; *Sporting Life,* 27 April 1901; *Sporting News* 4 May 1901.

31. *Philadelphia Press,* 18 May 1901; *Philadelphia Inquirer,* 18 May 1901, 20 May 1901, 27 May 1901; *Sporting Life,* 25 May 1901; *Sporting News,* 20 May 1901. For a full discussion of this lawsuit, see White, *Creating the National Pastime,* 47–54. Overviews can be found in Burk, *Never Just a Game,* 153; Murphy, "Lajoie," 23; Seymour, *Baseball,* 1:314–15.

32. *Philadelphia Inquirer,* 18 May 1901; *Sporting News,* 8 June 1901.

33. *Sporting Life,* 25 May 1901; *Sporting News,* 13 April 1901.

34. This anecdote is reported in *Sporting Life,* 23 March 1901; L. Allen, *The Hot Stove League* (New York, 1952), 31–33. It is recited by Alexander, *McGraw,* 76; Burk, *Never Just a Game,* 150–51; R. Peterson, *Only the Ball Was White* (New York, 1992), 54–57; Voigt, *Baseball,* 1:278.

35. *Sporting Life,* 2 March 1901; *Sporting News,* 6 April 1901; *Philadelphia Press,* 28 February 1901, 15 April 1901.

36. *Sporting News,* 27 April 1901; *Sporting Life,* 20 April 1901.

37. *Sporting News,* 2 February 1901. His contract cost Chicago $2,000.

38. See the Philadelphia newspapers for the games played between 18 May and 22 May 1901. The *Inquirer* mistakenly identified Jimmy Delahanty as Joe Delahanty.

39. *Sporting News,* 29 June 1901, 9 November 1901.

40. Ibid., 3 March 1900; 26 August 1899.

41. *Philadelphia Press,* 18 December 1900, 21 December 1900, 6 January 1901; *Sporting Life,* 29 December 1900. Also see Alexander, *McGraw,* 36–37, 47–48, 77, and R. Tiemann, "Hugh Jennings," *Baseball's First Stars* (Cleveland, 1996), 81–82.

42. *Philadelphia Press,* 8 March 1901, 29 April 1901, 30 April 1901, 2 May 1901, 5 May 1901; *Sporting News,* 20 April 1901, 8 June 1901, 15 June 1901; *Sporting Life,* 29 June 1901; *Philadelphia Inquirer,* 29 April 1901, 1 July 1901. Alexander, *McGraw,* 77–78; Solomon, *Where They Ain't,* 208–10. Also consult Philadelphia newspapers for 10 June–29 June 1901.

43. *Sporting Life,* 29 June 1901; *Sporting news,* 27 July 1901; *Philadelphia Press,* 24 June 1901.

44. *Philadelphia Press,* 22 June 1901.

45. *North American,* 24 July 1901.

46. *Sporting Life,* 27 July 1901; 6 July 1901.

47. Ibid., 9 November 1901.

48. *Philadelphia Press,* 13 September 1901.

49. *Sporting Life,* 9 November 1901.

50. *Philadelphia Press,* 8 July 1901.

51. *Philadelphia Inquirer,* 2 September 1901.

52. Consult ibid., *Philadelphia Press,* and the *North American* from 13 July to 10 August 1901.

53. *Philadelphia Inquirer,* 22 July 1901.

54. *North American,* 8 August 1901; *Sporting News,* 28 September 1901.

55. *North American,* 16 August 1901.

56. Ibid., 12 August 1901, 13 August 1901, 14 August 1901, 16 August 1901, 22 August 1901; *Philadelphia Inquirer,* 14 August 1901.

57. *Philadelphia Press,* 22 August 1901; *North American,* 31 August 1901; *Sporting News,* 31 August 1901; *Sporting Life,* 17 August 1901, 24 August 1901.

58. *Sporting Life,* 17 August 1901.

59. See the cartoon caricature in *Philadelphia Inquirer,* 21 August 1901, and a picture in ibid., 1 September 1901.

60. *Sporting Life,* 28 September 1901; *North American,* 19 September 1901

61. *Sporting News,* 7 September 1901; *Philadelphia Press,* 5 September 1901.

62. *Sporting News,* 14 September 1901; *Sporting Life,* 21 September 1901, 28 September 1901; *Washington Post,* 30 December 1902.

63. *Philadelphia Inquirer,* 8 March 1902.

64. *Sporting News,* 8 March 1902.

65. *Philadelphia Inquirer,* 22 September 1901; *Sporting News,* 28 September 1901; *Sporting Life,* 28 September 1901.

66. *Philadelphia Inquirer,* 24 September 1901; *North American,* 24 September 1901.

67. Ibid., 23 September 1901.

68. *Philadelphia Inquirer,* 25 September 1901; *Philadelphia Press,* 23 September 1901; *Sporting Life,* 28 September 1901.

69. *North American,* 23 September 1901.

70. Ibid., 24 September 1901; *Philadelphia Inquirer,* 24 September 1901, 23 September 1901; *Philadelphia Press,* 30 September 1901.

71. *North American,* 25 September 1901; *Philadelphia Inquirer,* 26 September 1901; *Sporting Life,* 5 October 1901; *Sporting News,* 5 October 1901.

72. *Sporting News,* 26 October 1901; *Sporting Life,* 26 October 1901.

73. *Washington Evening Star,* 13 July 1903; *Buffalo Evening News,* 15 July 1903.

74. *Sporting News,* 28 September 1901, 5 October 1901; *Philadelphia Press,* 13 October 1901.

75. *Sporting Life,* 19 October 1901. The players got their bonus money for agreeing to sign. *North American,* 20 October 1901.

76. *Sporting News,* 5 October 1901.

77. Ibid., 9 November 1901.

78. Ibid., 16 November 1901; *Sporting Life,* 16 November 1901.

79. *Sporting Life,* 23 November 1901.

15. Cresting in Washington

1. *Sporting News,* 5 October 1901.

2. Florence Delahanty Randall's Correspondence, *Randall Papers.*

3. Ed Delahanty's Tally Book, *Randall Papers.*

4. *North American,* 10 July 1903.

5. *Washington Post,* 2 March 1902, 31 March 1902; *Philadelphia Press,* 10 April 1902; *Sporting News,* 22 March 1902.

6. C. M. Green, *Washington: Capital City, 1879–1950* (Princeton, N.J., 1963), 2:ix, 77, 87, 132; C. M. Green, *The Secret City: A History of Race Relations in the Nation's Capital* (Princeton, N.J., 1967), 128, 134, 200; Thomas Spalding, *The Premier See: A History of the Archdiocese of Baltimore, 1789–1994* (Baltimore, 1989), 133, 242, 253, 310. *Twelfth Census Population Report* (Washington, D.C., 1901), clxxiii, cxcv; Donald Dodd, ed., *Historical Statistics of the States of the United States* (Westport, Conn., 1993), 18–19; *Bicentennial Edition of Historical Statistics of the United States* (Washington, D.C., 1975), 25; Stephan Thernstrom, ed., *Harvard Encyclopedia of American Ethnic Groups* (Cambridge, Mass., 1980), 531.

7. For background on the American League Washington Senators, see: Morris Bealle, *The Washington Senators* (Washington, D.C., 1947), 46–54; Shirley Povich, *The Washington Senators* (New York, 1954), 35–38;

Sowell, *July 3, 1903*, 142–44; *Sporting Life,* 2 November 1901, 9 November 1901, 16 November 1901, 23 November 1901, 30 November 1901, 8 March 1902; *Sporting News,* 14 December 1901, 28 December 1901; *Philadelphia Press,* 29 October 1901; *Philadelphia Inquirer,* 5 January 1902; *Washington Post,* 30 March 1902.

8. For background to this crisis, see: Burk, *Never Just a Game,* 152–53; Levine, *Spalding,* 66–68; Spalding, *National Game,* 302–7; Seymour, *Baseball,* 1:317–19; Voigt, *Baseball,* 1:304–5. Also consult sports coverage in prominent newspapers for November 1901–February 1902.

9. Spalding, *National Game,* 302. Levine, *Spalding,* 67; *Washington Post,* 14 January 1902; *Philadelphia Inquirer,* 13 January 1902, 14 January 1902.

10. Spalding, *National Game,* 302.

11. For a more detailed coverage of this factional strife, see: Burk, *Never Just a Game,* 152–53; Levine, *Spalding,* pp. 66–69; Seymour, *Baseball,* 1:317–21; Spalding, *National Game,* 301–26; Voigt, *Baseball,* 1:304–5.

12. *Sporting News,* 8 February 1902.

13. *Washington Post,* 21 April 1902.

14. Ibid., 23 March 1902.

15. *Sporting Life,* 12 April 1902; *Philadelphia Inquirer,* 8 April 1902.

16. *Washington Post,* 19 March 1902.

17. Ibid., 8 April 1902.

18. Ibid., 9 April 1902.

19. Ibid., 10 April 1902.

20. *Sporting News,* 31 May 1902.

21. For general accounts and interpretations of this decision, see: Burk, *Never Just a Game,* 53–54; Lowenfish, *The Imperfect Diamond,* 68–69; Murphy, "Lajoie" 23–24; Seymour, *Baseball,* 1:314–15; White, *Creating the National Pastime,* 52–58; *Sporting News,* 26 April 1902, 3 May 1902; *Sporting Life,* 26 April 1902; *Philadelphia Press,* 22 April 1902, 23 April 1902; *Philadelphia Inquirer,* 22 April 1902, 23 April 1902; *North American,* 21 April 1902, 22 April 1902; *Washington Post,* 22 April 1902.

22. *Philadelphia Inquirer,* 22 April 1902.

23. Ibid.; *Philadelphia Press,* 22 April 1902.

24. *Washington Post,* 22 April 1902, 5 May 1902.

25. Ibid., 24 April 1902; *North American,* 24 April 1902; *Philadelphia Press,* 24 April 1902.

26. *Washington Post,* 25 April 1902.

27. *Spalding Scrapbooks,* 6:160.

28. *Sporting News,* 10 May 1902, 17 May 1902; *Sporting Life,* 17 May 1902; *Philadelphia Inquirer,* 9 May 1902; *Washington Post,* 11 May 1902; *North American,* 8 May 1902, 9 May 1902, 28 May 1902.

29. *Sporting News,* 17 May 1902.

30. *Washington Post,* 13 May 1902.

31. *Sporting Life,* 19 July 1902; *North American,* 12 July 1902.

32. *Washington Post,* 2 May 1902, 3 May 1902.

33. Ibid., 29 April 1902.

34. Ibid., 6 May 1902.

35. Ibid.; *Sporting Life,* 17 May 1902; *North American,* 4 May 1902.

36. *Washington Post,* 15 August 1902.

37. *North American,* 24 July 1902.

38. *Detroit Times,* citing the *North American,* 16 May 1903.

39. *Washington Post,* 12 July 1902, 16 July 1902; *Sporting Life,* 9 August 1902.

40. *Washington Post,* 6 May 1902; *Sporting News,* 24 May 1902.

41. *Washington Post,* 23 November 1902.

42. Ibid., 18 April 1902; *Sporting Life,* 12 April 1902.

43. *Sporting News,* 5 May 1902.

44. Ibid., 26 April 1902, 17 May 1902.

45. Ibid., 24 May 1902.

46. Ibid., 1 March 1902, 5 April 1902, 22 November 1902; *Washington Post,* 26 August 1902.

47. McGraw, *Thirty Years,* 130; Alexander, *McGraw,* 88–89. *Sporting Life,* 12 July 1902, 19 July 1902; *Philadelphia Inquirer,* 3 July 1902; *Spalding Scrapbooks,* 4:136.

48. McGraw, *Thirty Years,* pp. 131–32.

49. *Sporting Life,* 17 July 1902.

50. *Baltimore Sun,* cited by Alexander, *McGraw,* 91. Also consult Solomon, *Where They Ain't,* 224–30.

51. *Sporting News,* 29 October 1904.

52. McGraw, *Thirty Years,* 135.

53. *Washington Post,* 11 July 1902, 14 July 1902, 20 July 1902, 21 July 1902, 4 August 1902; *Sporting Life,* 27 July 1902, 2 August 1902.

54. *Washington Post,* 23 July 1902, 24 July 1902.

55. Ibid., 23 June 1902; 24 June 1902; *Sporting Life,* 28 June 1902.

56. *Sporting Life,* 12 July 1901.

57. *Washington Post,* 16 August 1902, 17 August 1902, 18 August 1902; *Philadelphia Inquirer,* 28 July 1902.

58. *Washington Post,* 24 August 1902, 21 August 1902.

59. Ibid., 19 August 1902, 23 August 1902, 25 August 1902; *Sporting Life,* 6 September 1902.

60. *Washington Post,* 16 August 1902.

61. Ibid., 20 September 1902.

62. *Philadelphia Inquirer,* 25 August 1902.

63. According to a game-by-game analysis of Lajoie's batting, taken from local newspapers, he had 129 hits in 353 at-bats for a .366 average. Researcher Bill Wagner of Highland, Maryland, conducted the survey.

64. *Washington Post,* 25 September 1902, 28 September 1902, 29 September 1902, 13 December 1902.

16. GET THE MONEY

1. *Washington Post,* 30 November 1902, 2 December 1902.

2. Ibid., 29 September 1902, p. 8; *Sporting News,* 11 October 1902; *Sporting Life,* 18 October 1902.

3. *Sporting News,* 3 December 1902; *Washington Post,* 3 December 1902, 4 December 1902.

4. *Washington Post,* 13 December 1902.

5. *Sporting Life,* 27 January 1903, 31 January 1903; *Washington Post,* 25 December 1902; *Sporting News,* 13 December 1902.

6. *Washington Post,* 2 December 1902.

7. Ibid., 9 November 1902, 16 November 1902, 2 December 1902; *Sporting Life,* 15 November 1902, 22 November 1902, 6 December 1902, 13 December 1902; *North American,* 5 December 1902. Court Transcript (1904), p. 32. *Randall Papers,* packet 5.

8. *Washington Post,* 28 November 1902.

9. Ibid., 2 December 1902; *Sporting News,* 13 December 1902; *Sporting Life,* 13 December 1902.

10. *Sporting Life,* 22 November 1902.

11. *Washington Post,* 3 December 1902.

12. *Sporting Life,* 3 December 1902; *Washington Post,* 4 December 1902, 5 December 1902; *Sporting News,* 13 December 1902, 27 December 1902.

13. *Washington Post,* 19 December 1902.

14. *Sporting Life,* 6 December 1902; *North American,* 9 December 1902; *Sporting News,* 13 December 1902, 27 December 1902, 3 January 1903; *Washington Post,* 15 December 1902.

15. *Sporting Life,* 27 December 1902.

16. *Washington Post,* 15 December 1902.

17. *Sporting News,* 6 December 1902, 13 December 1902.

18. *Washington Post,* 4 December 1902.

19. *North American,* 19 December 1902, 29 December 1902; *Washington Post,* 30 December 1902.

20. *Sporting Life,* 20 December 1902.

21. Court Transcript (1904), p. 33. *Randall Papers*, packet 5.

22. *Sporting Life*, 27 December 1902; *Sporting News*, 27 December 1902.

23. *Sporting Life*, 27 December 1902, 20 December 1902, 15 July 1903; *Sporting News*, 20 December 1902, 27 December 1902; *Cleveland Evening Star*, 13 July 1903; *Philadelphia Inquirer*, 13 July 1903.

24. For a fuller account of these proceedings, consult: Burk, *Never Just a Game*, 156–57; Lowenfish, *Imperfect Diamond*, 69–70; Sowell, *July 2, 1903*, 169–76; Seymour, *Baseball*, 1:322–24; Voigt, *Baseball*, 1:308–9. Also read *Sporting News* and *Sporting Life*, December 1902–January 1903.

25. *Washington Post*, 22 December 1902.

26. *North American*, 29 December 1902; *Washington Post*, 30 December 1902.

27. *Sporting Life*, 10 January 1903; *Washington Post*, 19 December 1902.

28. *Washington Post*, 19 December 1902.

29. Ibid., 26 December 1902.

30. *Sporting Life*, 24 January 1903.

31. *Washington Post*, 15 December 1902.

32. *Sporting Life*, 4 July 1903.

33. *Chicago Tribune*, quoted by the *Boston Herald*, 29 July 1903.

34. *Washington Post*, 28 June 1903.

35. *Sporting Life*, 19 December 1902, 24 January 1903, 8 July 1903; *Sporting News*, 14 March 1903; *Washington Post*, 19 August 1903; Sowell, *July 3, 1903*, 173–74.

36. *Sporting Life*, 17 January 1903.

37. *Sporting News*, 17 January 1903.

38. *Sporting Life*, 17 January 1903.

39. *Philadelphia Press*, 12 July 1903. The only surviving betting book of Ed Delahanty records a forty-eight-day season. No time or race track is cited. According to his ledger, he won $5,975 and lost $7,694. His deficit was $1,719. Delahanty's largest daily losses were $1,940, $852, $715, and $519. Delahanty Notebook, 1–14. *Randall Papers*, packet 6.

40. *Sporting Life*, 13 December 1902.

41. *Washington Post*, 12 January 1903.

42. Ibid., 30 December 1902, 19 January 1903.

43. Ibid.

44. *Sporting News*, 7 February 1903; *Washington Post*, 18 January 1903.

45. *Washington Post*, 17 January 1903.

46. *Sporting News*, 21 February 1903.

47. *Washington Post*, 9 March 1903, 14 March 1903.

48. Ibid., 9 March 1903.

49. Ibid., 16 March 1903.

50. Ibid., 15 March 1903, 16 March 1903; *Cleveland Press,* 7 April 1903.

51. *Sporting News,* 7 February 1903, 21 March 1903.

52. Ibid., 21 March 1903.

53. *Washington Post,* 20 March 1903.

54. Ibid., 21 March 1903; *Sporting Life,* 28 March 1903.

55. *Washington Post,* 21 March 1903; *Sporting Life,* 28 March 1903.

56. *Sporting Life,* 21 March 1903.

57. *Washington Post,* 21 March 1903.

58. Ibid.

59. Ibid., 23 March 1903, 21 March 1903; *Sporting News,* 4 April 1903.

60. *Washington Post,* 25 March 1903, 29 March 1903; *Sporting Life,* 28 March 1903; *Sporting News,* 4 April 1903.

61. *Washington Post,* 25 March 1903, 28 March 1903; *Sporting News,* 4 April 1903.

62. *Washington Post,* 25 March 1903, 26 March 1903, 6 April 1903; *Sporting Life,* 28 March 1903.

63. *Washington Post,* 6 April 1903, 13 April 1903.

64. Ibid., 29 March 1903.

65. *Sporting News,* 1 November 1902; *Boston Globe,* 8 July 1903; portrait (1903), *Randall Papers,* packet 4.

66. *Washington Post,* 30 March 1903.

67. Ibid., 6 April 1903; *Cleveland Press,* 7 April 1903; *Sporting Life,* 11 April 1903, 18 April 1903.

68. *Washington Post,* 25 April 1903, 26 April 1903, 2 May 1903, 9 May 1903; *Sporting News,* 11 April 1903.

69. *Washington Post,* 26 April 1903.

70. *Washington Post,* 12 April 1903, 13 April 1903, 15 April 1903; *Sporting Life,* 2 May 1903; *Sporting News,* 18 April 1903.

71. *Washington Post,* 13 April 1903.

72. Ibid., 12 April 1903, 13 April 1903; *Sporting News,* 11 April 1903.

73. *Sporting News,* 11 April 1903.

74. *Washington Post,* 12 April 1903.

75. *Sporting News,* 25 April 1903.

76. *Washington Post,* 22 April 1903, 23 April 1903; *Sporting News,* 2 May 1903; *Sporting Life,* 2 May 1903.

77. *Washington Post,* 23 April 1903; 25 April 1903; 26 April 1903; *Sporting News,* 2 May 1903.

78. *Washington Post,* 26 April 1903.

79. *Sporting News,* 8 August 1903.

80. *Washington Post,* 1 May 1903.

81. *Boston Herald,* 5 May 1903. *Washington Post,* 10 May 1903.

82. *Philadelphia Press,* 8 May 1903, 9 May 1903, 10 May 1903; *North American,* 8 May 1903; *Philadelphia Ledger,* 8 May 1903, 9 May 1903, 10 May 1903; *Sporting News,* 16 May 1903; *Washington Post,* 8 May 1903, 9 May 1903, 10 May 1903.

83. *Washington Post,* 5 July 1903, 8 July 1903; *Boston Globe,* 8 July 1903; *Sporting News,* 18 July 1903.

84. *Washington Post,* 5 July 1903.

85. Ibid., 7 June 1903, 8 June 1903.

86. Ibid., 15 May 1903, 14 June 1903.

87. For coverage of these events, see *Sporting News* and *Sporting Life* for May and June 1903. Also consult: Alexander, *McGraw,* 103; William Lamb, "George Davis," *National Pastime,* 17, 6; Sowell, *July 3, 1903,* 210–32.

88. *Washington Post,* 6 June 1903.

89. *Sporting Life,* 20 June 1903; *Sporting News,* 20 June 1903; *Washington Post,* 10 June 1903.

90. The Senators would ultimately lose 94 times in 1903 and finish 17 games out of seventh place. *Washington Post,* 5 July 1903, 20 June 1903, 21 June 1903.

91. Ibid., 10 May 1903, 11 May 1903, 24 May 1903, 7 June 1903.

92. Court Transcript (1904), pp. 33, 37. *Randall Papers,* packet 5.

17. THE FALL

1. *Detroit Times,* 1 July 1903.

2. *Chicago Tribune,* quoted in ibid., 13 July 1903.

3. *Washington Post,* 10 July 1903; Delahanty Notebook, p. 1. *Randall Papers,* packet 6.

4. *Sporting Life,* 11 July 1903.

5. *Boston Globe,* 8 July 1903; *Washington Post,* 5 July 1903; *Hall of Fame Clipping File,* 26 November 1904.

6. *Washington Post,* 22 June 1903.

7. *Washington Evening Star,* 23 June 1903; *Washington Post,* 21 June 1903, 22 June 1903, 28 June 1903; *Sporting Life,* 27 June 1903, 4 July 1903; *Sporting News,* 27 June 1903, 4 July 1903; *North American,* 21 June 1903; *Philadelphia Press,* 21 June 1903. For a full account of the fight, see M. Sowell, *3 July 1903,* 235–39.

8. *Washington Evening Star,* 23 June 1903; Hall of Fame Clipping File, 26 November 1904.

9. *Washington Post,* 8 July 1903.

10. Ibid., 9 July 1903.

11. *Cleveland Press*, 26 June 1903.

12. Delahanty Notebook, p. 2. *Randall Papers*, packet 6. *Washington Evening Star*, 24 June 1903.

13. *Sporting Life*, 4 July 1903; *Washington Post*, 26 June 1903.

14. *Sporting Life*, 4 July 1903; *Philadelphia Ledger*, 29 June 1903; *Boston Herald*, 28 June 1903; *Washington Post*, 27 June 1903.

15. *Buffalo Morning Express*, 9 July 1903.

16. *Washington Evening Star*, 27 June 1903; *Washington Post*, 27 June 1903; *Cleveland Press*, 27 June 1903.

17. *Cleveland Press*, 27 June 1903.

18. *Sporting Life*, 11 July 1903.

19. *Washington Post*, 5 July 1903, 8 July 1903; *Buffalo Morning Express*, 8 July 1903, 9 July 1903; *Boston Globe*, 8 July 1903; *Sporting Life*, 18 July 1903

20. *Sporting Life*, 1 August 1903.

21. *Detroit Times*, 29 June 1903.

22. Ibid., 29 June 1903, 8 July 1903; *Detroit Evening News*, 8 July 1903; *Washington Post*, 5 July 1903, 8 July 1903; *Buffalo Morning Express*, 9 July 1903; *Boston Globe*, 8 July 1903; *Sporting Life*, 18 July 1903; *Sporting News*, 18 July 1903.

23. *Washington Evening Star*, 6 July 1903.

24. *Detroit Times*, 1 July 1903.

25. *Washington Post*, 8 July 1903; *Buffalo Morning Express*, 8 July 1903; *Buffalo Evening News*, 8 July 1903; *Niagara Falls Gazette*, 9 July 1903; *Sporting Life*, 11 July 1903.

26. *Detroit Times*, 1 July 1903.

27. *Washington Post*, 5 July 1903, 6 July 1903, 8 July 1903; *Washington Star*, 4 July 1903; *Boston Globe*, 8 July 1903; *Cleveland Plain Dealer*, 8 July 1903; *Buffalo Morning Express*, 8 July 1903, 9 July 1903; *Buffalo Evening News*, 8 July 1903; *Niagara Falls Gazette*, 9 July 1903; *Detroit Evening News*, 8 July 1903; *Detroit Times*, 8 July 1903; *Philadelphia Press*, 8 July 1903. The court transcripts discussed the actual ticket destinations. Court Transcript (1904), pp. 46, 85. *Randall Papers*, packet 5.

28. Court Transcript, p. 59.

29. Ibid., pp. 19–20.

30. Ibid., pp. 20, 48.

31. Ibid., p. 72. Also see *Buffalo Evening News*, 9 July 1903; *Buffalo Morning Express*, 9 July 1903, 11 July 1903; *Cleveland Press*, 9 July 1903; *Philadelphia Inquirer*, 10 July 1903.

32. Court Transcript (1904), pp. 60–61, 80. *Randall Papers*, packet 5.

33. For details of his ill-fated train trip, consult Court Transcript, pp. 16–23, 26–30, 47–48, 57–82. Also see *Buffalo Evening News*, 9 July

1903, 10 July 1903; *Buffalo Morning Express,* 9 July 1903, 11 July 1903; *Cleveland Press,* 9 July 1903; *Niagara Falls Gazette,* 6 July 1903; *Philadelphia Inquirer,* 10 July 1903. For contemporary summaries that do not include court testimony, see: Norm Nevard, "The Strange Fate of Hall-of-Famer Ed Delahanty," *Baseball Digest* (July 1954): 13–16; Robert Summers, "His Ticket Said New York City, But Fate Said Niagara Falls," *Buffalo Courier Express Magazine,* 8 September 1974; Frank Fitzpatrick, "A Baseball Mystery Is 85 Years Old," *Philadelphia Inquirer,* 3 July 1988; Joel Stashenko, "Delahanty's Death Obscured His Baseball Achievements," *Richmond Times,* 26 September 1992; Sowell, *July 3, 1903,* 262–63.

34. The description of the bridge and the details of Delahanty's last moments come from court testimony. See Court Transcript (1904), pp. 2–11. *Randall Papers,* Packet 5. Also see: *Boston Globe,* 8 July 1903; *Buffalo Evening News,* 3 July 1903, 8 July 1903; *Buffalo Morning Express,* 8 July 1903, 9 July 1903, 11 July 1903; *Cleveland Plain Dealer,* 9 July 1903, 10 July 1903; *Cleveland Press,* 8 July 1903; *Daily Cataract Journal,* 9 July 1903, 11 July 1903; *Niagara Falls Gazette,* 9 July 1903; *North American,* 9 July 1903; *Philadelphia Press,* 9 July 1903; *Sporting Life,* 18 July 1903; *Sporting News,* 11 July 1903; *Washington Evening Star,* 8 July 1903; *Washington Post,* 8 July 1903, 12 July 1903. For modern accounts, see citations in note 33 above.

35. *Daily Cataract Journal,* 11 July 1903.

36. *Cleveland Press,* 9 July 1903.

37. *Buffalo Evening News,* 14 July 1903.

38. For the foul play scenario, consult: *Buffalo Morning Gazette,* 11 July 1903; *Cleveland Press,* 9 July 1903; *Daily Cataract Journal,* 11 July 1903; *Philadelphia Inquirer,* 10 July 1903; *Washington Evening Star,* 8 July 1903; *Washington Post,* 8 July 1903; 9 July 1903.

39. *Cleveland Plain Dealer,* 8 July 1903.

40. *Buffalo Evening News,* 3 July 1903.

41. *Boston Globe,* 8 July 1903; *Buffalo Evening News,* 8 July 1903; *Niagara Falls Gazette,* 9 July 1903; *Washington Post,* 5 July 1903.

42. *Buffalo Evening News,* 9 July 1903; *Washington Post,* 10 July 1903.

43. *Sporting News,* 17 January 1903; 24 January 1903; *Washington Post,* 14 January 1903.

44. *Niagara Falls Gazette,* 3 July 1903.

45. *Washington Post,* 5 July 1903.

46. Ibid., 12 July 1903. *Sporting News* said that Delahanty was convinced that Brush had smashed the peace settlement and he could play in New York. *Sporting News,* 18 July 1903.

47. *Washington Evening Star,* 11 July 1903.

48. Court Transcript (1904), p. 16. *Randall Papers*, packet 5. *Buffalo Evening News*, 8 July 1903; *Cleveland Plain Dealer*, 9 July 1903; *Niagara Falls Gazette*, 9 July 1903; *Sporting News*, 18 July 1903; *Washington Post*, 9 July 1903.

49. *Sporting News*, 18 July 1903.

50. *Washington Evening Star*, 8 July 1903.

51. *Philadelphia Press*, 12 July 1903.

52. *Boston Globe*, 8 July 1903; *Boston Herald*, 10 July 1903; *Buffalo Evening News*, 3 July 1903, 8 July 1903; *Buffalo Morning Express*, 8 July 1903, 9 July 1903, 11 July 1903; *Cleveland Plain Dealer*, 9 July 1903; *North American*, 10 July 1903; *Philadelphia Inquirer*, 10 July 1903; *Philadelphia Ledger*, 10 July 1903; *Sporting News*, 11 July 1903, 18 July 1903; *Washington Evening Star*, 8 July 1903; *Washington Post*, 8 July 1903.

53. *Buffalo Morning Express*, 9 July 1903.

54. Court Transcript (1904), p. 54. *Randall Papers*, packet 5.

55. Ibid., p. 11.

56. *Buffalo Evening News*, 8 July 1903; *Buffalo Morning Express*, 9 July 1903; *Daily Cataract Journal*, 9 July 1903. Court Transcript (1904), p. 7. *Randall Papers*, packet 5.

57. *Sporting Life*, 25 July 1903.

58. S. Squires, "The Hazard of Drunk Boating, High Seas," *Washington Post*, Health Section, 2 July 1996, p. 10.

59. Ibid., 6 July 1903.

60. *Cleveland Plain Dealer*, 8 July 1903. For reports on the first couple of days, consult: *Buffalo Evening news*, 8 July 1903; *Buffalo Morning Express*, 8 July 1903; *Cleveland Plain Dealer*, 9 July 1903; *Washington Evening Star*, 6 July 1903; *Washington Post*, 6 July 1903, 7 July 1903, 8 July 1903, 9 July 1903.

61. *Buffalo Evening News*, 8 July 1903; *Daily Cataract Journal*, 9 July 1903; *Niagara Falls Gazette*, 8 July 1903, 9 July 1903; *Washington Post*, 8 July 1903.

62. *Boston Herald*, 9 July 1903; *Buffalo Evening News*, 8 July 1903; 9 July 1903; *Cleveland Press*, 8 July 1903; *Daily Cataract Journal*, 9 July 1903; *Detroit Times*, 8 July 1903; *Niagara Falls Gazette*, 9 July 1903; *North American*, 8 July 1903; 9 July 1903; *Philadelphia Press*, 9 July 1903; *Sporting Life*, 18 July 1903; *Sporting News*, 18 July 1903; *Washington Evening Star*, 8 July 1903; 9 July 1903; *Washington Post*, 8 July 1903, 9 July 1903. Delahanty Notebook, pp. 17–18. *Randall Papers*, packet 6. The surviving Washington "blue book" has Edward J. Delahanty's name penned on the front cardboard cover. It is missing one ticket from the 17 June ballgame.

63. *Buffalo Evening News*, 9 July 1903; *Buffalo Morning Express*, 10 July 1903; *Cleveland Press*, 16 July 1903; *Daily Cataract Journal*, 9 July

1903; *Niagara Falls Gazette,* 9 July 1903, 11 July 1903; *Washington Post,* 12 July 1903. Court Transcript (1904), pp. 15–16. *Randall Papers,* packet 5.

64. *Buffalo Evening News,* 9 July 1903; *Cleveland Plain Dealer,* 10 July 1903; *Daily Cataract Journal,* 9 July 1903; *Niagara Falls Gazette,* 9 July 1903; *Washington Evening Star,* 10 July 1903; *Washington Post,* 10 July 1903, 12 July 1903.

65. *Buffalo Morning Express,* 11 July 1903; *Daily Cataract Journal,* 11 July 1903. Delahanty Notebook, p. 19. *Randall Papers,* packet 6.

66. *Buffalo Morning Express,* 11 July 1903; *Buffalo Evening News,* 9 July 1903; *Cleveland Press,* 9 July 1903; *Daily Cataract Journal,* 11 July 1903; *Washington Post,* 12 July 1903.

67. *Buffalo Evening News,* 9 July 1903; *Cleveland Plain Dealer,* 10 July 1903; *Niagara Falls Gazette,* 10 July 1903; *Washington Evening Star,* 10 July 1903; *Washington Post,* 10 July 1903.

68. *Niagara Falls Gazette,* 11 July 1903.

69. Morse Mortuary Receipt for Ed Delahanty, 9 July 1903. Delahanty Notebook, p. 20. *Randall Papers,* packet 6.

70. *Sporting Life,* 18 July 1903.

71. *Cleveland Plain Dealer,* 26 May 1963.

72. *Buffalo Evening News,* 10 July 1903; *Cleveland Plain Dealer,* 9 July 1903; *Cleveland Press,* 16 July 1903; *Daily Cataract Journal,* 10 July 1903; *Niagara Falls Gazette,* 10 July 1903; *Philadelphia Inquirer,* 12 July 1903; *Washington Post,* 10 July 1903.

Epilogue

1. *New York Journal,* 10 February 1912.

2. Florence Delahanty Randall's Correspondence, *Randall Papers,* packet 4.

3. *Sporting Life,* 25 July 1903, 18. *Washington Post,* 10 July 1903.

4. *Washington Post,* 14 August 1903; 12 July 1903.

5. Ibid.; *North American,* 22 July 1903; *Sporting News,* 18 July 1903.

6. *Washington Post,* 6 August 1903, 9 August 1903; 14 August 1903; 16 August 1903.

7. Ibid., 9 August 1903; 21 August 1903.

8. *North American,* 19 July 1903.

9. Fatal Accident Act, 1887. *Randall Papers,* packet 5.

10. Statement of Mr. George Sterr Jr., 1903. Ibid.

11. W. H. German to N. Delahanty, 3 November 1903. Ibid.

12. Defense's position on *Delahanty vs. Michigan Central Railroad,* 23 November 1903. Ibid.

13. Appeal Book, 4 May 1904, pp. 1–4, and Copy of the Judgement, 16 June 1904, pp. 83–87. Ibid.

14. *Ontario Weekly Register*, 29 June 1905. Ibid.

15. German and Pettit to N. Delahanty, 30 June 1905. Ibid.

16. German and Pettit to N. Delahanty, 9 September 1905. Ibid.

17. Reminiscences of Florence Delahanty, 1937. Ibid.

18. These anecdotes come from Florence Delahanty's reminiscences. Ibid.

19. Much of the family's history in Mobile, Alabama, was given by Norine's guardians, Earl and Dorothy McDonald. Their hospitality and generosity made the research on the Delahanty family possible.

20. James Delahanty to Florence Randall, 5 November 1925. *Randall Papers*, packet 4.

21. Consult Bridget Delahanty's Estate Settlement in ibid.

22. For details, see the brothers' correspondences for 1925 and 1927 in ibid.

23. Frank Delahanty interview, *Cleveland Plain Dealer*, 26 May 1963.

24. *Sporting News*, 25 July 1903.

25. *Sporting Life*, 18 July 1903.

26. Ritter, *Glory of Their Times*, 184.

27. An unidentified Jimmy Delahanty Clipping, 2 February 1943. From *Smith Clippings*, Grafton, Ohio.

28. An unidentified Ja. Delahanty Obituary, 17 October 1953. Ibid.

29. An unidentified Ja. Delahanty Clipping, ibid. A contemporary reported that Jimmy's "habitual scrappy temperament" put him under "a shadow of suspicion." Soden, "Great Baseball Family," *Baseball Magazine* (September 1912): 21.

30. *Baseball Magazine* (September 1912): 22.

31. From a phone interview with Katherine Krysiak (William's daughter), 5 February 1993.

32. F. Delahanty interview, *Cleveland Plain Dealer*, 26 May 1963.

33. William Delahanty's Obituary, ibid., 18 October 1957. The beaning is described in "Famous Families," *Sporting News*, 6 November 1946. William's daughter did not recall him having any visual impairments. She said he wore glasses only as an old man. See Krysiak phone interview, 5 February 1993. An article written in 1912 said William hurt his arm and retired from baseball. Soden, "Great Baseball Familiy," 20.

34. F. Delahanty interview, *Cleveland Plain Dealer*, 26 May 1963.

35. W. Delahanty Obituary, ibid., 18 October 1957. For background on the brothers and their families, consult the correspondence and estate papers in the *Randall Papers*. "Famous Families of Game—Delahantys," *Sporting News*, 6 November 1946; unidentified James Delahanty clipping,

2 February 1943. *Smith Clippings;* an interview with George Uhle, 9 July 1973 in E. Murdock, ed., *Baseball Players and Their Times: Oral Histories of the Game, 1920–1940* (Westport, Conn., 1991), 129.

36. Herne, "Delahantys," unidentified clipping, *Randall Papers,* packet 1.

37. David Voigt, *American Baseball: From Commissioners to Continental Expansion* (Norman, Okla., 1970), 2:65–67; Burk, *Never Just a Game,* 171, 159–60, 243.

38. Twenty-one players who were in the major leagues in 1890 were active after Del died. Eleven were Irish.

39. *Sporting Life,* 25 July 1903; *Sporting News,* 18 July 1903.

40. Burk, *Never Just a Game,* 171, 244. Burk draws a good many of his conclusions from Lee Allen's studies that are housed in the Hall of Fame Museum in Cooperstown, New York. Reiss, *Touching Base,* 184–92.

41. Fred Lieb, "Baseball—The Nation's Melting Pot," *Baseball Magazine* (August 1923): 393–95, 419; Reiss, *Touching Base,* 53–84.

42. Reiss, *City Games,* 87–91. Reiss, *Touching Base,* 157–65, 171–84, 237–38.

43. *Sporting News,* 3 March 1894.

44. *Sporting Life,* 11 December 1897.

45. *Detroit News Tribune,* 12 July 1903.

46. *Sporting Life,* 10 July 1889.

47. *Sporting News,* 18 July 1903.

48. *Philadelphia Inquirer,* 13 July 1903; *Washington Evening Star,* 13 July 1903.

49. *New York Journal,* 10 February 1912.

50. *Detroit News Tribune,* 12 July 1903.

51. *Sporting Life,* 18 July 1903.

52. *Sporting News,* 5 October 1901.

53. Mack, *66 Years,* 84.

54. *Sunday News,* 5 March 1939. Unidentified clipping, *Randall Papers,* packet 2.

55. McGraw, *Thirty Years,* 226, 229. Also see *Philadelphia Bulletin,* 23 February 1923 in *Randall Papers,* packet 2.

56. Fred Lieb, *Baseball As I Have Known It* (New York, 1996 ed.), 16–17.

57. *North American,* 10 July 1903.

58. *Sporting Life,* 6 February 1897.

59. *Boston Herald,* 12 July 1903.

60. *Philadelphia Inquirer,* 13 July 1903; *Washington Evening Star,* 13 July 1903; unidentified clipping, *Randall Papers,* packet 2.

61. *Washington Post,* 10 November 1902.

62. *Sporting Life*, 18 July 1903; *Washington Evening Star*, 14 July 1903; *Boston Herald*, 26 July 1903.

63. *Philadelphia Sporting Press*, 13 July 1903.

64. Unidentified clipping, *Randall Papers*, packet 2; *Philadelphia Sporting Press*, 13 July 1903.

65. *Philadelphia Inquirer*, 13 July 1903; *Washington Evening Star*, 13 July 1903.

66. McGraw, *Thirty Years*, 230.

67. G. Rice, "The Record," *Fantology*, cited in Mack, *66 Years*, 206.

68. *Philadelphia Inquirer*, 13 July 1903; *Washington Evening Star*, 13 July 1903.

Bibliography

PRIMARY SOURCES

Henry Chadwick Diaries and Scrapbooks. 2 vols., 1887–1904. Society for
American Baseball Research microfilm lending library, Cleveland,
Ohio.
Invitation Program of Philadelphia Ball Park. 2 May 1895.
National Baseball Library, Cooperstown, New York.
   1. Delahanty, Ed, clipping file.
   2. Picture Collection.
National Census, 1880, 1900, 1910, 1920 for Cleveland, Philadelphia, Buf-
falo and Mobile. National Archives, Washington, D.C.
Osterhout, Edward D. Unpublished reminiscences. Philadelphia, Pa.
Randall Papers (Letters, Papers and Documents of Norine Delahanty-
Lerio). Mobile, Alabama.
   1. Packet 1: Scrapbook Clippings, pre-1903.
   2. Packet 2: Scrapbook Papers, post-1903.
   3. Packet 3: Miscellaneous Articles, post-1903.
   4. Packet 4: Delahanty/Lerio/Randall Correspondence.
   5. Packet 5: Court Transcripts, *Norine Delahanty vs. Michigan Central
Railroad,* 1904, and Appeal.
   6. Packet 6: Ed Delahanty's Tally Book, 1903, and wife's court notes.
   7. Packet 7: Official Papers and Documents collected by J. Casway.
   8. Packet 8: Picture and Print Collection.
Smith Family Clippings (James Delahanty). Grafton, Ohio.
Spalding (Albert) Scrapbooks, reels 1–5. SABR microfilm lending library,
Cleveland, Ohio.

Allentown Morning Call, 1898–1900.

Augusta Chronicle, 1896–97.

Boston Globe, 1903.

Boston Herald, 1903.

Buffalo Evening News, 1903.

Buffalo Morning Express, 1903.

[Chicago] Daily Inter Ocean, 1896.

Cleveland Evening Star, 1887–1903.

Cleveland Plain Dealer, 1867, 1887–1904.

Cleveland Press, 1887–1903.

Daily Cataract Journal, 1903.

Detroit Evening News, 1903.

Detroit News Tribune, 1903.

Detroit Times, 1903.

Lorraine Journal (clippings of unknown dates).

New York Journal, 1903 and 1912.

Niagara Falls Gazette, 1903.

North American News, 1887–1904.

Ontario Weekly Register, 1905.

Philadelphia Evening Bulletin, 1887–1904.

Philadelphia Evening Bulletin (clippings file at Urban Archives, Temple University, Philadelphia, Pa.).

Philadelphia Evening Item, 1887–1904.

Philadelphia Inquirer, 1887–1904.

Philadelphia Ledger, 1901–1904.

Philadelphia Press, 1887–1904.

Players' National League Base Ball Guide, 1890.

Reach's Official [American Association] Base Ball Guide, 1887–1904.

Spalding's Base Ball Guide, 1887–1904.

Sporting Life, 1886–1904.

Sporting News, 1887–1904, 1943, and 1946.

Sunday Item, 1887–1904.

Sunday Mercury, 1888.

Universal Base Ball Guide, 1890.

Washington Evening Star, 1902–7.

Washington Post, 1902–4.

Wheeling Register, 1887–88.

Adelman, Melvin. (Baseball, Business and the Work Place: Gelber's Thesis Reexamined." *Journal of Social History* 23 (1989): 285–301.

———. *A Sporting Time: New York City and the Rise of Modern Athletics, 1820–1870.* Chicago, 1990.

Alexander, Charles. *John McGraw.* New York, 1988.

Allen, Lee. *The Hot Stove League.* New York, 1952.

Axelson, G. W., *Commy.* Chicago, 1919.

Bang, Ed. "Famous Families of Game—Delahantys." *Sporting News,* 6 November 1946, p. 13.

Baseball Encyclopedia. 8th ed. New York, 1990.

Bealle, Morris. *The Washington Senators.* Washington, D.C., 1947.

Bicentennial Edition of Historical Statistics of the United States. Washington, D.C., 1975.

Bjarkman, Peter. "Forgotten Americans and the National Pastime: Literature on Baseball's Ethnic, Racial and Religious Diversity." *Multicultural Review* 1 (1992): 46–48.

Bowman, John, and Joel Zoss. *Diamonds in the Rough: The Untold History of Baseball.* New York, 1989.

Briley, Ronald. "Baseball and American Cultural Values." *Organization of American History Magazine* 7 (Summer 1992): 61–63.

Brock, Darryl. "The Wright Way," *Sports Heritage* 1 (March–April 1987): 35–41, 93–94.

Bruce, H. Addington. "Baseball and the National Life." *Outlook* 104 (May 1913): 104–7.

Burk, Robert. *Never Just a Game: Players, Owners and American Baseball to 1920.* Chapel Hill, N.C., 1993.

Casway, Jerrold. "The Best Outfield Ever?" *Baseball Research Journal* 27 (1998): 1–6.

———. "From Camac's Woods: The Origins of Philadelphia Baseball." *Temple Review* (April 1992): 19–24.

———. "Irish American Factor and the Emerald Age of Baseball." In Glazier, M., ed., *Encyclopedia of the Irish in America* (Notre Dame, Ind., 1999), 42–47.

———. "A Monument to Harry Wright." *National Pastime* 17 (Spring 1997): 35–37.

———. "Locating Philadelphia's Historic Ballfields." *National Pastime* 13 (Spring 1993): 5–7.

———. "Philadelphia Baseball's Unappreciated Founders: Al Reach and Ben Shibe." *National Pastime* 23 (Fall 2003): 122–25.

Clark, Dennis. "Irish Americans." In J. Buenker and L. Ratner, eds., *Multiculturalism in the United States: A Comparative Guide to Acculturation and Ethnicity,* 77–102. New York, 1992.

———. "The Irish Catholics." In R. Miller and T. Marzik, eds., *Immigrants and Religion in Urban America,* 48–61. Philadelphia, 1977.

———. *The Irish in Philadelphia.* Philadelphia, 1984.

———. "Sport Cults among the Latter Day Celts," paper delivered at the American Conference of Irish Studies, April 1989.

Craig, Peter S., "Monopsony in Manpower: Organized Baseball Meets the Anti-Trust Laws." *Yale Law Journal* 62 (March 1953): 579–639.

Cronin, Mike. *Sport and Nationalism in Ireland.* Dublin, 1999.

DeValeria, D. and J. B. *Honus Wagner: A Biography.* New York, 1995.

DiSalvatore, Bryan. *A Clever Base-Ballist: The Life and Times of John Montgomery Ward.* New York, 1999.

Dodd, Donald, ed. *Historical Statistics of the States of the United States.* Westport, Conn. 1993.

Doyle, David. "The Irish as Urban Pioneers in the United States, 1850–1870." *Journal of American Ethnic History* 10 (1990–91): 36–59.

Eisen, George. "Early European Attitudes towards Native American Sports and Pastimes." In G. Eisen and David Wiggins, eds., *Ethnicity and Sport in North American History and Culture.* Westport, Conn., 1994.

Fitzpatrick, Frank. "A Baseball Mystery Is 85 Years Old." *Philadelphia Inquirer,* 3 July 1988, pp. 1a and 10a.

Foner, Eric. "Ethnicity and Radicalism in the Gilded Age: The Land League and Irish America." In *Politics and Ideology in the Age of the Civil War,* 150–200. New York, 1980.

Fullerton, Hugh. "Del's 4 Homers." Unidentified clipping in *Randall Papers,* packet 2.

Gelber, Steven. "Working at Playing: The Culture of the Workplace and the Rise of Baseball." *Journal of Social History* 16 (1983): 3–20.

Gilbert, T. W. "The 1890's—Baseball's Irish Decade." *Irish Echo,* Part 1 (11 March 1989): 78; and part 2 (18 March 1989): 122.

Green, C. M. *The Secret City: A History of Race Relations in the Nation's Capital.* Princeton, N.J., 1967.

———. *Washington: Capital City 1879–1950.* Princeton, N.J., 1963.

Haven, Jeffrey. "Baseball: The Origins and Development of the Game to 1903." Doctoral dissertation, Brigham Young University, 1979.

Herne, John F. "To the Delahanty Family." Unidentified clipping in *Randall Papers,* packet 2.

Ibson, John. *Will the World Break Your Heart? Dimensions and Consequences of Irish-American Assimilations.* New York, 1990.

Ignatiev, Noel. *How the Irish Became White.* New York, 1995.

Isenberg, Michael. *John L. Sullivan and His America.* Urbana, Ill., 1988.

Ivor-Campbell, Frederick, Robert Tiemann and Mark Rucker, eds., *Baseball's First Stars.* Cleveland, 1996.

James, Bill. *The Historical Baseball Abstract.* New York, 1986.

Kane, Robert A. "Billy McGunnigle." *Baseball Research Journal* 27 (1999): 17–22.

Kavanagh, Jack, and Norman Macht. *Uncle Robbie.* Cleveland, 1999.

Keats, Patrick. "Hall of Famer Ed Delahanty: A Source for Malamud's The Natural." *American Literature: A Journal of Literary History, Criticism and Bibliography* 62 (March 1990): 102–4.

Kingsdale, Jon M. "The 'Poor Man's Club': Social Functions of the Urban Working-Class Saloon." *American Quarterly* 25 (October 1973): 472–89.

Kirsch, George B. *The Creation of American Team Sports: Baseball and Cricket, 1838–1872.* Chicago, 1989.

Klingaman, Mike. "Baltimore Orioles." *Baltimore Sun,* 7 July 1996, pp. 1a and 6a; 8 July 1996, pp. 1c and 7c; 9 July 1996, pp. 1b and 5b.

Koetting, Eric. "Shamrocks on the Diamond: The Irish in Baseball." In Washington, D.C., St. Patrick's Day Program, 1990, pp. 58–61.

Kuklick, Bruce. *To Everything a Season.* Princeton, N.J., 1991.

Lamb, William. "George Davis." *National Pastime* 17 (Spring 1997): 3–8.

Laurie, Bruce. "Fire Companies and Gangs in Southwark: The 1840's." In Allen Davis and Mark Haller, eds., *The Peoples of Philadelphia: A History of Ethnic Groups and Lower Class Life 1790–1940,* 41–83. Philadelphia, 1973.

Lebovitz, Hal. "Delahanty Tragic Jumper, Brother Recalls," *Cleveland Plain Dealer,* 26 May 1963, p. 4c.

Levine Peter. *A. G. Spalding and the Rise of Baseball.* New York, 1985.

Lieb, Frederick. *Baseball As I Have Known It.* Rev. ed., New York, 1996.

———. "Baseball—The Nation's Melting Pot." *Baseball Magazine* (August 1923): 393–95, 419.

———. *Connie Mack: The Grand Old Man of Baseball.* New York, 1945.

Lieb, Frederick, and Stan Baumgartner. *The Philadelphia Phillies.* New York, 1953.

Longert, Scott. *Addie Joss, King of Pitchers.* Cleveland, 1998.

Lowenfish, Lee. *The Imperfect Diamond: A History of Baseball's Labor Wars.* New York, 1991.

Mack, Connie. *My 66 Years in the Big Leagues.* Philadelphia, 1960.

McCaffrey, Lawrence. *The Irish Diaspora in America.* Bloomington, Ind., 1976.

McConnell, Robert C., et al. *Minor League Baseball Stars,* vol. 3. Cleveland, 1992.

McGraw, John. *My Thirty Years in Baseball.* Rev. ed., Lincoln, Nebr., 1995.

Meagher, Timothy, ed. *From Paddy to Studs: Irish American Communities in the Turn of the Century Era, 1880–1920.* Westport, Conn., 1986.

Miller, Kirby. *Emigrants and Exiles: Ireland and the Irish Exodus to North America.* New York, 1985.

Miller, Kirby, and Bruce Boling. "Golden Streets, Bitter Tears: The Irish Image of America During the Era of Mass Migration." *Journal of American Ethnic History* 10 (1990–91): 16–35.

Mitchell, John S. "The Celt as a Baseball Player." *Gael* (May 1902): 151–55.

Murdock, Eugene, ed. *Baseball Players and Their Times: Oral Histories of the Game, 1920–1940.* Westport, Conn., 1991.

Murphy, J. M. "Napoleon Lajoie, Modern Baseball's First Superstar." *National Pastime* 7 (Spring 1988): 5–77.

Needham, Henry B. "The College Athlete: How Commercialism Is Making Him a Professional." *McClure's Magazine* 25, 2 (June 1905): 115–28.

Nemec, David. *The Beer and Whisky League.* New York, 1994.

———. *The Great Encyclopedia of 19th-Century Major League Baseball.* New York, 1997.

Nevard, Norm. "The Strange Fate of Hall-of-Famer Ed Delahanty." *Baseball Digest* 13 (July 1954): 13–16.

Peterson, Robert. *Only the Ball Was White.* New York, 1992.

Pope, S. W. *Patriotic Games: Sporting Traditions in the American Imagination, 1876–1926.* New York, 1997.

Povich, Shirley, *The Washington Senators.* New York, 1954.

Pringle, W. N. "Freaks on the Fly." *Baseball Magazine* 1, 3 (July 1908): 25–26.

Reiss, Steven. *City Games: Evolution of American Society and the Rise of Sports.* Chicago, 1991.

———. "The New Sport History." *Reviews in American History* 18 (1990): 311–25.

———. "Race and Ethnicity in American Baseball, 1910–1919." *Journal of Ethnic Studies,* 4 (Winter 1997): 39–55.

———. *Touching Base: Professional Baseball and American Culture in the Progressive Era.* Westport, Conn., 1980.

Renoff, Richard, and Joseph Varacalli. "Baseball and Socio-Economic Mobility: An Irish-Italian Comparison." *Proceedings of the Sixteenth Annual Conference of the American Italian Historical Association* (1993), 43–51.

Ritter, Lawrence. *The Glory of Their Times.* New York, 1966.

Roberts, Randy. "On the Field of Struggle: The Irish American Sporting Experience." *American Catholic Newsletter* 18 (Fall 1991): 9–11.

Rossi, John. "Glimpses of the Irish Contributions to Early Baseball." *Eire, Ireland* 23, 2 (Summer 1988): 116–21.

Royal, Chip. "Delahantys Top Brother Act." *Baseball Digest* 2 (March 1943): 16.

Sensenderfer, Robert. "Ed Delahanty's Big Day." Clipping, *Philadelphia Bulletin,* 18 June 1942, in *Randall Papers,* packet 2.

Seymour, Harold. *Baseball: The Early Years,* vol. 1. Rev. ed., New York, 1989.

———. *Baseball: The People's Game.* New York, 1990.

Shannon, William. *The American Irish.* New York, 1963.

Shieber, Tom. "The Evolution of the Baseball Diamond." *Baseball Research Journal* 23 (1994): 44–50.

Shipley, Robert. "Baseball Axiom No. 22." *Baseball Research Journal* 23 (1994): 3–13.

Smith, Robert. *Baseball: A Historical Narrative of the Game.* New York, 1947.

Spalding, Albert G. *America's National Game.* Rev. ed., Lincoln, Nebr., 1992.

Spalding, Thomas. *The Premier See: A History of the Archdiocese of Baltimore 1789–1984.* Baltimore, 1989.

Soden, E. D. "The Greatest Baseball Family in the History of the Game." *Baseball Magazine* (September 1912): 17–22.

Solomon, Burt. *Where They Ain't: The Fabled and Untimely Death of the Original Baltimore Orioles.* New York, 1999.

Sowell, Mike. *July 2, 1903: The Mysterious Death of Hall-of-Famer Big Ed Delahanty.* New York, 1992.

Squires, S. "The Hazard of Drunk Boating, High Seas." *Washington Post,* Health Section, 2 July 1996, p. 10.

Stashenko, Joel. "Delahanty's Death Obscured His Baseball Achievements." *Richmond Times,* 26 September 1992, p. D-4.

Summers, Robert. "His Ticket Said New York City, But Fate Said Niagara Falls." *Buffalo Courier Express Magazine,* 8 September 1974, pp. 22–24.

Takaki, Ronald. *Iron Cages, Race and Culture in 19th-Century America.* New York, 1990.

Thornstrom, Stephan, ed. *Harvard Encyclopedia of American Ethnic Groups.* Cambridge, Mass., 1980.

Thorn, John, and Peter Palmer, eds. *Total Baseball.* Rev. ed. New York, 1993.

Tiemann, Robert. "Hugh Jennings." In *Baseball's First Stars,* ed. Ivor-Campbell, Tiemann, and Rucher, 81–82. Cleveland, 1996.

Tiemann, Robert, and Mark Rucker. *Nineteenth-Century Stars.* Kansas City, 1989.

Verducci, Tom. "Bat Man." *Sports Illustrated,* 28 July 1997, pp. 40–47.

Vincent, Ted, *Mudville's Revenge: The Rise and Fall of American Sports.* New York, 1981.

Voigt, David Q. *American Baseball:* Volume 1, *From Gentleman's Sport to the Commissioner System.* Norman, Okla., 1966.

———. *American Baseball:* Volume 2, *From Commissioners to Continental Expansion.* Norman, Okla., 1970.

———. "1894." *Baseball Research Journal* 23 (1994): 82–84.

Walsh, Victor. "Drowning the Shamrock: Drink, Teetotalism and the Irish Catholics of the Gilded Age Pittsburgh." *Journal of American Ethnic History* 10 (1990–91): 60–79.

Ward, John Montgomery. "Is the Base-Ball Player a Chattel?' *Lippincott's Magazine* 40 (August 1887): 310–19.

Weir, Hugh. "Baseball: The Men and the Dollars Behind It." *World Today,* 17 July 1904, pp. 752–61.

Wescott, Rich, and Frank Bilovsky, eds. *The New Phillies Encyclopedia.* Philadelphia, 1993.

Whelan, Kevin. "The Geography of Hurling." *History Ireland,* I, 1993, 27–31.

White, G. E. *Creating the National Pastime: Baseball Transforms Itself, 1903–1953.* Princeton, N.J., 1996.

Wilcox, Ralph, "The Shamrock and the Eagle: Irish Americans and Sport in the Nineteenth-Century." In G. Eisen and D. Wiggins, eds. *Ethnicity and Sport in North American History and Culture,* 55–71. Westport, Conn., 1994.

Wittke, Carl. *The Irish in America.* Baton Rouge, La., 1956.

Wright, Marshall D. *Nineteenth-Century Baseball.* Jefferson, N.C., 1996.

Name Index

Williams, Lucky, 213
Williams, Ted, 302
Willis, Vic, 218
Wolverton, Harry, 175, 186, 189, 197–98,
   213–14, 216–19, 224, 226–27,
   229–31, 236
Wood, George "Dandy," 41–42, 45, 58, 61
Wright, Harry, 24, 31–34, 36–37, 41–42, 45,
   49, 53, 60, 64–67, 71–74, 78–86, 107–8,
   124, 299, 321

Wright (Harry's widow), 158
Wynne, Bill, 93

Young, Cy, 85, 93, 117, 202, 229, 303
Young, Nicholas "Uncle Nick," 154,
   168, 224

Ziegler (Phillies physician), 35–36
Zimmer, Charlie "Chief," 35, 78, 89, 185,
   189–90

Subject Index

JERROLD CASWAY is professor of history and chair of the Social Sciences/ Teacher Education Division at Howard Community College in Columbia, Maryland. He specializes in early modern Irish history and nineteenth-century baseball.